The Beginnings of Medieval Romance

Up to the twelfth century writing in the western vernaculars dealt almost exclusively with religious, historical and factual themes, all of which were held to convey the truth. The second half of the twelfth century saw the emergence of a new genre, the romance, which was consciously conceived as fictional and therefore allowed largely to break free from traditional presuppositions. Dennis Green explores how and why this happened, and examines this period of crucial importance for the birth of the romance and the genesis of medieval fiction in the vernacular. Although the crucial innovative role of writers in Germany is Green's main concern, he also takes Latin, French and Anglo-Norman literature into account. This study offers a definition of medieval fictionality in its first formative period in the twelfth century, and underlines the difficulties encountered in finding a place for the fictional romance within earlier literary traditions.

D. H. GREEN is Schröder Professor Emeritus of German at the University of Cambridge. He is a Fellow of Trinity College, Cambridge, and of the British Academy. He is the author of *The Carolingian Lord* (1965), *The Millstätter Exodus* (1966), *Approaches to Wolfram von Eschenbach* (1978), *Irony in the Medieval Romance* (1979), *The Art of Recognition in Wolfram's Parzival* (1982), *Medieval Listening and Reading* (1994) and *Language and History in the Early Germanic World* (1998).

CAMBRIDGE STUDIES IN MEDIEVAL LITERATURE

General editor
Alastair Minnis, *University of York*

Editorial board
Patrick Boyde, *University of Cambridge*
John Burrow, *University of Bristol*
Rita Copeland, *University of Pennsylvania*
Alan Deyermond, *University of London*
Peter Dronke, *University of Cambridge*
Simon Gaunt, *King's College, London*
Nigel Palmer, *University of Oxford*
Winthrop Wetherbee, *Cornell University*

This series of critical books seeks to cover the whole area of literature written in the major medieval languages – the main European vernaculars, and medieval Latin and Greek – during the period c. 1100–1500. Its chief aim is to publish and stimulate fresh scholarship and criticism on medieval literature, special emphasis being placed on understanding major works of poetry, prose, and drama in relation to the contemporary culture and learning which fostered them.

A complete list of titles in the series can be found at the end of the volume.

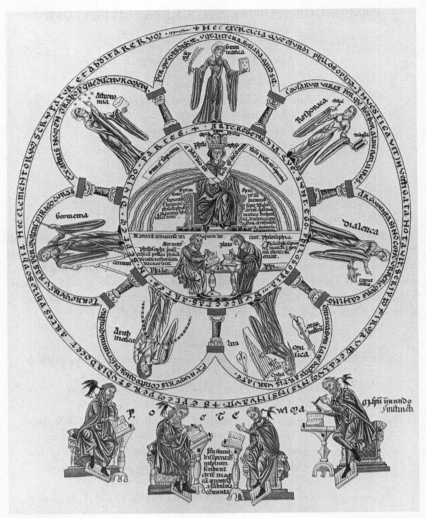

Truth and fiction: from the *Hortus Deliciarum* of Herrad von Landsberg
(ca. 1170, no destroyed). From Rosalie Green, '*Herrad of Hohenbourg, Hortus
Deliciarum*', Volume 'Reconstruction', facing page 56. Reproduced by kind
permission of the Syndics of Cambridge University Library.

The centre is dominated by Philosophia, inspired by God. Beneath her
sit Socrates and Plato, and around her are grouped the seven Liberal Arts.
Excluded from this circle of truth and wisdom are four figures of poets, the
authors of untruthful fables and inspired by unclean spirits.

The Beginnings of
Medieval Romance

Fact and Fiction, 1150–1220

D. H. GREEN
Trinity College, Cambridge

CAMBRIDGE
UNIVERSITY PRESS

PUBLISHED BY THE PRESS SYNDICATE OF THE UNIVERSITY OF CAMBRIDGE
The Pitt Building, Trumpington Street, Cambridge, United Kingdom

CAMBRIDGE UNIVERSITY PRESS
The Edinburgh Building, Cambridge CB2 2RU, UK
40 West 20th Street, New York, NY 10011-4211, USA
477 Williamstown Road, Port Melbourne, VIC 3207, Australia
Ruiz de Alarcón 13, 28014 Madrid, Spain
Dock House, The Waterfront, Cape Town 8001, South Africa

http://www.cambridge.org

First published 2002

Printed in the United Kingdom at the University Press, Cambridge

Typeface Adobe Garamond 11.5/14 pt.   *System* LATEX 2$_\varepsilon$ [TB]

A catalogue record for this book is available from the British Library

Library of Congress Cataloguing in Publication data

Green, Dennis Howard, 1922–
The beginnings of medieval romance : fact and fiction, 1150–1220 / D.H. Green.
p.   cm. – (Cambridge studies in medieval literature ; 47)
Includes bibliographical references and index.
ISBN 0-521-81399-9
1. Romances – History and criticism.   2. Literature, Medieval – History and
criticism.   I. Series.
PN671 .G74   2002
809.3′02 – dc21   2001052856

ISBN 0 521 81399 9 hardback

Contents

Contents

Preface

The problem of fictionality has come to the fore recently in research on the medieval German romance, even though, surprisingly in view of the seminal importance of Chrétien de Troyes, the same is not so true of French scholarship. The two most important representatives of German scholarship in this field are W. Haug and F. P. Knapp. Haug confines himself to medieval authors' reflections as found in prologues and digressions, whilst Knapp offers a more theoretical approach to problems of genre. By contrast, my aim is practical rather than theoretical (how did various authors make use of the potentialities of fictionality in organising their narratives?), but also genetic rather than generic (in concentrating on the period 1150–1220 I focus on a short period of crucial importance for the birth of the romance and of medieval fiction in the vernacular). German narrative fiction after 1220 reacts to the preceding generation, it rings changes on it, deviates from it, parodies it, but scholarship dealing with this later fiction suffers from the lack of consensus over the nature of narrative fiction before 1220. Like Knapp, I am convinced that the time is too early for a systematic treatment of this complex problem, so that, like him, I deal with it in interrelated approaches, homing in on it from different angles.

A word needs to be said about another delimitation of the problem. I am concerned with the emergence of fictional writing in the twelfth century in one genre alone, the romance. This means excluding from consideration such genres as the *chanson de geste* and the lyric, for to have included these as well would have been unmanageable within the confines of one book. Only when the problem has been dealt with for all three genres can their interaction and interdependence be worked out. But that is a task for the future.

ix

Preface

For similar reasons of space, and also to safeguard a clear line of argument, I have omitted (apart from a specific point treated in Chapter 3) any consideration of the connection between fictionality on the one hand and the interplay between orality and writing on the other. In an earlier book (*Medieval listening and reading*, Cambridge 1994) I devoted a chapter to literacy, history and fiction, but looked at the last two specifically from the point of view of literacy. What also needs to be done is to look at literacy (and orality) from the point of view of fiction, but that, too, is a task for the future.

This is the place to clarify two points in the terminology used in this book. I employ the word 'fictional' to mean pertaining to fiction as defined in Chapter 1 and as a property of some vernacular writing around 1200, whilst I use the term 'fictitious' (only very occasionally) in a broader sense, meaning that which has no real existence, and not necessarily applied to a work of narrative literature. I also distinguish between 'fiction' and 'fictionality', using the former to designate a specific example or body of fictional writing, and the latter to refer to its nature, to what sets it apart from other types of writing, especially of a factual or historical kind; where the occasion calls for it I also at times employ, as was also medieval practice, *poetria* or *poema* as equivalents for *fictio* or *figmentum*.

The second clarification concerns romances dealing with a theme from classical antiquity. Since examples exist both in antiquity itself and in the Middle Ages I refer to the former as 'romances of antiquity' and the latter as 'antique romances' (in specifically French cases as *romans antiques*). Since the term 'classical' has established itself as a designation for a group of German authors around 1200, distinguishing them from their 'post-classical' successors of the thirteenth century, I use the word 'classical' in this particular sense.

Whatever the restrictions (chronological and generic) I have felt it necessary to impose on my inquiry, it is wider in another sense since, although my first concern is German, I have also had to take in evidence from Latin, French and Anglo-Norman literature. This has given me the pleasure of ranging far and wide beyond my specialist field, enjoying what was already appreciated by Dante as the *ambages pulcherrimae* of Arthurian literature.

I owe a debt of gratitude to Mark Chinca and Nigel Palmer for reading through all the chapters in draft form and for giving me the benefit of their critical comments, as well as Laura Pieters Cordy for her skill with the computer and for not being daunted by the number of the endnotes. I also have to thank the Max Niemeyer Verlag for permission to reproduce, in modified form, as part of Chapter 3 my contribution to *Blütezeit. Festschrift für L. Peter Johnson zum 70. Geburtstag* (ed. M. Chinca, J. Heinzle, C. Young, Tübingen 2000).

Abbreviations

ABÄG	*Amsterdamer Beiträge zur älteren Germanistik*
AfB	*Archiv für Begriffsgeschichte*
AfdA	*Anzeiger für deutsches Altertum*
AfK	*Archiv für Kulturgeschichte*
AL	*Arthurian Literature*
ANS	*Anglo-Norman Studies*
BDBA	*Bien Dire et Bien Apprendre*
CCM	*Cahiers de Civilisation Médiévale*
CIMAGL	*Cahiers de l'Institut du Moyen Age Grec et Latin*
CL	*Comparative Literature*
CLS	*Comparative Literature Studies*
DVjs	*Deutsche Vierteljahrsschrift*
FEW	*Französisches Etymologisches Wörterbuch*, ed. W. von Wartburg, 24 vols. to date, Bonn 1928–83
FMS	*Frühmittelalterliche Studien*
FS	Festschrift
FSt	*French Studies*
GLL	*German Life and Letters*
GRLMA	*Grundriß der romanischen Literaturen des Mittelalters*
GRM	*Germanisch-Romanische Monatsschrift*
IASL	*Internationales Archiv für Sozialgeschichte der Literatur*
JAAC	*Journal of Aesthetics and Art Criticism*
JEGPh	*Journal of English and Germanic Philology*
JWCI	*Journal of the Warburg and Courtauld Institutes*
LiLi	*Zeitschrift für Literaturwissenschaft und Linguistik*
LSE	*Leeds Studies in English*
LwJb	*Literaturwissenschaftliches Jahrbuch*

MA	*Moyen Age*
MÆ	*Medium Ævum*
ME	Middle English
MGH SS	*Monumenta Germaniae Historica, Scriptores*
MHG	Middle High German
MLN	*Modern Language Notes*
MLR	*Modern Language Review*
MPh	*Modern Philology*
MPL	J. P. Migne, *Patrologia Latina*
MR	*Medioevo Romanzo*
NdJb	*Niederdeutsches Jahrbuch*
NM	*Neuphilologische Mitteilungen*
NT	*De Nieuwe Taalgids*
OFr	Old French
OLD	*Oxford Latin Dictionary*, ed. C. O. Brink *et al.*, Oxford 1968
OS	Old Saxon
PBB	*Paul und Braunes Beiträge.* (*T*) stands for the Tübingen series.
RF	*Romanische Forschungen*
RPh	*Romance Philology*
SLF	*Studi di Letteratura Francese*
TRHS	*Transactions of the Royal Historical Society*
WW	*Wirkendes Wort*
ZfdA	*Zeitschrift für deutsches Altertum*
ZfdPh	*Zeitschrift für deutsche Philologie*
ZfrPh	*Zeitschrift für romanische Philologie*
ZGL	*Zeitschrift für germanistische Linguistik*

CHAPTER I

Defining twelfth-century fictionality

The aim of this chapter is to propose a working definition of fiction applicable to the romances written between about 1150 and 1220, making no claim to wider validity. Even so, some assistance will be sought from elsewhere (classical literature, modern philosophical theory) on the grounds that, although some aspects of fiction vary widely over time, others are common to different periods.

To start by taking classical antiquity into brief account is not so irrelevant as it might seem. Plato's criticism of poetry was acceptable to early Christianity at odds with pagan literature and to early medieval thought dominated by Platonism before the relatively late reception of Aristotle,[1] whose *Poetics*, although available to the Latin West only from the thirteenth century,[2] provided arguments more favourable to fiction than those of Plato.

Plato's criticism rests on the view that the poet is a mere imitator, dealing with appearances rather than with what is real and therefore presenting a lie instead of the truth.[3] The basis of his argument is a radical distinction between poetry and philosophy, later adapted to Christian ends as one between poetry and theology.[4] As Plato's myth of the cave makes clear, the poet resembles the prisoners who, facing backwards, see only the shadows cast by the fire, so that the product of the poet is twice removed from reality. Plato's objections to the dangers posed by poetry (or by art at large) are fundamental: it accepts appearances instead of questioning them; it apes the spiritual and thereby degrades it; it aims at plausibility, so that its 'truthfulness' is a fake.[5]

As if these misgivings were not enough, Plato also has reservations about writing and therefore about literature which has found its way into writing.[6] For him writing is inferior to memory and the living exchange of dialectic discourse; it resembles poetry in providing yet another way of distancing oneself from truth and reality. Like art it can lie and amount to imitation and forgery. The importance of this criticism of writing is not merely that it reinforces the attack against poetry (in the specific form of written poetry), but that it is also relevant to fiction in particular, since the rise of fiction in classical Greece has been associated with the beginnings of literacy there.[7] (That these two developments may be causally connected is suggested by the parallel in the Middle Ages, where the genesis of vernacular fiction in the twelfth century coincides with a new place for literacy in the literature meant for laymen.)[8] For Plato poetry (and, more specifically, fiction) is untruth and unworthy of a philosopher.

With Aristotle the position is quite different. Fictionality is involved in his view of poetry as imitation or mimesis, so that his *Poetics* describes what can be recognised as a theory of fiction.[9] That this amounts to a defence, as opposed to Plato's critique, is clear when Aristotle, instead of contrasting the poet with the philosopher, differentiates him from the historian. Instead of ending up as a distinction between untruth and truth this defence argues that, whereas history makes particular statements, poetry makes general ones (and is therefore more philosophical!).[10] This universalising nature of poetry, telling not what has happened but what could happen, makes it of greater value than history. By claiming that this generalising function of poetry renders it more philosophical Aristotle meets Plato's critique on his own ground, but he also does this when arguing that in poetry we should even prefer plausible impossibilities to implausible possibilities.[11] He thereby grants a positive role to plausibility (whereas Plato saw this as a weakness, a shirking of truth) and points to a central feature of fiction: that it should not be judged by the standards of truth and untruth, like factual discourse (history or philosophy).[12] Aristotle therefore acknowledges the fictionality of poetry, whereas Plato rejects poetry because of that feature, and it is possible to read Aristotle's *Rhetoric* and *Poetics* as a defence against Plato's attack.[13]

Whereas Plato's thought dominated the early Middle Ages and his attack on poetry was acceptable to Christian fundamentalism, Aristotle's *Poetics* became available in the West in a thirteenth-century translation of an Arabic commentary that presented the theory of mimesis in a much altered form.[14] Because of this these two classical authorities appear to be irrelevant to our discussion: Plato's attack provided only a criticism of fictionality, whilst Aristotle's justification was known too late (and in a bowdlerised form) to preside over the genesis of vernacular fiction in the twelfth century. One way round this difficulty is to consider classical Latin authors who shared Aristotle's view and who were themselves known in the Middle Ages, especially in the twelfth century. In a century termed an Ovidian age it is fitting that our example should come from Ovid.

In *Amores* III 12 Ovid says[15] that, although he could have dealt with historical themes (Thebes, Troy, Caesar), he has instead sung only of Corinna (15–18), but that as a poet he is not to be believed as if he were a witness (19) and that no weight is to be attached to his words. That the authority which he disclaims is to be seen as historical (or biographical) reliability is suggested when the fertile licence of poets is said to be tied to no *historica fide* (historical trustworthiness, 41–2), so that the praise of the poetic figure Corinna is in fact a lie (43–4), but not in the sense of a wilful deception, for it is the credulity of his audience that prevents them from seeing, as they should, that his words are untrue.[16] In these lines Ovid reminds us of both Plato and Aristotle. Like Plato (and others) he equates his poetry with lying, but he resembles Aristotle in distinguishing the fictive nature of his apparently autobiographical poetry from historical truth (*poetas* and *licentia vatum*, poetic licence, as opposed to *testes*, witnesses, and *historica fide*). By insisting that the untruth of his poetry (*falso*) should have been seen through and should not have deceived his audience Ovid is making a point central to a definition of fictionality, that it rests on a contract between author and audience in which each consciously plays his allotted role.[17]

This example from Ovid, even though others could be adduced,[18] represents only an isolated case, too narrow a basis for showing how classical views on fictionality could have found their way into medieval theory or practice.[19] Another way, not so restricted, is to consider the theory of classical rhetoric, transmitted to the Middle Ages largely through Isidore of Seville, concerning the three types of narrative, *genera narrationis*.[20] According to this theory one of these types, *historia*, was a true record of events that had actually taken place, but at some distance in time from present memory. By contrast, *fabula* recounted fictitious events that neither had taken place nor could have conceivably done so (as in Aesop's fables or Ovid's *Metamorphoses*). Logically situated between these two extremes was the *argumentum*, dealing with events that had not happened, but could have. The direct value of this threefold division for the development of a medieval theory of fictionality has been described as meagre,[21] but this must be questioned in the light of Mehtonen's work on the adaptation of old (rhetorical) concepts to new poetics, above all in twelfth-century France.[22] She draws on a wide variety of sources (rhetoric, grammar, poetics, including medieval commentaries on earlier sources), ranging from antiquity through to the early thirteenth century, and shows that the threefold scheme defining degrees of truthfulness was inherited from classical rhetoric, but interpreted anew under changed cultural conditions. The scheme was utilised to legitimise poetics as a new, independent discipline in the twelfth century, so that what had originally been a rhetorical scheme could now be used for poetological distinctions and even for the reading of a poetic text.[23] The originally rhetorical distinction between *historia* and *fabula* could also be applied to the production of a fictional text, as when Chrétien's intertextual reference to Wace's *Roman de Rou* in his *Yvain* is employed as a signal to his fiction.[24] Also of interest is the way in which Dominicus Gundissalinus, for example, correlates the three types (which he expressly associates with *poetica* as a *scientia*) with the Horatian prescription that poetry should both delight and instruct,[25] for we shall see that this, too, played a role in finding a place for fiction in the twelfth century.[26] There is therefore every justification for taking account of these three types of narrative in the definition of fictionality that must now be attempted.

Even though Haug nowhere defines what is for him a revolutionary innovation of twelfth-century literature we must venture on a working definition adequate to the scope of this book. I propose the following.

> Fiction is a category of literary text which, although it may also include events that were held to have actually taken place, gives an account of events that could not conceivably have taken place and / or of events that, although possible, did not take place, and which, in doing so, invites the intended audience to be willing to make-believe what would otherwise be regarded as untrue.

A number of points in this definition require elaboration.

In equating fiction with literature this definition is deliberately restricted to one field, a focus made necessary by the wide use of the term 'fiction' (literary, but also legal, logical and mathematical).[27] The definition is not intended to be applicable to fields other than literature, where fiction is also a topic of current concern. These include philosophy, where I have nonetheless borrowed ideas from Searle, Rorty, Newsom, Currie, Walton, Lamarque and Olsen, without feeling it incumbent on me to provide a formulation reconciling my literary concerns with their philosophical ones.[28] The same is true of art in the case of Gombrich and Walton (even though the latter seeks a definition to embrace the visual and the verbal arts).[29] We need not press our definition that far, nor indeed, within the field of literature, beyond the circumscribed medieval period in which vernacular fiction in written form first arose.

A second point touches upon the inclusion in this definition of events that were held to have taken place, for this appears to smuggle *historia* or truth into the field properly reserved for *fabula* and *argumentum*. Although rhetorical theory distinguishes between history and fiction, historical details may still be included in fictional works, a fact acknowledged by modern as well as by earlier theory. Currie argues that a 'work of fiction is a patchwork of truth and falsity, reliability and unreliability, fiction-making and assertion'.[30] Others, having Tolstoy in mind, observe the conjunction of history (Napoleon's invasion of Russia) with fiction (Napoleon's conversations, invented by Tolstoy, or the story of Pierre and Natasha).[31] Lamarque and Olsen point out that works of fiction can also contain names of places or people from the extra-fictional world (Moscow, Napoleon again) alongside fictional ones.[32] Medieval parallels, such as the contrast in Wolfram's *Parzival* between Baghdad and Anjou on the one hand and Munsalvaesche and Schastel Marveile on the other, would not be far to seek.[33] Wolfram also introduces the figure of Prester John, regarded as historically credible, towards the close of *Parzival*, whilst other romances dealing with the fall of Troy introduce what could be regarded as a historical dimension by basing themselves on the written accounts of Dares and Dictys, held to be eyewitnesses of the Trojan War and therefore more reliable as 'historians' than the poet Homer who lived much later.[34] This presence of the extra-fictional even within the fictional world has been further stressed with the observation that fictions can re-assemble familiar details in new combinations, so that, whilst the constituents may be drawn from reality, it is their occurrence in a new combination that makes up the fiction.[35]

Earlier observers were also aware that, despite the distinctions made by theory, history could often percolate through fiction. Aristotle knew that, in addition to tragedies containing entirely fictitious names, there are others where some names are not fictitious.[36] Medieval critics of Homer agree with classical ones in attacking him for having mixed historical truth with impossible fictions such as the participation of the gods in human events.[37] Horace, on the other hand, while conceding that Homer lied, praises him for having mixed the true with the false in such a way that he remained consistent (and therefore plausible).[38] Macrobius' analysis of Virgil's *Aeneid* proceeds along similar lines: the Latin poet, too, added a fiction about Dido to an account of historical events involving Aeneas' departure from Troy and the founding of Rome.[39] This view of Virgil's work was still shared in the twelfth century. The *accessus* attributed to Anselm of Laon begins with Virgil's *intentio*: to praise Augustus, thereby suppressing much historical truth and adding certain poetic fictions.[40]

This mingling of fiction with factual details may well have been confusing to some members of a court audience for a fictional romance in the twelfth century, not because they were like the proverbial backwoodsman at a theatrical performance who leapt onto the stage to save the heroine from the villain,[41] but rather because they may still have been unacquainted with the new (and complex) phenomenon of literary fiction.[42] The reaction of an audience unused to such novel demands could have been to take the whole fiction (not just the historical, factual details in it) as representing actual facts or events. They mistakenly regarded a fiction as *historia*.[43]

To define fiction in terms of events that could not conceivably have taken place brings us, as the next step, to the rhetorical definition of *fabula*. In treating it now I abandon the sliding scale of the three types of narrative (moving progressively away from reality in the sequence *historia–argumentum–fabula*) in favour of a logical order, discussing the two extremes, *historia* and *fabula*, before the middle position, *argumentum*.

Fabula, sometimes explicitly designated 'untrue',[44] comprises events which are not simply untrue, but not even like the truth, not even plausible. Markers to make this clear include fictive happenings such as those in Ovid's *Metamorphoses* or the intervention of the gods in human affairs in Homer and Virgil. They can also consist of fictive creatures, those that fly in the face of reality (Isidore's definition of *fabula* includes the words 'contra naturam', against nature)[45] such as animals that speak. This raises the question, difficult to answer, how far these happenings and creatures were possibly believed in, how far the author could rely on their being seen through as fictitious.[46] Even if they were not seen through, this does not make of the fiction a lying deception, since by using such features the author has at least given a signal which is transparent for him and also potentially for his audience. In what follows we shall come across evidence for two possible reactions to these features: their acceptance as true, but also suspicion or scepticism. From this there follow two reactions to fictionality: an inability and an ability to recognise its presence, in other words the fact of a twofold audience.[47] In recognising this we must avoid assuming a straightforward replacement of credulity by scepticism over the course of time (Marco Polo, who had travelled to the Far East, still believed in the existence of Prester John, who also, even later, lurked behind the voyages of discovery of Henry the Navigator and Vasco da Gama).[48] Even those who did not acknowledge the presence of fictionality may not simply have failed to recognise signals to it, for they may have maintained (for example, as clerical rigorists) that the fiction stood in no relation to actual events or facts and was therefore simply untruth. Hence the equation of *fabula* and fictions based on it with lies.

As an example of *fabula* as the basis of a fiction I take the medieval Latin beast epic *Ecbasis captivi*. By its very genre, in the tradition of Aesop's fables regularly quoted as obviously fictitious, this work must be classed a fiction.[49] Quintilian says of this genre that the more simple-minded take pleasure in listening to 'quae ficta sunt' (what has been made up), while Isidore locates its fictionality in the fact that animals are presented with the gift of speech ('fictorum mutorum animalium inter se conloquio', conversation between invented dumb animals).[50] Although the *Ecbasis* belongs to a genre traditionally recognised as fictional, its novelty consists in the invention of a new narrative plot with a more ambitious structure than the beast *fabula* or *fabella* usually shows or than can be assumed for the stock of *vulgares fabellae* on which the author may have drawn.[51] The author makes his audience aware of his work's fictional status from the beginning. He first states what his undertaking is *not*, distancing himself from what used to be the practice, namely to concern oneself with deeds that had actually been performed (*res gestae*) and written up (*notator* and *scriptus*) on the basis of what an eyewitness (*visus*) or at least credible hearsay (*auditor certus*) had reported.[52] What the author here keeps aloof from is nothing other than *historia*, not merely because of his reference to *res gestae*, but because he sums up the traditional view of the historian. (For Isidore no one in antiquity wrote history who had not witnessed the events himself, and Konrad von Hirsau defines the *historiographus* succinctly as the 'rei visae scriptor', one who writes up what he has seen.)[53] Instead of history the author of the *Ecbasis* presents a 'rara fabella', strange fable (39), where the noun, a diminutive of *fabula*, denotes a fictional story and the adjective suggests that it is factually not entirely reliable.[54] This hint gives way to certainty, however, when the work is termed a lying book (40: 'mendosam cartam'), but useful ('utilia multa') because of its ethical content. If the work is described as lying this is hardly because of any rejection of its fictional nature, for otherwise it would not be recommended as useful, nor would the author conclude it by placing himself in the line of Horace's satires, giving delight together with instruction.[55] Instead, the word 'lying' was probably used because of the lack of a theoretical place and critical vocabulary for medieval fictionality,[56] so that it reflects the conventional contrast between historical truth and *fabula* or lies.

We come now to the third type of narrative, *argumentum*. Both Bernard of Utrecht and Konrad von Hirsau, by using the phrase 'dubiae rei fidem faciens' (conferring credibility on something doubtful), underline the ability of an *argumentum* to appear plausible.[57] Theoretically, *argumentum* occupies middle ground between *historia* and *fabula*: because of its fictional content it is linked to *fabula* and distinct from *historia*, but because of its plausibility it resembles *historia* and differs from *fabula*.[58] This middling position of *argumentum* made it attractive to authors of the twelfth century who sought the freedom to invent their narrative, but were constrained to present it as plausible or even (if by non-factual criteria) as truthful.

Gottfried's *Tristan* has been discussed in terms of *argumentum* or verisimilitude, in particular the episode of Tristan's combat with Morold.[59]

Chinca has shown that this was seen as a single combat both by received opinion ('al die werlde') and by the authoritative source (6870–1) which at the beginning of his work Gottfried took pains to equate with historical truth and which is here expressly termed 'diu wârheit', the truth (6881). Like the author of the *Ecbasis captivi* Gottfried then deviates from this historically true version (6875 ff.), so that his account, no longer of a *facta res* (something that happened), is a *ficta res* (something made up), but one which, in contrast to the manifest impossibilities of a beast fable, he proposes to show is *wârbaere* (6880), i.e. probable, plausible, fictionally true, by means of an imaginative interpretation of the episode. This he does by converting the combat between two men into a conflict of principle, for Morold may have the strength of four men, but Tristan is supported, on an abstract level which gains him victory over mere force, by God and the allegorical figures of justice and a willing heart (6881ff.). By thus going against historical truth Gottfried opens up a new perspective in his fiction but, in remaining within the bounds of plausibility, he invites his audience's complicity. To the poet's ironically expressed pride in his achievement (6896: 'als übel als ich doch bilden kan', as imperfectly as I can depict it) there corresponds the need for his audience to agree to the truth of his version (6901: 'nu habet ir ez vür wâr vernomen', now you have heard it as the truth). A consensus between author and audience has been established on the basis of its plausibility.

A comparable interpretation, even if it lacks the pointer to plausibility in *wârbaere*, is possible with another episode, where Tristan is clothed in readiness for his knighting ceremony.[60] With Tristan's thirty companions Gottfried has no difficulty in presenting them, for he will simply follow the source (4557), which we know already to be 'historically true'. Tristan himself is more difficult, so much so that Gottfried fully five times casts doubt on his ability to do justice to his description.[61] All this suggests that some special literary effect is aimed at, but it also insinuates a question: why does Gottfried not follow his source here, too? (Eventually he does, but only after insistently raising this disturbing question.) If the source is not (immediately) followed, this suggests a possible deviation from the historical truth incorporated in it, as later in the Morold combat. What follows at some length is confined to literature rather than history: the review of contemporary poets and a prayer for poetic inspiration to enable Gottfried to achieve his version. In the end, four allegorical figures prepare Tristan (4965 ff.), as they had his companions (4561ff.). The irony of this rhetorical build-up, achieved with so much difficulty, is that Tristan resembles his companions in outward clothing, but surpasses them inwardly, invisibly (4986ff.).

The fictionality of this episode in Gottfried depends on four features, in each of which the author is not tied to following his source and cannot therefore ultimately claim its historical truth for himself. One of the criteria for Gottfried's depiction is that it should be acceptable to his audience (4593: 'daz man ez gerne verneme', that you may gladly hear it; 4596: 'daz iu gelîche und iu behage' that it may please and suit you), whilst another is that it should fit in with the overall purpose and meaning of his narrative (4594: 'und an dem maere wol gezeme', and be fitting for the story; 4597: 'und schône an disem maere stê', and contribute to the beauty of this story).[62] Each of these points is repeated and, coming so close together, they drive out any idea that Gottfried's primary obligation is to source and attested truth, rather than to an imaginative interpretation of events that will meet with his audience's approval. This approval depends, thirdly, on his making his version plausible. When at the beginning of this episode (4558ff.) Gottfried challenges any objector to provide a better alternative he knows that no one in his audience can outdo him in studying the historical sources he claims to have consulted in the prologue. In other words, they are being invited to accept his version as plausible, as is the case with the game played by Hartmann von Aue with his (fictive) know-all interrupter in *Erec*.[63] This clothing episode in *Tristan* is meant to be as *wârbaere*, as much in conformity with verisimilitude, as the Morold combat. Like this episode it rests on complicity between author and audience. On reaching the point where Tristan is clothed allegorically the poet is confident that he has his audience with him (4963: 'mac ich die volge von iu hân', if I may have your agreement), so much so that when it comes to entrusting Tristan to the allegorical figures Gottfried does this in conjunction with his audience (4976: 'so bevelhen wir in vieren / unsern friunt Tristanden', so let us entrust our friend Tristan to the four of them). In both these episodes complicity with the audience is present, a collusion which is central to fictionality and to which we now turn.

The two most common ways of describing this collusion are Coleridge's 'willing suspension of disbelief'[64] and 'make-believe', the latter incorporated in our definition as an invitation to the audience to be willing to make-believe. Coleridge's phrase is still used occasionally,[65] but criticisms have been voiced. Walton calls it misleading, but unhelpfully gives no reason for this judgment, whilst Searle, talking of the logical status of fictional discourse, is more explicit.[66] Using his observation, we may say that we do not abandon or even suspend our disbelief when we encounter animals in the *Ecbasis captivi* gifted with the power of speech or, to take an extreme, but still valid example, when faced with the opening episode in *Sir Gawain and the Green Knight* in which the Green Knight, having just had his head chopped off, calmly picks it up and departs, warning Gawain that he will return the compliment at a given time.[67] On the contrary, we remain firm in our disbelief in the reality or truth of what is narrated in works like these. Even in less extreme cases only naïve or untrained members of the audience could be seen as suspending disbelief or as believing, whilst the reaction of others, accepting the invitation to complicity with the author, is both to disbelieve the reality of what is presented and to be willing to entertain the possibility of poetic or narrative truth.

More convincing is the term 'make-believe'. Of this concept, applied to fiction, it has been said that the author intends us to make-believe his text, but also to recognise that very intention, so that a tacit agreement is established.[68] To make-believe, as distinct from believing, implies that the make-believer adopts a dual point of view. At one and the same time he believes that Mr Pickwick is bald and also that there never was a Mr Pickwick, so that he cannot have been bald.[69] These conflicting beliefs are contradictory only for one who refuses to pretend or make-believe. In the knowing collusion between author and audience the latter undertake imaginatively to believe what they know to be fictive, so that author and audience are both playing a double game of belief and disbelief.[70] (How useful this concept can be, both in philosophical and in literary scholarship, can be seen from the fact that Walton has entitled his book *Mimesis as make-believe*, whilst Morgan's essay on the fictionality of the Greek romance is called 'Make-believe and make believe'.) Central to this game of make-believe is the fact that two parties are knowingly engaged on it.[71] This collusion between two parties in fiction has been described by various terms such as 'tacit agreement', 'convention', 'connivance' or 'contract'.[72] It involves the audience in consciously adopting an attitude which Lamarque and Olsen term a 'fictive stance': to make-believe that a fictional statement is true, while knowing that it is not.[73]

Such a fictive stance means that the audience cannot be deceived, that fiction for them is not the same as deception or lying (involving the conscious wish to deceive). The wish to deceive cannot be present when signals to the author's intention or meaning are given and are recognised by the audience (and even when they may fail to recognise them).[74] As long as they know that they are dealing with fiction they know that the author does not really have knowledge of the events he recounts.[75] Similarly, Sir Philip Sidney could absolve poetry (in our case fiction) of the charge of lying: 'Now, for the poet, he nothing affirmeth, and therefore never lieth. For, as I take it, to lie, is to affirm that to be true which is false.'[76]

Even though fiction cannot be stamped as lying, medieval sources often refer to what we should term fiction as if it were lying. Amongst the reasons for this we may adduce three. First, rigorist critics of fiction, refusing to adopt a fictive stance with which they had no sympathy, argued that if fiction did not purvey the truth, then it must indulge in lies. Already in Greek antiquity Solon, as reported by Plutarch, took up an uncompromising stand against the fiction of classical tragedy, arguing that an untruth was a lie, regardless of intention, effect or context.[77] With regard to the three rhetorical types of narrative Konrad von Hirsau refrains from saying that *argumentum* is characterised by verisimilitude; he thereby fails to acknowledge that, coming between *fabula* and *historia*, it may be fictional, but has the force of truth. For him secular, fictional literature is simply mendacious.[78]

Secondly, rivalry amongst authors means that one could denigrate the fiction of another by dismissing it as lies. This is a ploy frequently adopted by *ioculatores* (minstrels) in competition with one another and ready to assert that their own songs are historically true, whilst others are mere fables. Accusing rivals of mendacity need not even mean that one's own narrative is of unimpeachable veracity.[79] Thirdly, to refer to a fiction as a lie may be simply the result of a situation common to classical antiquity and the Middle Ages, namely the absence in both periods of a specific term and a theoretical home for the new genre of the romance and the fictionality that characterised it.[80] Lexical embarrassment may therefore lie behind Wace's hovering between *conte* and *fable* in referring to stories about Arthur.[81]

It can also happen that some modern scholars refer to a medieval work as fiction where there is no evidence that its author intended to be seen through and provided signals to that effect. Here confusion is sown by the ambiguity of the modern term 'fiction', possessing both the technical meaning that concerns us ('a fictive composition') and the non-technical, colloquial meaning ('falsehood, deceit, fabrication'). From our point of view: where there is no evidence for a conscious contract between author and audience the former is to be seen as tricking and deceiving his audience, not as colluding with them in a game of make-believe.

This is relevant to a work standing at the font of Arthurian literature, for Geoffrey of Monmouth's history has been termed a fiction, which can only be accepted in the colloquial sense of that word, not in the technical one. For example, Fichte makes no clear distinction between these usages of the modern term in applying it to Geoffrey's work. He calls it 'for the most part fictional', he refers to its 'fictitious plot' and can even designate it outright a 'fiction'.[82] This raises the question whether Geoffrey meant his work to be regarded as fiction or as history, however falsified the latter may have been. Anticipating our later argument, we may say now simply that it was presented as history (as Fichte himself concedes), even as quasi-history.[83] Geoffrey's work was meant to serve very real political purposes of the Anglo-Norman dynasty, to assist their image-boosting vis-à-vis the French royal house, so that we may ask how this aim would have been served (and how his work would have been received) if he had made it clear that he was presenting not a history (however bowdlerised), but a fiction to which no factual credence need be attached.[84] He did not mean his 'history' to be seen through as a fiction by those whose interests it was to serve.

The most important feature of our working definition is thus the complicity between author and audience in fictionality, the need for this to be made clear to the audience and their readiness to adopt a fictive stance. So far we have discussed this only in theoretical terms (apart from two episodes from Gottfried's *Tristan*), so that it is time to illustrate it in literary practice.

Once more, classical precedents may assist us. Our first example comes from Ovid, whose complicity with his audience underpins his *Metamorphoses*, where at one point two possible reactions for his audience are demonstrated.[85] Everyone, including Lelex singled out by name, is persuaded by Achelous into believing his story (8.612: *credentes*, trusting), they accept as a *factum* what is in itself *mirabile*, miraculous (8.611) because it is convincing. That is, everyone except Pirithous, for whom these stories are *ficta*, fictions. By building these two contradictory reactions into his poem Ovid makes it clear to his audience that they must be both Lelex and Pirithous, that a double stance, believing yet disbelieving, is a necessary condition for appreciating his fiction.

More explicit is what Macrobius has to say on the complicity between Virgil and his audience in understanding the Dido episode in the *Aeneid*.[86] For Macrobius, as for others,[87] this episode is without historical backing for, quite apart from the fact that Dido and Aeneas were not historical contemporaries, Macrobius is aware of the pointedly literary manner in which Virgil has gone to work here. He has borrowed the substance of this love-affair from the *Argonautica* of Apollonius, transferring what had been said of Medea and Jason to Dido and Aeneas. The procedure is one of an author of fiction, disposing of material from various sources, literary and historical, for his own purposes ('non de unius racemis vindemiam sibi fecit', he did not make his vintage from the vine of one grower) with no regard for overall historical veracity. Macrobius therefore feels justified in calling Virgil's work a *fabula*. As regards the reception of this *fabula* Macrobius is informative about the reaction not merely of himself, but of the whole world (*universitas*). He says that everyone knows this *fabula* to be false, presenting only the appearance of truth ('speciem veritatis', the appearance of truth, and 'pro vero', as if it were true), because they know that Dido was chaste and laid hands on herself only to safeguard her honour. Nonetheless, such is the beauty of Virgil's account ('pulchritudo narrandi') that they suppress within themselves the testimony of the (historical) truth ('intra conscientiam veri fidem prementes') and prefer to celebrate as true the charm of fiction ('malint pro vero celebrari quod pectoribus humanis dulcedo fingentis infudit'). Macrobius describes here how Virgil's audience, fully aware of the historical truth, nonetheless accept his fiction as if it were true by a process of make-believe of which they are conscious. In so doing they carry out their part of the fictional contract, and Macrobius describes their reaction as their connivance ('coniveant tamen fabulae', yet they connive with the story). A modern classical scholar still shares Macrobius' view today, for Feeney speaks of Virgil's 'awareness of the power of his fictive art to command credence even in the face of the audience's knowledge that the anachronistic affair between Aeneas and Dido is the poet's own created fiction'.[88]

In the twelfth century John of Salisbury was equally aware that fiction conflicted with history on this point ('Poetica licentia fidem peruertens historiae', poetic licence distorting the reliability of history), on the grounds both of Dido's chastity (*pudicissima*) and of time-difference (*ex ratione temporum*).[89] In his discussion of the *fictio auctoris* von Moos interprets the same author's prologue to *Policraticus* as amounting to a confession of fictional details in which his readers, alerted to them from the beginning, are to work with the author, not against him.[90] John confesses that he has made use of lies in the shape of invented authorities and adds that he will call his friend whoever may correct his errors. This admission, at such an exposed place, is seen by von Moos as an implicit invitation to educated readers to be on the alert in what follows, not to take every quotation at face value. Their task is to enter into cooperation with the author, to be his knowing accomplices.[91] In this they are as aware of what they are doing as was Macrobius (and John of Salisbury himself) in reading Virgil.

For a vernacular example of the fictional contract we come back to the *Tristan* story, this time to Gottfried's source, Thomas. When he narrates how Tristran was to send Guvernal to fetch Yseut to cure his wound Thomas refers to the traditional story and to how Breri differed from it (Douce 845 ff.), but then instead of following Breri as presumably providing the more trustworthy account Thomas goes his own way, giving his reasons why it cannot credibly have been Guvernal, too well known at court, who was the messenger.[92] The truth of this detail depends for Thomas not on any historically attested source, but rather on its imaginative plausibility. In rehearsing his doubts about Guvernal's suitability Thomas does not make authorial statements, but asks questions of his audience (Douce 871 ff.), inviting their response and participation. They are to join him in an imaginative experiment in which he seeks their connivance.

The last point in our definition which calls for comment is the fact that the object of the game of make-believe is what would otherwise be regarded as untrue, a formulation meant to suggest the replacement of historical or factual truth by a concept of truth that may be termed literary or imaginative or fictional. (Lamarque and Olsen may argue as philosophers against regarding fictionality in terms of truth at all, but for medieval fiction, breaking free from the absolute antithesis between truth and untruth and dependent in this on the three types of narrative defining degrees of truthfulness, this association was historically inescapable.) It is the opponents of medieval fiction, those still tied to this absolute antithesis, who criticise it for not corresponding to factual truth, for being therefore mendacious.[93] Not everything they called a lie is fiction (witness the attacks of clerical *litterati* on the inaccuracy of oral history or the criticisms by contemporary historians of Geoffrey of Monmouth),[94] but neither is fiction, as they claimed, a lie. Instead, by occupying middle ground fictionality is neither true nor untrue,[95] even though it may pretend in self-defence to convey truth (if not factual truth).

This middling status of fictionality was known to classical antiquity. The essays edited by Gill and Wiseman on fiction in the ancient world contain numerous references to or questions about fiction as 'a game of truth in which we pretend to forget that lies are lies; or in which the ordinary rules of truth and falsehood are both simulated and suspended' or as standing 'between "telling the truth" and "lying"'.[96] The episode in Ovid's *Metamorphoses* in which we are invited to be both Lelex and Pirithous concerns an account which is both true (*factum*) and untrue (*ficta*). More clearly defined and lasting through to the Middle Ages is the rhetorical position of *argumentum* in particular as the meeting-point of two binary oppositions.[97] The first is between the fictional (*fabula*, *argumentum*) and the non-fictional (*historia*), the second between what approximates to reality (*historia*, *argumentum*) and what is quite implausible (*fabula*). From this grouping *argumentum*, for our purposes the most interesting of these three types of narrative, is both fictional and also plausibly true in being verisimilar.

For a twelfth-century vernacular formulation we turn to the passage in Wace's *Roman de Brut* in which he distinguishes his own claim to have written a historical work from the tales about Arthur and the adventures of the Round Table.⁹⁸ These tales are recounted by professional minstrels whose work Wace dismisses as mere *fables* and who themselves are no more than *fablëors* (storytellers), so that Wace stands close to the equally critical attitude of William of Malmesbury towards the Arthurian *nugae*, *naeniae* and *fabulae* propagated by the Britons.⁹⁹ Important for our purpose is Wace's description of the content of these Arthurian tales, for they are neither completely lying nor completely true (9793: 'Ne tut mençunge ne tut veir,/ Ne tut folie ne tut saveir', neither all a lie nor all truth, neither all folly nor all wisdom). With this phrase it is difficult to imagine that Wace conceived these minstrels' tales as already incorporating what Chrétien only later achieved in his romances in express opposition to this kind of oral tale, namely the creation of fiction not as factual, but as narrative truth.¹⁰⁰ Instead, Wace conceivably had in mind the conflation of what were regarded as historical facts (9747ff.: the figure of Arthur and his establishment of the Round Table) with fictional accretions (9789f.: *merveilles* and *aventures*) such as troubled William of Malmesbury, who likewise accepted the historical figure of Arthur while rejecting the fables told about him.¹⁰¹ Wace's words show how well the *matière de Bretagne* lent itself to the subsequent development of fiction by Chrétien. They represent the first 'theoretical' formulation in the medieval vernacular of a break with the dichotomy between true and untrue, the first suggestion that these stories, like Chrétien's romances soon afterwards, could occupy middle ground between these two poles.¹⁰² To judge fictionality in terms of this dichotomy is therefore to apply a foreign criterion to it, but at least Wace saw that these exclusive categories did not apply.

In this Wace may even be said to have anticipated modern theorists on fictionality.¹⁰³ Walton puts it that part of a person believes something in fiction which another part of him disbelieves or that to half believe something is to be not quite sure that it is true, but also not quite sure that it is not true.¹⁰⁴ Morgan argues that within the world of the novel (we could say equally: of the romance) the statements that make it up are fictionally true, but outside that literary world they are factually untrue, and both author and audience acknowledge them to be so in their rational minds.¹⁰⁵

CHAPTER 2

Vernacular fiction in the twelfth century

Because of the historical variability of the concept and practice of fiction the definition attempted in the last chapter was meant to be applicable to a relatively short timespan on either side of 1200. Not merely does fiction vary across cultures, it is also changeable over time within one culture and between literary genres (which is why we are to concentrate on the romance).[1] Within the romance attention has been drawn to different features that make up its fictionality and emerge at different times, not all at once, so that the process of fictionalisation is a gradual one.[2] We must avoid a revolutionary model, positing a 'discovery' of fiction once and for all rather than the possibility that different conditions may encourage its emergence (and its loss) at different times. This suggests the relevance of the first section of this chapter, namely the possibility that vernacular fiction in the twelfth century may have had predecessors.

PREDECESSORS

The emergence of fictionality amongst the Greeks has been treated by Rösler in terms of the interplay between orality and writing.[3] The early Greek poets, like their critics, held that poetry should tell the truth, as befits an oral culture in which the task of poetry was to transmit traditional lore,[4] but with the advent of writing this gradually changed and the possibility of fiction arose. How this new possibility was reflected in Greek theory we have seen briefly with Plato (negatively) and Aristotle (positively). Of lasting importance for the history of literature was the emergence of the late Hellenistic and Roman romance, a genre of narrative fiction, no matter whether we regard it as pure fiction or as a fictionalised version of other genres.[5]

For Haug medieval fiction was essentially the discovery of Chrétien de Troyes, even though he is somewhat ambivalent in formulation, sometimes stating pointblank that Chrétien was the father of medieval fiction, sometimes qualifying this, more correctly, by saying that medieval *vernacular* fiction began essentially with him.[6] It is this latter view, with the implication that the concept and practice of fiction may have been present in medieval Latin before Chrétien, that underlies the following.

As an example we may take the Latin epic *Ruodlieb*, composed towards the end of the eleventh century. What has been said of Chrétien as the creator of the Arthurian romance can also be said of the author of this epic a century earlier, for he, too, drew upon a range of disparate genres, combining material from them to form a new experimental whole.[7] This material includes undoubtedly fictional genres such as the folktale (*Märchen*), in particular the type known as the folktale of good counsels.[8] Several aspects of this feature of *Ruodlieb* are fictional: the author draws on a fictional genre, the first three counsels give rise, quite implausibly, to the first three adventures on Ruodlieb's way (in exactly the same order), and even if this detail is 'relativised' this is not in the direction of any conformity to reality, but so as to replace the folktale by other fictional material, such as the *fabliau* and reminiscences of romances of antiquity.[9] The author of *Ruodlieb* also makes occasional use of the fictional device of the *ordo artificialis*.[10] Vollmann may have reservations about Haug's suggestion of a *Wegschema* as an overall structure, saying that it is too much dictated by the pattern of the Arthurian romance, whilst he stresses instead the frequency of 'contrasting responsions' in the Latin work's structure, features which are just as fictional, just as artificially contrived to convey meaning.[11] The author also employs signals pointing to the unreal nature of his plot, as in the folktale: the anonymity of the characters, the indefinite nature of time and place, the presence of animals that speak.[12] Vollmann sees this as characteristic of the folktale, received as fictional by the audience, which would imply, as a central feature in our definition of fictionality, an agreement or contract between author and audience.[13]

Alongside this, however, the author of *Ruodlieb* takes over some material from heroic tradition, regarded by laymen in a still predominantly oral society as a reliable source of knowledge of the past, but not by all clerics[14] and certainly not by the author of *Ruodlieb*, whose story is pronouncedly ahistorical and for whom this heroic tradition provided only a few random details.[15] He also makes use of legendary material, once more not as historically true (as the Christian legend was felt to be), but as free to be adapted across genres to the new needs of secular literature.[16]

The fictional status of *Ruodlieb* therefore rests on a variety of points. Its material derives from a number of recognisably fictional genres, but even where it comes from non-fictional, 'historical' genres it is freely adapted to new ends, so that the whole amounts to a novel combination of disparate material.[17] Behind this lies the invention of a new story, not one derived from history or from a source for which a truth-status could be claimed,[18] so that for these reasons *Ruodlieb* may justifiably be termed an example of fiction. More important from our point of view than any suggestion that it could be described as a predecessor of the twelfth-century romance is the conclusion that the Latin author, like his vernacular colleagues a century later, made use of fictionality to experiment with new forms of literary structure.[19]

Equally fictional is the medieval Latin beast epic, as represented by the eleventh-century *Ecbasis captivi*, whose fictional status we looked at earlier, or *Ysengrimus*, completed in the twelfth century, but shortly before Chrétien began work. Already in classical antiquity, although moral lessons might be drawn from animal fables, they could make not the slightest claim to literal truth or even plausibility.[20] Because of this they were *fabulae* in the conventional sense of a fictional type of narrative and were classified as either Libystic (men and animals speak with one another) or Aesopic (animals only are involved).[21] This distinction, as well as the status of such *fabulae*, was known to Isidore of Seville and also to medieval authors such as Konrad von Hirsau and Engelbert von Admont.[22] There can be no doubt that the Latin-speaking audiences for such beast epics realised, not merely on the basis of rhetorical theory, that these works were fictions. In view of the quality, length and complexity of works like the *Ecbasis captivi* and *Ysengrimus*, however, we cannot dismiss them, as does Haug, in terms of their fictionality as mere *Fabeln* or as providing no more than a narrative shape for already given truths.[23] Instead, they belong together with *Ruodlieb* to the Latin prehistory of what Chrétien later accomplished in the vernacular.

Also from the (late) eleventh century comes a revealing statement by Baudri de Bourgueil about the various guises of impersonation he adopts in his poems.[24] Thoroughly familiar with Ovid, he follows the Roman poet's example in composing a pair of letter-poems, purportedly sent between Paris and Helen, and another pair between Florus and Ovid himself.[25] Like Ovid with his disclaimer in *Amores*,[26] Baudri makes his position clear. He confesses that he writes about things as if they were real, attributes to various *personae* (including himself) words and feelings which are however not the truth, but all made up (85, 39: 'Crede michi: non uera loquor magis omnia fingo', Believe me, I do not speak the truth, I make everything up). Baudri likewise insists elsewhere that his love-poems are not private confessions and that if he were really in love he would not declaim it in public.[27] In view of Baudri's debt to Ovid we may see him as likewise disclaiming factual truth in favour of fiction, making this clear to his audience by such statements and occupying the middle ground between truth and lie which is characteristic of fictionality.[28]

What is best described as a tentative approach to fictionality or a flirting with it is also seen with the Latin historians of twelfth-century England discussed by Otter (William of Malmesbury, Geoffrey of Monmouth, William of Newburgh, Walter Map, Giraldus Cambrensis).[29] Otter focuses on a number of 'other world' episodes in these authors' works, involving fairytale motifs outside normal time and geography, allowing them to articulate the hypothetical, the ironic, the uncertain, to probe the limits of truth-telling, to ponder the authenticity of such episodes, whilst disclaiming any responsibility.[30] Two points in Otter's argument concern us. First, the historiographic works she treats only approach the practice of fiction, touching upon its possibilities tentatively, and even then piecemeal, episodically, temporarily, in interpolated stories, so that we may still regard the surrounding narrative as a historical account.[31] Any fiction present therefore does not inform the whole work, as with *Ruodlieb* and Chrétien's romances. Secondly, Otter stresses that even this tentative playing with fictionality in Latin historiography weakens the case for seeing fiction as a discovery of vernacular writing (Chrétien), marking its emancipation from the Latin ecclesiastical tradition.[32] Any emancipation from ecclesiastical tradition achieved by fictionality had its predecessors in Latin, even though they did not succeed in establishing a fictional genre.

Corresponding to the literary practice of such works that made it clear that they were fictional and should be received as such there are a number of indications that the status and legitimation of fiction was also under theoretical discussion in Latin before Chrétien, in the first half of the twelfth century. Concentrating on the literary-theoretical implications of Abélard's theory of language von Moos argues that theology of this period could provide a legitimation for secular fiction, an emancipation that belongs to the prehistory of a much later, modern conception of literature.[33] In a chapter devoted to the literary theory of early scholasticism Grünkorn has concluded, with whatever qualifications, that this theory found a place for fictionality, not merely with Abélard, but also with Alanus ab Insulis and John of Salisbury.[34] Burrichter, basing herself largely on von Moos, goes beyond him in questioning the tenability of Jauss's view that there was simply no distinction between fiction and reality in the period before Chrétien.[35] Mehtonen shows that the twelfth century saw not merely the development of poetics as an independent discipline, but also the appropriation of traditional rhetorical concepts to defining a Latin poetics of fiction.[36]

With Zeeman's discussion of the licence given to the poets by the schools, however, we reach a point germane to the next stage in our argument when she makes the transition from Latin to the vernacular. She reminds us that grammatical teaching about poetry in the Middle Ages was formulated for moral and scholarly purposes, but had a potential significance for those with other agendas, including expressly the vernacular romance, so much so that she suggests that the composition of romances could not have proceeded as it did without the impetus of the commentators' ideas about poetry.[37] Another significant link between Latin and vernacular is provided by the classical themes (Troy, Aeneas, Alexander) rendered into French and German in the twelfth century. Commentaries on and *accessus* to the classical works, both in antiquity and in the Middle Ages, frequently point to features that are historically true and those that are fictional. Clerical authors of their medieval versions would thus know from their schooling of the fictional possibilities of their themes.[38] The same can be assumed of clerical authors of the *matière de Bretagne*, who would learn of fiction in the same way and apply it to their different themes.

So far we have been concerned with the idea and practice of fiction before Chrétien in Latin, but the position is nothing like so clearcut when we turn to vernacular storytelling in the same period. This is hardly surprising given our lack of evidence since, although vernacular storytelling in one form or another may be characteristic of any human society at whatever time, we are dealing in this period with narratives on an oral, subliterary level. If such narratives survive at all it is only because at one stage they were transposed into writing, with changes in the act of transposition which make it difficult to assess their precise nature in the preliterate stage.[39] The difficulties which this creates for judging their fictionality (or otherwise) may be illustrated by three examples.

With the first we return to *Ruodlieb*, specifically to the folktale of good counsels on which its narrative is in part based. This folktale type is widely attested throughout Europe, and if *Ruodlieb* represents the earliest written example known to us, the later examples cannot possibly all descend from it, but must like it derive from oral tradition.[40] This is also the case with other material incorporated in *Ruodlieb*, likewise of oral rather than written literary origin. That this oral narrative material was of a fictional nature seems clear, particularly in the case of folktale or *fabliau* themes, but the exact nature of this oral fictionality escapes us.

The obstacle erected by the transition to written form to our understanding of an earlier stage, representing a possible oral fictional narrative, recurs in another genre, the so-called *Spielmannsepen*, whose written versions date from the late twelfth century, but which are held to be largely based on oral narratives. Like *Ruodlieb* they therefore represent the point of intersection between oral tradition and preservation in written form.[41] The difficulty with these works for our question is that we have no means of telling how these oral predecessors were regarded (as true or as fictive). The fact that historical elements in some of these works (e.g. *Herzog Ernst*), like legendary elements in others (e.g. *Orendel*), were regarded as historically reliable might suggest that their oral forerunners were held to be truthful, but on the other hand if such elements are 'buchepische' accretions to original tales of popular entertainment then it is conceivable that these tales were indeed fictive (as might be suggested by the fabulous journeys in the East narrated in

Herzog Ernst).[42] Again, while oral fictional tales may well have existed before our chosen period their very orality makes it difficult for us to lay hands on them.

The same remains true when we come to the threshold of Chrétien's revolutionary innovation in the vernacular. The prologue to his first romance, *Erec*, is commonly accepted as proclaiming the superiority of his written and structurally meaningful version to the oral and disjointedly composed *conte d'avanture* (tale of adventure) on which he drew.[43] But how are we to judge the relationship between Chrétien's work and the oral *conte* in terms of fictionality? We shall see that belief in the historicity of King Arthur need not imply belief in the reliability of tales circulating about him.[44] More specifically in this case: did Chrétien regard the *conte d'avanture* itself as already fictional or rather as material that he could treat fictionally? Even if this *conte* was regarded as fictional, is it at all likely that the oral *conteurs* so despised by Chrétien had a conception of fictionality close to his own? How far is it likely that their tales were regarded as truthful and hence non-fictional (especially if not always comprehensible)?[45] In other words, even if they betray fictional elements in their material these cannot go so far as the structural sophistication on which Chrétien prided himself, so that we are driven to assume, like Ridder,[46] different stages in realising the full potentiality of fiction.

Fictionality, in the strict sense of our definition as distinct from the colloquial usage of 'fiction' to mean 'untruth', may therefore be problematic in these vernacular examples before Chrétien (the oral material drawn on by *Ruodlieb* and the *Spielmannsepen*, and present in Chrétien's sources), but the same is not the case with medieval Latin works such as *Ruodlieb* itself and the *Ecbasis captivi*, whose fictional status is unquestioned. This justifies us in correcting Haug's ambivalence and in claiming that what begins or is discovered in the twelfth century is not narrative fiction itself, but the application of fictionality, previously recognised and practised in medieval Latin, to written vernacular literature. This by no means weakens Chrétien's importance, but underlines his clerical status (denied by Vitz)[47] in enriching vernacular literature from what was available in Latin. It is not surprising that the intellectual unrest which Haug himself dates from 1100[48] should be visible in Latin literature earlier than in the vernacular, in the case of fictionality a century earlier than Chrétien. This specific case offers yet another argument for regarding the twelfth century as modern historians view the nineteenth: as a 'long century' stretching beyond its opening and closing dates. By seeing fictionality predominantly in terms of the double cycle structure of the Arthurian romance (even though there are other possibilities of fictional structuring), Haug has been drawn towards seeing medieval fiction as beginning with Chrétien.[49] If instead, with Huber and in accord with our definition, we see fictionality more essentially in terms of a contract between author and audience[50] this opens up different aspects of the problem of fiction and grants a place to the Latin examples which came before Chrétien.

Another point where Haug's theory of medieval fictionality has drawn criticism from his reviewers concerns the position which he attributes to the literature which incorporates it. He refers to the 'disengagement' (*Unverbindlichkeit*) of that literature, but also, more drastically, to its autonomy, thereby anachronistically importing into the Middle Ages a modern view of literature which arose only in the eighteenth century.[51] (It is true that Haug also talks more warily of 'a certain autonomy' and in the second edition of his monograph answers his critics by toning down the force of his assertion, which however still stands in principle.)[52] We do not have to accept in its entirety Köhler's thesis that Chrétien's romances are a response to a crisis in feudal society towards the end of the twelfth century to recognise that there may be some force in a 'social' reading of Chrétien's work in the specific sense that his writings are significantly connected with centres of opposition to the centralising force of the French monarchy and arose in that politically charged and far from 'autonomous' context. Even Chrétien's *Erec*, his first romance in which he proudly proclaims the novelty of his achievement, cannot be claimed as autonomous if, as has been suggested, it is meant to serve the political interests of the Angevin dynasty, as had been the case with Geoffrey of Monmouth's history.[53] The postulated autonomy of these romances is further weakened by their extraliterary function in propagating an ideal of chivalry meant to serve ends which pass well beyond anything like art for art's sake, but also in the context of their actual performance as a social occasion at court.[54] Despite the first beginnings of private reading this remains the dominant context of reception in the Middle Ages, far removed from the position since the eighteenth century in which an autonomous fictional literature may well accompany a less pronouncedly social reception. To stress this difference between the Middle Ages and the modern period is yet another indication of the variability of fictionality over time and of the need to shun such anachronisms.

In answering his critics Haug also argues that even in literature serving particular external interests there remains the possibility of the occasional vacuum (*Freiraum*) granting more freedom of scope for the author's own concerns.[55] If so, that must be true not solely of Chrétien, for it opens up the possibility of fictionality within such a vacuum before him, perhaps not so fully fledged as with him. This is particularly relevant to medieval treatments of classical themes (Troy, Aeneas, Alexander) where we are dealing, as with the Hellenistic romance, if not with fiction itself, then at least with a fictionalised version of another genre.[56] This makes it regrettable that, apart from the *Alexanderlied*, Haug should have omitted these themes from his survey.

The changing nature of fictionality over time, its 'discovery' (or better: the conscious recognition of its possible existence) in classical antiquity, its displacement from reputable literary practice in early Christianity and in the early Middle Ages, its re-emergence in the high Middle Ages (not merely with Chrétien, but even before him) and, yet again, its renewed development at the hands of Cervantes[57] – all this immensely complicates the problem of defining fictionality so as to accommodate such a range of possibilities. We avoid this difficulty by using a definition purposely geared to the short timespan with which we are concerned.

FINDING A PLACE FOR FICTION

Difficulties, both theoretical and terminological, were encountered in finding a place for the novelty of a fictional romance, difficulties strikingly common both to classical Greece and to the twelfth century. The new genre of the romance in antiquity has been described as drastically undertheorised, since no satisfactory home could be found for it in established genres, whilst Knapp has argued similarly that the medieval romance could not be accommodated within the traditional scheme of poetics.[58] This difficulty in placing the innovation in an acknowledged theoretical framework is reflected in terminology: first, in that antiquity, although developing a range of possibilities, possessed no word corresponding exclusively to fiction, whilst for the Middle Ages Knapp has spoken of a 'terminologischer Notstand' (terminological emergency);[59] secondly, in that the failure to cope with this novelty meant that there was no term to designate the romance as a genre. Greek used a number of terms, but these applied only to some aspects or could be used of other genres as well.[60] The position was no clearer in the Middle Ages. French *romanz* meant at first any work translated from Latin into a Romance vernacular, and came only later to denote a work of narrative literature, including not only the romance, but several other genres.[61] German lacked a corresponding term, so that words like *liet*, *âventiure*, *rede* and *maere* are all used of works that we should describe as romances, whilst even the potentially most promising of these, *âventiure*, was also applied to genres other than the romance.[62] At two historical points where the fictional romance emerged in Europe its novelty meant that it was difficult to find a place for it, theoretically or semantically.

Whether we start with Chrétien or with the medieval Latin examples that preceded him, a justification had to be found for fiction, a place for it within the conceptual framework of a period still dominated by the Christian condemnation of poetry as lying. To the age-old charge that poets lie, presenting as reality what they have invented, they could respond by using devices like irony, allegory, *integumentum* or, more crucially, by blurring the border between history and fiction.[63] These defensive reactions were out of place in literature with a religious theme, hence true, or which dealt with what was regarded as under divine control, such as the *significatio rerum* (meaning of things) imparted to natural phenomena by God, in the *Physiologus* tradition, or in history seen as an unfolding history of salvation, or in hagiography in which historical truth was seen against the background of a higher truth, metaphysical or ethical.[64]

Even outside the religious context truth could be found in what is unreal and fictive, above all when, as was also the case with hagiography, appeal could be made to ethical as distinct from factual truth.[65] For Thomasin the mendacity of court fictional literature can convey *wârheit* (truth) as long as it teaches a lesson of *zuht*, right conduct in life, just as Johann von Würzburg attributes the power of moral improvement, *bezzerunge*, to such works, no matter whether they are the truth or a lie.[66]

Of a similar shift towards fictivity in Middle English works it has been said that they treat moral issues in a literary way, not by direct didactic address, but by author and audience joining in contemplation of an imagined world, in other words engaged in the conscious contract that is central to our definition.[67]

This defence needs to be placed in a wider context, however, for a twofold claim could also be made to safeguard a place for fiction in medieval literary practice: first, as just mentioned, that it could convey instruction or set up ethical examples, but secondly that it provided justifiable pleasure and entertainment. Taken together, instruction and pleasure are what Horace claimed for literature in his *Ars poetica*[68] and it is from this source that these two defences of fiction descend through the Middle Ages. Horace distinguishes three functions in what he expressly terms fictional literature (338: *ficta*, 339: *fabula*):[69] first, that it should teach a lesson ('prodesse', 'idonea . . . vitae', 'praecipies', 'utile', 'monendo', to benefit, the fitting things of life, give precepts, useful, instructing), secondly, that it should grant pleasure by being verisimilar rather than totally incredible ('delectare', 'iucunda', 'voluptatis causa', 'dulci', 'delectando', to delight, joyful, for the sake of pleasure, charming, giving pleasure),[70] and thirdly, that it is preferable for both these qualities to be combined in the one work (343: 'omne tulit punctum qui miscuit utile dulci,/lectorem delectando pariterque monendo', he won all votes who mixed the useful with the charming, giving the reader equal delight and instruction). There is no doubt but that this Horatian view of poetic fiction was well known in the Middle Ages, both in theory and in literary practice: his name is frequently mentioned in this context, but even when it is not the strength of this tradition is such that he must stand behind such cases. They run from late antiquity *via* Isidore of Seville to the early Middle Ages, the eleventh and twelfth centuries and beyond.[71] They also include vernacular examples (e.g. in Old French and in Chaucer)[72] and constitute, alongside the rhetorical distinction between three types of narrative, the most persistent justification of fictional writing known to the Middle Ages.[73]

Horace's ideal was that poetry should combine *prodesse* with *delectare* and it has been claimed that, in conformity with his demand, this was also an overriding feature of the medieval view of literature.[74] This does not mean, however, that it was the exclusive view and that either of these claims could not be put forward in isolation. When distinguishing his three functions Horace lists them not by *et* (and), but by *aut . . . aut . . . aut* (or),[75] and many of the medieval cases use a similar disjunctive (*vel* or *-ve*). When Augustine criticised the fables of Plautus and Terence for offering nothing but delight (by contrast to Aesop, who also provided instruction) he reveals that the Horatian joint ideal of fiction was not always observed in practice.[76] From a rigorist's point of view it was clearly more difficult to justify fiction when it offered only delight than when it provided something *utile* (not necessarily only instruction). For this reason, in the examples that follow, those that argue in terms of *prodesse* may afford to include a reference to *delectare* as well, whilst those that stress *delectare* are restricted to that function alone. They represent the heart of the problem in legitimising medieval fiction.

The 'usefulness' of medieval literature, as discussed by Olson, rests mainly on what he terms its hygienic and recreational justifications.[77] The somewhat offputtingly termed hygienic defence by no means excludes literary pleasure, for such *delectatio* instils in the audience an emotional state useful 'in preserving health, but also in attaining the finest disposition of mind and body'.[78] Anything (including fictional literature) that induces moderate cheerfulness is thus felt to serve the good of preserving health by inducing the mental attitude necessary for good health. Olson dwells on the medieval category of *theatrica*, under which he includes the performing arts and therefore the public recital of literature to an assembled audience.[79] It counts as a 'mechanical art' because it serves physical needs; such entertainment is justified because of its restorative value to mind as well as body. Entertainment involves delight, but conceived in such 'hygienic' terms it is also useful and profitable, so that it incorporates the double goal of literature as conceived by Horace ('miscuit utile dulci'), as St Bonaventure, for example, fully saw when referring to the Latin poet in making this point in his discussion of *theatrica* amongst the mechanical arts.[80] For Thomas of Chobham, judging various kinds of narrative recital in his day, performers who sing licentious songs are reprehensible, but those who sing of the deeds of princes ('gesta principum et alia utilia') and of the lives of the saints ('vitas sanctorum') bring solace to people in illness or mental discomfort ('faciunt solatia hominibus vel in egritudinibus suis vel in angustiis suis').[81] Saints' lives needed no justification, but the inclusion of what

29

must be regarded as *chansons de geste* (a genre closely related in its genesis to hagiography) amongst *utilia* amounts to a medical legitimation of this genre of secular literature.

The recreational justification of literature is treated separately by Olson, but cannot always be kept distinct from the hygienic argument. Recreation or relaxation in the form of temporary pleasure or entertainment can be seen as an *utile*, since the release it offers for a time from work and other pressures enables people to return later to more effective labour. Recreation in the etymological sense of 're-creation', a rebuilding of mental and physical health after strain and exhaustion, is therefore a valuable service, even if strictly secondary to the task of life's work.[82] With (false?) modesty Walter Map offers his *De nugis curialium* to those engaged in affairs of state as a temporary relaxation, as trifles (*nugae*), for the sake of pastime and pleasure ('recreacionis et ludi gracia').[83] He thereby grants a place to literary entertainment in court society. Petrus Cantor may not go so far when he concedes that minstrels who sing of exploits to give relaxation and perhaps instruction ('cantent de gestis rebus ad recreationem uel forte ad informationem') are close to being legitimate, but at least he is ready to tolerate some form of literary relaxation.[84]

The difficulty of defending literary fiction was much greater, as with Augustine's rejection of Plautus and Terence, when only *delectare* was involved, with no apparent trace of *prodesse*, so that the examples that follow present a much more negative picture. Augustine, this time more theoretically, defines *fabula* as a lie composed for usefulness or delight ('compositum ad utilitatem delectationemve mendacium'), where *-ve* shows that in his eyes not all fictions can claim to be useful.[85] Macrobius similarly distinguishes between fables which merely delight the ear and those which teach morality (the former he confines to the nursery).[86] Isidore of Seville differentiates poetic fictions created 'delectandi causa' (in order to delight) from those concerned with the nature of things and with human behaviour (under the first heading Plautus and Terence again make an appearance).[87] This tradition, damning literary entertainment that provides only pleasure, continues into the Middle Ages. The gloss on Horace in the *Scholia Vindobonensia* makes clear the author's view that fables only delight. By his repetition of *uel* (like Horace's of *aut*) Dominicus Gundissalinus likewise distinguishes poetry that delights from that which instructs in knowledge or behaviour. A thirteenth-century *accessus* to Ovid's *Amores* sees in its frivolous and amusing episodes ('ludicra . . . et iocosa') the intention to delight (*delectet*) defined by Horace in the case of fiction.[88]

We must go further than this, however, for some of these critics of poetic fiction devoted to entertainment alone recognise the unpalatable fact that this is what the audience so often prefers; their criticism is therefore not abstract theory, but directed at contemporary practice.[89] They can perhaps accept the *delectatio* of literature as a necessary relaxation or as a bait for moral instruction, but criticise it as an unwarranted diversion from higher, more serious things.[90] A telling example in the vernacular comes in the prologue to the *Vie de saint Edmund* by Denis Piramus.[91] His rejection of earlier secular concerns may be no more than a topos, but not the precise terms in which he expresses it, for he refers to an earlier romance, *Partonopeus de Blois*, whose fictionality is for him simply untruth (29–30: *fable, menceonge, sounge*), but nonetheless popular with the court audience (33: *mult amez, loez*) because of the *delectatio* it brought (52: *dilitables*; 58: *tel deduit*). By contrast, the religious theme which is now presented is felt to be superior in Horatian as well as Christian terms, for to listen to it will be pleasurable (61: 'deduit'), even more pleasurable (63: 'plus delitable'), but also supremely useful in saving souls (64: 'les almes garir'). Knowing that his audience takes delight in poetic recitals Denis hopes to win them by offering them more of the same, together with spiritual import. In one of his *miracles* Gautier de Coinci likewise argues that his religious tales are superior to secular fiction, that his aim is to give profit more than pleasure (64: 'A porfiter be plus que plaire'), thereby following the 'prophets', John and Luke, rather than the poets, Lucan, Juvenal and Virgil (65–6).[92]

So far we have listened to the voice of the opposition, but on the principle that there is no smoke without a fire may conclude from these criticisms that literary entertainment aiming largely, if not exclusively, at giving pleasure was a factor to be reckoned with. Alongside religious or ethical truth there was also present, especially in court literature, an element not merely of entertainment, but even of playfulness as part of the social ideal of *curialitas* (courtliness) investigated by Jaeger and finding expression in linguistic and literary form specifically in the Arthurian narratives in the Latin tradition treated by Echard.[93] The training in rhetoric undergone by a court author was a preparation for the serious, but also playful, manipulation of language and demanded a literary inventiveness which stood him in good stead in the complexities of fictionality. The linguistic facility required from the writer, but also ideally from the courtier, included such features as *subtilitas* (sophisticated subtlety),[94] *facetia* (a witty, ironic protective covering for truth-telling that avoided offensive or dangerous bluntness),[95] *iocunditas* (jesting as another way of implying the truth without offence)[96] and *ironia* (the language of indirection).[97] All these features employ in one way or another such a language of indirection; they hover between truth and untruth, just as fictionality does.

In this connection even the blanket accusation that fiction is untruth has to be qualified, for three types of *mendacium* could be acknowledged in theological tradition.[98] Lying to bring about harm ('mendacium perniciosum') was naturally condemned, whilst playful lying ('mendacium iocosum'), as in irony, was fully acceptable. The third type, lying to provide assistance ('mendacium officiosum'), could be used positively to include poetic fictions, of which it has been said that they were acceptable because they were perceived by the audience obviously not to be meant as the truth.[99] These listeners, as in our definition, have entered into a contract with the authors of these fictions. Augustine, too, recognises that literature (mimes, comedies, poems) may be full of lies, but with the wish to please rather than to deceive ('delectandi potius quam fallendi voluntate').[100]

The element of playfulness or recreation in the sophisticated language of the court can also extend to fictional literature, not merely for the court, but for other kinds of audience, too, and before the rise of court literature in the vernacular. Lucian, to take a very early example, advised his readers to take his work only as a refreshing interlude, providing mere entertainment, and warned them that they should not look for any record of the truth with him.[101] In classical Latin literature *ludus* and *ludere* (play) are used for certain branches of poetry.[102] The *ludus poeticus* (poetic play) requires leisure, it represents a jest or witty game by contrast with serious literature; it can be used almost synonymously with *nugae* 'trifles' and be equated with *iocus* 'jest'; and on rare occasions it can designate poetry at large as opposed to serious, political work. This range of usages lies behind what is found in medieval Latin. Although there are no grounds for assuming that Hrotswitha meant her poetic legends to be regarded as fictional, she nonetheless dedicates them with a wish that they be read to pass away the time when the reader is worn out by labour.[103] A similar contrast between relaxation and the more serious participation in the liturgy is drawn in the opening of *Waltharius*, dedicated to Archbishop Erkanbald, when it is hoped that time will be found for reading it in the intervals for entertainment between the duties of divine worship (Prologue 19: 'Ludendum magis est dominum quam sit rogitandum', whenever it is time for entertainment rather than for worship).[104] The timing is reversed, but the contrast is the same when the *Ecbasis captivi* closes with the admonition that it is time to lay aside these trifles (*nugae*) and such play (*ludus*) in favour of the singing of psalms.[105] Yet the entertainment this work provides is not meant to exclude instruction: even when admitting that it is a 'mendosa carta' (lying book) the author adds that it contains much that is useful (41: 'sunt tamen utilia quę multa notantur in illa'), thus meeting the Horatian prescription which can even be quoted at a later point (588: 'delectando pariterque monendo'). Drawing attention to the complaint of Froumund von Tegernsee that his pupils prefer amusing fictions to serious literature Vollmann stresses the element of fun and play (*iocus*) in *Ruodlieb* (together with the feature of *prodesse*).[106]

To devote himself at suitable times to such frivolities (including literature) was not felt to be beneath the dignity of a wise man (*sapiens*). John of Salisbury admits as much with regard to the recreational force of leisure (although he refers specifically to music and dancing the same would hold of literature).[107] William of Rennes presents his *Gesta* to his episcopal patron as a *ludus*, an entertaining diversion to refresh him after studying the scriptures.[108] The *Vita Merlini* opens with the author's intention to sing the madness of the prophet Merlin and the *musam jocosam*, words which hark back to Ovid's *Musa iocosa* (playful Muse), invoked in defence of the fictionality of his work (*Tristia* II 355: 'magnaque pars mendax operum est et ficta meorum/plus sibi permisit compositore suo', the greater part of my work is a pretence and fictitious, and has allowed itself more licence than its author).[109] In suggesting that responsibility lies with his audience as well as with himself Ovid provides another example of the fictional contract, but his importance for us rests with the conjunction of literary entertainment with what is admittedly

33

a fictional untruth. We have seen this already with Lucian, with Ovid's *Amores*, with the *Ecbasis captivi* and with Baudri de Bourgueil. John of Salisbury also suggests that fiction, even frivolous, can serve the serious purpose of philosophy, refusing to promise that all he writes is true, but suggesting nonetheless its usefulness to the reader.[110] Finally, with Marie de France, or rather with what Denis Piramus says of her *lais*, we reach the threshold, in dating and in the use of the vernacular, of Chrétien's decisive innovation in fictionality. In addition to rejecting his own earlier work Denis also mentions Marie, criticising her work, too, for being untrue ('Ki ne sunt pas del tut verais', which are not at all true), whilst recognising its popularity at court and the pleasure it brings (*delit, pleire, joie, gré*, delight, please, joy, pleasure).[111] Even in withholding his approval Denis testifies to the widely acknowledged entertainment value of tales that are known to be fictive.

CHAPTER 3

Fictive orality

Whereas in an earlier book I looked briefly at fiction from the point of view of orality and literacy,[1] in this chapter our concern will be with a restriction on the use of the term 'fiction', in opposition to what I regard as unsatisfactory views that have also been put forward. Basically, this chapter deals with how readers were more easily able, in the act of reading, to recognise the presence of fictionality than were listeners, since for readers any narratorial references to an oral recital were not immediately relevant and were therefore imaginary (*fiktive Mündlichkeit*). The position was not so obvious for listeners. Although they would recognise these references as bearing on their reception of a work, as being therefore 'real' (as they were not for readers *qua* readers), they could also see that Hartmann von Aue, for example, imputed questions to his fictive audience which no one in the real audience had actually asked, but which they could well imagine being asked at a recital and could therefore make-believe were possible. This situation (questions were not in fact asked that could conceivably have been asked) links the theme of this chapter to the definition of *argumentum* considered above.[2]

The main thrust of the earlier book was to argue against a binary model, against the view that a reading reception of literature was necessarily in contradiction to hearing its recital and that the two modes of reception were mutually exclusive. I proposed instead that we abandon such an either–or antithesis. The Middle Ages were characterised by a long-term symbiosis of oral with written, of hearing with reading, but the links between these two spheres go much further than a *litteratus* reciting from a written text to those who could not read it for themselves, for many works contain evidence for a reading reception alongside

pointers to their being heard in recital.³ The clearest evidence for this
is the double formula, suggesting reading and hearing as complementary possibilities and originally at home in classical and medieval Latin
(e.g. *audire aut legere*, to hear or to read), but also found in various
vernaculars (OFr *oïr et lire*, MHG *hoeren oder lesen*, ME *herkne or rede*).⁴
The wide spread of this formula (chronologically through to the early
modern period, but also over a range of various languages) shows that
even in the literate culture of Latin, but more so in vernaculars slowly
making their way into writing, public delivery was anticipated as well
as individual reading.

In arguing thus we have to protect ourselves on two flanks against
alternative readings of the double formula.⁵ One alternative is to suggest
that the verb *lesen* refers not to private reading for oneself, but to reading
aloud to others (*vorlesen*),⁶ so that the formula embraces the two poles
of a recital situation: the reciter declaiming from a written text and
his listeners. The other possibility stresses *und*, rather than *oder*, as
the conjunction linking the verbs and sees in the formula the common
practice of reading aloud to oneself. In neither case is a twofold reception
entertained: one suggestion focuses on recital, the other on individual
reading.

The first suggestion was made by Kartschoke in questioning the speed
and extent which Scholz attributed to the spread of a reading reception around 1200.⁷ In his turn Kartschoke feels misunderstood when
I suggested that in interpreting *lesen* in the double formula as 'to read
out, recite' he was playing down the possibility of private reading.⁸
His later defence of his position would be relevant if I had accused
him of denying, rather than playing down, the reader. His wording
suggests this: only after putting forward his interpretation of the formula
('to read out or to hear') does he add the other possibility ('to read
for oneself or to hear'), only to question how frequent this may have
been.⁹

Various aspects of the medieval usage of verbs meaning 'to read'
enjoin hesitation in accepting Kartschoke's interpretation as an overall
explanation. These concern cases where the verb (and derivatives) more
probably refers to the individual reader rather than a reciter.¹⁰ With
reading in the context of private devotions the only addressee – if they
were said aloud – must be God. In monastic literature the *studiosus lector*

whose needs in close reading are consulted by the author arranging for chapter headings or other markers is best seen as the individual reader wishing to learn more, not simply as a *lector* in the sense of 'reciter'. The vernacular *leser* who is instructed how to solve an acrostic is likewise the individual reader, not a reciter – who could not do this orally for his audience with acrostics scattered over distant points in the work. When an author hopes that blemishes in his work may be ignored by those who read it, when he recommends his writing to their careful attention, when he requests the exercise of their critical judgment and consults their convenience: in all these cases it make better sense to see the author as flattering the readers in his audience rather than insinuating himself with a possible reciter who sat well below the salt at court and occupied no position of permanent importance in the monastery.[11]

Such examples, where *lesen* is used of the individual reader, are relevant to the use of this verb in the double formula. In works which refer to readers and listeners by means of the formula (*ir horer und ir lesere*), but also contain other criteria suggesting a reception by readers, this pole in the formula cannot be dismissed quite so easily in favour of a reciter.[12] If these works are also addressed to listeners a reciter must still be present, but is not designated by the word *leser*. Thus William of Malmesbury says that in his leisure hours Robert of Gloucester either read himself or listened to others reading ('aut ipsi legere, aut legentes possitis audire').[13] William does not picture the earl demeaning himself by reciting at his own court, but rather as an occasional individual reader, even though there may be an element of flattery in that suggestion.

Kartschoke's reading of the double formula was made as a suggestion in passing, but his stress on public recital has been developed at greater length for English and French literature in the late Middle Ages by Coleman.[14] In this case, too, the thrust of her argument leads her to under-estimate the role of the individual reader. Fully to be welcomed is the importance that Coleman attaches to public recital from a written text to an assembled audience,[15] for this is the context in which the double formula was at home (a manuscript was read out to listeners, but was also available to the occasional private reader). To distinguish this mode from pure orality (extemporising formulaic composition or memorisation, in either case without benefit of writing) Coleman uses the term 'aurality',[16] although given the difficulty in English pronunciation of distinguishing 'aurality' from 'orality' it is ironic that in a book emphasising the lasting importance of acoustic reception this key distinction should be more apparent to the modern reader.

Another advantage is that Coleman sets her sights against any evolutionary determinism, against the view that, once a more efficient storage mechanism (writing) was available, orality would soon fall away or survive only as a chance residue.[17] Instead of a smooth replacement of orality by writing she argues the coexistence of public recital and private reading, with the public dimension retaining its hold long after the growth of lay literacy had made recital theoretically superfluous.[18] So far from being a non-functional survival of an extinct mode, public recital remained a vital part of a mixed oral–literate tradition throughout the Middle Ages. Between the two extreme poles of orality and full literacy the medieval literary scene is mixed, with literature predominantly addressed to listeners, but also to readers.[19] Interaction between the two is recurrent: within the listening audience were some who could also act as readers, whilst even those who could only listen were exposed to work that had been composed in writing and could be appreciated in its higher reaches only by readers devoting as close a scrutiny to it as had the author in composing it.

The actual situation underlying Coleman's 'aurality' is repeatedly stressed by her, the reception of literature as a social event, a performance situation that 'aurality' shares with pure orality.[20] Literature received as a shared experience was common on festive occasions at court (as also in religious communities of various kinds), where it promoted a sense of group solidarity, an affirmation of shared values and interests. If literature received in this way was an effective form of propaganda or social or spiritual affirmation, it was in the interest of patrons to encourage public readings, not merely in order to hear the texts themselves, but to ensure that their propaganda value was appreciated by as many as possible.[21] A work read out in such a context drew its force from the performer's recital skills and his affective gestures, but also from the reactions of the audience, their attentiveness, applause and even tears. It is a dimension of medieval literature inevitably lost to us, apart from isolated references.

In view of the mixed nature of 'aurality' it is not surprising that, although Coleman does not discuss it in its own right, her material includes many examples of the double formula as a pointer to a twofold reception.[22] These cover medieval Latin as well as English and French literature, mainly from the late Middle Ages, but sometimes extending into the sixteenth century. They form a useful supplement to the material collected in my book (classical and medieval Latin, but above all German). On some occasions, as in German, Coleman's evidence for a twofold reception may go beyond the strict limits of the formula, as when John Twyne in 1537 recommends 'every man to rede this boke/or [those] that cannot rede to geue dylygent eere to the reder' or when the two indicators, to listening and to reading, occur in the same work, but far apart.[23] The formulation may be different, but the ghost of the double formula is still discernible.

However, we cannot always accept Coleman's interpretations without qualification, for the very force with which she conducts her case for 'aurality', the reception of a written text read out to listeners, means that undue weight sometimes falls on listening and excessive restrictions can be placed on private reading. Thus, in the brief discussion of Chaucer's use of the double formula *herkne . . . or rede* Coleman concedes that one meaning of this may be 'to read privately or to listen to a public reading', but then entertains an alternative possibility 'to read publicly [i.e. to read aloud to others] or to listen to a public reading'.[24] Having proposed such an uncertainty she classifies this example as 'format-neutral' and ignores its significance (which, of course, given the wide spread of the double formula, goes far beyond this solitary case from Chaucer). The alternative possibility proposed here agrees with Kartschoke's, so that the reservations called for with him also apply here. There are, however, other considerations that cast doubt on whether the verb for reading in the formula (whether in English or in German, in Latin or in French) can simply be disposed of in this way.

For example, when the double formula is applied to the audience alone it denotes their private reception of a work (by reading) or their public reception (by hearing), as when Pliny expressed a preference for hearing a work recited by another to reading it for himself, or when Ulrich von Zatzikhoven sees the audience for his *Lanzelet* as listeners or readers.[25] Reading for oneself, rather than reading out to others, is also suggested when the formula, used of someone in authority, describes his ability to read as well as to listen to others whom he commands to recite (*audio et lego*, I hear and read, but also *lego et legi facio*, I read and have read out).[26] Finally, as the history of the formula and its entry from Latin into German shows, two of the three strands in this development (literary, historical, legal) establish a parallel between the beginning of the transmission process (seeing and hearing) and its conclusion (reading and hearing), so that reading is to be seen as a visual reception, not as reading out loud to others.[27]

Stemming from the priority that Coleman grants to listening to a public recital is her unwillingness to take 'to hear' as sometimes metaphorical.[28] The demonstration of this possibility is one of the strengths of Scholz's argument, as when the reader of the *Mariengrüße* is invited to 'listen' or when nowadays we can still talk of 'hearing' from a correspondent.[29] In view of this ambiguity (is the verb to be taken literally or metaphorically?) it will not do simply to list verbs of listening or hearing statistically, as Coleman does, to indicate an acoustic, as opposed to a visual, reception.[30] They may do, but they need not.

A converse bias is betrayed over the use of the verb 'to read' in the sense of individual reading. Coleman does not deny this function, but minimises its importance for the reception of literature by largely confining it either to the author's preparatory work in consulting his written sources or to the activity of scholars or professionals needing to consult works of reference.[31] Reading in these contexts certainly took place (there is evidence from Germany, too),[32] but that does not exclude the possibility of private recreational readers, however slowly they may have carved out a niche for themselves. Such readers are implied in many different ways by German authors, not least when they see the possibility of women readers in particular: these readers can be alerted to the presence of an acrostic, they can be expected to compare one passage with another and it is they whose approval the authors seek to win.[33]

A final point concerns the chronological implications of Coleman's argument with regard to the position in England. In her demonstration of the persistence of public recital throughout the Middle Ages, even to those in the audience who were literate, she suggests that 'aurality' may have been driven downmarket (restricted to *illitterati*) by the spread of literacy, but only in the late Middle Ages.[34] She claims that the word 'read' slowly drifted, through the fifteenth and sixteenth centuries, towards the sense 'to read privately for oneself', so that this meaning, although conceded, is dated late enough not to affect the overall importance of public recital in the Middle Ages. Whatever the position may be in England, this cannot be accepted for the continent. Not for France and not for Germany (even though lay literacy was slower to establish itself there), for the evidence for personal reading (*lesen* = 'to read privately') reaches back to the late twelfth century for court literature and even earlier for clerical.[35] In view of this it is possible (but needs to be investigated) that the lateness claimed by Coleman may well concern literature in English (relatively late in establishing itself in a multilingual cultural realm and less precocious than literature in Latin, French or Anglo-Norman), but not necessarily literature in England. If so, the position in England, if not in English, would be comparable with that on the continent in granting a place for private reading alongside recital far earlier than Coleman is ready to entertain.

The second flank on which we have to protect ourselves has to do with the converse argument, of which Scholz is the most important representative. For him private reading established itself more quickly and thoroughly in Germany than had been considered likely before. He concedes the fact of public recital, but in practice lays more stress on individual reading, even neglecting to consider the interplay between the two modes or to analyse the double formula thoroughly (even though the title of his book might have led one to expect this). Whereas with Kartschoke and Coleman we had to restore the balance by emphasising private reading, with Scholz we have to pay more attention than he to public recital.

Five years before his book Scholz published an article which, ranging as far as Italian and Spanish examples from the late medieval and early modern periods, placed his later argument in a wider context.[36] As in his book, he registers two types of anticipated reception, recital and individual reading (for Boiardo's *Orlando innamorato*), which he regards as irreconcilable.[37] Adopting a method similar to Coleman's, but directed to an opposing conclusion, he concedes the possibility of oral recital, but only occasionally[38] and threatened with a loss of function once written literature came to be addressed to readers.[39] Scholz resolves what for him is a contradiction in favour of actual readers as opposed to pointers to a recital situation which he regards as unreal and fictive.[40] He maintains that Boiardo *pretends* that his work was destined for public recital, but in fact meant it for readers by whom pointers to reciting or listening were to be understood as fictive, because they were now unreal.[41]

Scholz interprets the *Libro de buen amor* similarly, seeing references to a written book as implying reception by a reader, even though, as with Coleman's 'aurality', the book from which a performer recites in public could also suggest listeners.[42] That these, as well as readers, could well be meant is suggested by the presence of a double formula, mentioned by Scholz, but not discussed.[43] That the double formula and the twofold reception that it signalised could persist into the late medieval and early modern period has been shown for England by Coleman and for Germany by myself in random examples to suggest the continuity of this literary bimodality.[44] If written literature, from classical antiquity through to the sixteenth century at least, could be listened to by an assembled audience and also read privately by an individual we are absolved from any need to regard the two types of evidence with Boiardo as contradictory, and from any compulsion to resolve this by attributing reality to the reader, but a fictive existence to the reciter.

Despite its clarification of many key terms used of the reception of medieval literature, Scholz's book is informed by the same fault. On a rare occasion when he discusses the double formula he suggests that, dependent on whether the conjunction linking the two terms is *oder* or *und*, two alternative modes of reception are implied: in the first case reading or listening as complementary possibilities and in the second the unity of reading and hearing, the situation of an individual reading aloud to himself.[45] Whereas Coleman saw the double formula (in the case of Chaucer) more in terms of public recital, Scholz entertains the possibility of private reading (to oneself, but aloud). Scholz is also inclined to interpret *hoeren* figuratively, rather than literally.[46] In theory this is certainly possible, but it is mistaken to assume that because this is possible it must necessarily be so, and arbitrary to take references to reading as literally true, but to empty those to listening of real import by classifying them as merely figurative. If there is no contradiction between a hearing and a reading reception there is no necessity to overcome this supposed difficulty by depriving hearing as part of a public recital of any real content and seeing it as fictive or pretended orality.

This is not meant to deny the concept of fictive orality as such, but rather to criticise the use to which Scholz puts it. That it has an important part to play in our understanding of medieval literature is now commonly accepted.[47] With the dissociation of author and narrator in a written text the latter plays the role of the fictive 'I' of the former, so that in Hartmann's *Iwein* the author, in order to train his audience to a higher level of comprehension, can attribute a deficient understanding to the narrator, just as Wolfram presents his narrator, not himself as author, in the guise of an *illitteratus*.[48] The audience, too, can be presented in fictive form, as in the many passages where the narrator addresses them or where they play a part in an invented dialogue with him. Despite a partial correspondence over some details between actual and fictive audience the equation is by no means complete, so that what we are told about the audience in a fictional text is part of the fiction.[49] If both narrator and audience are fictive entities, then what binds them together – the recital situation itself insofar as this is presented – must also be regarded as a fictive element.[50]

The partial agreements and disagreements on which these distinctions rest serve the overall aims of narrative strategy.[51] By creating positive links between the fictive audience and a character in his narrative Wolfram imparts some of the latter's idealised features to the former, which in turn alerts the actual audience to the gap between themselves and the character. When Wolfram in his function as narrator makes often humorous remarks on the narrative action he increases the distance between narrator and action, but lessens that between narrator and audience, which can only have assisted his control and guidance of his audience's reactions. This is especially so when Wolfram has his narrator pretend that his imagined audience are in control of the action, deciding what is to happen next and thereby sharing responsibility with the narrator. By implying that the course of the action lies in their hands the narrative is revealed as a fiction, subject neither to source nor to historical truth.[52]

Fictive orality, like the narrator as a fictive 'I' and like the fictive audience, is therefore a concept with which we may work in medieval literature, but we need not accept it in the context in which Scholz uses it. It is a concept which he has possibly derived from studies in Middle English, but he makes use of it in order to resolve what he perceives as a contradiction in his evidence. If, thanks to the double formula and other classes of evidence, we no longer regard the evidence as contradictory there is no need to regard the recital situation as a fictive construct built into a work meant only for readers. Two German examples, discussed by Scholz, may illustrate the nature of our disagreement.

The first comes from Hartmann's *Erec*, a work intended for two modes of reception.[53] Scholz proceeds from a comment by Drube on the narrator's interventions in the course of the action (they convey the impression of an orally recited work), but qualifies this, saying that they need not reflect an actual recital, but are meant to achieve a fictive effect.[54] To support this Scholz quotes Drube: 'Hartmann erzählt hier unter der Fiktion, sich inmitten eines Kreises interessierter Zuhörer zu befinden, die in den Gang seiner Erzählung lebhaft eingreifen.' We have to read this sentence in its entirety: for Drube the fiction lay in the presence of listeners who interrupt with questions and comments. That is of course fictive, because these interruptions have been composed in advance, in the act of writing, by Hartmann before any contact with listeners at a recital of his work. Scholz, however, reads this passage as if Drube had said that the presence of the audience itself was unreal, which does not follow from Drube's remark or from the other evidence in Hartmann's work.

In my second example Scholz discusses a narratorial passage from the *Alexander* of Rudolf von Ems, which he correctly sees as meant for readers, whilst dismissing a contrary reference to hearing it read out by calling it a *Hörerfiktion*.[55] The passage 20651–64, however, can only be termed such by one who accepts the reading mode of *Alexander* as in necessary conflict with a hearing mode. But a bridge between the two modes is provided in this passage by two phrases: *hoeren sagn*, to hear said (20663, implying reception by ear) and *hoere lesn*, hear read out (20656, recital from a written text). Together these suggest an audience listening to a performer reciting from a manuscript (to which the individual reader could also have access).

That the reading reception should not exclude a listening reception is implied by the wider context of this passage. Rudolf goes on to talk of various literary genres requested by a potential audience, not all of whose needs can be met. Amongst these genres he mentions the heroic epic in the form of the Dietrich cycle (20667ff.) and the Arthurian romance (20670–1). The wording in the first case ('einer hoeret gerne', one is glad to hear) agrees with the oral transmission of the heroic epic, whilst that in the second ('wil ouch einer hoeren sagn', and another wants to hear said) points to recital of the Arthurian romance, which we know of as a possibility, even the dominant one, alongside a reading reception.[56] These allusions to two other genres fall outside the context of Rudolf's Alexander story, so that there was no need for him to construct a *Hörerfiktion* for two genres on which he was not engaged, and there is equally no need for us to take *hoeret* and *hoeren sagn* as anything but meant literally. If so, the same is likely to be true of *hoeren sagn* and *hoere lesn* with reference to the reception of Rudolf's own work, even though the last phrase implies that it could be received by the eye as well as the ear. If this passage is to be termed a *Hörerfiktion* at all, then it is so not exclusively, but only for potential readers for whom, at the moment of reading, recital had no immediate relevance.

Criticism of fictive orality has been voiced by Coleman in defence of the reality of the recital situation and with regard to work on Middle English which has made use of the concept. She accuses those who employ it of conducting a circular argument, in that pointers to a listening reception are interpreted by means of this concept to be really indicative of a reading reception.[57] Demoting pointers to listening to a metaphorical or fictive status, whilst evidence of reading is taken as factually true,[58] leaves no room for the written text read aloud to listeners (to safeguard this position was the aim of Coleman's book) or for the interplay between listening and reading, as suggested by the double formula (to emphasise this was the purpose of mine). Once we pay attention to these two possibilities the compulsion to assume fictionality of this kind is weaker.

These two possibilities are also bypassed when, in the belief that medieval literacy as a new communications technology rapidly made orality obsolete, fictive orality is invoked to explain any surviving references to an oral situation in a written text.[59] These references may be preserved out of carelessness or to conjure up for the reader the feeling of a live performance (what Coleman has called a *nostalgie de la bouche*). They are felt to have lost their original function and can be described as 'fossilised', 'remains' or 'residue', survivals from a past where they once had a real role to play. Unsurprisingly, Scholz also describes this condition with the word *Relikt*.[60] It can only be that, however, for those who ignore the twofold reception of medieval literature.[61]

For Coleman this fictive orality argument may have been put forward first in connection with Chaucer by Burrow, who argued that, in a new age of widespread literacy and book-production, the older face-to-face relationship between reciter and audience was internalised and fictionalised within the written poem.[62] Burrow's argument rests on an undifferentiated conception of orality and the recital situation. Orality in the shape of oral-formulaic composition or recital of a memorised work may well have been in decline in Chaucer's day, but not orality in the sense of a written text read out to listeners (Coleman's 'aurality'). This failure to differentiate between two types of orality could well be a scholarly hangover from the days of the ascendancy of the Parry/Lord oral-formulaic school, for whom composition-in-performance was the only kind of oral composition.[63] The failure to see that acoustic reception, in the sense of listening to the recital of a written text, survived the eclipse of oral-formulaic or memorial recitals means that the upholders of this view of fictive orality[64] lack any real situation to which they can attach Chaucer's narratorial tags. They are therefore driven to regarding them as mock orality, a sophisticated play with a past practice. The sophistication may appeal to us (it has its place in a private reading of Chaucer's work, for us as for his medieval readers), but its fictive nature needs to be qualified by the recognition that it was not perceived as such by those who were only listeners.

If fiction is present in the orality we have been discussing, it exists only for the reader and arises from the conjunction of his reading with his knowledge that the work was also meant for recital and was available to some only as listeners. We may agree with Scholz that it was the reader who was confronted with the task of learning what the rules of this fictionality were,[65] but we must also take into account the non-reading listener for whom the recital situation was a reality that blocked his awareness that fictionality could be at issue here. Fictionality arose not from literacy alone (in Scholz's terms: not from the reader with no contact with literature for recital), but from the interplay between oral and written, from the meeting of the spoken with the written word.[66] This conclusion does not deny fictive orality as such, but instead questions its use to play down the continuing reality of oral recital from a written text throughout the Middle Ages.

EXCURSUS: ORALITY AND PERFORMANCE
IN EARLY FRENCH ROMANCE

Where Coleman concentrates on English and French literature of the late Middle Ages, Vitz in a book with the same title as this excursus directs attention to French literature of the twelfth century.[67] Where Coleman concedes a reading alongside a hearing reception, Vitz theoretically accepts this, but in practice plays down the former even more than did Coleman.

Vitz's argument has two aims: first, to show that the early romance in France represents a blend of oral and written cultures, but secondly, more radically, that orality was more decisively present, even to the extent that Chrétien himself, she suggests, was not a literate cleric, but a probably illiterate minstrel. In pursuit of this double aim Vitz asks a number of questions.[68] Do vernacular authors display evidence of their *clergie* or literacy? What hints do they give of their mode of performance? What do we learn about the transposition of their work to written form? Is the audience addressed literate or not? The book falls into two parts, one dealing with problems of orality and literacy, the other with performance before a listening audience. Underlying the argument is the conviction, unlikely to be contested, that Benoît de Sainte-Maure, the author of the *Roman de Troie*, was a cleric and a *litteratus*,[69] but also the opinion that the same cannot be said of the author of the *Roman de Thèbes* or even of Chrétien. It is about this use of Benoît as an absolute yardstick (if what he says about himself is not said by others, this suggests their non-clerical status) that doubts are called for.

This is not to say that we have nothing to learn from this book. First, it provides a survey (how complete we are not told) of this problem over a wide range of French and Anglo-Norman works of the twelfth and early thirteenth centuries. Secondly, it gives many examples of recital performance of French works at feasts and official occasions, including accompaniments like gestures, music and dancing, stressing the dramatic and festive qualities of such occasions.[70] In organising her material Vitz sets up a theoretical performance spectrum, for which she claims that at one end (festive occasions) performance was *exclusively* recitation from memory[71] and that only at the other end (non-festive) did reading from a written text to listeners take place, even then but rarely.[72] The private reading of a romance was likewise very rare.[73] At this point, where doubts arise more insistently, we pass to criticisms of Vitz's thesis.

Although she twice refers (briefly) to Scholz's book she nowhere takes issue with his arguments in favour of romance reading around 1200, nor with his demonstration that verbs of hearing and saying can no longer be equated uncritically with an oral–recital situation without further evidence.[74] In the light of this, *oïr nomer* need not by itself imply learning from an oral source,[75] nor can it be sustained that the author of the *Roman de Thèbes* may not have read a source because, 'more orally', he says that the book of Statius 'says' this ('Si com dit li livre d'Estace').[76] Equally lacking in force, given the association of verbs of seeing with the act of reading, is the suggestion that Béroul may not have actually read a source, because he says merely that he has seen the story written ('La ou Berox le vit escrit').[77] More personally I must dissociate myself from Vitz's appeal to what I have said of MHG *lesen*, meaning 'to recount, tell'.[78] She uses my pages to support her view that Chrétien's Laudine may not have read the psalter ('et list en un sautier ses saumes', and read her psalms in a psalter), but merely looked at it,[79] whereas I expressly said that when the German verb was used in combination with the psalter, with a book, reading from a written text was implied.[80]

In her wish to lay the ghost of literacy Vitz has recourse to the restrictive definition of *litteratus* put forward by Grundmann.[81] Following him, she maintains that the word meant an ability to read and write Latin, so that literacy in the vernacular did not count,[82] so much so that when in *Perceval* Chrétien says that he has read the words of St Paul ('Sainz Pols le dist et je le lui') Vitz can even suggest that the poet 'might' have read St Paul in the vernacular, so that he should not strictly be described as *litteratus*.[83] Apart from this special pleading, I have argued against Grundmann's definition, urging that it is calculated to prolong the medieval cleric's far from disinterested view of literacy as a clerical monopoly and fails to do justice to the position in vernacular literature.[84]

In playing down Chrétien's literacy Vitz grants more importance to the role of memory in composing and reciting his works. Although she is aware that memory need not 'belong' to oral tradition, in the same breath she argues that Béroul's insistence on the accuracy of his memory ('Berox l'a mex en sen memoire') is a claim coming from oral, rather than written tradition.[85] This ignores the possibility that the written tradition also conserves memory, for example with Isidore of Seville and Einhard in Latin or with Wace's *Roman de Rou* and the *Lai de l'aubépine* in the vernacular.[86] To strengthen her argument that early romances were recited not merely orally, but by memory without benefit of writing, Vitz devotes several pages to the memorability of these works, enabling them to be memorised by heart.[87] Many of these pages are irrelevant, for she fails to distinguish memorability in this sense from a more general one, referring to memorable figures in the action, unforgettable characters.[88] Memorability in this broader sense pertains to the audience and the lasting impression the work makes on them, whereas it is the oral performer's ability to retain the work in his memory that should be Vitz's concern. It is not 'our memory' or points 'memorable to . . . audiences'[89] that are relevant here (they could apply as much to readers as to listeners),[90] so that only belatedly do we touch on the real problem, the performer's ability to store a work in his memory.[91]

Even here the argument is far from convincing. On the question of the 'memory-friendliness' of the romance Vitz draws inspiration from a work by Jousse (1925).[92] This datedness of Jousse tells against Vitz when she refers to his claim that Yugoslav guslars knew as much as 100,000 lines of poetry (from the context it is clear that she has knowing by heart in mind), for Lord's later work on Yugoslav oral tradition showed that it rested on no such strict verbal stability.[93] Vitz restricts herself to the performer's memory storing the work in his mind and dismisses the issue of how the work was composed orally (if not by the improvisation of the oral-formulaic school).[94] She thereby ignores a very real problem for her thesis. A poem of the brevity of Caedmon's *Hymn* could have been composed mentally and then stored in the memory, but this is already questionable with the OS *Heliand*, in the same alliterative tradition, but of incomparably greater length.[95] With the early romances, however, we are dealing not merely with the quantitative difficulty of composing lengthy works in the head, but with the qualitative one of works of great structural complexity, involving detailed parallels and contrasts, symmetries and gradations, all with a bearing on the work's meaning.

On how such works could be composed without writing, as distinct from being memorised, Vitz has little to tell us.

Vitz is well aware that the twelfth-century court was a centre where orality and literacy came together in a fruitful symbiosis, but with the solitary exception of the *Roman de Troie* she stops short of applying this insight to the individual court poet, who took this position into account in addressing listeners at a recital, but also appealed to the occasional reader. Vitz's concentration on the oral context to the detriment of literacy is carried over into her view of the *Thèbes* poet and of Chrétien, for she sees them as court minstrels, as oral performers, not as clerics or *litterati*.[96] Here long ago Faral, for whom a court poet could be both a minstrel *and* a cleric, was closer to seeing the cultural symbiosis of the court reflected in the twofold function of the court poet.[97] Faral's view that almost all the early romance authors in French performed such a double function is also true of the early romances in Germany.[98] Where Vitz sees her (largely illiterate) minstrels acquiring what knowledge they display from constant contact with clerics at court, others see this contact as much more close, as a *Personalunion* of cleric (with a clerical training, if not ordained as a member of the clergy) and poet in the same individual.[99]

In maintaining that Chrétien, with whatever learning he displays, was not a cleric Vitz realises that she is flying in the face of established opinion. She suggests, but does not demonstrate, that bookish references to Ovid or Macrobius need not be proof of clerical education, but could be the 'pseudo-clerical court packaging of a still essentially oral product'.[100] It is equally no more than a hypothesis when she questions whether Chrétien acquired his learning from books and suggests that 'it could as easily have been picked up from court talk, or from sustained social intercourse with learned men'.[101] At this point she seeks support from me which I am reluctant to give. After seeing a parallel between *Cligés* (25: 'Par les livres que nos avons / Les fez des anciens savons', from the books we possess we know the deeds of the ancients) and a German phrase like *wir lesen*, we read (neither need actually mean reading as distinct from general knowledge stemming from written tradition) Vitz applies this to *Erec* (6674: 'Lisant trovomes an l'estoire', reading we find in the story).[102] She suggests that 'perhaps' Chrétien found things that were told him by others, so that he may have based his knowledge of

Macrobius in this passage on hearsay. Although I argued that a phrase like *wir lesen* is ambiguous, needing support from other criteria if we are to take it as a pointer to individual reading, this is what we find with Chrétien, for a few lines later he confirms that it was he, as the author, who read Macrobius (6680: 'si con je l'ai trové el livre', as I found it in the book). When Vitz, looking further at the description introduced in this way, judges that there is nothing suggesting training in the schools about it,[103] it does not follow that Chrétien lacked such training, for he could equally well be adjusting his speech to the requirements of an audience only marginally involved in reading.

Vitz's argument can be faulted on two general scores. The first is the frequency with which she relies on negative evidence and unwarrantably draws a positive conclusion from it. Of the kings and aristocrats in the *Roman de Thèbes* she says that not one of them is said to be able to read, even though they may be wise and eloquent.[104] On this negative basis she postulates that a work composed by a literate cleric will 'tend' to include at least some literate characters (why? how far are we to take 'tend'?), whereas the absence of such characters 'appears to be more telling of minstrelsy'. To argue thus is to confuse the internal dimension of a fictional narrative with the external position of its author and his composition of the work. Another argument *ex negativo* is employed when it is said that Chrétien, like the author of the *Roman de Thèbes*, never speaks of himself as a cleric or as writing.[105] If Vitz contrasts this with the *Roman de Troie* it must be asked why Benoît's explicitness on this point should be privileged as an absolute criterion of literacy whose absence in other cases is a pointer to illiteracy. In talking about performances in festive settings (one of the most informative sections of her book) Vitz says that in most cases 'there is no reference to books or reading at great events at court – which presumably means that songs and stories were performed from memory'.[106] For this no positive evidence is adduced.

Another major fault is Vitz's readiness to indulge in special pleading. Of Chrétien's words about oral storytellers in the prologue to *Erec* (21: 'Depecier et corronpre suelent', are accustomed to mutilate and mangle) she says that his criticism 'is nothing more than the backbiting common among performers'.[107] It is more than that, since literate authors also distanced themselves from such oral entertainment,[108] so

that Chrétien's words permit no clear conclusion about his status. As part of her would-be demolition of Chrétien's literacy Vitz quotes the forged letter received by Gauvain in *Lancelot*, remarking that it hardly redounds to the glory of writing if letters can lie and are less trustworthy than witnesses.[109] But spoken words can also lie and has she not heard of the saying common in Eastern Europe: 'He lies like an eyewitness'? It presses the argument too far when Vitz, discussing Wace's programmatic wish to record in writing the feats of ancestors and to read their stories at feasts (*Roman de Rou* 1ff.), seeks to undermine the force of this by suggesting that Wace's intention to read his work aloud is no guarantee that it was so read.[110] A similar doubt is in order when, in the description of a court feast and its entertainments in *Le chevalier à l'épée*, a mention of reading romances aloud (803: 'Cil list romanz et cist dist fables', one read romances and another recited fables) is emptied of import by the suggestion that *list* is no more than a prestigious synonym for *dist*, also providing an internal rhyme.[111]

At some points Vitz would have done well to take fictionality into account. We have seen that it is wrong to confuse different dimensions by inferring from the presence of characters in a fiction who are not depicted as literate that the author of that fiction must therefore be illiterate. We have also seen that the length of a work, more particularly the complexity of its structure, has a bearing on whether it was composed in the head or in writing, but since there is an intimate connection between consciously devised structure and fictionality the latter is also relevant to Vitz's problem.[112] At another point, when defining what she means by a romance, she mentions fictionality, but only to qualify it by saying that medieval authors do not always see it in that light.[113] Her example (king Arthur, she says, was thought by many to have been a real person) is ill-chosen, for the fictionality of the Arthurian romances attaches not to Arthur, whose historicity was accepted, but to the exploits of his Round Table.[114]

Much work remains to be done. Although Vitz maintains that the internal evidence of the French works must be looked at carefully, her scrutiny is not rigorous enough, so that a revised survey that is prepared to grant weight to reading alongside hearing is called for. However unequal their incidence may have been in the reception of romances in the twelfth and thirteenth centuries, it is reading which is the decisive innovation, to which attention must be paid as a theoretical possibility realised in some cases, if not in all. Considering both possibilities will mean seeing the court, but also the court poet, above all Chrétien (like his German colleagues), at the meeting-point of literacy and orality, actively conveying his own clerical, Latin learning to laymen and not just passively acquiring, as a mere minstrel, scraps of knowledge from clerics at court.

We also need to be assured how extensive the survey of material is, for Vitz nowhere says explicitly that she has covered the whole field of romances in the French-speaking world of the twelfth and thirteenth centuries. In my own survey for German literature up to 1300 I discussed a range of lexical criteria for assuming that works were expected to be received by listeners and then a similar range for anticipated readers.[115] Although Vitz occasionally refers to my points she does not proceed systematically herself, even though some of her examples are strikingly parallel to mine. Thus, the phrase 'to read before/in front of someone' (*Yvain* 5364: 'lisoit . . . devant lui') corresponds to German *lesen* + *vor*;[116] the construction *lire* + *a* (*Li chevalier as deus espees* 8952-3) parallels German *lesen* + dative object;[117] the conjunction of *faire* with *lire* in the sense of having something recited (*Hunbaut* 3052f.) has its echo in German *lesen lân* or *lesen heizen*.[118] What is telling about theses parallels between French and German is that they all refer to the context of recital to listeners. In other words, we are given no information by Vitz about possible lexical criteria for private reading in French and are left wondering whether this is because they do not exist (which would be surprising) or because she has not considered them.

What emerges from Vitz's book is her view of a marked discrepancy between the Anglo-Norman realm and France with regard to orality and literacy, with the former making earlier use of reading and writing.[119] Arguing for too pronounced a time-lag in the case of French literacy creates difficulties when we compare France not with Anglo-Norman England, but with Germany, especially in the case of the romance. Vitz is aware of the discrepancy between her findings for France and mine for Germany, acknowledging that German authors stress writing and reading more than their French colleagues, that private reading is referred to earlier in Germany than in France, and even the opportunities of private space for such reading appear more in Germany.[120] In view of

France's cultural lead in so many respects at this time this is precisely what we should *not* expect, and Vitz confesses her inability to explain it.[121] This question clearly needs further investigation, but one possibility suggests itself. If Vitz had systematically treated the whole range of lexical criteria in French, for reading as well as for listening, might not the result have been significantly different?

Not merely does the twelfth-century court stand at the junction of orality and literacy, but individual authors, above all Chrétien, also do the same, writing as literate authors for an audience predominantly of listeners, even though it also includes readers. Although the position was different, more complex, for these readers, the recital situation was the only reality for the majority, for those who could only listen: it was for them a reality, not a fictive orality. The fictionality visible to some was not so obvious to others.

CHAPTER 4

Fiction and Wolfram's *Parzival*

This is the only chapter in which we focus our attention on one work alone, but one which looms large as regards the problem of fictionality. It illustrates how the author developed his fiction not by inventing it from scratch, but by taking over narrative details from earlier works, seeking out gaps and filling them with new material. It also provides telling examples of the fictional contract between author and audience, central to our definition of fictionality around 1200. Finally, it highlights in acute form the relationship between fiction and history, best treated here rather than in the wider ranging Chapter 6.

INTERTEXTUALITY

In his treatment of intertextual references to the classical Arthurian romances found in the post-classical works of Der Pleier Kern talks of the construction of a 'werkübergreifende Erzählwelt', whilst in his more philosophical work Currie uses terms such as 'interfictional carryover' and the 'interfictive use' of fictional names.[1] What I prefer to call the 'interfictive world' of the Arthurian romances (certain names, of people and of places, and certain events are common to, or presupposed in, a number of works) is certainly not confined to this medieval genre. Currie quotes as a modern example the many stories about Sherlock Holmes, some by Doyle and some by others, producing consistent extensions of the original character across a number of different fictions.[2]

This interfictive world of the Arthurian romance is already found with Chrétien, the action of whose various works presupposes, at least in part, the same general background: the court of king Arthur with the same figures at its centre (and varying ones at its fringe), the same time and much the same geography.[3] In addition, Chrétien can incorporate a romance into an overarching wider narrative world by including in it references to the action of another. In his *Yvain*, for example, reference is made on three occasions to the action of *Lancelot*, in part to explain why Gauvain was not present at Arthur's court at a given time, in part out of fondness of the interlace technique of intertwining one narrative action with another.[4] In his German adaptations Hartmann not merely follows Chrétien's lead in this detail,[5] but shows that he has understood the potentialities of this technique by developing it independently of his French model. In his *Iwein* he therefore has Gawein warn his friend against committing the fault of which Erec has been guilty in the romance devoted to him, an intertextual reference not to be found in Chrétien's version.[6] (Even though Erec may not actually appear, his story is placed in the past by reference to the present work, so that both form part of the same fictive world.) By thus linking the narrative of the later romance with that of the earlier Hartmann creates the impression of a wider narrative world in which both romances are located.

In Wolfram's *Parzival* the creation of this wider world is taken very much further, once more beyond what is to be found with Chrétien. In addition to the core membership of Arthur's court (Arthur, Guinevere, Gawan and Keie) a host of other named figures appear, many of whom were known to a German audience from the lengthy list of members of the Round Table given in Hartmann's *Erec*.[7] Kinship, a theme of overriding importance in *Parzival*, is another way of placing the personnel of this work in a wider context already known to the audience. Jeschute and Orilus are presented as the sister and brother-in-law of Erec, and most of the figures whose names were not previously known to a German audience are incorporated into the same narrative world by kinship relations to well-known figures.[8] Since kinship plays a less far-reaching role in Chrétien's work[9] Wolfram goes well beyond him in constructing an interfictive world which passes beyond even the heavily populated Arthurian realm by links with the worlds of the Grail and of the East. Finally, Wolfram extends his narrative world not merely geographically, but also chronologically in his prehistory.[10] In this not merely does Parzival's father appear, but also the fathers of Arthur, Gawan and Erec, known by name since Hartmann's romances.

These two German authors therefore do not merely follow Chrétien's example, they also take it further, so that it will pay us to consider the ways in which their interfictive world was constructed, paying attention above all to *Parzival* and to the implications for its status as fiction. Work on the methods that could be employed has been done particularly with regard to the post-classical romance and its intertextual references to its forerunners.[11] Der Pleier not merely refers to episodes that took place in an earlier romance, he also develops his narrative from an earlier one, extending it in time and adding to this model. This is true not merely of Der Pleier: the importance of intertextuality for the genesis of fiction lies not in any invention *ex nihilo*, but in the exploitation of gaps or blank spots in a previously existing narrative for new ends.

The first method of creating an Arthurian narrative world was to incorporate the names of actors from other works. The mere mention of recognisably Arthurian names in a new work (especially towards the beginning) is enough to achieve this effect, but it can also act as a signal, for if the audience (or some of them) are already alert to the fictionality of Hartmann's Arthurian romances they will be predisposed to assume the same with *Parzival*.[12] A more detailed pointer is provided by the mention of Meljahkanz in Book III of *Parzival* (even if he does not appear on-stage), for an audience acquainted with *Iwein* will recognise that the young hero is indirectly confronted with the unchivalrous abductor of women referred to by Hartmann.[13]

Place-names provide a second opportunity. When Parzival departs from his mother for the 'fôrest in Brizljân' (129, 6) we know from Hartmann's use of this same name as a place of knightly encounters that the hero, true to his wish for knighthood, is moving into the established Arthurian world.[14] How far Wolfram deliberately appeals to the previous knowledge of his audience is clear from the form of the name he gives to Arthur's castle at *Karidol*, thereby avoiding Chrétien's *Carduel* in favour of the form used by Hartmann.[15] However, when it comes to places not previously known from the geography of the Arthurian world Der Pleier creates the impression that in locating the action of his narrative he is merely filling in a gap, occupying a blank space in an otherwise well-known landscape.[16]

Chronology can also be used to the same end. Of the sons of Gurnemanz who met their death in knightly combat two are linked with the Arthurian world in the not too distant past before the onset of the narrative dealing with Parzival: one was a victim of Iders, the other of Mabonagrin, both known from Hartmann's *Erec*. By thus incorporating allusions to Erec's first and last opponent Wolfram has placed the whole of the *Erec* narrative chronologically before *Parzival*, so that between them the illusion of temporal continuity is created.[17] Wolfram suggests in this way that his romance continues from the point where Hartmann's left off and that both stand on a common quasi-objective time-axis.

Wolfram's exploitation of genealogical connections (between his characters and those of earlier romances, but especially in view of the kinship ties of most of the figures in his own work) created an opportunity for later authors, too. Der Pleier, for example, devises a genealogical home for Garel by inserting him into the Mazadan family tree, as elaborated in *Parzival*, filling out his predecessor's pattern with this new detail.[18] By seeking the authority of Wolfram in this way the later author equips his own innovation, the story of Garel, with the appearance of an attested truth which can be confirmed from beyond the limits of his own work.

Recurrent in these various methods of creating an interfictive world is the way in which authors, by no means only post-classical ones, seek out blank spots or narrative gaps in earlier works which give them the opportunity to place their own figures or to develop implications only latent (or not even intended) in their predecessors' works.[19] Underlying this is the suggestion of a vast Arthurian world whose detailed story cannot be captured in any one work, so that others may supplement or continue it. This opportunity is made use of in *Diu Crône* with the early statement that the previous neglect of Arthur's childhood and youth will be made good in this work or when, here as elsewhere, figures established in literary tradition are shown in a new light, not always complimentary.[20] Authorial competition may well be at work here in the post-classical examples (the need to find a thematic free space for a new romance on an already crowded stage), but significantly this competition still takes place within the interfictive Arthurian world with its fixed points of reference. Intertextuality of this kind demands of the later author that he successfully harmonise his own work with those to which he refers and avoid contradictions,[21] but it also presupposes an audience sufficiently versed in literature to take up his allusions. In addition, intertextuality and the wider Arthurian world which it helped to construct possibly served another end, alleviating difficulties caused by writing fiction in a still clerically dominated age which did not find it easy to find a place for fiction.[22] Viewed in this light, the author of a later text could seek shelter with the authority of the texts to which he referred, so that the interfictive world at large provided a cloak of objectivity, extending beyond his own work, for his inventiveness, however restricted to the vacant spaces he could find this may have been.[23]

Intertextuality, as practised from the beginning of the romance in France and Germany, displays therefore two apparently contradictory features. On the one hand, it possesses the illusive power of conjuring up an infinite realm, independent of any one author and passing beyond the frame of any individual work, suggesting experience of a reality beyond it and thereby boosting its credibility.[24] The audience of such a work, encountering references to what is already known to them from elsewhere and seemingly complementing and confirming it, can be tempted into regarding it as an objective, non-fictive account. (This may well not have been the author's intention, but the result was unavoidable with the less sophisticated members of his audience and even acceptable if he was exposed to rigorist criticism for dealing in lies.)

On the other hand, the interfictive world created by intertextuality is, as indicated by the term itself, a fictional construct stemming from the author's imaginative control over his material as he seeks out lacunae in previous works and reshapes their narrative in the light of his own purposes.[25] In the development of his fiction, as we shall see, Wolfram makes it clear that it was not his aim to present his narrative world as factually true, no matter whether some in his audience were persuaded of this or whether others, judging it by the criterion of truth/untruth, found it wanting. Despite the appearances of the interfictive world, the factual truth of one work of fiction cannot be established by its consistency with another, but only by its conformity to aspects of the extrafictional world. Intertextuality makes no claim to do this because of its literary, written, 'made' nature.[26] Its references are to other works of literature, which draw attention to its own status as literature, playing variations on inherited fiction even when expectations are occasionally thwarted. The self-enclosed, self-generating nature of intertextual references can claim self-consistency, but cannot transcend its own fictional realm.

These two features of intertextual references in the Arthurian romance are only apparently contradictory.[27] They can be reconciled if we take into account the heterogeneous nature of the audience for this genre at court, consisting of some who were attentive at recital and others who were not, some who could only listen and others who could savour more subtle points in reading, some whose reading ability was on a lower level than the Latinity of others.[28] Wolfram's use of intertextuality, to which we now turn, is nothing if not subtle and dependent for its effects on the literary knowledge of his audience, who can therefore be seen as fully capable of recognising the literary nature, and hence the fictive status, of the interfictive world.[29] Others in the audience may have taken it at face value, but it was not for them primarily that Wolfram wrote.

Wolfram constructs isolated details of his interfictive world by making free use of the given material he found in Hartmann's romances, which he could assume were well known to his audience. By expanding on this material he was doing no more than was theoretically prescribed, as when Matthew of Vendôme recommends the author's correction of his *materia* in different ways (for example, he found fault with Ovid's version of Jupiter's rape of Io for omitting certain stages that needed to be included).[30] We shall see that Wolfram faulted Hartmann in a similar way. Wolfram is not alone in using intertextual references inventively, but others can introduce even more drastic changes. Heinrich von dem Türlin, presumably because he could not entertain the prospect of Iwein's lion as permanently present at Arthur's court, removes the difficulty by conveniently having the animal die.[31]

In what follows we shall be concerned with Wolfram's references to Chrétien's and Hartmann's romances insofar as they cast light on the fictional nature of *Parzival*. It will emerge that the biographical sequence in which these works were composed by their authors is also the chronological sequence of the events they narrate in the interfictive world to which they all belong. In other words, the events that take place in *Erec* come before those that occur in *Iwein*, whose action precedes that of *Parzival*.[32] In making references both to *Erec* and to *Iwein*, but also in basing himself on Chrétien as well as Hartmann, Wolfram was confronted with the complex task of harmonising such different features of his interfictive world, and also making his dispositions clear to his audience if they were to become conscious participants in his make-believe.

A counter-example may illustrate this last point. Wolfram has Orilus confess that Erec defeated him in a joust at Prurin (134, 12–13).[33] This place-name does not occur in Chrétien's *Erec*, but in Hartmann's version a tournament takes place in the vicinity of Prurin in which Erec is involved (2240ff.), but none of his opponents is named as Orilus (2231ff.). Nonetheless, it has proved possible by means of a detailed comparison to reconstruct how Wolfram came to associate Orilus with the place Prurin.[34] In *Perceval* Wolfram's Orilus bears the name 'li Orguelleus de la Lande' (3817) and a further opponent of Erec at Prurin is called 'der hôchvertige Landô' by Hartmann (2576), whilst this same knight in Chrétien's *Erec* is likewise called 'li Orguelleus de la Lande' (2175). In other words, Hartmann's Landô and Wolfram's Orilus can be identified with each other only by reference to Chrétien's *Erec* and *Perceval*, where they have the same name. This means that for Wolfram to make this identification he must have known not merely his source, Chrétien's *Perceval*, but also his *Erec* (as well as Hartmann's). This detailed comparison of Wolfram's text with three other works shows us how Wolfram, working inventively on these other works, may have had the idea of having Erec defeat Orilus at Prurin. Even if we concede that some of Wolfram's audience may have been acquainted with French as well as German romances, it is difficult to imagine them (as distinct from Wolfram and modern scholarship) possessing such detailed knowledge and indulging in such complicated comparisons.[35] If the contemporary audience was therefore unable to reconstruct the process by which the author devised this new narrative detail, we cannot, if we place any importance on the fictional contract in which author and audience consciously collude, regard this detail as fiction, but rather as an example of *inventio* by Wolfram.

The position is different, however, when we consider a victory of Orilus,[36] who boasts that he defeated Erec in a joust at Karnant (134, 14ff.). Karnant, the capital of Erec's realm, could derive from either the French or the German version of *Erec*, but for Wolfram's audience the latter is more likely. Neither version of *Erec*, however, knows anything of such a combat at Karnant, which must have been freely invented by Wolfram elaborating on a predecessor's work, just as he independently constructed the defeat of Orilus at Prurin.[37] This fictional elaboration of Hartmann's story has critical implications for Wolfram's attitude towards

Hartmann's hero. One possibility of synchronising Wolfram's account with Hartmann's is to assume that the events recounted are contemporaneous, so that both Chrétien and Hartmann must have remained silent about an encounter detrimental to the victorious reputation of their hero, whilst Wolfram more openly reveals the truth. On the other hand, it is more likely that Erec's defeat at the hands of Orilus, as described by Wolfram, is meant to be later than the events narrated by Hartmann.[38] It cannot have come before Erec's wedding tournament, for this was the hero's first tournament (2252–3), or during this tournament, where Erec was victor, or during the period of his 'verligen' (inactivity) at Karnant, when precisely no knightly combats took place. We are therefore led to believe that this combat, for which there is no lacuna in Erec's journey of adventures, must have occurred after the conclusion of Hartmann's romance, in the period when Erec no longer neglected chivalry (10122–3), but before the events in *Parzival*. Wolfram thus places a question-mark against the successful conclusion of the earlier romance by adding to it a defeat of Erec at Karnant. The shadow that falls on Erec in Wolfram's work serves the polemical purpose of heightening the esteem of his own hero, for if Parzival in turn defeats Orilus (265, 27ff.) this shows him as superior to the Erec whom Orilus had bettered.[39] Basing himself on *Erec*, Wolfram has inventively constructed a new event which defines his attitude towards the hero of the first Arthurian romance, but in such a way that his audience, needing no more than an acquaintance with Hartmann's work, could follow him. In this instance we are dealing not merely with Wolfram's *inventio*, but with a fictional expansion of an earlier work in which his audience could keep pace with him.[40]

We come now to a cluster of intertextual references to Hartmann which again reflect Wolfram's reservations about his predecessor. As Parzival takes his leave of Gurnemanz his knightly mentor tells him how each of his (Gurnemanz's) three sons met his end in knightly combat, two of them at the hands of the first and last opponent met by Erec in Hartmann's account.[41] One of these sons, Lascoyt, was killed by Iders (defeated by Erec in the sparrow-hawk adventure) and the other, Gurzgri, by Mabonagrin (overcome by Erec in his crowning adventure at Schoydelakurt in Brandigan).[42]

The killing of Lascoyt is put forward by Wolfram in terms of the criticism of knightly violence that informs his work.[43] Hartmann has it that Iders, defeated by Erec at the beginning of the work, can do no more than threaten to kill Erec (712ff.) and we are informed only in passing that his knightly reputation rested on violence.[44] These suggestions are exploited by Wolfram, who takes them to the point, absent from Hartmann's narrative, that he actually killed a knight, Lascoyt, for no more reason than the token of a sparrow-hawk. In depicting Gurnemanz's grief Wolfram has not simply hinted at death in knightly combat, he has also presented us with its tragic results.[45] These negative implications Wand has sought to play down by arguing that the combat with Iders (and later that with Mabonagrin) has a positive role to play in *Erec*, marking the course of the hero's rise to supreme chivalry, and that it would have been unwise of Wolfram, if he had wished to call his chivalry into question, to refer to combats with a positive function.[46] However, what one author sees as a positive function in his work need not be seen as such by another, who could indeed heighten his effect by revealing the shadow side previously glossed over. Moreover, Wand's attempt at a positive reading rests on her view of a non-polemical attitude of Wolfram towards Hartmann which has been rendered unlikely by Draesner's more probing analysis of the former's intertextual allusions.[47]

With the killing of Lascoyt by Iders we face the same problem as with Orilus' defeat of Erec: where do we place it chronologically with regard to the events in *Erec* and *Parzival*?[48] Two possibilities occur here: either Lascoyt was killed before the action of *Erec* began or he met his end later, but before that of *Parzival* began. Wand argues for the first possibility on the grounds that Iders was 'pacified' by Erec's victory over him and that he even became a member of the Round Table (1281–2),[49] but Hartmann's optimism on this score cannot simply be transposed to another author whose views on knightly violence were much more critical. This argument is also undermined by the fact that both Chrétien and Hartmann stress that, before Erec, no one had dared engage with Iders in combat.[50] Even if we were nonetheless to place this killing before the action of *Erec*, this would still mean that Chrétien and Hartmann had given no reference to the victory of an evil knight and had optimistically introduced him only in time to have him conveniently defeated. If on the other hand Lascoyt encountered Iders *after* the conclusion of Hartmann's sparrow-hawk adventure Wolfram's critical voice is more deeply disturbing, for the encounter can now only mean that Iders' pacification was no more than skin-deep and that he lapsed into his former ways once Erec had passed out of his ken. On behalf of this view speaks the general consideration that the action of *Parzival* takes place later than that of *Erec*, but also the conclusion reached by Draesner that Lascoyt's death possibly followed after the defeat of Mabonagrin, but probably after Erec's sparrow-hawk combat, after Iders's presumed pacification.[51] Underlying this less than optimistic view is the conviction that Hartmann's world was too well regulated (because it was fictionally contrived) to be credible. Wolfram criticises this, but himself makes use of fiction in doing so, inventing further implications from Hartmann's material. In other words, Wolfram does not criticise Hartmann's use of fiction as such, but rather the implausibility of his fiction.

The other son of Gurnemanz to be killed by a character from *Erec* is Gurzgri (178, 20ff.), the victim of Mabonagrin.[52] Hartmann had contrived things in favour of his optimistic view of knightly violence by depicting Erec's last opponent just before the restoration of the 'hoves vreude' (joy of the court) and Mabonagrin's pacification, locating his violence safely in the past. Wolfram, however, places the emphasis differently, depicting this knight as a victor who shows no mercy and focusing more closely, therefore more effectively, on one person's grief (Gurnemanz) rather than dispersed amongst Hartmann's flock of widows. My earlier view that the killing of Gurzgri came after the conclusion of *Erec* (so that Mabonagrin was to be seen, like Iders, as continuing his reign of terror beyond the chronological frame of *Erec*) can no longer be maintained after Draesner's demonstration that Mabonagrin's pacification by Erec was final.[53] If Mabonagrin therefore does not lapse into his old ways again, the same cannot be said of Clamide, a character not to be found in *Erec*, but according to Wolfram king of Brandigan (the site of Erec's crowning adventure)[54] and related to Mabonagrin not merely by blood but also in his predisposition to violence,[55] causing bloodshed at Pelrapeire and killing Gurnemanz's son Schenteflurs. Even if Mabonagrin may have been finally pacified, Clamide still causes bloodshed, so that the kingdom of Brandigan remains unredeemed, a hotbed of knightly violence even after the conclusion of *Erec*. Hartmann's narrative is therefore spun out by Wolfram in its further ramifications, as he imaginatively develops them, to throw a critical light on knightly practice. If he show doubts about Hartmann's pacification of violent knights, but is also ready to make use of it himself, he significantly sets limits to its universality, acknowledging that there are some, such as Lähelin and Meljahkanz, who remain irredeemable.[56] Wolfram's fiction is thus generated from Hartmann's fiction, which he knows to be fiction.[57]

Wolfram was manifestly aware of the problems of synchronisation posed by any ambitious intertextuality.[58] As far as his references to the violent knights in *Erec* are concerned Wolfram's *Parzival* suggests the following chronological stages. Before the onset of the action of *Erec* Mabonagrin must probably have killed Gurzgri.[59] During the course of this work Erec defeated Iders and pacified Mabonagrin. After the close of the action of *Erec* but before that of *Parzival* Clamide attacked Pelrapeire and killed Schenteflurs, whilst Iders killed Lascoyt and Orilus defeated Erec at Karnant. Finally, in the course of the action of *Parzival* the hero defeated both Orilus and Clamide. This complex, but consistent chronology illustrates how very carefully the interfictive Arthurian world had to be constructed so as to avoid contradictions. Although historiography must also avoid chronological contradictions, the consistency we find in *Parzival* should not be taken as a pointer to historicity,[60] which is established not by internal, self-referential consistency within a closed fictive world, but by agreement with chronological facts outside the work itself. The consistency of *Parzival* is rather an ambitious feature of a literary fiction seeking the appearance of plausibility.

The last intertextual example I wish to look at for what it reveals about fictionality is Wolfram's address to Hartmann (143, 21ff.).[61] It is placed at the point when the young Parzival comes to Arthur's court for the first time: the narrator Wolfram demands of Hartmann that he arrange for the court to receive Parzival kindly and not to make fun of him, otherwise two of Hartmann's characters (Enite and her mother) will have to pay for it. What does this internarratorial passage tell us about Wolfram's (and Hartmann's) fiction?

Immediately apparent, even though Wolfram addresses Hartmann, is the close relationship between himself and Parzival ('mîn gast', a guest of mine, and 'mîn friunt', my friend) as well as between Hartmann and 'his' characters ('frou Ginovêr iwer frouwe', your lady Guinevere, but also 'iwer hêrre der künc Artûs', your lord king Arthur, and 'iwer frouwe Enide', your lady Enide). From this close relationship between each narrator and the figures in his narrative there derives the importance attaching to the narrators, who between them act as intermediaries between the hero of Wolfram's romance and those of Hartmann's and are presented not merely as telling their stories, but also as capable of intervening in the course of the action and dictating its development.[62] By suggesting this capability Wolfram reveals (in a manner obvious enough to invite his audience's collusion in this make-believe) that his work is a fiction, made up as the product of his own decisions, but also that he recognises the same of Hartmann's work. That other authors, not merely his audience, recognised that Wolfram was in charge and could dispose of his fiction as he thought fit has been shown in the case of Heinrich von dem Türlin with regard to the same segment of the *Parzival* narrative.[63]

This can also be shown by a linguistic detail in Wolfram's passage where he seems to have developed a hint found in Hartmann's *Erec*.[64] At two points in this earlier work the narrator uses a form of polite address of two feminine characters: Guinevere is 'mîn vrouwe diu künegîn', my lady the queen (1526) and Enite is 'mîn vrouwe', my lady (3462). These phrases are not the equivalent of *madame* (they do not precede the personal name), but instead have the full force of 'my lady' or 'mistress', suggesting therefore an actual relationship between Hartmann and these figures within his narrative. Wolfram knew *Erec* closely enough to be aware of these examples and to follow them in his address to Hartmann (especially since the first example concerns Enite's arrival at Arthur's court and is therefore a parallel situation to that in *Parzival*). In his address to Hartmann Wolfram refers to Guinevere as 'iwer frouwe' and to Arthur as 'iwer hêrre' (Hartmann had introduced them in the first Arthurian romance in German and was therefore responsible for them, they were 'his' characters), but he also refers to Parzival as 'mîn gast' and 'mîn friunt'. Just as Wolfram feels responsible for his fictional creation, Parzival, so he demands the same attitude from Hartmann towards his own.[65] This again implies that all these figures (not merely Parzival, but also Guinevere, Arthur, Enide and her mother) are at the disposal of their respective authors. It is these authors, and not any authoritative source, who are ultimately responsible for them.[66]

This line of argument, stressing authorial responsibility rather than a source as a feature of fictionality, reaches by a different path a conclusion similar to that proposed by Nellmann in his discussion of the appearance of 'frou Âventiure' (lady Adventure) at the beginning of Book IX. He stresses, as does Wolfram, that this imaginary figure, the guiding spirit of the story, seeks admission to the narrator's heart and argues that, located there, *Âventiure* cannot strictly be a source (one of the meanings of this word) in any external sense.[67] On the contrary, the narrator here shows himself to be independent of any transmitting authority (oral or written) and to be speaking exclusively on his own behalf and with the same responsibility for his fiction that he showed in his address to Hartmann and assumed to be true of him as well.[68]

SOURCES

Wolfram's freedom to dispose of earlier narrative details in his inter-textual references, as well as the authorial independence he displays in his address to Hartmann and invocation of *frou Âventiure*, raises the question of his source-references in *Parzival* at large. The conventional function of source-references (they are a guarantee of the truthfulness of an author who follows what is attested from the past)[69] can be called into question whenever the suspicion arises that they are not genuine, are meant ironically or as a parody.[70] This is what we find repeatedly in Wolfram's *Parzival*, despite the first impression (he appeals to a source as many as ninety-one times)[71] that he is as conventional as any of his predecessors in early medieval literature.

The frequency of such formulas, with Wolfram as with his contemporaries in vernacular literature, has been contrasted with the position in classical and medieval Latin, where authors are mostly content with an initial indication of their source or truthfulness without any need of further repeated asseverations.[72] Several reasons have been suggested for this, each of which may point to one aspect of a complex situation. These include the need to ward off clerical criticism (of the untruth of poetry at large, of the treatment of a secular theme, of the inferior status of the vernacular), but also the need of literate authors to set themselves apart from rivals amongst oral minstrels, thus re-drawing the boundary of what is acceptable in literary entertainment to their own advantage.[73] Also relevant is the possible literary status of the German audiences (or a part of them) of court literature in its beginnings, untrained in the novel demands of vernacular fiction and conventionally expecting that literature should simply purvey the truth and needing to be assured of this.[74] For an audience still to be introduced to the novelty of fiction, literature would be, initially at least, as truthful as history, an expectation that was fed by repeated assurances of truthfulness and adherence to what had been handed down. (In the particular case of *Parzival* it has been suggested that the introduction of Kyot as a fictitious source in Book VIII was a response to the possible criticism that the author, for all his many source-references, had nowhere yet mentioned a specific source.)[75]

We should, however, not exaggerate the extent to which a German lay audience was incapable of meeting the demands of Wolfram's sophisticated fiction. There are indications enough that such an audience was sufficiently trained in literature at large and in fiction in particular. Literary knowledge on the part of his audience, and a capacity to deal with the subtlest allusions, are presupposed by Wolfram in his intertextual references to detailed episodes in Hartmann's works.[76] What he expected from them was the ability to pick up his hints and apply them to their knowledge of his predecessor, even when Hartmann may not be explicitly named and when Wolfram's allusion may be so brief or concern such a detailed point that considerable demands are made on the associative powers of the audience.[77] In making such demands Wolfram must have felt that there was some hope that they could be met, by some at least.[78] We shall see that there are cases where the author feels confident enough to draw the audience into cooperation with him (the 'fictive contract').[79] If he even goes so far as to plant the seed of scepticism about his source-references in them, implying the privilege of an author of fiction to break free from a slavish dependence on tradition, Wolfram continues what was hinted at only in isolated cases by Hartmann, as when, despite an explicit reference to Chrétien as his source, he comments on the truth of a hyperbolic detail in the description of a combat with a throw-away gesture (*Erec* 9209: 'got lône im derz geloube,/wan ich niht drumbe geswern enmac', May God reward him who believes it, since I cannot swear to it).

The two types of audience for *Parzival*, those who were insufficiently trained and those who were capable of appreciating its fictionality, have been seen as contradictory on the grounds that one possibility excludes the other.[80] However, this unrealistically presupposes a homogeneous audience (all are untrained or all are capable), whilst Draesner more persuasively postulates a differentiated reception, with some needing to be trained and others already equipped.[81] This echoes a similar differentiation of the court audience as regards literacy and the ability to appreciate literature: just as the acoustic reception of a work need not exclude its reading reception, so too the expectation of source-references by some need not exclude an awareness of fiction by others.[82] It is on the latter that Wolfram focused his attention, and so must we.

Although medieval literature, whether clerical or secular, could not always dispense with oral source-material, the dominance of clerical literate culture meant that greater reliability was seen in written sources, in dependence on a book in which the truth had been transmitted.[83] Source-references with this background take the simple form of 'the book tells us' or 'I have read', sometimes with an accompanying claim for truth ('the book tells us as true'), but not always, since the appeal to a book-source was felt to be persuasive enough. Behind this equation of the book with truth lies the clerical view of truth: in the case of religious literature its origin in the bible as authoritative scripture and in the case of historiography the view that history was the unfolding of God's plan of salvation.[84] So prevalent was this equation that it could retain its force when divorced from its original biblical background, so that (even in secular literature) merely to substantiate a fact in a written source was to proclaim its truth.[85] Since medieval literacy was predominantly literacy in Latin, the truth of a source-reference can often lie not just in its written source, but also in the Latin form of that source, as in *Herzog Ernst* 4474: 'ze latîne ez noch geschriben stât:/dâ von ez âne valschen list/ein vil wârez liet ist' (It is written in Latin, so that it is a true poem, written without any false deceit).[86] Finally, even if transmission in writing in the Middle Ages suffered from the textual *mouvance* and variations on which the New Philology has laid such stress, its fixity, hence its reliability, was far greater than that of oral tradition. This difference could often come to a head explicitly, as when clerical authors, writing in Latin or even in the vernacular, could argue for the truth of their historiography against what was handed down orally in heroic tradition by challenging their rivals to produce written testimony for their versions.[87] So great was the pressure on oral tradition to conform to literacy and the truth it was felt to embody that a number of heroic epics, after the lead given by the *Nibelungenlied* in being transferred to writing, no longer justify themselves from within oral tradition, but manufacture a written source for themselves.[88]

Written sources could be claimed not merely for these heroic epics, but also for other vernacular works with a secular theme. Even though vernacular sources might lack the kudos of Latin, their written status could only reinforce the claim for truth. The so-called *Spielmannsepen* resemble the heroic epics in going back to a largely oral and vernacular tradition, but like them they also claim a written source, sometimes even in Latin as the language of literacy.[89] With a change of source-language the authors of German romances could claim (initially, at any rate) that they derived from a written French source, which put them in a better position than, say, Chrétien, who derived his narrative material from oral tales of Celtic origin.[90] Gottfried can refer to his source as a book or as something he has read, which justifies him in also referring to this source as 'diu wârheit' (the truth).[91]

These constant appeals to what tradition has handed down, orally or in writing, imply the need for the poet to conform to this tradition and not to go his own way by invented additions or by omissions.[92] This view of the author's relationship to his material grants him the privilege of trustworthiness, but at the cost of largely depriving him of freedom of scope. Its conception of truth makes little generic distinction between history and literature (both are to conform to factual truth), which is why Gottfried presents his source, 'diu wârheit', not merely as a book, but more specifically in historical terms as a *geste* or *istôrje*.[93] How far such traditionalism was felt to be opposed to innovations is shown by Chrétien's reference to his 'ancient' book source for *Cligés* as a stronger guarantee of the truth (24: 'Li livres est mout anciiens, / Qui tesmoingne l'estoire a voire; / Por ce fet ele miauz a croire', The book testifying to the truth of the story is very ancient. Hence it deserves more to be believed). Whether these conventional nods in the direction of established views actually impeded these authors in their revolutionary development of fiction is quite another matter, however, for the case of Wolfram suggests that conformity to what is expected by some can be a cloak for what is suggested to others who have ears with which to hear.

Conformity to conventional expectations is the last thing offered by Wolfram when he disclaims anything to do with literacy (115, 27: 'ine kan decheinen buochstap', I know nothing of letters) and argues that his work proceeds without the guidance of books (115, 29: 'disiu âventiure/vert âne der buoche stiure', this story goes its way without the help of books). These lines have been interpreted on several different levels,[94] to which we may add the point that this twofold denial amounts to an authorial rejection of the practice of deriving the truth of the narrative from adherence to a book-source. This is borne out by the fact that none of Wolfram's many source-references makes mention of a book, writing or reading.[95] This is in marked contrast to the conventional practice of his day, more particularly of the three authors to whom he makes intertextual references (Eilhart, Veldeke, Hartmann), who he could therefore assume were known to his audience and could offer a yardstick against which his own waywardness would stand out the more clearly.[96] Eilhart, for example, makes it clear that information derived from a book-source is a hallmark of truth when he says how long the love-potion exercised its power over the lovers (*Tristrant* 4730: 'alsô sprechin die/die ez an dem bûche hân gelesin/daz mag wol ungelogin wesin' (this is what those say who have read it in the book. That may well be true). Veldeke can likewise settle a contentious issue by equating truth with what the books have to say (*Eneasroman* 145, 10: 'nû wizzen wir daz wol vor wâr,/die wir diu bûch hân gelesen/daz daz niht ne mac wesen', now we who have read the books know this to be the truth: that cannot be so). These are both authors who indicate that their own works are books,[97] but the significance of passages like these is that they bring out the function of books to convey and confirm the truth. Hartmann is of interest in a different way. Although conventional formulas of the type 'as I read in a book' occur in his *Erec*,[98] this is not the case with *Iwein*, whose prologue contains a sketch, however, of the literate author reading books just before composition of this work is mentioned (21 ff.), so that the books could conceivably refer to his source. In either case, the bookishness of Hartmann's procedure is clear, so that Wolfram's reference to many authors starting their work from books (115, 28: 'dâ nement genuoge ir urhap') could refer to Hartmann's emphasis on his literacy in the opening lines of *Iwein*.[99]

In disclaiming literate status for his work Wolfram flies in the face of what he elsewhere makes clear, namely that his *Parzival* exists in written form and that he reckons with women readers (337, 1ff.) alongside listeners to whom it is read out.[100] Maintaining that *Parzival*, unlike the romances of Eilhart, Veldeke and Hartmann, is not a book is therefore meant ironically, and Wolfram's purpose in using this irony is possibly to distance himself from the equation of books with factual truth found in the first two of these predecessors (the truth of *Parzival* may therefore be of a non-factual kind) and to pour scorn on the whole convention of book-references.[101]

Although this long-established convention served the useful purpose of legitimising vernacular literature in the face of the superior claims of Latin writing (more learned) and the inferior status of oral tradition (less reliable), Wolfram is not the only author to stand aloof from the convention, even if his reservations are much more pronounced. Against the naïve assumption that writing is a guarantee of truth there speaks the realisation that written tradition need not be unanimous and that not all versions are reliable. The *Alexanderlied* speaks out against the view that Alexander was the son of a magician and not of Philip of Macedon, calling its upholders 'bôse lugenâre', wicked liars (Vorau MS 71) and Gottfried makes it clear that an alternative version of the episode of the swallow with the golden hair, with which he has no truck, is in fact a written text (8605, 8626–7).[102] Other cases go even further, for they play with or express doubt about the very idea of traditional book-references. Instead of safely sheltering behind the authority of a written source the author of the *Alexanderlied* insinuates a doubt by saying that if his source lies, so does he (17: 'nîman enschulde sîn mich:/louc er, sô liuge ich').[103] He may still pass off the responsibility, but at the cost of needlessly raising a doubt, possibly because of his clerical unease in dealing with a secular theme, one moreover which already in antiquity had attracted doubts as to its veracity.[104] Doubts are also raised (purposely, so as to open the door to fictional, rather than factual truth) in Hartmann's *Erec*, expressly dependent on Chrétien's written text, when the narrator refuses pointblank to swear that a detail is true

(9209–10). These examples, where references to a written source are not meant quite straightforwardly,[105] all concern secular themes where traditional clerical doubts could certainly be expected, but they also come from the romance genre (in the case of the *Alexanderlied* from a romance theme) in which fictionality was now establishing itself.[106] To cast doubt on their factual truth is a way of suggesting not their untruth, but the possibility of their fictional truth.[107]

Wolfram goes much further than these isolated parallels, for he systematically undermines the source convention in that his source-references do not hold – they do not substantiate what he claims for them. They have been closely analysed by Lofmark, whose conclusions I largely take over at this point. In *Parzival* the author inserts a large number of conventional references, giving the impression that he shares the assumption that fidelity to his source is a guarantee of the truth of his work and that he must render the whole source and invent nothing new. He thereby suggests a sustained commitment to the acknowledged rules of source authority.[108] There is reason to doubt these statements by Wolfram, however, which are not confined to the problem of Kyot, a source that Wolfram claims to follow in preference to Chrétien, even though most scholars are at present inclined to regard him as a fabricated figure. Lofmark (who later presented his reasons for questioning the existence of Kyot as an independent source)[109] established his doubts by comparing Wolfram's text with Chrétien's over those parts of the narrative where the German author could base himself on the French work. His conclusion is that in fully eighty-two of the ninety-one cases in question Wolfram's claim to be in agreement with his source is false, a finding which only in its high proportion, but not in the tendency it reveals, echoes the similar situation with Hartmann's source-references in *Erec*.[110] Only five of Wolfram's references are reliably true, whilst there are forty that are reliably false, so that the majority of references are deliberately false and the truth of a handful of cases is likely to be accidental. These conclusions are telling, but we must part company from Lofmark when he talks of Wolfram 'deceiving' us, of his 'intention' to 'deceive'.[111] I question whether we can talk of deception in these cases (and Lofmark later corrects himself),[112] for if Wolfram's technique is that of a source-fiction, then in accordance with what we have seen of the fictional contract between author and audience, and what we have yet to see of Wolfram inviting his audience to connive with him in establishing fiction, there can be no deception of listeners to whom all this is made clear.

What Lofmark has established of Wolfram's source-references at large is also true more specifically whenever the word *âventiure* in the sense of 'source' is employed in the same kind of context, for here too he claims poetic licence for himself while still putting forward the protective screen of a pretended source. Since Thomasin von Zerclaere *âventiure* in its literary sense had been associated with lying (and significantly is not used of source-references found in chronicles),[113] and nearly half of the cases where Wolfram uses this word in a source-reference occur in passages of hyperbolic description where this accusation could most justifiably be made.[114] In addition, if we confine ourselves to examples of *âventiure* where direct comparison with Chrétien is possible we register that in only two cases out of twenty does the reference to the source accurately reflect Chrétien's point, but that even here the reference is quite general.[115] The remaining eighteen cases are all false references, creating the impression of an agreement between German text and French source where in fact none exists. As we saw with Wolfram's dialogue with *frou Âventiure*, his use of a word meaning 'source' implies less a dependence on the factual truth of his source than the freedom to go his own way.[116]

If modern comparative scholarship can cast doubt on the truth of Wolfram's source-references, how far were similar doubts open to a medieval audience, how seriously did they take his claims? The position with him is not the same as, for example, with medieval biblical epics where not all source-references agree with the source, for this illustrates no more than the looseness of medieval quotations.[117] By contrast, Wolfram's references are not merely inaccurate in the modern sense, he also plays with the very idea of source-references and makes this clear to his audience. Like a handful of his immediate predecessors in Germany, but more emphatically than they, he can introduce a doubt into his references, saying that events unrolled as he depicts them *if* his source (*âventiure*) tells the truth (210, 18) or has not deceived him (224, 26), *if* Kyot spoke the truth (776, 10) and *if* Wolfram himself as narrator has not lied to his listeners (216, 9).[118] Wolfram also goes out

74

of his way to provoke doubts about his seriousness in this. His remark on matter which is his own invention (435, 1: 'swerz niht geloupt, der sündet', whoever does not believe it, commits a sin) effectively passes the buck to the audience, inviting them to share his joking disrespect for source-authority (cf. also 381, 28: 'geloubetz, ob ir wellet', believe it if you like).[119] Can it be meant seriously when source authentication is required to establish that in jousting knights are knocked off their horses backward (73, 9–10) or to support the unreal hyperbole that a lady's beauty outshone the light of candles (638, 15 ff.)?[120] We are left, like Düwel, to wonder at the possibility of irony when Wolfram maintains his inability to dispose as he thinks fit over the material of his source (734, 20ff.).[121] The sheer triviality of what the source is meant to substantiate must also make us doubt whether such authentication serves factual truth of any kind, as when we are assured in all seriousness that before leaving Schampfanzun Gawan took breakfast (431, 1–2).

Underlying examples of this kind is the question how far the undermining of source authority was visible to the audience of Wolfram's day. This question may not be so acute as with Lofmark's comparison of Wolfram's source-references with Chrétien's text (we cannot imagine a member of a medieval audience going to work so philologically), but we still need to know whether some of Wolfram's audience would be led by his disrespectful tone to see the wider issue here – the abandonment of the factual truth which source-references were usually held to support. Lofmark entertains the possibility that Wolfram's audience may have shared this disrespect with him and that his real attitude was betrayed to them,[122] but we need to consider further cases, where Wolfram reveals his hand more clearly.

One class of evidence concerns passages, like his address to Hartmann and dialogue with *frou Âventiure*, which make it clear that the narrator disposes of the details in his story, that the truth he presents derives not from an authoritative source, but from the author's inventiveness.[123] When the elderly king Uterpandragun is unhorsed in a joust the narrator intervenes to praise himself for having so courteously contrived to land him amongst flowers where never peasants set foot (74, 11ff.). In doing this the narrator advertises that it lies within his power to shape such an event and that his work is a fictional construct.[124] When Parzival encounters Feirefiz we are not told anything of a source (certainly not

Chrétien, whose work was broken off long before this and knew nothing of any character corresponding to him), but instead the narrator says that it is he who has guided the hero to this point (737, 25: 'ich sorge des den ich hân brâht', I am worried for the one I have brought here), just as, in concluding the whole work, it is he, the narrator, who has brought Parzival to the goal for which he was destined (827, 17: 'Parzivâls, den ich hân brâht/dar sîn doch sælde het erdâht', Parzival, whom I have brought to where destiny intended him).[125] In all these cases the narrator displays that events, details as well as long-term developments, are under his control, so much so that any factual dependence on a source that is not even mentioned is edged into insignificance.

However, authorial inventiveness alone does not suffice for fictionality, as we saw in the case of an intertextual reference concerning Orilus. Also necessary is the knowing collusion between author and audience of the kind revealed by Gottfried in his preparation of Tristan for his knighting ceremony, where his description no longer conforms to the source, but is dependent on collusion between author and audience in a shared fictional enterprise.[126] We need evidence similar to this from *Parzival*, too, given the centrality of the fictional contract to our definition.[127]

There are various ways in which the narrator involves the audience, making them complicit with him. A simple form is when he seeks their agreement over a detail, but whereas examples of this before Wolfram are normally in the first person plural, involving audience and author (e.g. *Kaiserchronik* 16615: 'nû lâzen wir die rede sîn', now let us abandon the account), Wolfram more commonly employs the second person plural (e.g. 777, 8: 'dâ mite lât die rede sîn', let the matter rest at that).[128] Although the technical function of these formulas is clear (they usually continue the narrative from one scene to a new one), Wolfram's change of pronoun involves the audience more closely in the narrative task, suggesting that its continuation depends on them, not on Chrétien's (discontinued!) text or on the narrator as an intermediary. Even this formulaic emphasis on the audience does not undermine their cooperation with the author, for their agreement to abandon one episode can be linked to listening to what is to come (e.g. 354, 3: 'die rede lât sîn als si nu stê:/nu hoeret wiez der stat ergê', let the matter be at that and hear

76

how things stand with the town), so that their decision still leaves them dependent on the narrator, they still have to work with him.

We go a step further when the narrator, pretending indecision as to whether to continue or not, makes a make-believe appeal to the wishes of his audience on this score, only to continue after having momentarily heightened the tension in this way (e.g. 403, 10: 'welt ir, noch swîge ich grôzer nôt:/nein, ich wilz iu vürbaz sagen', If you want, I can be silent about such grief. But no, I will continue the story for you).[129] From this it is a short step to pretending that the listeners are not merely nominally in charge of continuing the narrative, but can actually control the course it takes.[130] (Hartmann has one or two examples of this pretence, whilst in France the narrator of *Le bel inconnu* suggests that his lady can dictate the course of the action to him and even provide an alternative conclusion.)[131] In *Parzival* the audience, again with a *lâzen* construction, are supposedly in charge of the hero's journeying at the start of a new stage in the narrative as he leaves Pelrapeire (224, 5: 'lât rîten Gahmuretes kint', let Gahmuret's son ride on), but here, too, they cooperate with the narrator on whom they still depend (224, 1: 'Swer ruochet hoeren war nu kumt...' whoever wishes to hear...). When the description of a meal is concluded by the narrator he excuses this by implying that his listeners can decide that, but for any glutton, enough has been eaten (639, 1: 'Ezn sî denne gar ein vrâz,/welt ir, si habent genuoc dâ gâz', If you agree, they have now eaten enough, but for any glutton). In all this the audience are not merely involved or consulted, they are also jokingly allowed to believe that their wishes are paramount in the course of the tale (327, 26: 'waz welt ir daz man mêr nu tuo?', what more do you want to be done?). It is they who are to give permission for Gahmuret to change his coat of arms (14, 12ff.). A narrative apparently so dependent on their preferences (but really on a narrator who manipulates their wishes) cannot claim conformity to an authoritative source as its overriding principle. The passages we have been considering testify to a threefold fictionality. They are built on fictitious dialogues between the narrator and an audience which he has invented and built into his work; they pretend that the overall plan of the work is not yet fixed, but still *in statu nascendi*[132] and therefore capable of being re-arranged at will; the work is not derived from a fixed source on which it depends for its truth, but from a contract between narrator and audience which is still negotiable over details.

An audience so involved in arranging the course of the action, even to the extent that, if they say so, the story must be true (59, 27: 'Gebiet ir, sô ist ez wâr', if you will have it so, then it is true), shares responsibility with the author for the truth. The collusion that Wolfram imposes upon them is most obvious at a peak of narrative incredibility (the miraculous food provided by the Grail) when a statement is substantiated not by the narrator's oath, but by that of his listeners (238, 8: 'man sagte mir, diz sag ouch ich/ûf iwer ieslîches eit', I was told and I tell it, too, on your oath).[133] As a result, if the narrator is lying (as he had earlier admitted as a possibility, 216, 9: 'ob ich iu niht gelogen hân', if I have not lied to you), then so must be his audience (238, 11: 'sol ich des iemen triegen,/sô müezt ir mit mir liegen', if I deceive you on this, then you must be liars with me). Wolfram may use the verb for lying here to show that we are dealing not with factual, but with poetic or fictional truth, but he cannot be accused of deception (*triegen* occurs in a hypothetical statement) when he lays his cards so openly on the table and invites his audience to play their part in the game he is playing, not contract bridge but fictional contract.

The focus of any discussion of Wolfram's source-references and their fictive nature has long been the figure of Kyot: was his work Wolfram's actual source or is he no more than a fabrication? An early approach to the latter possibility was provided by Wilhelm in a wide-ranging article.[134] No clear distinction is made over the use of the term 'fiction' ('deception' or 'fictitious composition'),[135] but the point is made that although the figure of Kyot is a fabrication Wolfram cannot be accused of lying, which ties in well with what we have just seen of his fictional contract.[136] The wide range of fabricated sources discussed by Wilhelm includes cases where pretence is made of a written source (when there is every reason to doubt its existence) as a guarantee of truth as opposed to the unreliability of oral tradition.[137] This is relevant to the case of *Parzival*, for although Wolfram denies its written status, the literary tradition which he fabricates for Kyot is a literate one (even if of an unusual kind in going back ultimately to writing in the stars). However, Wolfram does not simply suggest an (ultimate) written source, as do the other examples given by Wilhelm; he also exaggerates the origins of this source in such a fabulous way as to provoke incredulity as regards its factual truth.[138] This has not prevented some scholars from hunting down clues to the existence of a 'real' Kyot, even though the majority opinion seems now to be in favour of his fictive status.[139] This division in modern scholarship may reflect a division in the medieval reception of *Parzival*, with some accepting Kyot as a guarantee of factual truth and others aware that he was a signal to fiction.

Kyot is explicitly mentioned in *Parzival* on six occasions, three of them in digressions, the other three more in passing.[140] Two points need to be made about these references, the first of which is that the earliest (416, 17ff.) occurs as late in the narrative as Book VIII. The second is that, since Kyot is cited as a guarantee of the conclusion of the story that Chrétien's fragment had not delivered (827, 5 ff.) and since what Trevrizent reports on the Grail goes back to Kyot, but also harks back to what preceded Book III, Kyot acts as an informant for those parts of *Parzival* which could not be based on Chrétien (prehistory, expansion of the encounter with Trevrizent in Book IX, conclusion).[141] This prompts the question whether this material derived from a Kyot who was used as a cover for Wolfram's deviations from and additions to Chrétien. Nellmann has pointed the way in which the decision between fact and fiction may best be made: by trying to reconstruct how a contemporary audience was led to view the situation.[142] Were they in a position to see through what I take to be a fictional pretence by the author and therefore enter into collusion with him?

Some of the facts associated with Kyot by Wolfram, however fantastic and incredible they may appear to us, need not have been seen in that light by contemporaries, so that they could have been credible in principle.[143] Astronomy was a reputable discipline in which the Arabs held a lead, especially at Toledo, so that knowledge of their language was a requirement, whilst for Kyot to seek a historical base for knowledge derived from this source by studying Latin chronicles from Britain, France and Ireland was fully acceptable in a period in which Anglo-Norman historiography flourished, a point underlined by the mention of Anjou.[144] These details are all mentioned in connection with Kyot, and have their real counterparts in the world of Wolfram's day, so that a contemporary audience would not have faced the difficulties that confront us in taking this fabulous figure at face value. In addition, there is the practical point that no audience at that time would have been remotely in a position to disprove what is said about Kyot, so that for some of them at least he was conceivably a real entity, a guarantee of the literal, factual truth of what Wolfram said.[145]

There remain, though, a number of uncertainties, ambiguities and contradictions that cannot be accounted for in this way and that open the door to another view of Kyot. These have been discussed by Lofmark, who stresses that, contrary to the tendency of modern scholarship to interpret ambiguities in one direction or another and thus produce clarity, Wolfram's picture of Kyot and his activity is imbued with uncertainty, so that what outwardly could be considered as acceptable fact is instead ambiguous, intangible and unclear in the extreme.[146]

This uncertainty is one of the reasons why the figure of Kyot, regarded as a fabrication, has been held to be a defence by Wolfram mounted against those in his audience who were untrained in fiction. That this was certainly possible in the twelfth century is clear from the polemics of Adelard of Bath against the blind acceptance of past authority, the rejection of what the *moderni* may have to say, so that whoever has something new to say is constrained by the prevailing conservatism of the day to conceal it under a pseudonymous author who can act as an authority or to affirm that what he has to say goes back to the Arabs.[147] By making use of Kyot and having him do his research in Arab Spain Wolfram could be said to combine both the possibilities suggested by Adelard.

What the specific occasion was for Wolfram to introduce the figure of Kyot at the point where he did is not so clear. At least two reasons have been adduced, which need not be mutually exclusive. One suggestion is that, on the brink of launching his narrative into details of the fabulous realm of Munsalvæsche in Book IX, Wolfram was prompted to meet criticism from his audience, used to factual, historical truth, for not having named a source-authority, since up to 416, 20ff. all his many source-references had been nameless.[148] This defence points backwards (no specific details about the source he followed hitherto) as well as forwards (the need to authenticate Book IX), but there is no reason why the two directions should not complement one another. Another explanation looks further afield and sees Kyot as a defence of the inventiveness forced upon Wolfram in continuing *Parzival* beyond where his source left off.[149] This use of Kyot would be far from making a virtue out of necessity, for the German author's inventiveness embraces Books I and II, but also the greater expansiveness of Book IX. Again, the crucial importance of this Book may have occasioned the detailed digression on Kyot in 453, 5 ff., with 416, 20 ff. and 431, 2 as preparatory passages, inserted either in anticipation of Book IX or in a subsequent re-working.

These reasons concern only the attitude of those who may have felt uneasy at the absence of an authoritative source, but the transparency of some of the Kyot passages suggests that other members of the audience, alert to literary fiction, were also expected. Nellmann makes the telling point that only the educated members of the audience would have entertained doubts about what was told them, but that it is precisely with these that an understanding of fiction could be presupposed.[150] Beyond this general consideration, however, there are detailed points that can only have aroused suspicion, and were intended to, amongst which the very first mention of Kyot belongs.[151] He is adduced as guarantee of the name of Liddamus (416, 19–20), who is however so peripheral to the action that one questions why such authentication should be called for. Moreover, the name sounds Latin and can hardly be typical of Schampfanzun, as is made clear when Wolfram makes him refer to Veldeke's *Eneasroman* and quote from German heroic tradition (Wolfhart, *Nibelungenlied*, Dietrich). To a German audience it would have been clear that this figure was a creation of an author on the German side of the linguistic border, not of a Provençal Kyot who wrote in French. To introduce Liddamus so contradictorily under the auspices of Kyot casts all too obvious doubt on the veracity of any Kyot reference. This is true of source-references that arouse suspicion as to their seriousness when they belabour a trivial point. That Gawan took breakfast before leaving Schampfanzun (431, 1) is of no importance to Wolfram's story, so that for him to go to the trouble of saying that he has this from Kyot (431, 2: 'ich sage iu als Kyôt las', I am telling you what Kyot read) undermines the importance of Kyot to the point of absurdity. Equally, when ladies' lips are said on one occasion to be red without the use of cosmetics (776, 8–9), do we really need to be assured that the authority of Kyot stands behind this, especially when this is expressed with a slight element of doubt (776, 10: 'ob Kyôt die wârheit sprach', if Kyot spoke the truth)?[152] Kyot may be used to introduce the important revelations about the Grail in Book IX (453, 5 ff.), but to associate him with such trivialities calls into question how necessary he was for Wolfram's task of composition.[153] He may serve as a useful screen when the author faces criticism (why has he not named his source? what is his authority in deviating from Chrétien?), but we are allowed to suspect that his role in the genesis of *Parzival* is minimal.

So minimal, in fact, that the distinction between Wolfram and Kyot is at times very unclear, as when the latter's authority is invoked over matters which we know are characteristic of Wolfram himself[154] or when the technique of releasing information in carefully controlled instalments, typical of Wolfram's work at large,[155] is attributed to Kyot (453, 5: 'mich batez helen Kyôt', Kyot asked me not to reveal it). The narrator may praise Kyot (against Chrétien!) for having told the whole story of Parzival unto the very end (827, 5 and 11), but only a few lines later he praises himself for having brought, together with *sælde* (destiny), Parzival to this successful conclusion (827, 17–18). The final impression is therefore of the German author's self-conscious pride in his achievement, demonstratively naming himself (827, 13) in pushing Kyot to one side.[156] The function of Kyot is also exposed to doubt in the dialogue with *frou Âventiure* at the opening of Book IX, where the exchange takes place in direct discourse between the narrator and the presiding genius of the story, behind Kyot's back, as it were.[157] Moreover, in seeking admission to the narrator's heart (433, 1ff.) *Âventiure* is revealed as no external source, but as identical with the author himself, in much the same way as when Virgil in the *Aeneid* asks the Muse to 'unroll the huge boundaries of the war *along with me*' (9.528: 'et mecum ingentis oras euoluite belli').[158] Wolfram's self-consciousness, equating himself with and seeing himself as the presiding genius of *Parzival*, leaves little room as a factual source for a Kyot who can be shown in an absurd light, pushed to the limits of triviality, shown up as doubtful in much of what is said of him and, at the most, serves only as a useful screen for the author's own purposes.

The transparency of many of Wolfram's source-references and the manner in which he involves the audience in his fiction made the fictional nature of *Parzival* apparent to them, but also to other authors of his day and later, even if they were not always ready to accept it. One way to see this is to return to the beginning of this chapter, to the question of intertextuality. By definition, the interfictive world on which it rests is built on the relationship between two or more literary works; it opens up not a relationship between a literary work and the external world, but a discourse within literature. This is true of both the text and the pre-text: both are *verfügbar*, at the author's free disposal in constructing his fiction. Wolfram's Arthurian world is part of his fiction, as was seen by later authors who refer intertextually to his work in much the same way as he had to earlier authors.[159] In *Parzival* it is made clear that Hartmann's romances, the pre-texts of most of Wolfram's references, are fictional (in the address to Hartmann as Parzival comes to Arthur's court the earlier author is presented as in control of his own fictive world) and therefore at the free disposal of Wolfram, too, also engaged in fiction. This is true at a later intertextual stage, for other authors show that they in their turn are aware of the fictional status of *Parzival*. In *Diu Crône*, for example, Heinrich von dem Türlin makes an intertextual reference to the earlier romance, quoting from Wolfram for ironic purposes, much as Wolfram had done with Hartmann.[160] Heinrich seeks leave from Wolfram in doing this. He 'quotes' briefly the episode in Soltane where the young Parzival encountered the knights, but then refers to the subsequent action (Parzival's departure from Soltane for Arthur's court), saying of Wolfram: 'der in von sîner muoter nam / und hât in ze hove brâht', who took him away from his mother and brought him to the court (6381–2). In saying that it was Wolfram who took Parzival from A to B and that, but for him, Parzival would have remained with his mother (6383 ff.) Heinrich sees Wolfram as in charge of the action, just as Wolfram had similarly proclaimed that it was he, as fictional puppet-master, who had taken Parzival to his final success (827, 17–18). It may not be fortuitous that Heinrich makes Wolfram's control of events clear by a reference to that part of the *Parzival* narrative (the hero comes to Arthur's court) where Wolfram had placed the intertextual address to Hartmann in which he demonstrates that both he and his predecessor freely dispose of figures in the Arthurian world.[161]

An earlier and critical voice, saying that Wolfram's fiction is concerned not with truth but with lies, is raised by Gottfried in his polemics against the 'vindaere wilder maere', fabricators of wild stories (*Tristan* 4663).[162] Although Nellmann sees the force of this criticism of Wolfram as lying in the words *wildiu maere* (a narrative in which the *sin* (meaning) is not made clear or is not even present),[163] this need not of itself exclude a further criticism conveyed by the word *vindaere* (one who finds or invents and thereby conveys untruth).[164] For Schröder the words *wildiu maere* refer even more closely to the question of Wolfram's sources; since they point to the unauthorised, lying content of *Parzival*, they betray his irresponsible attitude to sources, dabbling in inventions by himself or others, put forward as true.[165] In his analysis of Gottfried's use of *vinden* and *vunt* Schröder shows that, although they can be used positively,[166] they can also occur in a context devoid of truth. When Tristan fabricates a story to the pilgrims (3091: 'sîn âventiure vinden', invent his tale) his account has no factual truth, but is at least plausible,[167] which is more than Gottfried is ready to concede with Wolfram's fantasies. Deception, even self-deception leading to disastrous results, is more obviously present in the words composed by Tristan for the songs he sings to Isold with the White Hands (19200: 'Tristan der machete unde vant', Tristan composed and invented; 19204: 'er vant ouch . . . /den edelen leich Tristanden', he also made up the noble song of Tristan). In attacking Wolfram as belonging to the 'vindaere wilder maere' Gottfried is attacking not fictionality as such (of which he is himself a past master), but the fiction put abroad by Wolfram and others (significantly he uses *vindaere* in the plural).[168] In doing this he is re-drawing the frontiers within contemporary literature in favour of himself and so as to discredit a rival and those with whom he associates him, just as Wolfram himself does in distancing his own truthful account (338, 12: 'lop mit wârheit', praise in accord with truth) from what others produce (338, 17: 'valsch lügelîch ein maere', a false and mendacious tale).

HISTORY

If, in the three types of narrative, rhetorical theory placed *historia* at the opposite pole to *fabula* and also distinguished it from *argumentum*, but saw these two latter types as constituting fiction, this raises the question as to what the place of *historia* may be in a work like *Parzival* which we have suggested is fictional.

We may start from what can be termed the doubly visual dimension of history,[169] as passed on to the Middle Ages by Isidore of Seville. He based his definition on the two features of an eyewitness and written tradition, so that in antiquity, in his view, no one wrote history who had not witnessed the events himself.[170] This doubly visual conception of history, continued by clerical authors in the Middle Ages, is most succinctly summed up by Konrad von Hirsau, who defines *historia* as *res visa* and the *historiographus* as the *rei visae scriptor* (one who writes up what he has seen).[171] The author of a romance who was consciously engaged in fiction and wished to subvert the view that *historia* might be applicable to his work could in theory deny both these aspects of *historia*. Given his denial of bookishness (no matter whether we regard this as true or not) there was no call for Wolfram to dwell on the lack of a written tradition (it may be present, in however fantastic a form, between Flegetanis and Kyot, but the break comes with Wolfram himself, so we are led to believe). This proclaimed 'illiteracy' of Wolfram stands apart, however, since other authors pointedly stress their own literacy and adherence to a written tradition. For them (but also for Wolfram) any subversion of *historia*, any suggestion that their work is to be regarded as fiction, must proceed from a denial of eyewitness authentication.

Two other authors of fictional romances, expressly literate and there-fore forced to focus on the eyewitness argument, may illustrate this. Hartmann makes fun of eyewitness verification, showing that it has no place in a work of fiction, in *Erec* when he has an imagined member of the audience ask the narrator for details of the dress worn by Mabonagrin's mistress (8946). In reply to this request the narrator states that he does not know because he never saw it himself, but that the questioner should ask her chamberlain (8947: 'des vrâget ir kamer-aere:/ich gesach in weizgot nie,/wan ich niht dicke vür si gie'). These lines are compressed fiction on several levels. First, the dialogue between listener and reciter is not real, but invented. Secondly, the chamberlain is not a character that appears in *Erec*, so that he possesses not even a fictional existence. Thirdly, to argue the truth of a fiction by appealing to a 'witness' within that fiction, rather than outside it, is to move in a vicious circle.[172] On different levels Hartmann makes fun of the eye-witness convention, but by raising this convention at all when there was no need for it he has given himself the opportunity to imply that his romance, for all its literate status, does not conform to the second requirement of *historia*.

The eyewitness is similarly dispensed with in Hartmann's *Iwein* where he points out, with regard to the single combat between the victorious

Iwein and Ascalon, that the hero was too well-bred to have boasted about his exploit, but that no one else had been present as a possible eyewitness informant (1032: 'sî wâren da beide,/unde ouch nieman bî in mê/der mir der rede gestê', they alone were there and no one else who could give me an account).[173] If the author is writing here on an event on which no eyewitness report is possible, this has the drastic result that this crucial episode, on which the rest of the work hinges, is left in an unauthenticated, unhistorical void. As an indication of his fiction Hartmann has thus turned Isidore's definition on its head, for he makes it clear that his written version cannot go back to an eyewitness. How far this fiction stands from history can be shown from a counter-example.[174] In his *Kindheit Jesu* Konrad von Fussesbrunnen forgoes the description of a meal because he had not been present himself (2443 ff.), so that what for lack of an eyewitness was not possible in a genre, the legend, that counted as *historia*[175] was permissible to Hartmann in a fictional genre.

Another example is given by Gottfried, who concludes his description of the love-grotto by apparently putting himself forward as an eyewitness to what he has just described (17104: 'Diz weiz ich wol, wan ich was dâ', I know this indeed, because I was there).[176] This claim has been interpreted as an *attestatio rei visae* (attestation of what has been seen), which in a written text would bring it into line with Isidore's view of *historia*, but against this speaks the narrator's further remark that although he knew the love-grotto he had never been to Cornwall (17140ff.). His attestation is therefore meant not literally or historically, but figuratively (he does not claim to have 'seen' the grotto, but uses the verb *erkennen* (to know), 17140, of his knowledge of love).[177] How far this 'eyewitness' authentication is removed from history can be shown, as with Hartmann, from the counter-example of a legend, for in the *Väterbuch* the truth is testified on the grounds that the martyr's sepulchre, unlike Gottfried's love-grotto, has actually been seen (10074ff.)[178]

If for these two contemporaries of Wolfram fiction involved their breaking free from the idea that their romances derived from an eyewitness who transmitted an account to them, as with *historia*, there is no reason why Wolfram should not also go out of his way to disclaim eyewitness authentication. A first example concerns the extent of Gahmuret's travels, of which the narrator says that he will speak in accordance with the source, for he has no other witness (15, 13: 'als mir diu âventiure giht./ine hân nu mêr geziuges niht', as the source tells me. I have no other testimony). We have seen that the term *âventiure* is a dubious quantity as regards Wolfram's conformity to a source, but when Wolfram later says (115, 29–30) that his story goes its way without the guidance of books (sources), it is probable that his account of Gahmuret's travels proceeds without either eyewitness confirmation or a written transmission, in other words without the two features that could qualify it as *historia*. Much the same is true of a combat fought by Gawan, for here too *âventiure* as the source is invoked, together with a lack of witnesses (381, 29: 'geziuge sint mir gar verzagt, / wan als diu âventiure sagt', I have no witnesses, except what the source says), whilst the uncertainty of such deliberately unhistorical attestation is underlined by the throw-away nonchalance of the preceding line (381, 28: 'geloubetz, ob ir wellet', believe this if you like).[179] In the description of the wedding festivities at the close of Book VII eyewitnesses may not be mentioned expressly, but they are implied in a particular way (397, 7: 'wie diu hôchzît ergienc, / des vrâgt den der dâ gâbe empfienc', on how the wedding went ask those who received a gift there). In asking his (invented) questioner to request further details from those who were present and received largesse the narrator proceeds just as unhelpfully as in Hartmann's *Erec* when the questioner is directed to the chamberlain of Mabonagrin's mistress. Wolfram's narrator, unlike Hartmann's, may not actually say that he was not present himself, but he implies as much, whereas those whom he does put forward as supposedly present and receiving gifts are imagined creatures of his own fiction and in no position to authenticate it as *historia*. Something similar is present when the Gawan narrative is resumed at the start of Book X. Again, imagined questioners are behind the inquiry as to what had happened to him in the meanwhile (504, 1ff.) and again they are fobbed off by being recommended to consult those who witnessed his journey (504, 5: 'des jehen diez dâ sâhen', let those tell you who saw it), who are also internal to the fiction, not external. These examples where eyewitness verification is debunked may not be many in number, but in every case there was no pressing need for eyewitnesses to be mentioned at all. By bringing them in only to question their relevance Wolfram reminds his audience at repeated points that his fiction is subject to criteria other than those of *historia*.

That Wolfram's technique was recognised at the time, even if it was not accepted as justifiable, is shown in *Seifried Helbling*, where the author points out (XIII 78 ff.) that he will praise only what he had himself seen, unlike the praise lavished on Gahmuret and Parzival by Wolfram 'der ir einen nie gesach' (who never saw either of them).[180] The mention of Gahmuret ties up with the first example of this technique in *Parzival* (15, 13 f.), but heightens its implications for satirical purposes: whereas Wolfram says that no eyewitness reported on events, it is now claimed that he was not an eyewitness himself. Wolfram's high-handed dispensing with eyewitness authentication could therefore call forth objections from those who were not prepared to accompany him into the realm of fiction, of the historically unattested.

Wolfram's stress on the fictional status of his work and his flying in the face of *historia*, as based on eyewitnesses, justifies a questioning of attempts to overdraw the extent to which *historia* may be found in *Parzival*. This is not to deny the presence of historical features or details of contemporary reality in the work, but rather to ask whether they are not subordinate to an overall fictional purpose.[181] (Does the presence of Napoleon's campaign in Russia make Tolstoy's *War and Peace* any less fictional?) Three suggestions have recently been made concerning the historicity of *Parzival* that call for further refinement.

In the first of these Nellmann concludes that Parzival was believed by Wolfram to have been a historical figure.[182] In support of this the presence of historical features has long been recognised, but not always with the necessary distinction between history and the appearance or fictional pretence of history.[183] Hence, a number of features adduced by Nellmann are not so unambiguously historical as he suggests. The emphasis placed on genealogy in *Parzival*,[184] including family trees and the extension of the narrative backwards into the parents' generation and forwards into that of the descendants, could contribute to a historical dimension, but does not constitute it. The internal chronology of the work, even though worked out more consistently than in any other work of the time, is likewise a presupposition of historical writing, but not identical with it or confined to it. It could equally well be a particular aspect of the internal consistency required of fictional writing since Horace (*Ars poetica* 119: 'sibi conuenientia finge', make up consistently). Nellmann also suggests that the care with which Wolfram gears the action of *Parzival* into the earlier one of *Erec* and the later one of *Lancelot* implies a chronological view of all these events.[185] That may be so, but still not constitute history, since we saw in connection with intertextuality that this technique was part of an interfictive world in which one fiction was linked with another, suggesting no more than the illusive impression of historical continuity.[186]

In his discussion of Wolfram's possible knowledge of Wace's *Roman de Brut* Nellmann draws attention to manuscript R (on the assumption that Wolfram may have known it and learned from it).[187] The manuscript is a codex beginning with the Troy and Eneas romances, followed by the *Roman de Brut*, which is interrupted at the point of an interval of peace in Arthur's reign for the insertion of Chrétien's Arthurian romances before Wace's work is taken up again. From this the conclusion is drawn that the scribe, inserting Chrétien's works into a collective historical work in this way, must have regarded them as quasi-historical. We must distinguish, however, between the poet (Wace or Chrétien), and the scribe (or the patron who commissioned him), but also between the time when these poets were active and the time when the manuscript was compiled, the second quarter of the thirteenth century, a time when a greater need was felt to defend fiction against the accusation of untruth (by the transition from verse to prose or, as here, by suggesting its historicity). Moreover, since we shall later see that the scribe of this manuscript goes against both Wace and Chrétien[188] it is hazardous to use his product as evidence for anything but his situation in the thirteenth century, let alone for Wolfram's work.

From this postulated knowledge of Wace by Wolfram Nellmann concludes that he must also have known the lines, considered at the close of our definition of twelfth-century fictionality, in which Wace dismisses the adventures recounted about Arthur's knights as neither completely lying nor completely true (1253–4). Nellmann is not ready to take these lines to show that Wace regarded these adventures as fictional.[189] He argues instead that they indicate that facts are mixed with fiction (but that in itself is a recognised feature of fictionality)[190] and that these facts contain a nucleus of (historical) truth. However, for Wace this nucleus of truth concerned Arthur and his court as well as the wars he waged outside the period of peace. Like William of Malmesbury, Wace does not extend this truthfulness to what is reported of the adventures of

Arthur and his court in this period (the subject matter of the Arthurian romances).[191] If Wace was on the brink of realising or formulating the nature of Arthurian fiction, we cannot use his testimony as an argument for historicity. Belief in the historicity of Arthur does not entail a similar belief about Parzival, as little as the presence of Napoleon in *War and Peace* means that Natasha and Pierre are also historical figures. The matter may not be quite so clearcut with certain figures of the Arthurian world, for in their histories Geoffrey of Monmouth and Wace mention, in addition to central figures of the court like Gauvain and Keu, the occasional protagonist of a romance such as Yvain, to whom therefore historical credence could be given.[192] But there are in other romances figures who are not historically accredited in this way, such as Erec and Lancelot, and Parzival is among these.

We have seen Wolfram playing with source-references, fabricating Kyot, dispensing with eyewitness authentication, generating something new out of Hartmann's fiction, presenting himself as controlling the course of narrative action as he thinks fit. He does all this and makes it visible to those in his audience who have eyes with which to see and advertises his work as a fictional construct. What historical material is present in his work is applied, rather than organic to the plot.

This is relevant to the second suggestion made about historicity, for if Nellmann is persuaded that Wolfram took Parzival to be a historical figure, Knapp suggests that we should regard the work at large as *historia*, not as *fabula*.[193] In proposing that *Parzival* should be seen more as a historical romance (like *Willehalm*) and less as a fictional romance (like Chrétien's *Perceval*) Knapp bases himself on the suggestion (which he admits has not yet been fully worked out) that the element of marvels in it does not conform to what we understand as *märchenhaft*, to what we should expect of a folktale. We may agree that the *Märchen* is one possible constituent of fiction,[194] but still question whether it is also a necessary feature. In other words, it is doubtful whether showing *Parzival* not to be *märchenhaft* is the same thing as demonstrating that it is not fictional.

Like Nellmann, Knapp adduces codicological evidence to support this view (which he concedes it does only sometimes).[195] The example he quotes is the Codex Sangallensis 857, containing in addition to *Parzival* works which were regarded as eminently historical, such as the

Nibelungenlied, the *Klage, Karl der Große* by Der Stricker, and Wolfram's *Willehalm,* so that *Parzival,* Knapp suggests, must have been felt to be similarly historical. Here too, as with Nellmann's suggestion, we must distinguish between Wolfram's intentions and how his work was viewed by the later compiler of the codex and recognise that with the noticeable shift in the course of the thirteenth century from fiction to historiography[196] the two need not be the same. The danger of extrapolating from other works included in a codex is particularly clear in the French example quoted by Nellmann (manuscript R of Chrétien's *Perceval*), for the scribe of the codex inserted Chrétien's romances into an otherwise historiographical compilation, but precisely at the point where Wace placed his critical comment on the fictional nature of these adventures. If we do not on this account describe Chrétien's romances as historical,[197] recognising that a codex compilation may reflect a range of literary interests and not simply one single point of view, there is no reason to assume otherwise with the inclusion of *Parzival* in the St Gallen codex. Certainly Gottfried did not regard Wolfram as engaged on factual *historia. Seifried Helbling* exposes the non-historical nature of his writing, whilst those authors who make intertextual references to *Parzival* recognise it as belonging to the same fictional world as their own romances.

As a third suggestion, Knapp has returned to this question in another article in which he takes issue with Brunner's view that in *Parzival* Wolfram, in full accord with what has been said of fiction since antiquity, endeavoured to combine fictional with extraliterary, recognisably 'real' features.[198] Even if we accept *Willehalm* as historico-legendary, this does not oblige us to see *Parzival* as either exclusively fictional or as non-fictional, historical. Even Knapp has to concede that Wolfram refrains from pinning *Parzival* down chronologically, and its historical status cannot therefore be equated with that of *Willehalm.*[199]

The dividing line between *argumentum* and *fabula* on the one hand and *historia* on the other was no sharp one. Rhetorical embellishments, criticised by rigorists as untrue, could be found a place in history as in fiction; history could make use of poetic devices, just as fiction could incorporate historical details.[200] Despite Knapp's objections Brunner does justice to the complex position of *Parzival* in its interplay between history and fiction. This interplay may grant a greater role to history than in Hartmann's romances and thereby prepare the way for what has been called Wolfram's 'return' to history in *Willehalm*,[201] but not to the extent of an abandonment of fiction. Wolfram's contemporaries, especially those critical of him, saw this clearly enough, and Knapp has to concede that his successors such as Heinrich von dem Türlin and Der Pleier built on his fictional Arthurian world.[202]

CHAPTER 5

Fiction and structure

Underlying the medieval view of poetry was the distinction between the way in which the narrative was arranged (*dispositio*) and its stylistic adornment (*ornatus*), each of which can be seen to be closely associated with fictionality. Stylistic adornment can take the form of rhymed verse instead of prose, with the former being seen often as harmful to the truth of an account.[1] But *ornatus* embraced much more than this, covering figurative language as such and including features like metaphor, irony, ambiguity, all of which belonged to the realm of *fictio*.[2] (This explains why Lucan could be seen as a *poeta fingens* as regards his literary style, but as a *historicus non fingens* as regards his subject matter.)[3] This point was made in a similar way by Lactantius, who argued that the poet does not make up the events he narrates, but instead converts what actually happened into other forms by indirect figurations, by obliquity and inexplicitness ('ut ea quae vere gesta sunt in alias species obliquis figurationibus cum decore aliquo conversa traducat').[4] For this reason, too, Grünkorn includes in her survey of the literary theory of fictionality a section on *equivocationes* and *multivocationes*.[5]

In this chapter, however, we are concerned with the other side of the distinction, with *dispositio* as a meaningful patterning of a fictional narrative. The unified structure of fiction, coherent rather than arbitrary as opposed to the fortuitous incompleteness of history, was already clear to Aristotle, just as for one twentieth-century scholar fiction narrates a series of situations so related to each other by the author as to achieve a significant unity of meaning.[6] As opposed to 'real life' with its scrappy, disordered contingencies, fiction patterns its narrative so as to convey a meaning. The presence of a contrived symmetry, for example, in a narrative suggests that history is subordinated to the demands of fiction and that we are dealing with an 'artistic control of signification', while to recognise a close parallelism is to be aware of its improbability, to see that a fictional plot has been consciously designed by its author.[7] Thus, parallels (and contrasts) between the Perceval and Gauvain parts of Chrétien's *Perceval* suggest that their respective adventures are to be seen as complementary and as casting light on one another.[8] Haug has drawn attention to the greater complexity and ambitiousness in patterning which is open to the author of a written work by contrast to the simpler linearity of narrative in oral composition.[9] This is relevant to the problem of fictionality in the medieval romances, composed in writing by literate authors at a time when writing was making inroads into the hitherto predominantly oral culture of laymen,[10] especially since greater complexity of plot-structure presupposes the freedom to contrive which fictionality provides.

Structure in fiction therefore projects an order on events that in real life would suggest no such order.[11] It does this by means of purposeful organisation to make artistic sense as opposed to the random nature of the contingent world.[12] To achieve this end the author of a medieval fiction had to cut free from any absolute obligation to an authoritative source or to the truth of events held to be historical, he had to enjoy the liberty to create imaginatively, to create not absolutely (*ex nihilo*), but in the sense of providing his own structure and organisation of events and thereby his own view of their meaning.[13] One form that this narrative liberty took in the medieval romance was for the author to combine material from other works in the new context of his own work, as when Johann von Würzburg says in the prologue to *Wilhelm von Österreich* that he intends to compose an *âventiure* (story) from a number of other *geschihten* (tales).[14] This guarantees that any factual truth that may (or may not) have been present in these *geschihten* will no longer be found intact in his *âventiure*, a fact clear to the author's audience both from their general literary knowledge and from this explicit statement of intent.[15] The author's fictional liberty in such a case does not amount to any freedom to invent, but still allows him to combine in a novel way. Insofar as one work of fiction is composed as a variation on another fiction, this opens up a metaliterary dimension such as we saw with Wolfram's intertextual references to Hartmann. How important this play on variations was for the history of the Arthurian romance in France has been shown by

Schmolke-Hasselmann, who traces the extent to which Chrétien's model was adapted, simplified or undermined by his successors, all within the framework, in the widest sense, of what he had first devised.[16]

Although these variations occur markedly in the post-classical phase of the romance (and have often earned their authors the title 'epigones'), they existed as a possibility from the beginning of the genre. Chrétien himself, after devising the structural model of *Erec*, rang the changes on it subsequently,[17] whilst his *Cligés* is patterned largely as a response to the challenge of the *Tristan* story.[18] In Germany Hartmann re-composed the conclusion of his *Erec* in the light of Chrétien's *Yvain*, while Wolfram drew on both Hartmann's *Iwein* and Chrétien's *Yvain* in finding a conclusion for *Parzival*.[19] All this implies a fictional freedom of scope from the beginning of the Arthurian romance, not merely in its later stages, a fact best illustrated from Chrétien's much discussed term *conjointure* (*Erec* 14).

Like Johann von Würzburg, Chrétien combines a number of *contes* (tales) into the new whole of his *Erec*. The first part of this work joins the adventure of the White Stag (the *premiers vers*) to the tale of the Sparrowhawk,[20] a meshing of separate *contes* into a new unity which echoes what Thomas says more explicitly about his unification of diverse material to constitute his *Tristan* (Douce 835: 'Seignurs, cest cunte est mult divers,/E pur ço l'uni par mes vers/E di en tant cum est mester', Lords, this tale is very variegated, and for that reason I unify it by my verses and say what is necessary), omitting what he does not regard as acceptable.[21] Such a technique, picking and choosing what suits the author's intention rather than conscientiously following a source from which nothing is omitted and to which nothing is added,[22] enables Chrétien to describe his *conjointure* as *bele* (it expresses the truth of his narrative) and Thomas to maintain that rival versions of his story 'sunt del cunte forsveié/E de la verur esluingné', have deviated from the tale and distanced themselves from the truth (Douce 879–80). By contrast with the relatively homogeneous sources of the antique romances, the variety of the material drawn on by Chrétien and the contradictory nature of the versions of the *Tristan* story before Thomas made it more difficult for them to handle and unify their material.[23] But it offered them infinitely more scope to adapt it to their own ends, to choose, to add, to omit, to re-group as they thought best.

There are many types of structural patterning to be found in narrative literature, especially in the romance. Of these I have chosen four for discussion, because of the particular light they throw on the fictionality of such patterning. Amongst these is included the double cycle structure which dominated research until recently, especially in Germany, and whose overall importance I seek to play down. We turn now to the first of these four forms of *dispositio* used to convey the truth of fiction.

ORDO NARRATIONIS

The rhetorical handbooks recognise two main ways of organising a narrative: either the *ordo naturalis*, arranging the sequence of a story to conform to the chronological succession of events, or the *ordo artificialis*, re-arranging this succession in accordance with the author's overall purpose.[24] Although there is no hard and fast distinction, the former *ordo* is commonly regarded as the hallmark of the historian and the latter as characteristic of fictional writing.

The *ordo naturalis* was commonly seen as exemplified by Lucan and Statius in their capacity as historians, and in the definition of *historia* given by Engelbert von Admont ('Historia autem est rei gestae, prout gesta est, ordinata narratio' History is an account of what happened in the sequence in which it happened) the last two words mean not simply an 'ordered narrative', but more specifically one in the same order as the events took place.[25] Such a chronological ordering of the narrative best befits a historical work and is often put forward as the historian's method. For Gregory the Great, for example, what is recounted in a vision by St Benedict is so undoubtedly true that it had to be presented in a historical manner ('vir Dei per ordinem, quae fuerant gesta, narravit', the man of God recounted events in the order in which they happened).[26] A saint's life demands similar treatment (the legend was also known as *historia*),[27] so that in the *Vita s. Guthlaci* Felix of Crowland makes it clear that he adopts a historical sequence ('principium in principio, finem in fine compono', I compose the beginning at the beginning, the end at the end).[28] The same point is made by William of Malmesbury in his *Vita s. Wulfstani* ('nichil turbaui de rerum ordine; nichil corrupi de gestorum ueritate', I have disturbed nothing of the order of events or distorted the truth of what occurred),[29] as also in a more secular context in the same author's *Gesta regum Anglorum*, where he stresses the uninterrupted sequence of his history ('continuam Anglorum historiam ordinauerim', recount in order the continuous history of the English).[30] As part of his claim to be a genuine historian Geoffrey of Monmouth argues similarly in the dedication of his *Historia regum Britannie*, presenting not merely a consecutive survey from Brutus down to Cadwallader, but one in the correct historical sequence of his source ('actus omnium continue et ex ordine', all their deeds continuously and in sequence).[31] In his vernacular translation of this work Wace, as a historian who took Geoffrey seriously as such, could make no use of his predecessor's dedication, but he makes the same historian's point in his opening. He therefore presents the successive kings of England (2: 'De rei en rei e d'eir en eir', from king to king, from heir to heir) in their proper chronological sequence (5: 'Quels reis i ad en ordre eü,/E qui anceis e ki puis fu', what kings there were in sequence, who came before and who came after).

By contrast, the *ordo artificialis* disturbs the chronological sequence of events in accordance with the author's own plan (in the words of Remigius of Auxerre: 'voluntate et ingenio' by choice and ingeniously).[32] The leading example of this re-grouping of events for fictional purposes was Virgil's *Aeneid*, frequently quoted in this context. In his commentary on this work Servius sees it explicitly as part of Virgil's artistry ('artem poeticam') that the fall of Troy and Aeneas' first wanderings are narrated after, not before his arrival at Carthage and that Anchises' prophecy projects the narrative forward to the age of Augustus.[33] This commentator's reference to the artistic nature of this re-arrangement is more specific, however, for he also mentions Horace's *Ars poetica* as prescribing this technique (the poet 'semper ad euentum festinat et in medias res . . . auditorem rapit', always hastens to the outcome and plunges the listener into the midst of things).[34] Horace may have had only Homer in mind, but Servius legitimately applies his observation to Virgil, too. This view of the poetic nature of the *ordo artificialis* survived into the Middle Ages. The ninth-century *Scholia Vindobonensia*, commenting on Horace's work, refer to the example of the *Aeneid* and recommend the author of a poem to love the artificial order and avoid the natural.[35] Fromm has drawn attention to the fact that the use of *explanatio* by Servius was apparently known to Bernard of Utrecht in the eleventh century, who interpreted it to mean a subsequent elaboration and clarification of what had earlier been said.[36] A century later Konrad von Hirsau quotes the *Aeneid* as an example of the *ordo artificialis*, and later still Geoffrey of Vinsauf, basing himself on Horace's *Ars poetica*, is lavish in his praise of the artistic fecundity of this *ordo*.[37]

Between these two ways of arranging narrative material there was, however, no absolute contrast. Despite the recommendation of the *Scholia Vindobonensia*, the author of a poetic work could, if he so chose, follow the *ordo naturalis*, as is done, for example, by medieval adaptations of the *Aeneid* (the *Roman d'Eneas*, Veldeke's *Eneasroman*) in the opening of the work, narrating the fall of Troy, Aeneas' first wanderings and his arrival at Carthage in chronological sequence.[38] An *accessus* to Lucan makes no bones about the theoretical possibility of a poet working in this way, saying of him: 'iste dicitur proprie poeta. Ordinem quoque habet naturalem' (He truly is termed a poet. He uses the natural order).[39] The author of a work of fiction therefore has a choice which in theory is denied to the historian: he can follow the *ordo artificialis* or the *ordo naturalis*, or he can combine both (*ordo commixtus*)[40] in one work. From the use of the *ordo naturalis* it is quite unsafe to infer that the work in question was meant as historical.

Although the *ordo artificialis*, as described by grammarians and commentators, may appear to be a somewhat arbitrary or even banal feature, the example of Virgil to which they so often refer illustrates the artistic possibilities of a more complex structure, its ability to convey meaning by abandoning strict chronology. Virgil's hero is caught at a point in time 'between a dead past and a future which has not yet come', between the fall of Troy and the founding of Rome.[41] If past and future intrude upon the poem's present in this way, it makes good artistic sense to highlight this by disturbing the natural time-sequence, bringing the Trojan past to bear on the events at Carthage and opening up Book VI to the distant future of a new Troy, a future which reaches as far as Virgil's own present. An example of such quality is best fitted to demonstrate the aesthetic potentialities of the *ordo artificialis*, but our question now is whether, quite apart from any invidious comparison with Virgil, the same *ordo* was utilised by medieval authors to convey the meaning of their fictional narratives.

The expansive and multiple narrative of most romances provided ample opportunity for the *ordo artificialis*. Following the adventures of their heroes in their temporal sequence, they cannot avoid this *ordo* whenever an antagonist is introduced, often as a stranger, *in medias res*, whose motives and prehistory have to be recapitulated, however briefly, in a flashback.[42] A romance with more than one narrative strand cannot avoid similar flashbacks when taking up one strand again after another. In Wolfram's *Parzival*, for example, these flashbacks can be accompanied by a careful synchronisation of the two strands, so that the *ordo artificialis* of the flashback leads over to a return to the *ordo naturalis*.[43] In what follows, however, we must be highly selective, looking at three authors only.

Pride of place belongs to Chrétien, all of whose romances apart from *Cligés* adopt the *ordo artificialis*, plunging into the midst of events and giving subsequent accounts of the prehistory as called for – even in the case of *Perceval*, whose theme of the hero's slow progress might have suggested a strictly linear biographical pattern.[44] In most of his romances Chrétien also adopts a technique, reminiscent of Servius' *explanatio*, of introducing his protagonist at first anonymously (or, in the case of *Yvain*, without making it clear who is the protagonist) and only subsequently equipping him with a name, for the most part at a meaningful point in the narrative.[45]

The *ordo artificialis* plays a significant role in *Yvain* and *Perceval*.[46] In the first of these romances Calogrenant, like Virgil's Aeneas, recounts events which lie some time in the past, before the story opens,[47] but this initial example prepares us for other cases. Thus, Lunete's past (her accusation and condemnation) is recounted by her, not the narrator, and since the two strands, Yvain and Lunete, come together here Yvain (and the audience) need to be informed of events in the past.[48] Similarly, the woman acting on behalf of the Count's younger daughter seeks Yvain for help, asking several people *en route*, each of whom gives partial information about a stage of Yvain's recent journeying, so that a joint description of his past is conveyed.[49] More complexity is reached when two episodes are not in sequence, but each meshed with another episode: the rescue of Lunete has intercalated into it the combat with Harpin, while the inheritance dispute of the two sisters is interrupted by the *Pesme Aventure*.[50] Not merely does this technique deprive this part of the story of the directly continuous sequence of time characteristic of the *ordo naturalis*, but its very artifice stands out forcefully: twice Yvain is engaged in combat with giants, twice in legal conflicts, and twice he has severe difficulties in keeping a promised deadline. Although the suspense and tension created in this way must have been welcome to Chrétien, it is the double risk of Yvain's failing to observe a deadline that is the issue here, for it reflects the cause of the crisis that arose between Laudine and himself.[51] In a sense utterly different from Virgil's *Aeneid*, time is of the essence in this romance, a fact brought home to us by the disturbance of linear narrative chronology.

In *Perceval* the suspension of linear chronology is practised on the small as well as the large scale. Continuing the technique used in *Yvain*, Chrétien arranges the first part of this later romance in such a way that four episodes (the death of his mother; the girl in the tent; Blanchefleur; the Red Knight) are left in suspense, each involving an interruption of the preceding one, with each then being resolved in turn, culminating in Perceval's admission to the Round Table.[52] On an even larger scale Chrétien interrupts the story of Perceval by interposing the story of Gauvain, intending by the parallels between them that each should pass comment on the other. How such interlace narrative is connected with the *ordo artificialis* is shown by the fact that when Chrétien interrupts the Gauvain story to interpose Perceval's stay with the Hermit and then returns to the Gauvain story he reverses the chronological disturbance of the Hermit episode by taking us back five years.[53] In making such switches from one strand to another Chrétien can be quite explicit (e.g. 6214: 'De monseignor Gavain se taist/Ichi li contes a estal,/Si comenche de Percheval', here the tale is silent about lord Gauvain and begins to deal with Perceval),[54] and if such interlace pointers lack the subtlety of 'gliding transitions' they have the advantage of revealing the hand of an author disposing of the arrangement of his fictional narrative as he thinks fit.[55]

For Gottfried's *Tristan* I give one example only, but a revealing one: the passage in which the lovers walk in the early morning in the surroundings of the love-grotto (17351ff.).[56] These lines combine interlace (they switch back to the lovers after we have been following the strand of Marke's hunt and of his huntsman following tracks that lead him to the vicinity of the grotto) with the *ordo artificialis* (in 'actual' time the lovers' walk had preceded the huntsman's arrival, so that the tracks he has followed merge into the footprints left by the lovers in the dew). By abandoning the *ordo naturalis* (and signalling this by an interlace comment, 17351:

'Des selben morgens', on that same morning) Gottfried shows us that the lovers' idyll is threatened and that the world of the court is moving in again on the lovers, not merely within the context of this work, but as a comment on the dangers to which love is exposed in the world at large. Here, too, the *ordo artificialis* conveys a meaning that passes well beyond the isolated point at which it is employed.[57]

In Wolfram's *Parzival* the *ordo artificialis* informing the opening of Chrétien's *Perceval* (we learn the prehistory of the protagonist's parents only some way into the work by a flashback)[58] may have been converted into the *ordo naturalis* (in Books I and II the story of his parents precedes that of Parzival, which begins in Book III), but this does not exclude the occurrence of the *ordo artificialis* elsewhere in the German work. One example is the start of Book VI (280, 1ff.), concerning Arthur's departure in search of the Red Knight, for this takes place at a point in time earlier than the conclusion of Book V, on which it immediately follows.[59] Another example, likewise strategically placed, is the start of Book IX (433, 1ff.), the dialogue between the narrator and *Frou Âventiure* dealing with Parzival's adventures since he was lost to view at the end of Book VI for, although no precise details may be given, the whole passage is given over to past time. This dialogue with *Frou Âventiure* allows the narrator to plead ignorance about the time of Parzival's journey (435, 5: 'ine weiz ze welhen stunden', I do not know at what time) and to pass this ignorance on to his audience, which in turn they share with Parzival himself, as he makes clear in his statement to the pilgrim-knight (447, 20ff.).[60] Behind this detail, a disruption of time brought about by a flashback, there lurks a central problem of Wolfram's work, for the fact that Parzival's restoration to time is seen in explicitly religious terms (448, 5ff. and 460, 22ff.) means that his falling out of time, his disorientation, was a sign that, as a stranger to liturgical time, he was unreconciled to God.[61]

Although it has been suggested that an explicit reference to an author's rhetorical disposition is not to be expected in a purely literary work,[62] this takes no account of Chrétien's pointers as he switches between the Perceval and Gauvain strands of his narrative, or of a passage in Hartmann's *Erec* (7825 ff.) in which the narrator, engaged in a fictive dialogue with an impatient member of his audience, keeps him at bay and promises to release the information he craves only in due course.[63]

A similar stance is developed at greater length by Wolfram's use of Kyot as an excuse for deferring information, even though it may not always be narrative events that are deferred, but rather the information necessary for understanding them (the *explanatio* of Servius). At three points (241, 1ff.; 452, 29ff.; 734, 1ff.), all of them meaningful turning-points in the story, the narrator explains and justifies his dispositions to his listeners, revealing the required information to them in progressive instalments that match Parzival's gradual enlightenment.[64] This strikingly recalls Horace's recommendation to the poet not to overwhelm the reader with everything at once, but rather to say at the moment what should be said then, postponing and omitting much for the present.[65] Wolfram may not have known Horace (just as Chrétien may not have been directly inspired by the Virgilian model), but both vernacular authors betray a knowledge of the *ordo artificialis* in structuring their fictions.

The so-called *Bogengleichnis* (241, 1ff.) can also be seen as a defence of Wolfram's practice of long-term deferment of necessary details.[66] Eleven lines of this passage (241, 8–18) appear to acknowledge the principle of straightforward narrative, but this impression is undermined by the fact that, as if in accord with Horace, the narrator says this just after telling the audience (241, 1–7) that he will not give them now all they may want to know about Munsalvaesche, but will come back to it later ('her nâch').[67] At this point the narrative is anything but straightforward, rather is it circuitous, its principle is *krümbe*, roundaboutness (241, 15). Such circuitousness is even to be seen, against appearances, as direct, as is suggested much later in lines that recall this passage (805, 14: 'ez ist niht krump alsô der boge,/diz maere ist wâr unde sleht', This tale is not bent like the bow, but true and straight).[68] What appeared to be a circuitous narrative is in fact *sleht*, because in direct accord with the author's wishes. It is also *wâr*, because justified within the economy of the work and capable of conveying its narrative truth.[69] The use of the *ordo artificialis* is justified whenever such a form of narration conforms to the author's intentions, to what Remigius of Auxerre saw as his 'voluntas et ingenium'. This was already the case with Virgil, but medieval authors such as Chrétien, Gottfried and Wolfram were fully capable of realising its potentiality for conveying meanings that could not have been presented so effectively by following the historical sequence of events.

TYPOLOGY

One respect in which typology differs from the interlace narrative considered in the last section is that interlace encourages the reader to move on a horizontal axis, following the meandering course of the narrative and alert to internal references, whereas typology offers vertical connections between the narrative and the theological level of God's control of history.[70] This difference does not mean, however, that typology cannot also be employed self-referentially, as we shall see with what has been termed 'internal typology' (confined to one work) and with typology used fictionally.

Central to typology is a turning-point in time, characterised by Christ, between the old and the new, in which the type, coming before Christ, anticipates and is surpassed by the antitype, coming in and after Christ, as when Adam foreshadows Christ, the *novus Adam*.[71] In that the antitype surpasses its type there is an element of discontinuity in typology, but in that it also reflects its forerunner an element of continuity, so that typology is made up of the conjunction of both these features.[72] The presence of typology is generally (but not always) indicated by some sort of signal. Common examples include referring to the antitype as the 'true' (*verus*) fulfilment of the old (Christ as the true Samson or the true Isaac, dependent on whatever function is being stressed), as the 'new' embodiment (Christ as the new Adam), or the use of *noster* (Christ is not merely the *sol novus*, but also *sol noster novus*, our new sun).[73] Another signal is the use of a grammatical superlative like *summus*, *supremus* or *altissimus*, so that Alanus ab Insulis can refer to the Christian God as *supremus Iupiter* (or simply as *Iupiter*).[74]

Thanks mainly to the labours of Ohly it is now generally accepted that there are various categories of typology.[75] Its home and its most important function are the bible and the interpretation of the Old Testament in the light of the New, but it can also be employed outside this restricted context in what can be termed semi-biblical typology (only one pole, type or antitype, is biblical, the other is not) or extra-biblical (neither pole is biblical). The acceptance of these further possibilities means regarding typology more as a way of thinking than as a method of exegesis restricted to the text of the bible, an extension of scope which is all the more likely in view of the wide range of examples collected and discussed by Ohly from early Christian sources through to the late Middle Ages and beyond.

Biblical typology (typology in the strict or narrow sense) is too well known to need dwelling on. Examples range from the New Testament itself, where Christ as antitype surpasses Moses (2 Cor. 3, 7ff.) and Adam (Rom. 5, 12ff.), just as Mary also came to be regarded as undoing what Eve had wrought,[76] through to the north portal of Bamberg cathedral, where the apostles are depicted standing on the shoulders of the prophets.[77]

Semi-biblical typology falls into two classes, in the first of which the type is biblical, but the antitype non-biblical. Examples include the concordance between Solomon and Constantine (the former built the temple at Jerusalem, the latter founded the Church in Rome), between Ezechias and Theodosius (the former defended Jerusalem from its enemies, the latter the Church from heretics), between the events of Exodus and those of the crusading present (in both poles a crossing of the sea, associated exegetically with baptism, leads to military conquest of the Promised Land).[78] The second class is the reverse, containing a non-biblical type (most commonly from classical antiquity) in relation to a biblical antitype, and resting on the view that select aspects or figures of the pagan past were granted partial access to a truth fully revealed only by Christ.[79] Figures from the classical past conscripted for this purpose include Ulysses (tied to the mast he foreshadows Christ on the cross), Hercules by virtue of his heroic exploits, Socrates because of his wisdom, but especially Orpheus (as one who tames wild beasts or descends into the underworld).[80] Other aspects of the classical past include, for example, the mysteries of Eleusis (anticipating those of Christ), Mount Cithaeron (as the type of Mount Zion) and even Roman triumphal processions as prefigurations of the Church's celebration of Christ's victory.[81]

Finally, with extra-biblical typology employed by clerical authors both type and antitype are still subservient to a Christian interpretation, but are taken from a non-scriptural source. Under this heading the founding of Rome by Romulus and Remus is related to the founding of the new Rome by Peter and Paul, whilst in his Christian epic Juvencus takes Virgil as his model, but is assured of the typological superiority of his own work by virtue of its religious truth, granting him not merely the 'longa fama' (long-lasting fame) of his pagan forerunner, but the promise of an 'aeterna laus' (eternal praise).[82] When the Roman Church in the third century settled on December 25, the birthday of the pagan *Sol Invictus*, as the official date of Christ's birth its concern was to proclaim Christ as the *Sol novus,* typologically superior; but this was later taken very much further by Notker Balbulus. Combining this typological example with the idea of a *translatio imperii et studii* from the east to the west Notker can even view the Irish founder of his monastery, St Gallus, as a *Sol novus* coming miraculously from the west, and argues that God at the moment of creation foresaw that in the sixth age Bede, too, would rise as a new sun in the west to illuminate the whole world with his learning.[83]

One important consequence for us comes from the possibility of semi-biblical and extra-biblical typology, for together they can at times involve the presence of fiction in one pole, in the type. This is already the case with early Christian exegesis whenever the type that is surpassed comes from classical mythology or poetry, from what was regarded as *ficta,* not the *facta* of *historia,* which were reserved for the Christian antitype.[84] (The theoretical objection that applying the same typological method to classical texts as to the Old Testament ignored the difference between fictional *fabulae* and biblical *historia* appears to have presented no long-term obstacle to this practice.) Exegetes who employ this method were perfectly aware that one of their poles was fictional and the other factual. Thus, when Gerhoh von Reichersberg correlates Ulysses with Christ he expresses doubt about the former's historicity ('Etiamsi non ficta, sed facta crederentur', although believed not as fictive, but as facts), but none about the antitype ('facta, et non ficta sine dubio creduntur', believed as facts and without any doubt not as fictive), suggesting that the accounts of the former were made up (*fingere*) by a mixture of truth with falsehood ('falsa veris miscere')[85] whilst the biblical text knows of no such adulteration ('absque omni admistione totius falsitatis').[86] Much earlier, when Ambrose adopted Plato's myth of Gyges and his ring in order to establish the superior truth of biblical testimony he argued by means of a similar contrast, setting *fictae fabulae* (fictitions fables) against *verissima exempla* (truest examples), *figmenta* (figments) against *res gestae* (what in fact happened).[87] When Juvencus argued the higher value of his Christian epic by contrast with Virgil, this was not merely because he was sure of eternal praise as opposed to long, but finite renown, but because of what lay behind this certainty: the addition of *mendacia* (lies) to Virgil's account of heroic deeds by contrast with the truthfulness of his own account of Christ's deeds ('falsi sine crimine').[88]

Examples such as these, associating the type with the lies or fables of classical literature, are of a twofold nature. On the one hand, to place the type so obviously on a lower level makes it the more credible that Christian texts, by virtue of the truth claimed for them, typologically surpassed those of classical antiquity. On the other hand, of greater importance for our concern is the fact that they introduce the possibility of finding a place for fictionality within typology, even if, in these cases, with a negative function.

Before we turn to the further penetration of fictionality into typology, this time under positive auspices, a word must be added on what has been termed 'internal typology',[89] involving no longer the conjunction of two separate texts, the type and the antitype, but the incorporation of the two poles of typology within the same work, imbuing it with a structural tension. An early example is provided by the *Vita s. Martini* of Sulpicius Severus.[90] In place of a historical contrast between a past pagan epoch and the superior Christian present, the saint's life is presented in the biographical terms of his earlier service as a soldier in the Roman army and his later military service in a spiritual sense, as a 'miles Christi' (soldier of Christ). This biographical contrast is summed up in St Martin's words: 'Christi ego miles sum, pugnare mihi non licet' (I am a soldier of Christ and am not allowed to fight),[91] presenting, as in typology at large, both continuity (*miles* describes the saint in both parts of his life) and discontinuity (as a spiritual warrior he does not fight physically or in a secular cause). What Sulpicius illustrates here was not intended by him as fictional or unworthy of belief, but by incorporating typological correspondences between the saint's life before and after conversion he certainly makes use of literary artifice in his composition.[92] We move from literary artifice to a fictional work when in Wolfram's *Parzival* the two stages in the protagonist's career are similarly brought out. Gurnemanz sees in Parzival a potential feudal ruler (170, 22: 'ir mugt wol volkes hêrre sîn', you may indeed be the lord of a people), an office which he assumes on marriage to Condwiramurs, whereas he is ultimately brought to the higher office of Grail kingship (477, 21: 'von art des grâles hêrre', by birth the lord of the grail).[93] Here, as with the *Vita s. Martini* and with typology at large, continuity is combined with discontinuity: continuity in the fact of rulership (*hêrre*), discontinuity in the radical difference between a feudal kingdom and the realm of Munsalvaesche.[94]

We have so far only briefly touched upon the possibility of fictionality within typology, but may be encouraged to inquire further by the presence of semi-biblical and even non-biblical typology, by the examples of internal typology we have looked at, but above all by the occasional presence of fictionality in one pole, the type, for this opens the door to the possibility of fictionality in both poles, to the fictional use of typology. The text where this can be shown most effectively is Gottfried's *Tristan*, where typology, as in semi-biblical or extra-biblical cases, is employed to show the action surpassing what was achieved in antiquity, but also in secularised parallels to biblical typology.

Gottfried's use of typology falls into two classes, the first of which (short-range typology) operates between two generations, i.e. between two segments of a biographically conceived narrative (a usage which reflects the fact that biblical typology hinges on the birth of Christ as the turn of an era).[95] Particular stress falls on the way in which Tristan radically surpasses his father Riwalin in their typological relationship. The secular use of religious imagery when Riwalin falls in love and is granted 'ein niuwe leben', a new life (936), whether or not we regard this as a typological turning-point comparable to St Martin's conversion, is later echoed by the similar experience of his son and the imagery used of him (8316: 'im was ein ander leben gegeben:/er was ein niuborner man', he was granted another life, he was a new-born man).[96] Whereas the father was granted a new life, however, the son is more emphatically described as reborn,[97] and in his case the typological implication is more clearly conveyed by this passage coming immediately after Tristan's ecstatic praise of Isold's beauty with the unmistakably typological reference to her as 'diu niuwe sunne', the new sun (8284). In the case of both father and son the new life brought by love is intimately associated from its inception with death: Riwalin is mortally wounded in battle (1287), whereas Tristan willingly embraces the 'êwiclîchez sterben', eternal death (12506) of his love for Isold.[98] What for the earlier generation was imposed from without in physical terms is positively accepted by the son and transposed to a metaphorical level.[99]

The later generation typologically transcends the earlier also in the case of Isold, in a twofold sense. On the one hand she is shown surpassing Blanscheflur in the scene of the latter's first union with Riwalin, in particular with regard to the idea of medicine.[100] In order to come undetected to the wounded Riwalin Blanscheflur has to disguise herself as an *arzâtinne*, doctor (1276), and if her love restores Riwalin to life this is not described in terms of any metaphorical medicine. The position is quite different with Isold and Tristan, for they are led to one another by the supernatural agency of 'Minne diu arzâtinne', Love, the healer (12168) and each exercises a healing power over the other (12174: 'ein ander z'arzatîe'). The physical disguise as a doctor in the prehistory is thereby transposed to the higher level of the antitype. Something similar is true of the theme of magic.[101] When pondering the cause of her emotional turmoil in falling in love Blanscheflur considers the possibility of a magic charm (1001), even though she later sees that the cause lies in her heart and not in any magic (1033 ff.). With Isold, however, even though she and Tristan have drunk a love-potion there is no thought of physical magic, even temporarily.

The other sense in which Isold is presented typologically in a change of generations is in regard to her own mother (of the same name).[102] Whereas the mother is termed 'daz morgenrôt' (dawn) the daughter is repeatedly described as 'diu sunne' (the sun),[103] but the comparative force of these two terms is best seen when they are employed together, as in Tristan's praise on his return to Cornwall (8284: 'diu niuwe sunne/nâch ir morgenrôte/Îsôt nâch Îsôte', the new sun after the dawn, Isold after Isold) or when both women appear at the court in Dublin (10889: 'Sus kom diu küniginne Îsôt,/daz frôlîche morgenrôt,/und fuorte ir sunnen an ir hant', thus came queen Isold, the joyful dawn, leading her sun by the hand). The religious source of these epithets, as well as their typological function, is quite clear, for to the description of Christ as the *sol* (sun) there corresponds the term *aurora* (dawn) for Mary. Just as the sun outshines the first signs of light at dawn, so does Christ surpass His mother, and Isold hers. The chronology on which typology depends (the new transcends the old) is here, as in the other examples, seen as a change in generations, and this temporal gradation is also brought out in the first example quoted, where the sun comes after (*nâch*) the dawn. That by no means exhausts the typological richness of this terminology, but fittingly leads on to the second class of typology in Gottfried's work.

This may be termed long-range typology, operative between two 'historical' periods and placing the narrative in its wider 'historical' dimension. I have placed the word 'historical' in inverted commas because the last sentence does not mean that Gottfried's fiction is historical, but that he uses the typological way of thinking to organise his fictional narrative, to present a 'fictional history'.[104]

Our first example takes the dawn–sun metaphors a stage further, for Gottfried uses them typologically to relate Isold not merely to her mother, but also to Helen, the classical paragon of feminine beauty.[105] The passage just considered (8284ff.) is part of a double typology, short-range in linking Isold as the sun with her mother as the dawn, but also long-range in the preceding lines by setting her above Helen (8267ff.). More for the sake of analogy than in error Helen is presented as the daughter of Aurora (8270),[106] thereby prefiguring the relationship be-tween Isold and her mother, but under the force of his experience Tristan abjures his belief that the sun of feminine beauty rose in Greece (8277ff.), convinced that it now rises in Ireland. This is why Isold is described not simply as the sun, but as 'diu niuwe sunne', the new sun (8284), for she surpasses not merely the dawn, her mother, but also the old sun, Helen. This linkage between Greece and Ireland is typo-logical also in combining continuity with discontinuity, for Tristan's claim that 'ganzlîchiu schoene', perfect beauty (8279) did not appear in Greece, but now in Ireland presupposes that Helen at least had some of the beauty in which Isold now transcends her.[107] Moreover, in transposing the sun's appearance from Greece to Ireland, from east to west, Gottfried strikingly parallels what Notker Balbulus had said of the *Sol novus* (St Gallus or Bede) coming from the West, even down to a detail: Bede provided 'illuminationem totius orbis' (illumination for the whole world), just as Isold 'erliuhtet elliu rîche' (illuminates all kingdoms).[108]

Typological surpassing of a past age of a different kind is exemplified by the love-grotto.[109] At the beginning of this episode Gottfried des-cribes how the grotto had been constructed in the distant pagan past by giants who resorted there for their love-making (16693ff.), but a tenuous

link with classical antiquity is provided by the allusion to Corinaeus, a
figure derived from Virgil or Geoffrey of Monmouth.[110] At a later point
this allusion to the past is taken up again, but with specific reference
to Tristan and Isold in the present, when they are put forward as the
typological fulfilment of what was imperfectly adumbrated in the pagan
past:

> Swaz aber von der fossiure
> von alter âventiure
> vor hin ie was bemaeret,
> daz wart an in bewaeret.
> diu wâre wirtinne
> diu haete sich dar inne
> alrêrste an ir spil verlân.
> swaz ê dar inne ie wart getân
> von kurzewîle oder von spil
> dazn lief niht ze disem zil.
> (17229ff.)

(Whatever was once recounted in the old stories about the grotto was
shown to be true in their case. The true mistress of the cave had for
the first time given herself to her game. Whatever pastime or game
there had earlier been in the grotto bore no comparison with this.)

Typological pointers in this passage include the temporal turning-point
between past ('vor hin', 'ê') and present ('alrêrste'), the surpassing of the
past by the present ('niht ze disem zil') and the description of the antitype as true ('bewaeret', 'diu wâre wirtinne'). How carefully Gottfried
goes to work linguistically in distinguishing the pagan past of the grotto
from the lovers' present is suggested by his use of the nondescript word
hol ('cave') before the lovers come there and its replacement by a term
with religious, even eremitical associations, *klûse* (hermitage), once they
occupy it.[111]

Gottfried's adaptation of typology to secular purposes has led to his
work being termed a 'Heilsgeschichte der Minne',[112] falling, as clerical typology does, into three consecutive periods (antiquity, the time
of Tristan and Isold as the turn of the era, the community of the
edeliu herzen who are to take their lesson to heart).[113] If we accept
this term for *Tristan* it must be as an analogy or a secular calque, not as

identity with the Christian concept of salvation history. The salvation that Gottfried preaches is secular (*innerweltlich*)[114] and erotic, not religious in a Christian sense and lacking the historicity that Christianity claimed for itself. Similarly, history in Gottfried's use of typology is not referentially verifiable, but the poetically imagined process of the realisation of an ideal love. In accepting the term *Heilsgeschichte* we are therefore not smuggling history into Gottfried's fiction. In clerical usage typology was applied to the interpretation of the bible in order to discover the meaning and historical truth of events and deeds in God's work. Gottfried uses typology to convey the meaning and narrative truth of events and deeds in his literary work.[115]

Examples such as these, however sustained, from one work alone might be regarded as fortuitous, or too isolated to suggest that typology plays any important part in the structure of romance fiction at large. For the possibility of a wider application we may now refer in passing to another kind of structure that will occupy us later, the double cycle of the Arthurian romance.[116] Whatever reservations may be called for concerning its universal validity, they are less necessary with two classical examples at the start of the genre's history, Chrétien's *Erec* and *Yvain*, both of which feature a bipartite narrative with echoes between both parts and an underlying pattern of enhancement. Warning has termed this a 'Prinzip der steigernden Reprise' which he sees as derived from clerical exegesis of the bible in terms of prefiguration and fulfilment and which, like its biblical model, turns on a crisis of death and a new beginning, involving therefore continuity alongside discontinuity.[117]

Whether in Gottfried's *Tristan* or in Chrétien's Arthurian romance, the employment of typology as a structural device presupposes two things. First, that it was possible for these authors, and is necessary for us in interpreting them, to distinguish between typology in the strict biblical and in a less restricted sense. This is why those opposed to Schröder's attempt to confine typology to biblical exegesis alone are careful to qualify their use of this term, referring to a 'typological way of thinking', 'an analogy to typology', 'figurative [or typological] thinking' or a 'thought pattern indebted to typology'.[118] Secondly, as Gottfried's theme of adulterous love makes strikingly clear, we are dealing with a secularised application of typology,[119] with an attempt to challenge the cultural hegemony of the clergy by exploiting a hitherto clerical technique for new ends.[120] The authors who made this attempt were themselves clerics or at least clerically trained, but composed for a lay audience works with secular themes on which they conferred greater dignity by using the intellectual apparatus of the clergy.[121] Gottfried's use of the word *klûse* for the love-grotto sums up this tendency *in nuce*. It is a historical irony that in so doing these clerical authors of secular romances were reversing what the Church had done centuries earlier in appropriating features of classical culture for its own ends, a policy justified by Augustine with reference to the Egyptian treasures taken by the Israelites on their exodus.[122] It would be difficult to exaggerate the importance of this enrichment of lay culture by breaking the clerical monopoly, but equally difficult not to agree with Ruh's passionate attack on those who take the presence of originally clerical features in romances to mean that their authors were conveying a clerical, religious message.[123] This is why the signs of clerical alarm at what court literature was attempting are so unmistakable. If it was still necessary in the thirteenth century for clerics (including Thomas Aquinas) to debate whether typology could justifiably be used outside the context of the bible,[124] this suggests, on the principle that there is no smoke without a fire, that the practice was still in force and needed to be condemned.

What an author does in disposing of events in his fiction typologically is analogous to what God does in disposing of events in history. Already in the Old Testament God is seen as disposing (Wisdom of Solomon 11, 21)[125] and biblical typology reveals the order of His dispositions, allowing as it were a bird's eye view, or better a view of things through God's eyes.[126] The planning intelligence of an author, controlling the destiny of his creation, stands likewise at the centre of his fictional universe. But the difference is equally clear, since God alone creates *ex nihilo*, whilst the author re-fashions or re-combines pre-existent material, which is why his activity may be described by the verb *fingo* (form) or *facio* (make), never by *creo* (create).[127] In an essay significantly entitled '*Solus creator est Deus*' Cramer suggests that Thomas Aquinas' restrictive definition of creation may result from a defensive reaction to contemporary movements[128] (as could also be the case with his rejection of a less restrictive use of typology). Cramer sees the earliest trace of these movements in the utopianism of the Arthurian romance of the twelfth century, its freedom from the time and space of creation.[129] The originality of these authors lay in the transposition of biblical typology to a non-biblical, secular context and in their work of *compilatio*, of *conjointure*, combining pre-existent patterns into a new whole. Whereas God patterns history and allows its meaning to be seen by typology, romance authors make use of a secularised typology (amongst other methods) to pattern their fiction and allow its meaning to be seen. Clerical exegetes read a divinely ordained pattern out of what otherwise appears to be the disorder of secular history, which is thus revealed as a meaningful salvation history. By contrast, romance authors work a typological pattern into their narrative in order to convey the meaning of their fiction.

FOLKTALE PATTERN

We need not go as far as Novalis ('Alles Poetische muß märchenhaft sein') to acknowledge that folktale elements play a central part in the romance.[130] The wonders that occur in works of this genre are at odds with the miracles that characterise the saint's legend: in the latter the miracle, however exceptional, is an event in the real world pointing to a higher, transcendental reality, whereas in the folktale, abandoning the world of reality for one of wish fulfilment, the wonder is instead the rule.[131] Whereas the legend is held to be historically true, the folktale is consciously fictional – even more so if, with Propp, we take the *Zaubermärchen* to be the folktale in the proper sense of the word,[132] for this lays greater stress on the element of magic, on what, according to the definition of *fabula*, did not happen and could not have happened. In the folktale this element is present in actors (dragons, giants, animals that talk), objects (a magic potion, ointment, pillow or ring) and places (an enchanted garden, a castle under a spell, a magic wood).

This remoteness from historical reality is brought out by further aspects that characterise the folktale as a fictional construct. It is remote from contingent reality in presenting a world where the course of events is no longer complex, unclear and incomplete, but transparently meaningful.[133] The high degree of abstraction which this involves means that the action of the folktale is essentially timeless: it may contain elder and younger sisters, but not characters that are depicted as growing old, whilst the typical opening 'Once upon a time' may refer to time, but leaves it unspecified.[134] Events in the folktale unfold similarly against a placeless background, and characters may be defined by their function (a king, a princess), but generally not so far as to be actually named.[135] The imperfection of the real world is also left behind by the regularity with which the success of a folktale hero is pre-ordained: he arrives back on the very day when his betrothed is about to be married to someone else, or returns in the nick of time to save someone from the stake.[136] This success of the hero is best summed up in the typical ending of the folktale (often involving marriage and throne for him), so that the concluding formula 'And they lived happily ever after' is as characteristic as its timeless opening.

Unlike the chaotic fortuitousness of real life, events in the folktale follow an ordered pattern and betray an obviously artificial structure. Many folktales are recognisably bipartite, but a threefold division is more common (three tasks are set the hero, three helpers assist him, three opponents confront him).[137] To this structure belongs a frequent climactic sequence (the third task is the most difficult, the third combat is the most dangerous, two failed attempts are surpassed by final success),[138] but also the artifice, when events are repeated, of having various episodes unfold in exactly the same sequence. Even the reverse of this feature, namely variability instead of an artificially fixed sequence, can be claimed as fictional if we take into account the thirty-one 'functions' under which Propp has classified the structure of the typical folktale, for these can be subjected to a range of variations.[139] In the folktale, not located in history, variations on the underlying model are therefore possible: it has the freedom to dispose of individual 'functions' as it pleases, a freedom of scope that must have been attractive to romance authors seeking freedom to find a literary form for their own concerns.

That such features as these could be recognised as unreal, as fictional, in the Middle Ages is suggested by those cases where romances betray dissatisfaction with motivation of a folktale nature because of its manifest implausibility.[140] The authors of romances, for the most part educated clerics, cannot simply be dismissed as credulous and unaware of the rhetorical distinction between what is possible and impossible in real life, and of literary reflections of that distinction. If we proceed from the view that the folktale is a fundamentally fictional genre, it follows that a romance, insofar as it adopts folktale elements and uses them as the basis for generating its narrative events, will also contain fictional features, even to the extent of its overall structure being fictional. Our concern in this section is therefore to ask how far the folktale contributes towards the structural composition of the fictional genre of the romance.

In what follows I use the term 'folktale' rather than 'fairytale' if only because the figure of a fairy is by no means essential to every case of *Märchen*. (This is presumably the reason why Simon finds it necessary to distinguish between *Märchen* and *Feenmärchen*.)[141] At times I also refer not simply to 'folktale', but to 'folktale material' or 'folktale elements',[142] meaning by that narrative elements in the romance comparable with what is found in the folktale, not necessarily derived from it as a source (the genetic question of the relationship between these two genres I leave on one side).

An indirect way of hypothesising the presence of folktale material in the romance is the dissatisfaction felt by some authors: if their discontent with the implausibility of this material had a cause, or at least an occasion, this suggests that for them folktale elements were a recognisable feature. However acceptable such material may have been to authors seeking freedom of movement, limits were set to this by the extent of implausibility in the folktale. How firm this limit could be is shown by an example coming before the rise of the Arthurian romance and concerned not with the folktale as such, but with the magic or enchantment that characterises it, the *Roman de Rou* of Wace. As a conscientious historian Wace felt it incumbent on him to put a magic fountain to the test, about which the Bretons tell many a fable and which is reminiscent of the fountain in Chrétien's *Yvain*.[143] This fountain was reputed to have otherworldly features (6409ff.: *fees, merveilles*, fairies, marvels) and in search of these Wace set out, but was disillusioned and came back cursing himself for his folly (6415ff.).

Under different auspices, as a writer of fiction and not as a historian, Chrétien may shortly afterwards have made use of a similar motif for artistic purposes, but nonetheless the plausibility required by successful fiction meant that not every magical element in a folktale was acceptable. The motif of a fairy assisting a mortal lies behind Enide taking care of Erec's horse and arms, but Chrétien distances himself from this, at the same time showing what he is rejecting when he adds that Enide cast no spell or charm (710).[144] Much more telling is the position in Chrétien's *Cligés* where, in proving his polemical case against Thomas's *Tristan*, the plot machinery creaks audibly when Chrétien has to employ blatantly improbable magical, folktale motifs (a potion inducing sleep to create the impression of Fénice's death, but also a grotesque potion putting her hoodwinked husband to sleep and persuading him that he has made love with his wife, who is thus preserved for her lover).[145] Do such unreal details betray the author's suspicion that his ideal of love, reconciled with marriage and society, had as little plausibility as the folktale motifs on which he falls back here? If so, then Chrétien's folktale motivation is *faute de mieux*, not meant to be taken as seriously true.[146] The same is the case with the magic tower in this work which the lovers imagine will allow them to escape from reality, for Chrétien, having lured us together with them into this realm of make-believe, later explodes the fiction and returns us with a jolt to reality.[147]

The folktale feature most exposed to critical scrutiny because of its implausibility is the conventional happy ending, often in the form of a happy marriage, combined with rulership. In Hartmann's *Iwein* doubts that may have been raised about the strength of the final reconciliation between Iwein and Laudine are hardly laid to rest when the commentary, apparently laudatory, on the couple's future happiness at the end of the work (8139ff.) is meant to be questioned more closely, first by a lengthy conditional sentence with an accumulation of conditions that will have to be met and then by a concluding surmise (8148: *waenlich,* presumably) instead of a final affirmation.[148] Where in other cases Hartmann does supply a happy ending, it is left to someone else to question this folktale conclusion, as we have seen Wolfram do with his intertextual undermining of Hartmann's pacification of Iders and his suggestion that, even after the defeat of Mabonagrin, Brandigan remains unredeemed as a site of bloodthirsty violence.[149]

In view of this it does not surprise us that Wolfram questions this same convention in his own work. His *Parzival* does not conclude in the same wishful way as Chrétien's *Erec* in that it does not finish with the protagonist asking the redeeming question at Munsalvaesche, rejoining wife and sons and assuming Grail-kingship.[150] He does all this, but Wolfram then takes the story further, for more than 1300 lines in which more questions are raised than answered, putting the harmony of the folktale conclusion into second place, a sop for those who convention-ally expected it. For others, however, this is replaced by an open ending, questioning whether the succession to Grail-kingship has in fact found a permanent solution and whether the conclusion is really a conclu-sion. If Wolfram thus goes out of his way to disappoint conventional expectations this means that a folktale happy ending was anticipated by some, and that this critical point in a romance was felt to be governed by this traditional motif, with which Wolfram in this way expressed his dissatisfaction.

Clerical critics of the vernacular romance also occasionally expressed their dissatisfaction, thereby equally confirming in general terms the conformity of folktale and romance. Killy's observation, expressed in the context of German *Kitsch* and referring to light fiction, that many novels are really folktales for grown-up children rests on the view that folktales are above all meant for children.[151] This is paralleled by the con-descending attitude shown by clerics towards the vernacular romance which in the eyes of Latinate *litterati* could make no claim to intel-lectual or aesthetic distinction. Alanus ab Insulis shows his scorn for such works by likening them to pap for babes, while Thomasin von Zerclaere, although prepared to grant a restricted positive function to the romance, still sees it essentially as literature for the young or those otherwise disadvantaged.[152] This criticism goes far beyond the folktale presence in the romance which is our present concern, but opens the way to considering how romance authors could make use of folktale material for what we regard as ambitious literary purposes of high quality. I shall restrict myself to Chrétien's *Yvain* and Wolfram's *Parzival*.

The basis of the *Yvain* plot is a folktale of what is known as the *Lanval* type.[153] It consists of the love of a knight for a fairy (here at least we can talk more correctly of a fairytale), his breaking of the taboo which she imposes and his consequent loss of her, grief and ultimate regaining of her. This pattern was adapted by Chrétien to the circum-stances of his feudal world by presenting the breaking of the taboo in terms of Yvain's neglect of his duty as lord and protector of the realm he has won by marriage. This romance, taken as representative of the classical Arthurian romance in France as well as Germany, has been analysed by Nolting-Hauff (with the help of the range of 'functions' established by Propp for the folktale) as a series of different folktales combined into one work.[154] This implies that a folktale quarry has been exploited for narrative material which has been incorporated (along with much else, especially topical adaptations to feudal life) into a new literary whole. (To vary the title of Meyer's book: we are dealing here with the 'Verfügbarkeit des Märchenmaterials' in the genesis of fiction.)[155] Using the episode of the *Pesme Aventure* as her starting-point, Nolting-Hauff demonstrates that its separate phases can be correlated with the various segments in Propp's analysis of the typical folktale, still recognisable beneath courtly and feudal accretions.[156] She then extends her method to other parts of the romance and comes to the same conclusion: Yvain's second path of adventures is made up of five separate folktales, all centred on the theme of liberation,[157] but this is enclosed within a more complex *Hauptmärchen* (beginning and conclusion of the romance) focusing on marriage to a fairy.[158] In his discussion of this analysis Cormeau casts doubt on its implication that the romance arose genetically from the folktale, the *Großform* from the *einfache Form*.[159] This genetic question can, however, be ignored by us in favour of another point. Whether derivatively or independently, whether causally connected or not, this romance is built up of a number of narrative elements closely paralleled in the folktale. What concerns us is the fact that it is composed of such elements, the manner in which they are structured as parts of a greater whole and adapted to its overriding aim, the presentation of a knightly code of social behaviour.[160]

Further work on folktale elements in the romance has been done by Simon, who likewise makes use of Propp's scheme and considers both of Hartmann's romances, as well as Wolfram's *Parzival* and Gottfried's *Tristan*.[161] In the case of *Iwein* he introduces a novel aspect, seeing this work not simply as an Arthurian romance based on a folktale pattern (as does Nolting-Hauff), but also as incorporating a *Feenmärchen*, which complicates the structure of the romance and relativises the force of the Arthurian programme.[162] Also, more consistently and emphatically than others, Simon argues that the Arthurian romance was not simply built of folktale elements, but grew out of them genetically. In agreement with Nolting-Hauff he therefore calls the romance an 'Uminterpretation des Zaubermärchens': it is dependent on it, it distances itself from the folktale style, but arises out of the folktale.[163] To the extent that the structure

of the folktale is fictional the same is true of a romance genre which
derives from it.

The folktale structure of *Parzival* is more complex and needs looking
at in closer detail. In his analysis of this work Simon applies Propp's
method to the protagonist's career only insofar as it is covered in Book iv,
i.e. from the time when he leaves Gurnemanz to the point when he gains
wife and kingdom at Pelrapeire.[164] In going no further Simon follows an
early lead by Ehrismann, who regarded the second part of the Arthurian
scheme (as introduced by Hartmann) as taken over by Gawan,[165] so that
Simon feels justified in cutting short his analysis of a folktale pattern for
Parzival's career so early. Since he also fails to look at Parzival's course before the Gurnemanz episode (even though he concedes folktale elements
for it),[166] the protagonist is given very short measure indeed. Instead,
Simon abandons his previous structural analysis in favour of a thematic
one, stressing the importance of kinship, specifically the avunculate, in
the Parzival action. This need not contradict any approach from the
point of view of folktale elements, however, since we shall see that this,
too, confirms the role of the matrilinear avunculate. There are also ramifications from folktale elements in Book iii that persist long afterwards.
To some of these elements that Simon has ignored we now turn.

The fact that Parzival grows up as a simpleton (*Dümmling*) and in
isolation, but sets out, proves himself, gains a wife and lives happily in
renown is recognisably the biographical pattern of countless folktales.[167]
One recurrent feature of the *Dümmlingsmärchen* (the simpleton is generally the youngest of three brothers, scorned for his inexperience) is
apparently missing from *Parzival*, whose hero is the only son of his
parents. By contrast, Chrétien's *Perceval* stands closer to the folktale
since the boy's mother has lost not merely husband, but also two sons
in combat.[168] Perceval is therefore the youngest of three sons and ultimately succeeds not because of his brothers' failure (as in the folktale),
but because death has robbed them of any opportunity. Wolfram takes
Chrétien's motivation to its logical conclusion: if the elder brothers are
eliminated from the narrative action, they are now superfluous and need
not even be mentioned.

Parzival's initial ignorance before setting out on his uncertain course
means that he is in need of instruction (Herzeloyde, Gurnemanz),
of factual enlightenment (Sigune), of religious advice (Trevrizent).[169]

However ramified their further implications, these scenes owe their existence to the patterning of Parzival's career in terms of the *Dümmlingsmärchen*. His departure from the wilderness and entry into the world is also a feature of the folktale, where the action generally begins with the hero's decision to leave home to seek his fortune.[170] Into this motif is inserted another, also with folktale parallels, for in the *Märchen von den guten Ratschlägen* a young man setting out into the world is given a number of wise counsels, and encounters on his way situations disposed so as to allow him to try out each piece of advice.[171] The exploitation of this particular type of folktale arises from what precedes Parzival's departure (his *tumpheit*, inexperience), but it also governs what follows, since the events that befall him illustrate each piece of advice given him by his mother.

As is also possible in the folktale,[172] but much more so in the expansive *Großform* of the romance, these folktale elements do not always follow immediately on one another, but can be interwoven in a manner at times close to the interlace technique. Thus, the *Dümmlingsmärchen* in *Parzival* is intertwined with the *Märchen von den guten Ratschlägen*, and both of them with the folktale theme of a young man setting out into the world. Embedded in this same sequence is the episode of the young Parzival's encounter with the knights, analysed by Mohr in relation to the folktale as an *einfache Form*.[173] All this illustrates how complex and ramified this opening segment of Parzival's story could be made by incorporating a variety of folktales. On a larger scale the same is true, for just as the folktale can sometimes deal with two characters who go on a quest,[174] so does Wolfram, following Chrétien, intertwine the quests of Parzival and Gawan, each of whose stories is composed of several folktales.[175]

Wider implications are present in the theme of the advice or instruction given to Parzival. Just as the folktale can be organised on a bipartite or tripartite pattern, so does Parzival undergo three sets of instruction (Herzeloyde, Gurnemanz, Trevrizent), the first two of which are so closely enmeshed that the last recommendation by his mother to be followed by Parzival (to pay attention to advice by an old man) leads directly to Gurnemanz's instruction.[176] But the matter is much more complex than that, for these first two sets of advice are carried out on two levels of application, the second of which comes very much later in the narrative,[177] so that we are dealing here with a change of perspective (what Herzeloyde and Gurnemanz mean by their counsel is surpassed by what the author means by it), with long-term reverberations of these early scenes through the wide span of the whole work, in short with a structural complexity that takes this romance far beyond the range of the folktale. If these three sets of advice together make up a gradation such as can also be found in the folktale,[178] it is not simply the case, as modern readers might be tempted to assume, that, internally, Parzival gradually achieves more of his potential, but rather that, externally, events are so contrived as to depict this achievement. This arrangement of events is a feature of the folktale, but it is also a pointer to the deliberate artistry of the romance, a fictional fashioning of events that can make no claim to historical truth.

Several details of this first part of the Parzival story require further comment. First, a number of the 'functions' in Propp's scheme for the folktale may still be recognisably present, but have been reinterpreted in the new context of the romance. By his function *Verrat* (betrayal) Propp meant a threat or danger to the folktale hero, but this is present in the figure of the knight Karnahkarnanz only in the eyes of Herzeloyde, for whom he incorporates the danger of knighthood from which she wished to protect her son.[179] Another function, *Betrugsmanöver*, deception (the folktale hero's opponent adopts a disguise), undergoes a similar transformation, for the deception presented by the knightly splendour of Karnahkarnanz is rather self-deception on the part of Parzival himself, who takes him to be a god (121, 30–1).[180] The expectations of anyone still awaiting folktale motivation are reversed in another function of Propp's, *Schädigung* (harm) or *Mangelsituation* (deprivation) (often the theft of an object from the hero by an opponent), for the perpetrator turns out to be Parzival's own mother who in keeping him away from courtly society deprived him of the royal status which was his by birth (117, 30ff.).[181]

These examples concern only details, but a wider field is opened up by Wolfram's reinterpretation of another motif. In the folktale the hero may be a wanderer, but his journey, far from being arbitrary, has its direction firmly determined, so much so that God does not need to be invoked for this purpose.[182] The *Dümmlingsmärchen* is again the type where this is most apparent: the fact that each of three brothers encounters the same adventure one after the other shows that events are following a preordained pattern and that each separate journey is subject to an overall control.[183] What did not need to be invoked in the folktale, however, is gradually shown to be at issue in *Parzival*. Of Parzival's initial journeying we are allowed to think that he is given miraculous guidance through to Munsalvæsche in Book v: his speed and directness are not the result of chance, but appear to be the gift conferred on a typical folktale hero.[184] Only later is it made clear that this guidance was instead extended by God: where we thought that we were in the world of the folktale, events are in fact transposed to the realm of providential guidance.[185] If the narrator can rely on his listeners, being deceived by their expectations, assuming folktale dimensions in a narrative that transcends them, this suggests that Wolfram, following Chrétien, was building his romance out of folktale material.

The motif of the son searching for his father, unaware whether he is still alive or not, is a recurrent one in the folktale[186] but, because Parzival learns of Gahmuret's death from Herzeloyde, can find no literal echo in Wolfram's work. It is rescued, however, by being transposed to the symbolic plane, in that Parzival now sets out to seek a place in the knightly world of his father in the rest of Book III and above all in Book IV at Pelrapeire.[187] A parallel folktale motif (the hero sets out this time in search of his mother)[188] occurs at the end of Book IV when Parzival announces his intention of leaving Condwiramurs for a while to seek for adventure and his mother. We know, as he does not, that because of her death he cannot fulfil the second wish, but his journey from Pelrapeire takes him, if not back to Soltane, then in a profounder sense into the realm of his mother at Munsalvaesche, the possibility she has bequeathed him.[189] In both these quest motifs the *einfache Form* has been converted into a longer narrative sequence, but with a change into a symbolic dimension.

How far-reaching Wolfram's conversion of details into a longer sequence can be is shown by his treatment of the instruction given to Parzival first by his mother, then by Gurnemanz. As in the *Märchen von den guten Ratschlägen* each piece of advice generates a subsequent narrative event in which it may be tested in action,[190] but again Wolfram takes their ramifications unexpectedly further. Thus, the four pieces of advice given by Herzeloyde call into being the episodes her son encounters after leaving Soltane, just as the recommendations of Gurnemanz give rise to the events in Book IV to illustrate them.[191] However, Herzeloyde's injunction to accept advice from an old man of experience has a double application. What she had in mind was her son's need to seek further advice before very long from someone like Gurnemanz, but what the narrator also has in mind is an anticipation of Parzival's need of profounder advice from Trevrizent in Book IX.[192] Of this longer span only the consciously planning author, not Herzeloyde in Book III, can have had advance knowledge. Similarly, the first piece of advice given by Gurnemanz (170, 21ff.) points to the future in two ways. It anticipates in detail the kind of situation at Pelrapeire which the old man could assume his pupil, destined to chivalry and kingship, would soon come across, but also, in equal detail, the position when Parzival comes to Munsalvaesche.[193] Of this Gurnemanz can have had as little foreknowledge as had Herzeloyde that her son at some time in the future would be in existential need of Trevrizent's help. These two occasions in the remoter future (meeting with the hermit, Munsalvaesche) were intended by neither the mother nor Gurnemanz, but instead by the narrator speaking through them, manipulating them fictionally for his own ends.[194] By prolonging the reverberations of a folktale motif Wolfram has devised a structure that extends from Book III in the one case to Book V and in the other as far as Book IX. Together with other romance authors who made use of folktale material he had the liberty to dispose of it as best suited him because he was dealing with a Utopian genre not tied to reality, whether historical or religious, and therefore easily susceptible to rearrangement.[195]

DOUBLE CYCLE

The theory of a double cycle structure, first put forward in detail by Kuhn for Hartmann's *Erec*, but then applied by German Romanists to Chrétien, too, rests on the meaningful distribution of Arthurian scenes throughout the work.[196] The hero sets out from the court of Arthur, accomplishes a mission and returns successfully to the court, but awareness of an inner fault drives him forth again on a longer and more difficult quest to rectify it. At a point in this second quest he rejoins the court for an interim stay but, conscious that his reintegration is still incomplete, departs again and returns to it finally only once this has been fully achieved. The punctuation of the hero's knightly questing by

Arthurian scenes conveys the meaning of the work, for the Round Table and the hero are dependent on one another: the ideal status of the court, initially called into question, is restored by the hero's success, but for its part the court acts as the criterion by which this success is measured.[197] Within this framework the adventures that befall the hero are grouped in a complex pattern of parallels, contrasts and gradations which suggests a conscious artistic control of signification, possible only in fictional writing, so that the double cycle structure amounts to the most contrived (but not the only) patterning to be found in the early Arthurian romance.

This theory has come in for increasing criticism, with talk of Kuhn's 'fateful invention' and of its 'hermeneutic automatism'.[198] Underlying this criticism are a number of different points. First, the view that the complexity of the romance is such that its structure cannot be subsumed under one pattern alone.[199] Secondly, the fact that what was first suggested for the specific case of Hartmann's *Erec* has been unwarrantably generalised and held to be true not only of Chrétien's version, but of other romances at large.[200] Although this particular structure may have been accepted for Chrétien's *Erec*, and with qualifications for his *Yvain*, difficulties arise in applying it to his *Cligés*, *Lancelot* and *Perceval*.[201] Thirdly, insofar as this structure postulates the hero starting and finishing at Arthur's court, this may be true of Chrétien's *Erec*, but not of Hartmann's version, or of *Yvain* or *Iwein*, let alone of Wolfram's *Parzival*, in all of which the action culminates not at Arthur's court, but in rulership elsewhere.[202] Fourthly, the exemplary functioning of the double cycle depended on Arthur's court remaining intact as a literary ideal, about which doubts have been expressed with regard to Chrétien's *Lancelot* and *Perceval*.[203]

In view of these doubts is it at all justified to devote a section of this chapter to this type of structure? One reason for doing so is that, for all these doubts, Chrétien's *Erec* as the first Arthurian romance is commonly, if not universally, held to exemplify the double cycle pattern, so that there is every point in giving space to this type of structure employed in the first example of vernacular fiction. Another reason is that, however untypical of the Arthurian romance at large this structure may be, the meaningful patterning it reveals is so well worked out that its very complexity is an unsurpassed example of Chrétien's structural control of his fictional material.

Since the double cycle was first proposed in detail for the German *Erec*, and then applied to Chrétien's version, we may best start with Hartmann's text, where the parallels and cross-references are so detailed that they must proceed from the organising hand of an author freely disposing of narrative material so as to produce order and convey meaning. This first German Arthurian romance constitutes an overall double cycle in which the first part of the action takes Erec away from Arthur's court and then, after he has gained knightly renown and love, back to it again, while the second part leads to a new departure on a quest for a series of adventures, finishing with a successful return to the Round Table. This overall bipartite pattern is repeated in greater detail within the second part, which is similarly patterned into two sub-cycles of matching adventures.[204] In the first sub-cycle the three encounters (with robbers, with a would-be seducer count, and with Guivreiz) are echoed in the three episodes of the second (encounters with giants, the would-be seducer count Oringles, and Guivreiz).[205] In between these two sub-cycles is inserted Erec's interim stay at Arthur's court, which acts as an axis, showing us that from this point the second sub-cycle reduplicates the first. Similarly, Erec's final return to Arthur's court tells us that this reduplicating quest has been successfully completed.

However, the complex artifice of this structure goes much further. In the first place, the episodes in the second sub-cycle are meant to surpass or enhance the corresponding ones in the first (whereas the robbers were quickly disposed of, the giants bring Erec to the brink of death; whereas the first count was merely wounded, the second was killed; whereas Erec defeated Guivreiz in their first encounter, in their second he is saved only by Enite's intervention).[206] Secondly, in each of these two sub-cycles the three episodes are themselves arranged in an order of progression.[207] Thus, in the first sub-cycle, whereas Enite merely has to warn Erec of the presence of the robbers, in the second episode more urgent steps (her deception of the count and the couple's flight) are required, whilst the third adventure confronts Erec for the first time with a truly chivalric opponent in Guivreiz and is accordingly a far greater test than anything before (4269–70).[208] Erec's victory thus qualifies him for the following interim stay with Arthur and his companions. The second sub-cycle is similarly patterned as a progression. The danger represented by count Oringles in the second episode is inevitably greater, since the preceding encounter with the giants had left Erec apparently dead, whilst the overriding importance of his following defeat at the hands of Guivreiz is that it teaches him that knightly exploits should involve service of others, rather than headlong unprovoked aggression.[209]

So far, this pattern leaves out of account the *Joie de la Curt* episode, inserted between Erec's second encounter with Guivreiz and his final return to Arthur's court. It stands outside the two sub-cycles with their matching episodes and is the only encounter without a corresponding one, since it is meant to sum up the whole action of the romance and convey its meaning.[210] This is why Erec is so insistent on facing this adventure and is convinced that it is the fulfilment of his whole quest (8521ff.), for what he encounters in the magic garden, in however distorted a form, is recognisably the antisocial seclusion of lovers to which Erec and Enite had fallen victim at Karnant, so that in defeating Mabonagrin Erec overcomes and lays aside his past self.[211] Only at this point is the balance between love and knighthood restored for Erec, who now feels able to return to Arthur's court, the sign that his quest is over.

The first part of the action (up to Erec's triumphant return with Enite to Arthur's court for marriage and rulership at Karnant) is governed by a symmetrical pattern outwardly demonstrated by the hero's initial departure from Arthur's court and eventual return there.[212] The meaning of this part (that knightly renown and love of a woman belong reciprocally together) is a fundamental conception of Chrétien's romance,[213] but if this work were a folktale that might be the happy end at which it concluded. In going beyond this point, however, and in opening out into the wider range of adventures in the second part, in which Erec is gradually brought to practise chivalry in the service of others, this romance passes beyond a purely personal achievement (knightly success and marital happiness) to an integration of these gains into an awareness of social commitment.[214] In that sense of wider obligations the second part of the work (after the crisis at Karnant) surpasses the first, so that the structural pattern of the whole work repeats what was true, within the second part, of the relationship between the first and second sub-cycles.[215]

In Hartmann's *Iwein* the overall structure of his *Erec* is still detectable. In this second romance the path followed by the hero is again, at first, that of a beginner who finds personal fulfilment in knightly renown and marriage to Laudine, but who then forfeits these by his own fault and has to gain them anew by a series of adventures geared to the service of others.[216] This action therefore falls into two parts. In the first of these Iwein, like Erec, gains a wife and rulership (2747ff.) and his success is confirmed by the presence of Arthur's court, while the second part, again as in *Erec*, begins with a crisis, brought on by Gawein's advice to avoid Erec's fault of *verligen* (inactivity) at Karnant. The significance of this intertextual pointer (Erec's crisis, the hinge between the two parts in the earlier work, is quoted at the comparable point of Iwein's crisis) is that it shows that this romance, too, is governed by a double cycle structure.[217] Accordingly, an interim stay also comes in the middle of the hero's adventures in the second part, but with the significant innovation that it takes place not at Arthur's court, but at Laudine's.

The general outlines of the double cycle pattern are therefore present, but with an innovation pointing to its constructed, fictional nature. Avoiding a simple repetition of the *Erec* model, Chrétien and Hartmann introduce variations, adjusting it inventively not to narrating a different historically attested event, but to expressing the narrative truth of a different literary theme. At this stage we are dealing with a fictional variation on an already fictional structure, with fiction at two removes from any pretence of reality. The innovation of locating Iwein's interim stay at a court other than Arthur's, moreover the emphasis on a second centre other than the Round Table, a centre which is also Iwein's ultimate goal, amounts to a significant relativisation of Arthur's court, no longer the unchallenged structural centre of the work, and thereby to a weakening of the double cycle structure.[218] In addition, the second part (from the crisis on) is itself not constructed, as it was in *Erec*, with two sub-cycles, but differently (by interlace) so as to stress the pressure of time in keeping a promise, the cause of Iwein's offence against Laudine.[219] The double cycle which informed the second part of *Erec* may thus have been abandoned in *Iwein*, but the structure of the later work is just as skilfully contrived to convey meaning. In his adventures at this stage Iwein proves himself in three ways so as to undo his offence: by helping and protecting women in need (as he should have done by returning to Laudine), by demonstrating *triuwe* (as he should have done in keeping his word to her) and by keeping deadlines against all difficulties (as he failed to do in her case).[220] The contrivances of fictional structure are no mere decoration, but convey meaning: the nature of Iwein's offence and rehabilitation.

We now leave Hartmann's reflection of two of Chrétien's romances, turning to three other works by the French author (*Cligés*, *Lancelot* and *Perceval*) whose distance from the double cycle pattern is unmistakable, even to the point of its abandonment, so that not even Chrétien himself always employs this structure as an organising principle.

Even though a place is found for Arthur in *Cligés*, this is by no means at the centre, since the absence of a quest in this work involves a demotion of Arthur's court as confirmation of its success.[221] This romance appears to resemble the double cycle model only insofar as it falls into two parts, but these are loosely connected with one another and are in any case devoted to different protagonists of different generations. Although the opening of the second part may represent a clear turning-point, it does not begin with a personal crisis, as in *Erec* and *Yvain*. Bipartition of this looser kind probably derived from the *Tristan* story, as known to Chrétien in the version of Thomas.[222] In other respects, too, apparent echoes of the double cycle cannot be taken at face value. The first part of the work appears to conform to the pattern in beginning at Arthur's court (but significantly displaced to the second episode) and also in ending there, and although the second part may end there (but only in the penultimate position) it has an interim stay there on a much reduced scale. As in *Tristan*, Arthur is little more than a remote point of reference for the love-story of Cligés and Fénice.[223]

Cligés resembles *Tristan* in much more than its bipartition into two generations. The Arthurian romance, as devised by Chrétien in *Erec* and *Yvain*, promoted an ideal unity of chivalry and love, but also the reconciliation of these values with social obligations, including marriage.[224] In this the *Tristan* theme, specifically in the version of Thomas, confronted Chrétien with a problematic challenge.[225] He dealt with this in *Cligés* by inserting a number of isolated critical references to the *Tristan* story, but more sustainedly by building into his work a comparable constellation of actors and a number of similar episodes, even in the same sequence.[226] Where this sequence is retained over lengthy stretches of the narrative the absence of any double cycle pattern in

Thomas's work means that Chrétien could not find a place for this
pattern in his adaptation of Thomas, changed so as to express a critical
view of the *Tristan* story. Like *Yvain* (modelled freely on the structure
of *Erec*), *Cligés* (modelled parodistically on *Tristan*) is an expressly literary work, a fictional variation on a fictional construct, fiction at two
removes from any claim to historical truth, despite the evocation of
'historical' features at the opening of the work.[227] These literary details
were taken over from *Tristan* and re-employed by Chrétien to support
an opposing *sens*, which in this case is far from being a meaning read
out of pre-existent facts from a reliable source or a *sensus* read out of
historia.

The compositional liberties that Chrétien allows himself in *Lancelot*,
described as the most episodic of his romances, further demonstrate
that the double cycle, suggested for this work only with difficulty, was
no constant feature even in the works of the founding father of the
Arthurian romance.[228] This work's resemblance to the double cycle pattern goes no further than its possible division into two parts, and it
contains only two structurally significant Arthurian episodes, hardly
enough to serve as structural supports.[229] The first part of the narrative may start at Arthur's court, but it does not finish there, whilst the
second part finishes, but does not begin there. These two parts hinge
together, not with an Arthurian scene as in the double cycle, but with
the stay at Bath; yet even this substitute for an Arthurian scene does not
serve a comparable function, for the Bath episode, far from resolving
one adventure and creating a new one, merely delays the climax until
the end of the work.[230]

Cligés and *Lancelot* show few of the detailed correspondences found
in *Erec* and *Yvain* and they make no fundamental use of the double
cycle as a structural artifice. Just as any employment of this particular
device was invalidated in *Cligés* by the parodistic imitation of *Tristan*, so
is it cut across in *Lancelot* by another structural pattern, symmetry, not
merely for the key events at Bath, but also for the work as a whole.[231]

If the double cycle pattern remained meaningfully valid only as long
as the ideal of the Round Table around which it was organised remained
intact, we may doubt its applicability to Chrétien's *Perceval*.[232] Into this
work, alongside the Arthurian world, Chrétien built a second narrative

sphere, the realm of the Grail.[233] Although he had done something apparently similar in *Yvain* (Laudine's independent realm, from which Lunete comes to accuse Yvain, just as the Hideous Damsel accuses Perceval), Chrétien goes much further in the later work, constructing a mysterious otherworldly realm of the Grail which is not on the same footing as the Round Table. Arthur's court is overshadowed by this realm as it had not been by Laudine's.[234]

This demotion of the Arthurian realm is confirmed by numerous details. *Perceval* does not open at Arthur's court, but in a wilderness far from it, already outwardly suggestive of the inaccessible realm of the Grail. After winning the hand of Blanchefleur Perceval, unlike Yvain after marriage to Laudine, does not rejoin Arthur's court, but seeks to visit his mother and instead comes to the Grail-castle, so that a structural turning-point previously occupied by the Round Table has been taken over by this other realm.[235] When Perceval does rejoin Arthur's court on the second occasion it is the Round Table that seeks him out, not Perceval who returns to them.[236] Although this can be compared with Erec being tricked into re-joining Arthur briefly against his will, much greater weight falls to this order of priorities in *Perceval* because of the other critical qualifications present in this work. Chrétien's work remained uncompleted, but there is enough to suggest that the Round Table has been ousted from its earlier central organising function and that the double cycle model, in which Arthurian scenes occupy key positions, is present only fragmentarily, not as a meaningful structure of the whole work.

To the extent that Wolfram follows Chrétien, the latter's dislodgement of the Round Table, involving a disruption of the double cycle, also applies to the former. But Wolfram takes this disruption further, above all in questioning Arthur's status and the recurrent function of the Round Table as a structural pillar in the narrative.[237] Thus, the Round Table is displaced from its conventional initial position not merely by a preceding episode (Soltane), but more emphatically by the prehistory of Parzival's parents, and even when the young Parzival is on his way to Arthur's court two further encounters intervene.[238] By contrast with Chrétien's hero, Parzival sends his defeated opponents initially to Cunneware rather than to Arthur himself, and later not to Arthur's court at all, but to his wife Condwiramurs.[239] At one point (286, 5 ff.) Arthur himself makes it clear that Munsalvæsche marks the limit set to his authority. This is confirmed conversely when the criticism of Parzival made by the Grail messenger Cundrie also pointedly includes the Round Table for having accepted him in their midst, a detail that goes beyond the apparent parallel in *Yvain* and *Iwein*, where the court remained unaffected.[240] A feature of *Yvain* and *Iwein* is also retained in Parzival's combat with Gawan, but differs from the earlier pattern, first in making it clear that Gawan runs the danger of being defeated and is therefore no longer the absolute standard by which the hero is to be judged, but also in dislodging this encounter from its climactic position by having it followed by Parzival's combat with Feirefiz.[241] Details like these cumulatively weaken the position of Arthur's court so that at a number of critical points it no longer sustains a double cycle structure. Wolfram's freedom of manoeuvre in all this is such that, although *Parzival* may share parallels with *Erec* and above all with *Iwein*,[242] it is too complex to be subsumed under the double cycle that governed their structure. Again, as regards the theme of fictionality, we reach the same conclusion as before. Insofar as *Iwein* was already a fictional variation on the fictional structure of *Erec*, in other words at two removes from 'reality', those newly devised parts of *Parzival* where Chrétien's fragment provided no model and Wolfram had recourse to *Iwein* are at three removes distant. In all this a tradition is in process of being formed in which a literary work is freely based on another literary work, not on any fixed, unalterable source, let alone on events that actually took place.[243]

It is noticeable that, whereas most German Romanists have adopted Kuhn's analysis of Hartmann's *Erec* and applied it to Chrétien's version, French (and other) Romanists have been more reluctant to do so, as is perhaps best brought out by the different structure of the French work proposed by Lacy.[244] Clearly, the double cycle is not the be-all and end-all of Chrétien scholarship, and not even Chrétien himself remained true to this pattern in all his works, whilst in the French romance tradition after him this is even more manifest.[245] It is to Lacy that we owe a careful registration of other structural devices employed by Chrétien, including interlace, analogy, parallelism, symmetry, but also progression and binary division (not as part of a double cycle).[246] We could not do better than adopt his view of the multiplicity of structures to be

found in Chrétien's works, of his multistructural composition,[247] thus
breaking free from the dominance of the double cycle theory, whilst still
acknowledging that work on this has opened our eyes to the subtleties
and complexities of romance structure, which is our justification for
including it in this chapter.

That something similar is true of German literature, that the double
cycle is not the sole key to the structure of the German romance, has also
been argued in two contributions to the discussion of intertextuality in
the romance. Haug contrasts the Arthurian romance, and its double
cycle structure, on the one hand with *Tristan*, and its episodic additive
structure, on the other (at least after the discovery of the lovers' affair).[248]
For him *Tristan* is therefore structurally the odd man out, so that there
are in his eyes two romance types, to only one of which the double cycle is
at all relevant (but not even then, as we have seen, in every case). For
Mertens the position may be different, but leads to a similar conclusion.
He starts with a contrast between two romance types, one represented by
Hartmann's *Iwein*, with its double cycle structure, and the other by the
Lanzelet of Ulrich von Zatzikhoven, with its linear sequence of episodes
and lack of any midway crisis.[249] It is this latter model which Mertens
argues was followed by later German romances such as *Wigalois*, *Diu
Crône* and *Garel vom blühenden Tal*, so that if, seen from this point of
view, *Lanzelet* is now the odd man out, it is by contrast with the *Iwein* or
double cycle type of romance. To focus on *Tristan* and *Lanzelet* in this
way brings out the fact that the romance, even the Arthurian romance,
cannot be explained structurally only by reference to the theory which,
since it was advanced by Kuhn, has enjoyed an inflated popularity.

Lacy repeatedly draws attention to correspondences between the formal structure of Chrétien's romances and their meaning, a fact which
is true of the romance at large, whether French or German. An author
devises fictional events and arranges their sequence so as to convey meaning, whereas the task of a clerical exegete was to lay bare the meaning
inherent in events that unrolled according to adivinely preordained plan.
This parallel between the author's relationship to his work of fictional
art and God's relationship to His work of creation in the historical dimension is therefore true not merely of typology, secular and clerical,[250]
but of any structure freely devised so as to be meaningful. Given this

potential competition, we need not wonder that medieval clerics voiced criticism of court literature and of the romance in particular.

The careful artistry and complex structure underlying these romances are much greater than any single one of the patterns we have looked at (*ordo artificialis*, typology, folktale structure, double cycle), since several of them can often be employed in the composition of one work.[251] The more these patterns are employed together, interwoven with each other and contributing to a meaningful complexity (but still clearer than the random, often inexplicable fortuitousness of reality), the more the work stands out as the careful product of a conscious and freely disposing control by the author, in short as a work of fiction.

CHAPTER 6

Fiction and history

In a book with a title similar to that of this chapter Knapp presents a wide-ranging and theoretical discussion of the medieval classification of literary genres and the place found within it (or not) for the romance as a representative of literary fiction.[1] This present chapter is concerned with the relationship between fiction and history in another sense, posing a genetic, rather than generic question, asking how the romance arose out of contact with historical writing.[2] Examples from medieval, but also classical literature will be discussed because both faced the problem of accommodating the new genre of the romance and the novel phenomenon of literary fiction.

TYPES OF NARRATIVE

Under this heading we revert to a classification that proved its usefulness in our definition of twelfth-century fictionality.[3] In doing so we are not taking up Knapp's generic question (for these types of narrative are not strictly identical with what could be called genres), but rather the genetic question how far these types were the occasion for the emergence of fictional writing from historiography. At issue are the three categories of narration (originally at home in classical oratory but in the twelfth century applied to poetics)[4] in their relation to reality as discussed systematically by Mehtonen from classical antiquity through to the thirteenth century.[5] *Historia* treats of what actually happened in the past, *argumentum* treats a hypothetically possible case as if it had really occurred, whilst *fabula* is a fiction dealing with what had not and could not have happened. This classification is to be found as early as the *Rhetorica ad Herennium*, but also in Cicero and Quintilian.[6] Through

Isidore of Seville it finds its way into medieval tradition, where it occurs, for example, in the *Scholia Terentiana* and in Bernard of Utrecht and John of Garland.[7] The constant factor in this classification is the distinction between *historia* on the one hand (what actually happened) and *argumentum* and *fabula* on the other (what had not happened and for which no claim to historical or factual truth could be made). Seen in this light, the threefold classification could imply a binary opposition between actual events (*res factae*) and imagined ones (*res fictae*).[8] It is this contrast that concerns us in this chapter.

By dealing with what had once taken place *historia* can obviously make a claim to truth (*veritas*),[9] although what counts as historical truth must be what medieval authors, as distinct from modern historians, regarded as such.[10] In medieval historiography past events can be distorted and adapted to a later historical situation,[11] but thereby still retain a historical function and be regarded as true.[12] Moreover, the truth of history in the Middle Ages rested on metaphysical assumptions no longer shared by modern historians: on the view that God controlled the course of events in this world (their truth stemmed from divine authority) and that the bible was the prime example of unassailably true historical writing.[13] The equation of *res gesta* with *res vera* is therefore frequently attested, even in classical, non-Christian sources (Cicero, Lucan or Servius), given the definition of *historia* as what had indeed happened.[14] Isidore's concise definition ('Historiae sunt res verae quae factae sunt', Histories are true events that took place)[15] sums this up and constitutes a bridge to the Middle Ages, where terms like *veritas historiae*, *veritas rerum* or *veritas gestarum* (the truth of history, of events, of happenings) are frequent.[16] This view of the truth of *historia* finds its way into the vernaculars, where Anglo-Norman historians agree with their Latin-writing colleagues in distinguishing between truthful, authentic historiography and the fictional status of the romance.[17]

Argumentum and *fabula*, by contrast, belong together in mapping out the field of poetic fiction.[18] Already in the *Rhetorica ad Herennium* the first of these[19] is defined as dealing with what could have happened, but did not, and therefore as a fiction ('Argumentum est ficta res quae tamen fieri potuit'), a view still repeated, for example, by Bernard of Utrecht and John of Garland.[20] Whether augmented by such concepts as verisimilitude and self-consistent plausibility[21] or not, *argumentum*

retains its relevance to the medieval concept of fiction. A similar continuity is to be observed with the term *fabula*.[22] The view of Macrobius
that the name of *fabula* points to the recital of untruth ('falsi professio')
is continued by Isidore ('Fabulas poetae a fando nominaverunt, quia
non sunt res factae, sed tantum loquendo fictae', The poets termed
fables from speaking, because they are not events that happened, but
made up solely in the act of speaking).[23] This definition served the
Church well in its polemical encounters with pagan myths or heretical
opinions, stamped as *fabulae* and therefore false by contrast with
Christian truth.[24] For Konrad von Hirsau Aesop's fables are 'false
fictions', and with Engelbert von Admont the *fabula* is still a 'sermo
de rebus non factis, sed fictis inventus et compositus' (a discourse made
up and composed of fictive events that did not take place).[25] Similar
contrasts between fact and fiction can be made in the vernaculars, as
when, for example, Jordan Fantosme employs *fable* and *geste* to imply
'Never was there heard tell, in romance or in history', i.e. in no narrative,
false or true.[26]

The separation of *argumentum* and *fabula*, together constituting
poetry, from *historia* amounted to branding poetry as lies (*mendacium*).
To the extent that poetry had a rhetorical basis it was subject to the age-
old criticism of rhetoric for its mendacity (the orator's trick of decking
out a lie with fragments of truth, his dealing in feelings rather than facts,
and his suppression of facts).[27] There were of course classical precedents
for branding poetry as lying (Solon, Plato, Ovid, Augustine on Terence
and Plautus),[28] but these were given a new lease of life by the claim
of Christianity to incorporate the truth against the lies of pagan poets.
Sedulius sets up his *Paschale carmen* against the lies (*figmenta*) of pagan
poets, Arator presents a new type of poetry, a *carmen verum*, a true
poem (hitherto an oxymoron), and Notker Balbulus rejects the *fabulae*
of pagan poets in favour of works by Christian poets (e.g. Prudentius,
Juvencus, Sedulius).[29] With this reinforcement Christian rigorists could
criticise poetic fiction as such with as much fervour as had Plato. Bernard
of Clairvaux therefore warns Christian knights against 'mimi, et magi, et
fabulatores scurrilesque cantilenae' (mimes, magicians, storytellers and
scurrilous songs), while in the *Hortus deliciarum* poets are excluded from
the depiction of the seven liberal arts and equipped with the description:
'Isti immundis spiritibus inspirati scribunt artem magicam et poetriam

id est fabulosa commenta' (These are inspired by unclean spirits and write the art of magic and poetry, that is fabulous fabrications).[30]

Behind the antithesis of *historia* and *fictio* lies the wider opposition between truth and falsehood in literature, the different attitudes to what constitutes truth (and the need to affirm it). In early clerical literature in Germany claims to be speaking the truth are comparatively rare, because redundant: since the themes treated are biblical or unquestioned truths of Christian doctrine the need to affirm the truth of such literature is superfluous.[31] For quite a different reason the same was true of German heroic tradition (at least until the beginning of the thirteenth century), since for those who transmitted these largely oral works, as well as for their recipients, heroic literature was the main vehicle for knowledge of the past and as such reliable and beyond questioning.[32] If doubts about the truth of this oral tradition were expressed at all, they came not from within, but from without, from clerical *litterati* critical of oral transmission where it manifestly conflicted with written sources available only to them.[33] Even though a third literary genre, the legend, was held to convey the truth (and could even be designated as *historia*),[34] difficulties were caused by the fact that legends were not protected by biblical authority, so that the miracles they reported did not always escape sceptical comments – which called forth, in return, authorial claims that they narrated the truth.[35] Only here does the question of truth or falsehood arise, but even then marginally or sporadically.[36] For the rest, truth is no literary problem and therefore does not need to be affirmed. The position becomes acute, however, when we come to works with a secular theme (whose untruth is castigated in the prologue of the *Kaiserchronik*),[37] especially in the case of those of classical provenance (whose truth-claim may lack a Christian legitimation and even be jeopardised by their pagan origin),[38] and even more so with hitherto unknown themes from the Celtic realm, the *matière de Bretagne*.[39] At this point we may consider briefly a few examples of the tension between truth and falsehood in vernacular literature around 1200.

The binary opposition of *res factae* and *res fictae*, together with the fact that any criticism of the latter would concentrate more on the extreme case of *fabula*, means that untruth in literature was commonly associated with this term and its vernacular equivalents. In Old French the term *fable* (rejected by being attributed to 'novel jougleor', newfangled minstrels) can be contrasted with 'la plus veraie estoire' (the most true story) which the author is about to recite himself,[40] or the word *estoire*, for which *verité* (truth) is claimed, can be further defined by 'sans nulle fable' (without any fable).[41] Elsewhere, without the opposite pole *estoire* being mentioned, *fable* can simply be contrasted with *verité* or equated with *mençonge* (lie).[42]

It is with an often quoted passage from Jean Bodel, however, that the degree of truth or untruth is most strikingly apportioned to different literary genres, even if he makes no use of the term *fable*. In the *Chanson des Saisnes* he distinguishes between the *chanson de geste* (the genre on which he is himself engaged), the antique romance and the Arthurian romance.[43] Of the first of these genres, the *matière de France*, he says without more ado that it is true (11: *voir*), a claim readily acceptable in his day when the heroic epic was regarded by laymen as a record of the past, a source of identity and a token of legitimacy, in most cases the only record of secular history directly available to them.[44] However untrustworthy they may be to us, claims for veracity can often be made in the heroic epic by appeals to the authority of written sources,[45] as does Jean Bodel in his own work by sheltering behind 'li livre d'estoire' (the book of history) as guarantee (3). He goes even further, however, by arguing that of the three genres the *chanson de geste* (his own genre!) is the most truthful of all (12). In all this Bodel is clearly speaking *pro domo*, not merely for himself, but also on behalf of the French royal house and its encouragement of epics dealing with the Carolingian past as an ideological counter-argument to the Anglo-Norman propagation of Arthurian literature with its own dynastic implications.[46] That the political hegemony of France was not far from Bodel's thoughts in composing his epic is made quite clear soon after (13: 'La coronne de France doit estre si avant,/Que tout autre roi doivent estre a li apendant', The crown of France must be so much in advance that all other kings must be appendent to it).

Of the *matière de Rome* Bodel says that it is *sage* and 'de sens aprendant' (10), based on knowledge and also passing it on, teaching it. This strikes a note characteristic of this genre, transmitting knowledge of the classical past for the benefit of the present by translating into the vernacular in what amounts to an authorial *translatio studii*.[47] The author of the *Roman de Thèbes* begins by saying that whoever is *sage* should not conceal it, but demonstrate his *sen* (good sense) by passing it on, quoting

classical examples (Homer, Plato, Virgil, Cicero) in justification (5 ff.).
The same point is made at greater length by Benoît de Sainte-Maure in
his prologue to the *Roman de Troie* (3–4: *sen celer, demostrer*, without
concealing, demonstrate), whose *enseigner*, teach (10, 21) more explicitly
complements Bodel's *aprendre*. His use of this verb and of *sage* accurately
describes the transmission of these works to laymen from Latin sources
available only to *litterati*. This feature of the antique romance, however,
need not conflict with its historical veracity, with the way in which the
Roman de Thèbes, *Roman de Troie* and *Roman d'Enéas* were conscripted
for Anglo-Norman ideological service as a venerable prehistory of the
Normans' new realm.[48] Even though Bodel may not have accepted this
Angevin appropriation of classical themes for their own (anti-French)
ends, he could not deny the historicity of these romances. The fact that
he regards the *matière de France* as 'la plus voir disant', the most truthful
(12) still implies a degree of truth for the *matière de Rome*, in agreement
with what Benoît de Sainte-Maure had said of his work, that it was an
estoire (authenticated by Latin) and therefore *verté*, truth (34f., 44).

The position is quite different with Bodel's summing up of the
matière de Bretagne, which he describes as 'vain et plaisant' (9).[49] The
second adjective may have the positive force of 'giving pleasure or
entertainment',[50] but this in itself is not enough when no further positive value is to be found, if we recall Augustine's criticism of the fables of
Plautus and Terence for giving nothing but entertainment or the similar argument levelled by Denis Piramus against secular court literature
of his day.[51] Whatever value may attach to the other adjective used by
Bodel, *vain* certainly cannot have positive force. It may mean, as Guiette
suggests, 'empty, vain' and therefore even 'frivolous' because too
worldly,[52] but this need not exclude the further implication of 'untrue'.
Latin *vanus* could embrace such meanings as 'illusory, imaginary, pretended' and also 'containing no truth, false'.[53] Virgil can alternate between *vana somnia*, vain sleep, and *falsa insomnia*, false dreams (the
former translated in the *Roman d'Enéas* as *mençonges*) and Isidore denies
the truth of *historia* to *vanae fabulae*.[54] Similar meanings are attested in
Old French for *vain* ('sans fondement solide et raisonnable, illusoire'),
where *vain rêve* is defined as 'trompeur'.[55] The prologue to a vernacular
rendering of the *Vitae patrum* warns women against court romances
(*Cligés* and *Perceval* are named), equating these *romanz de vanité* with

mençonge, just as in the *Bestiaire* of Gervaise *mançonge et fables*, however entertaining they may be, are opposed to *verité* and equated with *vanité*.[56] There is no reason, therefore, why Bodel should not be criticising a genre which in his eyes propagates the vanities of this world and is also untrue. These are for him two aspects of the same deception; the romance genre suffers for him, as it did for Denis Piramus, from being untrue and merely entertaining.[57]

The equation of the fictional romance with untruth can also be attested from Germany.[58] From the ranks of the clergy the most explicit evidence is provided by Thomasin von Zerclaere, who concedes a qualified ethical usefulness of secular literature for the young in setting up examples of behaviour to be followed or shunned.[59] The literature he has in mind is the *matière de Bretagne* (he lists names from Arthurian literature and also refers to Tristan), but also the *matière de Rome* (Andromache, Alexander) and the *matière de France* (Charles the Great). Unlike Bodel Thomasin makes no distinction between these genres, they are all seen by him as *âventure* (1089),[60] as 'diu spel diu niht wâr sint', tales that are not true (1085). Even though these works may have a restricted ethical function, their essence for Thomasin is untruth (1120: 'diu lüge ist ir gezierde krône' lying is the crown of their adornment), so that what moral truth they convey (1125) is cloaked with the untruth of fiction (1126: 'daz wâr man mit lüge kleit'). Thomasin's attitude may be more sweeping and radical than Bodel's (he has no need to defend one of the three genres as historically true), but they both agree in characterising the romance as untrue, because fictional.

Another dismissal of untrue tales, even though they may not be specifically termed romances, but rather *fabulae*, occurs in Gottfried's *Tristan* at the point in his narrative where he refuses to be sidetracked into an account of the (for him) irrelevant adventures of Tristan in Germany. These have no direct bearing on the author's presentation of the love-story and are therefore rejected out of hand (18467: 'die fabelen, die hier under sint, / die sol ich werfen an den wint', The fables amongst them I am to cast to the wind). The image of separating the wheat from the chaff[61] implies that the *fabulae* are the chaff, whilst what remains in Gottfried's version is the wheat or the truth which he claims to be presenting (18469: 'mir ist doch mit der wârheit / ein michel arbeit ûf geleit', I have a great task set me with the truth). The contrast between *fabelen* and *wârheit* reflects the traditional rhetorical distinction between *fabula* and *historia*,[62] while the latter concept informs Gottfried's presentation in his prologue of his poetic task as that of a *historiographus*.[63] Whether Gottfried meant his role as a historian seriously and whether he indulged elsewhere in *fabulae* when it suited him is another matter.[64] What counts for us at the moment is the labelling of the *fabelen* he rejects as historically untrue.

The contrast we have been following through – on the one hand, *historia* as the historical truth (or what was held to be such) and on the other, *fabula* or *fictio*, stamped as untrue or even impossible – is a clearcut one. The reasons for the sharpness of this division are not far to seek. When theoretical definitions were required for the three types of narrative in rhetorical handbooks it was precise distinctions, rather than overlapping ones, that were called for. This was all the more necessary where polemics were involved and the two camps had to be set firmly apart, a tendency at work when the threefold rhetorical classification gives way in practice to a bipolar contrast between two extremes, between *res factae* and *res fictae*. True to this bipolarity clerical writers (such as the author of the *Kaiserchronik* and Thomasin von Zerclaere) maintain this clear distinction, but the same is also true of secular authors polemicising against rival works (such as Gottfried) or against rival genres (such as Jean Bodel in opposition to the Arthurian romance).

So much for theory but, as so often, practice was rather messier, and there are occasions when even theory made a less clean distinction than has hitherto been apparent. Hagiography and the belief in the *communio sanctorum* provide examples of a metahistorical interpretation taking precedence over what were known to be historical facts,[65] as when Reginald of Canterbury justifies his poetic version of the *Vita sancti Malchi* (in which he incorporated details from elsewhere which are not to be found in his source) on the grounds that what is true of one saint must be true of all.[66] The attitude to truth which this betrays was best expressed by Augustine: 'Utrum illa vera sit aut conficta narratio, nihil mea nunc interest' (it is of no concern to me now whether the discourse is true or fictitious), for what counts is the religious, not the factual truth.[67] In Augustine's eyes a narrative can express a truth even if it is a fiction, because a fiction that refers to a meaning is not a lie (*mendacium*), but a figure of the truth (*figura veritatis*), whereas only one devoid of meaning and presented as the truth is in fact a lie.[68] Moving from this metahistorical to the ethical plane, we find texts that are not historically true claiming to offer true morality. This was implied with the moral fables of Aesop, but also stated in defence of his fiction by the author of the *Ecbasis captivi*,[69] and it comes close to shedding a more favourable light on Thomasin's grudging admission about the ethical *wârheit* conveyed by the *lüge* of the court romance (1121 ff.).

We turn now to literary practice around 1200, to consider cases where the distinction between fiction and history can be blurred in two directions, by the incorporation of historical details into fictional literature and conversely by the way in which historical writing can make use of rhetorical and poetic devices and embellishments, even to the extent of incorporating historically untrue details.[70] In considering the complementary relationship between the historicity of fiction and the fictionality of historiography.[71] we have to take into account the problem of referentiality, distinguishing between two kinds. In support of its truth-claims historical writing is dependent on external references to people, places, events and dates (or even to other historical accounts with similar references) by which it can be confirmed or falsified. By contrast with this external referentiality, fictional writing, even though it may include such external references to the extent that it can also incorporate occasional historical details (Napoleon in Tolstoy's *War and Peace*), is fundamentally self-referential, it remains true to its own fabricated world and seeks consistency within its limits (cf. Horace: 'sibi conuenientia finge', make up consistently).[72] If a work of fiction makes reference to other works (as with intertextuality), this differs from the historian's references to other historical accounts by remaining confined to a world of fiction (Wolfram's pointers to Hartmann) conceived in the larger sense of an interfictive world.[73]

As an opening example of a historical feature incorporated into fictional writing we take the first written vernacular fiction in the twelfth century, Chrétien's *Erec*. He concludes the work with Erec's coronation by Arthur, where we find ourselves in a different world, no longer, as at Erec's wedding, at a scene where guests could come from so impossibly far afield as Cappadocia (1969) and the Antipodes (1994), but at 'Nantes an Bretaingne' (6553), with Arthur's vassals attending from recognisable parts of the contemporary Angevin empire, in Britain and on the continent (6644ff.).[74] It has been shown that this scene echoes details of Henry II's investiture of his son in Nantes at Christmas 1169, with the added compliment of allowing that king to appear as another Arthur.[75] The ivory chairs on which Arthur and Erec are seated (6713 ff.), presented to Arthur by Bruianz des Illes (6730), correspond to the thrones given to Henry by Brian de Wallingford, the leopards carved on the chairs (6728) agree with Henry's coat of arms, while the final description of Erec as a *rex doctus*, learned king (6736ff.) reflects the well-known intellectual interests of the Angevin ruler.[76] At the conclusion of his work Chrétien therefore latches recognisable details of contemporary history onto his fictional *conjointure*, but not completely, since Erec, whose realm was initially in Wales, apparently reached his residence in Brittany without the awkwardness of having to cross the sea.[77] History may graft itself onto fiction at Nantes, but without converting it into history.

A second illustration comes from the *Tristan* versions of Thomas and Gottfried. What the German poet says of Isold's father, king Gurmun of Ireland (5871 ff.), identifies him as a 'historical' figure playing a part in this fictional story. However, this figure was introduced by Thomas, whose innovation it is, even though it may have been inventively elaborated by Gottfried.[78] The historicity of Gurmun concerns the fact that he is said to have come from Africa, after seeking legitimation from the Roman emperor, in search of land to conquer, made himself king in Ireland and subdued Cornwall and England, forcing them to pay an annual tribute. However far-fetched this historical sketch may seem, it has been possible to see in it a reflection of events during the Anglo-Saxon invasion of Britain and a connection with events on the continent.[79] Distorted the history may have been, but not so much as to conceal its factual origin.

Knowledge of Gurmun and his prehistory reached Thomas from sources he regarded as historically reliable. Geoffrey of Monmouth knows of a Gormundus, king of the Africans, who fought victoriously in Britain, but also together with Isembardus against the Franks.[80] Although Thomas may have derived knowledge of this from Geoffrey's *Historia*, he also knew Wace's vernacular version on which it is more likely that he drew (Wace's version includes all the relevant details).[81] Wace's attitude to his material was very much that of a historian,[82] so that Thomas could regard him as no less factually reliable than Geoffrey.

In inserting such a historical detail into a fictional story Thomas faced a chronological problem.[83] Since the historical events to do with Gurmun fell in the period of the Anglo-Saxon invasions, the period in which Geoffrey's Arthur played so prominent a part, Thomas had to correlate these two figures and their stories in historical time. Rather than treat them as contemporaries (as with the none too edifying episode in Eilhart's *Tristrant* where the hero comes together with Arthur and his knights),[84] Thomas solved his problem by placing Arthur's reign earlier than the events in his own romance. To this end he invented a minor episode in which he refers to a giant who had earlier been an adversary of Arthur himself, and likewise the hall of statues is described as being in a cave dating from the time of king Arthur.[85]

By inventing such details (even if they are meant to solve a problem of narrative chronology) and by changing the relative chronology of Arthur and Tristan Thomas shows himself to be in charge of his material, rather than subject to his source or to historical fact. The same is true with other details, as when Tristan's speech objecting to payment of the tribute to Morold is lifted from a speech by Arthur in Wace's *Brut*, or when the scene in which Tristan arms himself for combat with Morold seems to follow one with Wace in which Arthur prepares for battle with the Saxons.[86] In view of this it has been said that the interpolations from Wace do not historicise Thomas's romance by making of it a chronicle.[87] His *Tristan* is not history, but historical fiction, alluding to historical events for interpretative purposes that have nothing to do with historical writing. In building in these occasional historical references Thomas felt free to proceed independently in several respects: by the invention of details, by transpositions from another author where apposite, and by the adjustment of chronology to his own ends. This latitude suggests that history did not have the last word with him.

Just as Chrétien had incorporated a historical event in the real world of Nantes into his fictional *Erec*, so too does Wolfram, but on a much larger scale, make use of the real world of the crusades in his *Parzival* romance.[88] He makes fictional use of geographical material in the form of European place-names, but also features of the East, building them into the folktale, largely 'placeless' realm of Arthurian fiction. For us many of these geographical features may be just as fantastic as the realm of Arthurian fiction, but in Wolfram's day they were accepted as factually unquestioned.[89] By including Prester John and his realm, however, Wolfram has incorporated not merely further geographical details, but also a figure regarded from the twelfth century as historically real. This figure's incorporation into Wolfram's fiction concerns not merely geography, therefore, but also history.[90]

In looking at the fictional use of historical material in *Parzival* we must distinguish between what Brunner terms the immanent, but what I prefer to call the self-referential, historicity of Book II and historicity proper (as understood in the Middle Ages) in Book XVI.[91] In Book II (therefore independently of Chrétien) Wolfram introduces a number of characters from a generation earlier than that of the main characters in the subsequent action.[92] This genealogical perspective, although reconcilable with history, is not identical with it. These characters in both generations are literary figures from Wolfram's romance or from other authors; their 'historicity' is therefore confined to the world of literature. Some of the characters occur in Geoffrey of Monmouth,[93] but could be regarded as historical only by acknowledging the truth of his *Historia* regarding not merely Arthur, but also the deeds of his followers – precisely what was questioned by numerous voices in the twelfth century.[94] If it is doubtful, therefore, whether we can equate this genealogical perspective with history (as distinct from the appearance of history), the same is not the case with the conclusion of *Parzival*, where a historical perspective is opened up with reference to extraliterary figures regarded as historical in Wolfram's day.

Wolfram could have concluded his work with Parzival's crowning success in attaining Grail-kingship at Munsalvaesche, a folktale happy ending that would have matched that of Chrétien's *Erec*.[95] He goes out of his way to avoid this by continuing for more than 1300 lines, in which he agrees with Chrétien in another way, by finally opening up his fiction to the realm of history (as Chrétien had done with the coronation at Nantes) in a manner characteristic of Wolfram, by raising a nagging question about the future of Grail-kingship.[96] These concluding lines open up two historical dimensions, closely related in the context of the crusades,[97] incorporated in two figures held to be historical. The first of these is Prester John, regarded as a real person known in Europe as such in Otto von Freising's chronicle and on the basis of letters purportedly sent by him to the Byzantine emperor Manuel Comnenus and pope

Alexander III.[98] Wolfram finds a home for him in his fiction by making him (or an ancestor of his) the son of Feirefiz. The other figure is held to be the swan-knight Loherangrin, genealogically connected with ruling houses of Brabant and with Godfrey of Bouillon, *advocatus* of the Holy Sepulchre after the successful outcome of the first crusade.[99] Wolfram finds a place for Loherangrin by presenting him as Parzival's son.

Whether Wolfram acted independently with whatever Loherangrin material was known to him, shaping it in accordance with his own purposes, is uncertain,[100] but the position is clearer with Prester John. The historical basis concerns not simply the person himself, but also the Latin letter sent to the Byzantine emperor, of which the parallels with details in *Parzival* have been analysed by Bumke.[101] But Wolfram makes independent use of this material for his own ends: first, by combining it with the story of Parzival (with no precedent in Chrétien's version), and secondly by transposing it from Prester John's realm in the remote East to the Grail-kingdom.[102] What was regarded at the time as historically true has therefore been added creatively by Wolfram to his romance narrative, subordinated to the purposes of fiction and meant to entice his audience to think further (and creatively in their case, too) about the implications of his work.[103] What has been said of the presence of historical material in Greek romances can also be applied to the German medieval example. Here, too, the historical material is applied, rather than organic to the plot; there is no attempt to accommodate the story as a whole to these historical details.[104]

The counterpart to the historicity of fiction we have been considering is the fictionality of history, or rather of historical writing. This last distinction arises from two senses of the word *historia*. On the one hand it meant what had actually happened and was therefore true ('Historia est gesta res', history is what happened), but on the other it meant an account of those events ('Historia est narratio rei gestae', history is an account of what happened), making use of rhetoric and poetic embellishments.[105] It is through this use of rhetoric and the distortions it imposed on a presentation of past events that historical writing can be said to have incorporated untrue details, even though its main outline conformed to what was recognised as the truth.

This fictional nature of historical writing was a traditional feature long before the Middle Ages. Already in classical antiquity the closeness of the historian to the poet, both being fabricators, came up frequently for discussion, and although greater latitude for embellishments was allowed to the latter, the difference between them in this respect was one of degree, not of kind.[106] Historical writing of any quality could be rhetorically as ambitious as poetry,[107] so that a clearcut distinction could not always be made between writers of history and writers of poetry, between fictional history and historical fiction. This difficulty is accentuated by the feature of plausibility common to both kinds of writing, for this was an aspect of some fiction[108] (if not an absolute requirement), but also one of the latitudes granted to historiography ('what could or should have happened' alongside 'what did happen'). This is true even of two religious genres commonly classified with *historia* where we might have expected no truck with rhetorical distortions. From early on there were what might be called apocryphal[109] romances like the pseudo-Clementine *Recognitiones* or the *Acts of Paul and Thecla*, neither pure legend (and therefore claiming historical truth) nor fully fledged romance.[110] Much later Jehan Malkaraume presents a verse adaptation of bible stories, arranged along the lines of a universal chronicle and therefore doubly historical, but still finds it permissible to insert literary, fictional interludes (Ovid's monologue for Medea is attributed to Potiphar's wife; the fountain of Narcissus becomes the well at which Rebecca met Abraham's messenger; the tale of Pyramus and Thisbe comes at the close of the story of Susanna and the Elders).[111]

The literary (we could also say rhetorical or fictional) and the strictly historical aspects were closely intertwined from the beginnings of European historiography.[112] With Herodotus and Thucydides this combination makes it difficult to describe their work in terms of either literature or history, of fiction or truth. Herodotus, the father of history, thus aligns himself with Homer, and the encomiastic features of his writing must affect the truthfulness of his representation of history. It has therefore been suggested that (corresponding to Aristotle's distinction between the specific, restricted truths of history and the universal truth of poetry)[113] Thucydides can focus at rhetorical high points on eternal questions of human behaviour, transcending past and present, so that his work contains a mixture of the specific and the general, of factual and of imaginative truth.[114] If the rhetorical embellishments of poetry qualify it as lies in the eyes of rigorist critics, then the same objection can be raised against historical writing that also makes use of such embellishments.

The mendacity of classical historians (for Seneca historians are liars) has been classified under seven headings.[115] Three of these are relatively straightforward – tendentiousness (e.g. flattery or malice), miraculous stories (e.g. Theseus and the underworld) and travellers' tales (e.g. the wonders of Alexander) – but the remaining four have to do with the influence of rhetoric or of a literary genre such as drama. In arguing this classification Wiseman makes a clear distinction between lies out of factual ignorance and lies from choice ('ad arbitrium suum'), where only the latter concern us. He also differentiates between *historia* meaning 'inquiry' and *historia* meaning 'narrative'. It is in the latter context that rhetoric made its influence felt, giving rise to the possibility of conscious untruthfulness in classical historiography. Accusations of deliberate fabrication are made repeatedly (Herodotus is the father, not merely of history, but of lies, and Lucian knows of historians who claim to have witnessed things they could not possibly have seen).[116] Livy, a model historian for posterity, begins his history of Rome with the fall of Troy because of the legend of Aeneas, but admits that such material is more fitted to the creations of the poet than to the historian's authentic record and refuses to commit himself as to its truth or untruth.[117] Seneca mischievously plays the irresponsible historian in claiming to know what business was transacted in heaven and, when asked for the source of his knowledge, refers his imagined questioner to the man who saw Drusilla on her way to heaven.[118] In recommending the impossible (the questioner is to seek in the extraliterary world what is confined to the literary realm) Seneca strikingly anticipates the similar trick played by Hartmann von Aue, referring his own invented questioner to the servant of Mabonagrin's mistress if he wishes to know more about her dress.[119]

Distrust of the truthfulness of rhetoric (and therefore of historical writing that avails itself of it) stems from the primary aim of rhetoric, to move and persuade an audience, to invite belief at all costs, making use of either truth or falsehood to achieve that end.[120] This subordination of content to technique means that in rhetoric plausibility is more important than truth,[121] a feature which in Cicero's discussion of rhetoric comes close on two occasions to what also characterises fictionality. In

De oratore he has Scaevola define the good orator as one who seems to the intelligent to speak with eloquence, but to the stupid to speak the truth. What he says may not be the truth, but it must sound like it if some are to be taken in.[122] This division of the orator's audience corresponds to what we have also seen with that addressed by an author of fiction,[123] but, more importantly, if the intelligent are not taken in this must be because they recognise the rules by which the game is being played, they have made a contract with the speaker. Cicero makes another point in *De inventione* when talking about plausibility.[124] No matter whether true or not ('sive id falsum est sive verum'), a plausible account is one that invites belief because it is a narrative of events that could have happened, a formulation that approaches the standard definition of *argumentum* as one of the constituents of fictionality.[125]

As with so much of the heritage from classical antiquity, the attitude of the Church towards rhetoric was ambivalent, either polemical or eirenic, either rejecting it (especially in the early period) or adapting it to its own ends.[126] It could be rejected on the simple ground that it implied words without conviction and betrayed the presence of corruption or flattery. Its legitimacy was the subject of debate, its partisanship could be equated with propaganda (the orator defending a client was expected to suppress damaging evidence and even to make skilful use of fictions).[127] Rhetoric was also accused of appealing to the emotions of listeners, not to their reasoned judgment, so that a historical work may claim impartiality by contrast with the biased hyperbole of mere oratorical display, amounting to deceit.[128] William of Malmesbury, like others, claims to avoid rhetoric, saying that his subject is worthy enough to dispense with unnecessary embellishments, but he does this in such stylish prose that his rejection of rhetoric is itself a rhetorical flourish.[129]

This last example shows that, despite such hostility, Christian writers were also willing to make use of rhetoric. The classical technique could be retained, but harnessed to morally defensible subjects, as with Augustine's recommendation to use the art of persuasion in order to spread the word of God more effectively.[130] Cicero had already held the view that the past could be manipulated so as to bring out moral or exemplary lessons, and his lead was followed centuries later by Philippe de Commynes who, although he claims eyewitness authority, embellishes what he saw in order to underline his moral lesson.[131] In cases like these 'truth' means what is regarded as exemplary, not just what actually happened, as with early Christian encomia on martyrs using the stylistic and compositional methods of pagan rhetoric and subordinating any strict concept of truth to the need to emphasise model behaviour.[132]

If it was felt justifiable to rescue rhetoric by using it for positive ends, it is not surprising that, in the Middle Ages as in antiquity, rhetorical devices were employed in historical writing. William of Malmesbury does this in the very act of denying it, but there are other medieval historians who, without a comparable stylistic display, expressly renounce any poetic style so as to avoid distortion of the truth, as when Reinbot von Durne in his prologue to *Der heilige Georg* (46ff.) forgoes 'tihten unde zieren,/mit lügenen florieren' (inventing and adorning, decking out with lies) for the sake of 'diu wârheit' (the truth).[133] By stressing what they are avoiding, however, such authors imply that there are others who were prepared to deck out (or compromise?) the truth of their account with these embellishments. These other authors, while claiming to represent events that had in fact taken place, employed the means of expression recommended by a rhetoric not free from the blemish of untruth.[134] If they added decoration to the events recounted by means of invented speeches, lengthy descriptions or moral commentaries they were doing what had been regarded as legitimate in historiography since classical times, but this freedom did not extend as far as the invention of new characters or episodes, let alone to altering the course of the story.[135] To do that would have meant crossing the line separating the restricted rhetorical liberty of the historian and the more thoroughgoing licence enjoyed by the poet.

Although restricted in this way, the types of rhetorical transformation available to the historian were still many.[136] He could depict what actors said or thought in accord with his understanding of their character; he could dramatise by using direct speech; he could expatiate on descriptions (a city, a storm, a battle); he could insert a love episode, and in all this still remain within the bounds of what was permitted to the historian. None of these transformations (especially the representation of speech or thought) was meant to make a truth-claim as to what actually happened, but corresponded rather to what might plausibly be expected to have happened in such circumstances.[137] The possibilities just listed fall under the rhetorical heading of *amplificatio*: they amount to rhetorical, often exemplary adornments to what were regarded as historical facts, whose truthfulness was not affected by these additions.[138] They allow scope for *inventio*, defined in rhetoric as the devising of matter true or probable (*verum* or *verisimile*) to make a case appear convincing,[139] and defended as honest invention and as an integral part of his work by a historian of the stature of William of Malmesbury.[140]

More far-reaching, but still reconcilable with the historian's task, are his interventions intended to convert the incomplete disorder of events in historical time into an ordered and patterned account, a task which most nearly resembles the structural organisation aimed at by authors of fiction.[141] Elaborations to bring this out and to make the past understandable therefore served a historical purpose, even if they edged away from strict historical accuracy.[142] Of the *Rhetorica ad Herennium* it has been said that a recital of bare fact could still lack plausibility if it were clumsily constructed and that a convincing narrative of fact required the same care as fiction.[143] Southern has stressed that the truth presented by such historians is the truth that Aristotle allowed to the poet, not the historian, but that in Aristotle's sense these writers were all poets, for they manipulated their materials to give form and universality to their works.[144]

With regard to Anglo-Norman historiography (Latin and vernacular) Burrichter has designated such stylistic embellishments as 'functional fictionality', distinct from what she terms the 'autonomous fictionality' of the court romance.[145] In place of her adjectives I prefer a distinction between 'rhetorical fictionality' (indicating the restricted field in which it is operative) and 'generic fictionality' (with reference to those genres held to be fictional). Although both may be termed fictional, there are telling reasons for keeping these phenomena apart.[146] Although the decorative, fictive elements in a historical narrative may serve to convince, please and hold the attention of an audience,[147] they play no part in determining whether the whole work is fictive or true. If Burrichter's functional fictionality was rarely discussed in the Middle Ages, an important exception was Lucan's *Pharsalia*,[148] but even here these ornamental details were not felt to disqualify the truth of the whole work and stamp it as a fiction, for with regard to his literary style Lucan could be regarded as a *poeta fingens* (a poet who invents), but concerning his historical material as a *historicus non fingens* (a historian who does not invent).[149] We have seen that William of Malmesbury found a place for *inventio* in his historical writing, and his work, like that of other Anglo-Norman historians, is replete with *exempla* and fictive speeches.[150] By the same token, the many rhetorical, decorative additions in the *Historia* of Geoffrey of Monmouth do not of themselves damage the claim of his work to be historical truth; not even William of Newburgh, his most pronounced critic, objected to him on that score.[151] In short, the rhetorical embellishments, utilised by medieval historians and accepted as contributing to an overall historical purpose and not endangering it, are best kept distinct from fictionality as characteristic of literary narrative, above all the romance.

This blurring of the boundary between history and fiction has given rise in classical scholarship to the question whether the Greek romance may have arisen out of Greek historical writing. A number of features suggest this possibility. Without committing himself to any evolutionary model Morgan proposes that it was within historiography that the fictional contract (central to our definition of fictionality) was first extended to prose narrative, 'thus allowing fiction . . . to enter a new form and generate a new and more equivocal literature of pleasure in prose: fiction in the form of history'.[152] It is for this reason that many Greek romances have titles that are outwardly historiographical (*Aethiopica*, *Babyloniaca*)[153] and take over characters and background from recognisably historiographical works, so that the impression is created that the action is located in gaps in real history.[154] Fiction thus emerges from such gaps and profits from their supposed existence.[155] It blurs the dividing line between truth and untruth and invites confusion between the real and the unreal.[156]

In the rest of this chapter I shall try to apply these suggestions to the romance around 1200, asking whether it, too, had roots in historical writing. Burrichter has sketched the development of the Arthurian romance from Anglo-Norman historiography, but we must go a step further, asking whether specifically the fictionality of the romance arose from this source, but also taking into account the antique romances (how far were they regarded as historical, how far fictional?). Of the three thematic fields touched on by Jean Bodel the *matière de France* can be left out of consideration because the *chanson de geste* was commonly regarded as historical (Bodel calls it *voir*, true). When clerics criticise oral history in German they criticise it for being faulty, mistaken history, not for being fictional.[157] Since the *matière de Rome* is attested earlier in France (and to some extent in Germany, too) than the *matière de Bretagne* we shall deal with them in that order.

MATIÈRE DE ROME

Under this heading we consider three classical themes in the sequence in which the historical events on which they are based allegedly took place (Troy, Aeneas, Alexander),[158] confining ourselves to those themes common both to French and to German literature of the twelfth century.[159] Our task, inevitably compressed, will be to look at the evidence in Latin, French and German for the historicity of these themes, but also for their penetration, tentative and episodic, by features that may be regarded as fictional or potentially so.

The Trojan War was regarded unquestioningly in antiquity and in the Middle Ages not merely as having actually taken place, but as the epoch-making event of pre-Roman history.[160] It is therefore recorded as a historical fact by historians of antiquity and by their medieval successors.[161] The basis of their accounts, the works of Dares and Dictys, however fraudulent as purportedly eyewitness accounts they are known to us to be, was accepted throughout at face value.[162] By claiming to be eyewitness accounts, but also by expunging the Homeric gods from the action,[163] they presented themselves as historically reliable, so much so that Dares, for example, could be regarded as the first pagan historian, a counterpart to Moses in biblical history.[164] The impression of historical accuracy, spurious though it may be, is further strengthened by the repeated and precise time-references with which Dares equips his work, as well as by his following the *ordo naturalis* of events, as expected of the historian, proceeding from the first causes of enmity through to the destruction of Troy.[165] Bernardus (Silvestris) regards Dares so much as a historian that he can compare Virgil unfavourably with him in this respect for not having written, like Dares, 'secundum historie veritatem' (according to the truth of history).[166] This distrust of poetic veracity means that Dares is more commonly set off against Homer, who lived long after the events he describes, as is categorically expressed by Benoît de Sainte-Maure in the prologue to his *Roman de Troie* (45 ff.).

How firm a place such knowledge of the events at Troy occupied in the historical imagination of the Middle Ages is shown by their key position in the doctrine of *translatio imperii* (the transfer of power from Babylon to Greece)[167] and by the way in which peoples like the Franks and the Britons sought their origins, and therefore their place in history, by tracing them, like the Romans, back to Troy.[168]

Already in classical antiquity there was, centred on Homer, another view of the Trojan War, since the later fabrications of Dares and Dictys were able to fasten onto existing misgivings about Homer's account.[169] These included the fact that Homer lived so much later and the sheer incredibility of some of his statements (pygmies fighting cranes, gods intervening in human combat).[170] Such mistrust does not amount to a recognition of Homeric fiction, but it renders acute the question of the poet's truthfulness[171] and prompts us to ask whether there are features suggesting the piecemeal genesis of fiction from what was regarded as a historical theme. In Augustine's eyes Homer wrote *fabellae*, fables (just as Virgil composed *poetica figmenta*)[172] and much later these two authors are again linked by virtue of their *inutiles fabulae*, useless fables.[173] We move closer to fiction, however, when it can be shown that Homer allows himself the freedom to re-fashion events to suit his own purpose.[174] He may take over already made-up stories from others, he may alter stories that he has inherited and he may invent some of his own.[175] His inventiveness involves abandoning the limits of the real world at times, changing them to some extent as an act of choice.[176] Examples of such fictional re-fashioning by Homer include the presence of Helen at Troy (when she was known to be in Egypt),[177] and the participation of the gods in the affairs of men (a feature criticised as insane by Dares, and also by Benoît and which, as in the comparable case of Virgil's *Aeneid*, was seen as mixing 'uera cum fictis', the true with the fabricated).[178] Homer's fabulous realm of Ocean (more frequent in the voyages of the *Odyssey*, but also referred to in the *Iliad*) has been expressly associated with 'a kind of imaginative literature we might loosely call fiction'.[179] To call this aspect of Homer's inventive artistry 'fabulous' ties up with a medieval *accessus* ('Ilias est fabula de destructione Troie composita', the *Iliad* is a fable composed about the destruction of Troy)[180] and with the *inutiles fabulae* attributed to him and to Virgil.

In passing now to Benoît's *Roman de Troie* we have to ask whether the twofold view of the Trojan War in antiquity (a historical event, presented by Homer in a factually untrue way) is reflected in the twelfth-century version. Some of the fictional features of this romance are the rhetorical embellishments found regularly in medieval historiography, but others are closer to what could be termed a fictional representation.

Certainly, Benoît puts himself forward as a historian, as he does also in his *Chronique des ducs de Normandie*.[181] He makes a point of saying that he conforms to Dares, rather than Homer, on the grounds that were already rehearsed in antiquity.[182] In addition, by describing Dares as writing up each night his account of the day's events on the battle-field, even to the point of interviewing participants, he puts him forward in the guise of the medieval view of the historian 'rei visae scriptor', he who writes up what he has seen.[183] In following such an authoritative source to the letter, without adding to it, Benoît can claim to recount *la verité* as his *auctor* reveals it.[184] (Because this principal source did not include an account of the end of the war Benoît had to turn for this to Dictys, equally a *bona fide* historian for the Middle Ages.) A striking fact about Benoît's dependence on such prosaic sources of no literary pretensions (by contrast with the *Thebaid* of Statius as the source of the *Roman de Thèbes* and Virgil's *Aeneid* for the *Roman d'Enéas*) is the avoidance of stylistic embellishments and distortions which this makes possible for an author claiming to offer historical truth.[185] Nor did others doubt the work's historicity, if we may go by its insertion into a thirteenth-century translation of the bible[186] or, more pervasively with regard to the work's subject matter, by the fact that Troy was regarded as the origin of the Franks, the Britons and the Normans, granting them a place in history.[187] It is probably the wish to propagate the Trojan origins of his Anglo-Norman realm that encouraged Henry II to commission this translation from Benoît.[188]

There is, of course, another side to Benoît's artistry, more important in terms of *literary* history. When he says that he has added nothing to his source he immediately qualifies this (as indeed he has to in view of his vast expansion of Dares),[189] admitting that he has inserted only 'aucun bon dit', some fine discourse (142–3), while keeping to the substance of his source (144).[190] What this amounts to has been discussed by Nolan, who sees Benoît as a translator following his *matire* faithfully, but as a composer organising and controlling it,[191] referring to Horace's advice in the *Ars poetica* about the careful composition of a literary work, its unification by the due proportions of a carefully contrived form.[192] This suggests two things: first, that Benoît has taken to heart advice that was meant specifically for the poet, the writer of fiction,[193] and secondly that his work differs from historical writing in his conscious manipulation of material to achieve a carefully calculated poetic form for the sake of his *intentio*.[194] This *intentio* of Benoît has been summed up as the discussion of *amor et militia* (love and knighthood),[195] achieved by means of *inventio*, devising a space for love in material traditionally dominated by the theme of warfare. He does this by interweaving into his repeated and lengthy battle-scenes a number of love-affairs which are only briefly touched upon, if at all, in his source (Jason and Medea, Helen and Paris, Briseida and Troilus together with Diomedes, finally Achilles and Polixena).[196] In these sketches he draws largely on Ovid, introducing subjective analyses of personal feeling characteristic of Ovidian fiction 'alien to epic and history',[197] assisted by the fact that most of the Roman poet's letter-writers in the *Heroides* were connected with the Trojan War.[198] In grafting fictive Ovidian love-stories[199] on to his historical material Benoît is repeating what Virgil had earlier done in transposing the story of Jason and Medea on to that of Aeneas and Dido, a procedure that Macrobius described in words that reveal it as consciously fictional.[200] Similarly, with reference to Benoît (as well as to the author of the *Roman d'Enéas*), Nolan has concluded that narrative fiction is used to explore history in relation to sexual desire,[201] but that the process of exploration itself, the fusing of fiction with history, is inventively, creatively fictional. Even though Benoît's controlling manipulation of events can occasionally be long-term in its effects,[202] his fictional interventions in the form of love-affairs are essentially episodic, interludes carved out of years of warfare, whilst for the rest he follows the course of events in his source (144: 'Mais la matire en ensivrai', but I will follow its material).[203] Chrétien's inventive dispositions with the *matière de Bretagne* will go radically further, involving the whole plot of each of his works.

After Benoît's work the *Liet von Troie* of Herbort von Fritzlar presents a very different picture, a realistic, even cynical view of love and warfare.

In avoiding any courtly embellishment of these themes he paints what is for him a more truthful, historical picture of events at Troy. He largely undoes the fictional elements introduced by Benoît. He and Lamprecht in the Vorau version of the *Alexanderlied* are the only authors of these vernacular works with a classical theme in which no fictional features can be ascertained.

That Herbort's work is meant to be historical is suggested by a range of features. It could appeal tacitly to the traditional view that the Franks came ultimately from Troy and that Xanten was a new Troy;[204] it has been seen on a par with the work of historians of the twelfth and chroniclers of the thirteenth century,[205] and was regarded in that light by the compiler of the only manuscript that transmits it, where it chronologically precedes Veldeke's *Eneasroman*.[206] Like Benoît before him, but with more justification, Herbort insists that it is Dares and his Latin 'translator' Cornelius Nepos whom he follows, as well as the French text (53 ff.). As becomes a historian, he presents his account in the *ordo naturalis*, but goes beyond his French predecessor in also devising a consistent overall time-pattern for his work, whereas Benoît, not so concerned with strict historical accuracy, had largely undone the time-scheme present in Dares.[207] As part of a general shortening of the French work Herbort also cuts back on any rhetorical embellishments, as well as on implausible elements of the marvellous (again in contrast to Benoît).[208] The feature of the French work that most obviously falls victim to this drastic shortening process is the series of love-scenes introduced by Benoît, so that the German work presents events at Troy historically as dominated by warfare, not as a courtly interplay between *militia* and *amor*.[209] It thereby sacrifices Benoît's major innovation, the theme which, like Virgil, he had inventively introduced, thereby demonstrating his fictional control of his material. In this avoidance of fiction Herbort's work stands out as an alternative form of romance, complementing its fictional contemporaries as a 'historical romance'[210] and filling what would otherwise be the gap between the largely historical tradition of German literature before the court romance and the renewed emphasis on historical genres such as the chronicle and the legend in the thirteenth century.[211]

In that the story of Aeneas proceeded from the Trojan War there was little doubt in antiquity and in the Middle Ages about its historical veracity. Although there were qualifications, Virgil's account could be regarded as *historia*: for Eberhard the German it was 'historialis apex' (the peak of history); Konrad von Hirsau maintained that Virgil derived his material and intention from history; and a commentary attributed to Anselm of Laon goes so far as to correlate the events in the epic with historical ones from the Old Testament.[212] For Servius the historicity of the epic rested on its theme, the founding of a nation and the links binding past with present.[213] Virgil's account of Aeneas therefore ends with the founding of a people destined for imperial rule;[214] the historical truth of it was so little questioned that the *Annolied* and the *Kaiserchronik* could base themselves on Virgil and the commentary of Servius in their historical surveys.[215]

Virgil's history, however, not merely looks backwards (how Rome was founded by refugees from Troy), but also forwards, as far as the poet's own present. The curse of the dying Dido on Aeneas, vowing enmity between her people and his, transposes her on to the historical plane as the initiator of the hatred between Carthage and Rome.[216] In this way even what Macrobius saw as Virgil's fictive invention of the Dido interlude is made to serve a historical end.[217] The prophecy made by Anchises likewise passes beyond the primeval time-frame of the narrative into a period of fulfilment in the person of Augustus in Virgil's own day.[218] The analogies between the poem and the Augustan present confer authority on the Emperor as descended from a semi-divine hero, but also on Virgil's account by tying it in with history.[219] The *Aeneid* thus presents history as linear progress from defeat at Troy to fulfilment in the person of Augustus, Virgil's own patron.[220] By virtue of this historical dimension of his poem Virgil, like Lucan, could be regarded as *poeta et historicus* (poet and historian): for Servius he presents history (but, as a poet, not openly) and Otto von Freising explicitly equates him with Lucan, saying that both mix *res gestae* (what happened) with *res fabulosae* (what was invented).[221]

This mixture of the historical with the poetic or fabulous opens up another aspect of Virgil's work, since there also existed a counter-tradition that cast doubt on his historical truthfulness. This alternative view presented Aeneas as a traitor,[222] which suggested the unreliability of Virgil's account, so that, as was the case also with Homer, Dares and Dictys can be claimed as historically more trustworthy.[223] By comparison with them, although the downfall of Troy may be true (*historia*), what Virgil says of Aeneas' virtue is not (*fabula*).[224] One reason for this mistrust of Virgil's version of events is his imitation of Homer, so that the criticism to which the model was exposed also affects his successor,[225] as when, for example, the gods intervene and take part in human affairs.[226] Another reason is the fact, well known to medieval commentators, that Virgil wrote to flatter Augustus, a fact adduced when Dares is given preference, but also (in an *accessus* attributed to Anselm of Laon) to explain the poet's suppression of many historical facts and insertion of *figmenta*.[227] Macrobius was aware that this was part of Virgil's fictional technique, as is borne out by the inventive transfer of Medea's story to Dido, by the pretence that Aeneas and Dido were contemporaries, by compromising the well-known chastity of Dido and by the description of the Punic Carthage in terms of its Spanish namesake.[228] Macrobius felt it justified to regard this technique as fiction, rather than lying, because these facts were known to Virgil's audience, to whom the poet makes his procedure expressly clear in having Aeneas emerge from the underworld by the gate of false dreams.[229] Virgil's fictional disposition of his material also explains his employment of the *ordo artificialis*, already commented on by Servius as a poetic technique recommended by Horace in his *Ars poetica*.[230] Although this was not enough for clerical rigorists, who simply accused the poet of lying,[231] others, especially the humanists of the twelfth century, saw it as a feature of his poetic art and acknowledged it for what it was, fictional inventiveness.[232] This conscious artistry means that the double formula used of Lucan, *poeta et historicus* (poet and historian), is also true of Virgil, as when Bernardus 'Silvestris' judges him to have interspersed historical material with his inventions ('ficmentis extollit') or when 'Anselm of Laon' says that he suppressed much (not all!) historical truth in adding poetic fictions.[233] When a fourteenth-century commentator distinguishes fact from fiction he signals this by saying that here the author passes from history to fiction ('Transit auctor de historia ad figmentum'),[234] which sums up the literary development that we are tracing on a larger scale in this section.

We now have to ask whether a similar conflation of history and fiction is to be found in two twelfth-century vernacular versions of the *Aeneid*. For all its preoccupation with the exploits, martial and amatory, of an individual knight the *Roman d'Enéas*, in following Virgil's narrative line, is also concerned with his historical theme, the founding of Rome.[235] It even goes beyond Virgil in extending the line of historical continuity backwards to the judgment of Paris which led to the Trojan War and forwards to the imperial descendants resulting from the marriage of Eneas and Lavine.[236] What the French author does in emphasising historical continuity is taken a step further in the manuscript compilations that transmit his work, for seven of the nine manuscripts present the *Enéas* together with other historical works (*Thèbes*, *Troie*, *Brut*) in varying combinations, thereby including it within a vast historical panorama.[237] The implications of these works were clear not only to the later compilers of these manuscripts, but also to the twelfth century in view of the Angevins' interest in establishing their prehistory and a model of empire for themselves.[238] These works, especially *Brut* and *Enéas* (with *Troie* as a forerunner), provided their dynasty, especially under Henry II, with historical legitimation.[239] Given the historical function that his theme could be made to serve it is not surprising that the author of *Enéas* should undo Virgil's use of the *ordo artificialis* and replace it by the eminently historiographical *ordo naturalis*.[240] In the same spirit, when Eneas reports the fall of Troy to Dido (this scene is retained in the French work, but in addition to, no longer in place of, an earlier account of the sack of the city) he does this with the historical justification of an eyewitness (857: 'la verité vos an dirai,/car jo i fui, sel vi et sai', I shall tell you the truth about it, because I was there and saw it and know).[241] Also conscious of factual credibility, the French author largely (if not entirely) eliminates the divine machinery that had already invited rational criticism in classical antiquity, even before Christianity added a further, religious dimension to the rejection of the gods' intervention.[242] Although the *Enéas* may contain its own wonders (largely of a scientific or architectural nature), these replace the pagan ones of the Latin work (e.g. a burning fleet of ships is metamorphosed into a group of water nymphs) that were credible only to those who accepted the Olympian deities.[243]

The *Enéas* also betrays, however, by contrast with Virgil a dehistoricising tendency which, whilst it may not of itself constitute fiction, assists a development in that direction. The central imagery of Augustus in the *Aeneid*, the ruler towards whom history has been moving, disappears in the French work, whose chronological prospectus at the end of the

work concludes well before Augustus.[244] Equally, the goal reached in
the vernacular text is not Rome, but the marriage of Eneas and Lavine
(to which the summary fulfilment of Anchises' prophecy is added only
as an appendix).[245] When the French author replaces Dido's curse on
Aeneas' line by an act of forgiveness, this deprives the scene of its historical role of accounting for the future wars of Carthage and Rome.[246]
Much more telling than this negative tendency, however, is the way in
which the French author has re-worked the second half of Virgil's work
(even externally, measured against the *Aeneid*, it is expanded to more
than twice the length of the first half).[247] The core of this expansion is
the figure of Lavine (Virgil had barely mentioned her at all) and with
her the theme of love, so that, true to the literary interests of romance,
this half of the work is dominated by the theme of *amor et militia*.[248] By
this creative and transforming innovation the author breaks free from
any slavish adherence to source and consults his own artistic interests;
he devises a role for Lavine as a balance, but also as a contrast to the
figure of Dido.[249] In his fictional invention of Lavine the French author
can be said to be repeating what Virgil had accomplished with his fictional invention of a role for Dido.[250] The author of *Enéas* was assisted
in this, in a way that we saw was characteristic of fiction generated by
intertextuality, by the fact that Virgil's text was open to expansion in
this way by an author concerned, like his audience, with the interplay
of *amor* and *militia* soon to be applied by Chrétien to the *matière de
Bretagne*.[251] The *Enéas* author even creates his own gaps to be filled with
the new theme of love, by allowing human emotions to come into play
during the periods of truce that separate the battles between Eneas
and Turnus.[252] In this expansion, in Lavine's talks with her mother and
above all in her self-analysing soliloquies, he draws largely on Ovid,
whom he also exploits in depicting Dido's love.[253] Especially helpful
here were the Roman poet's *Heroides* and their twelfth-century commentaries. Since most *accessus* to this work register the fictive character
of the epistles the French author shows his inventiveness by building
his own fiction on a predecessor's fiction.[254] The parallel with Virgil's
procedure is also clear. Where the Roman turned not to history for his
depiction of Dido, but to another work (the *Argonautica* of Apollonius),
thereby showing the literary, 'made' nature of his construct, so does his
French colleague turn to another expressly fictional source, the *Heroides*,

in depicting Dido and Lavine. Fiction finds a niche in history, but also grows out of other fiction.

For Veldeke's *Eneasroman* a historical dimension can be established on several fronts. In the first place, much more so than in the French work, its culmination is, if not Augustus, then the equally historical *translatio* of Trojan knighthood to a Roman context which opens out into a specifically Christian one.[255] The figure of Augustus may still be retained, however briefly (351, 28), but only because it was in his reign that Christ was born and, ultimately, a new Empire made possible. The line of salvation history sketched by Veldeke as his innovation (Eneas–Rome–Augustus–Christ) owes much to the pronounced historical tradition of German literature before him, but also to the revival of the idea of a Christian Empire under Barbarossa.[256] Whereas Virgil's historical conception was to link past with present by emphasising Augustus as a new Aeneas, in the twelfth century Gottfried von Viterbo draws a genealogical line between the Trojan rulers and the German ones of the present (Barbarossa and Henry VI), whilst the anonymous *Carmen de gestis* dated 1162 actually presents Barbarossa as a second Aeneas, so that Veldeke (or his patron) may have had every reason to assume at this time that a work on this subject would go down well in the Emperor's circle.[257] This possibility raises the question of Hohenstaufen affiliations and of the two so-called *Stauferpartien* in Veldeke's work (226, 16ff.: the discovery of the grave of Pallas when Barbarossa was crowned Emperor in Rome in 1155; 347, 13 ff.: the imperial court festival at Mainz in 1184).[258] Opitz dismisses such affiliations as mere speculation, but seems to be unacquainted with Dutch-language scholarship on this topic, in which Willaert and others have argued emphatically for an imperial background to Veldeke's work, in his lyrics and in the legend *Servatius* as well as in the *Eneasroman*.[259] This prompts Willaert to think that Veldeke had the Hohenstaufen court in mind from the beginning, whereas Thomas regards the *Stauferpartien* as later interpolations, but in either case, whether as original intention or as happy afterthought, they place the *Eneasroman* in a firmly political and historical context.[260] It is of a piece with this historical slant of Veldeke's work that he agrees with his French source in adopting the *ordo naturalis* (even making it somewhat more obvious), in using the historiographical device of an eyewitness account and in playing down the role of the pagan gods (no doubt for religious reasons, but also for the sake of historical veracity).[261] Others (not merely Hohenstaufen circles whose interests it may have served) regarded the *Eneasroman* as *historia*, if we are to go by its much abbreviated form in MS w, where it serves as a prelude to a fully fledged historical work, the *Weihenstephaner Chronik*.[262]

As a result of such historical features Opitz has read Veldeke's work as a historiographical text, not to be adequately understood by the fictional criteria of the court romance. This is justified to the extent that it can be placed within the context of the preceding historiographical tradition in German literature, but that is only part of the story with what was recognised at the time as a key work.[263] In addition to his central theme of love Veldeke innovates over against his French source by stressing the role of the narrator, the genesis of his work (thereby pointing to its written nature as an artificial construct) and the fact that, in contrast to the anonymous *Enéas*, the (implicit) author 'Heinrich' is responsible for this construct.[264] These features are not meant to underline the historical truth of what is recounted, but point rather to the work as an artefact, a precondition for any development of conscious fiction. Bastert even goes so far as to say that Veldeke, not merely chronologically but also in terms of his narrative technique, emerges as standing close to Hartmann and Wolfram.[265]

For the rest, Veldeke may agree with his French source, certainly not slavishly, but with understanding and is frequently independent of it.[266] Where they agree we may assume that Veldeke accepted the fictional innovations of the French work, including therefore the dehistoricisation of the Dido narrative, the inventive addition of the Lavinia story as a conscious counterpoint to that dealing with Dido, and the elaboration of the theme of *amor et militia*. In all this Veldeke may also borrow independently from Ovid (not always through the intermediacy of the French text),[267] so that the German author is responsible for his own fictional innovations, taking further what he found adumbrated in the *Enéas*. With him we encounter a combination of the historical and the fictional, resistant to any simple opposition of true and false.[268]

Of the three classical themes we are dealing with that concerned with Alexander, to whose lifespan we can even give dates, is the most obviously historical.[269] He was interested in the historical record himself in that he took with him on his campaigns the scholar Callisthenes to collect material to be written up, thus providing in reality for himself (a written eyewitness account) what Dares and Dictys falsely claimed for their account of the Trojan War.[270] (That such falsification, purporting to be history, was not absent in Alexander's case either is clear from the spurious *Epistola Alexandri ad Aristotelem*, regarded as a first-hand account of the wonders of the East.)[271] It is therefore little wonder that the story of Alexander's life is frequently treated by historians or regarded as history in antiquity (e.g. Quintus Curtius, Justinus and Orosius), but also in the Middle Ages (e.g. Honorius Augustodunensis, Vincent of Beauvais and Roger Bacon).[272] The historical importance of this figure was enhanced in the Middle Ages by the traditional interpretation of Daniel's dream (Dan. 8. 3 ff.) as signifying the transfer of world dominion from the Medes and Persians to the Greeks under Alexander.[273] He was thereby allotted a firm place in the Christian conception of history, and his historicity was further guaranteed by the fact that he was mentioned by name in the Old Testament (Macc. 1.1ff.)[274] Even the wonders of the East that cluster around the Alexander tradition, for us an apparent undermining of historicity, were often regarded already in antiquity as of factual, scientific interest, belonging to natural history and geography.[275]

But there was another side to the reception of this wonder material, casting a different light on Alexander's exploits. Long before him Greek myth encouraged the view that distant peoples were monstrously deformed, so that authors like Scylax and Ctesias gratified this expectation of monsters and marvels, writing to entertain rather than to inform.[276] The frank admissions by Strabo that 'the distant is difficult to disprove' or by Eratosthenes that remote regions are 'easy to lie about' suggest that the extent of Alexander's travels could become a cloak for fictional narrative, for opening the way to 'the most radical experiments in prose fiction ever attempted by ancient writers'.[277] The literary popularity of the Alexander theme was guaranteed by the Greek Alexander Romance, termed Pseudo-Callisthenes because ascribed to the historian who accompanied Alexander, but in fact a prime example of the invasion of history by romance fiction with all the elements of the wonderful and the intimate.[278] In view of this and other travel literature Strabo claimed categorically that those who wrote about India were for the most part a set of liars, and Aulus Gellius expressed disgust at such superstition.[279] There were some in antiquity who were worried by texts that could not be categorised as either factual or fictional, but also others who saw their intermediate nature rather as an opportunity to be exploited.[280] In Photius' *Wonders beyond Thule* the adventures recounted move from science to outright fabulous invention as we progress beyond Thule, in a way strikingly similar to what can be seen in later Alexander romances (only in the *loca fabulosa*, fabulous places, of India do we pass from geographical and historical reality to a novel realm of marked unreality).[281] To their critics such fabulous accounts were simply lies, but their authors can be assumed to have composed them as fictional works,[282] for they are characterised by two features central to our definition: they betray a fictional contract between author and audience and they set out to blur the boundary between fact and fiction, between truth and untruth.[283]

Because of the historicity of Alexander as a turning-point both in antiquity and for the Middle Ages the various works dealing with him in French can at least expect to be taken as true. That is reflected in the fact that the earliest of these versions, by Albéric of Pisançon, makes use of Quintus Curtius and that the only surviving fragment is found in a manuscript of the Roman historian's *Alexandri Magni Historiae*.[284] In a manner typical of the *chanson de geste* and the competition between *jongleurs* Albéric polemicises (27ff.) against other versions that deny that Philip of Macedon was Alexander's father, accusing them of untruth and thereby implicitly claiming truth for himself.[285] That is far from meaning that Albéric's own text is actually true, but it amounts to an expectation that it should be regarded as such. The kinship of Albéric's *Alexandre* with the *chanson de geste* that has been argued in terms of formal technique[286] could therefore conceivably extend further: both are to be seen as presenting the truth about the past.

Albéric's dependence on a historical source like Quintus Curtius does not exclude other non-historical possibilities, for he also based himself on Pseudo-Callisthenes, with his mixture of history and fiction, and permitted himself enough originality to qualify even the wisdom of Solomon on *omnia vanitas*, all is vanity (7f.)[287] More important as an innovation, even though it remains confined to one episode alone, is the introduction of the love-theme in the person of the queen Candace in other French versions of the twelfth century. In the decasyllabic *Alexander* women and talk of love make a brief appearance, while in

the *Roman d'Alexandre* the hero's encounter with Candace is an amatory one, which it had not been in earlier sources.[288] Although very
much attenuated, the addition of this theme is reminiscent of what
we saw as fictional innovations in the *Roman de Troie* and especially
the *Enéas*, even to the extent of also making some use of Ovidian
material.[289] Another episode with the (unrealised) potential for a love-
encounter is the scene of the flower-maidens, whose fantastic nature,
however, qualifies the narrative at this point as pure *fabula* or fiction in
the sense meant by Isidore of Seville (*contra naturam*, against nature).[290]
Different though they may be, these flower-maidens belong to those furthest regions where authorial imagination had long run riot, picturing
Alexander ascending to the sky, plunging to the depths of the ocean and
reaching the frontiers of the Other World.[291]

In Germany the Vorau version of the *Alexanderlied*, possibly in reaction against the fabulous accretions the subject had long since attracted,
lays renewed stress on its historical features.[292] There was one precedent
in particular that encouraged the author Lamprecht in this, since there
was a long tradition of tracing the Franks, like so many other peoples,
back to Troy, having them as one group settling between the Rhine and
the Danube, while another penetrated to Macedonia.[293] In claiming
an ancestral link with Alexander as part of their historical identity the
Franks had even less reason to question the historical validity of what
was reported of him. This does not prevent Lamprecht from authorising
his version, mainly for religious reasons, by seeking repeated authentication from his sources, above all from the bible, where he was initially
assisted by the biblical mention of Alexander.[294] Whereas Albéric mentioned the bible only to cast doubt on Solomon, Lamprecht differs
from him by gaining confirmation from the bible, seeking authentication from Maccabees in the opening lines (11–12), quoting Solomon
in order to agree with him (19ff.) and introducing Darius by referring
to Daniel (473). Since these two biblical books go no further than the
death of Darius and since Macc.1.1 has it that Alexander killed (*percussit*)
Darius, Lamprecht's text, to judge by the Vorau manuscript, goes no
further than this point, thereby remaining within biblically attested
historia and keeping free of the uncertain terrain of fabulous adventures
in India.[295] (In the same spirit Lamprecht introduces a new dimension
into his text by repeatedly correlating events and places in the Alexander

story with those of biblical history, so that the unquestioned truth of the latter is extended to the former.)[296] In referring to Daniel's dream when mentioning Darius Lamprecht is alluding to the clerical conception of how dominion passed to the Greeks, so that it is this Christian view of world-history that informs his work, just as it dictates the position of his work in the Vorau manuscript, at the chronologically correct point of intersection between works dealing with Old Testament themes and those beginning with the life of Christ.[297]

If there is reason to think that Lamprecht composed no further than Darius' death because of his commitment to *historia* and doubts about *fabula*, this suggests that he was uncomfortably aware of the dangerous presence of the latter in his theme. This could account for the otherwise surprising formulation of his source-reference to Albéric (19: 'louc er, sô liuge ich', if he lied, so do I),[298] betraying reservations about the theme's secular and pagan nature and the propriety of translating for the first time in German literature, not from time-honoured Latin, but from another upstart vernacular.[299] It could also imply that not the whole Alexander story could be authenticated by the bible: certainly his reign and defeat of Darius could be, but not necessarily all the exploits attributed to him,[300] which were therefore best omitted. That such a differentiation was feasible at that time has been shown by Szklenar's analysis of three German historiographers of the twelfth century, who distinguish clearly between historical and fictitious elements in the Alexander tradition of their day (where Otto von Freising, like Lamprecht, opts for excluding the fictitious).[301] This was not the attitude of the author who, true to tradition, continued the story of Alexander in the Strassburg version beyond the death of Darius. By this continuation he converted a work that had culminated in a providential turning-point in history into an individual *vita* in which Alexander's deeds are not merely the fulfilment of God's plan but acquire more importance for themselves, and in which the depiction of the fabulous realm of India is not subject to the need to be factually or historically true.[302] It is only in these further reaches that the *loca fabulosa* are situated,[303] only here that the historical narrative of the Vorau text gives way to a narrative that is itself a *fabula*, devoted to the *wunder* that plot Alexander's journey to the ends of the earth.[304] By comparison with this it is less important, but still significant, that the Strassburg text also finds room for the fictional themes of love (Candace) and the flower-maidens known from French versions after Albéric,[305] and replaces the density of biblical place references in the Vorau text with a contrived spacelessness, as Alexander penetrates eastwards, that is reminiscent of the folktale.[306]

The authors of these vernacular versions of three themes from antiquity could learn from their schooling in classical and medieval commentaries and *accessus* about the fictional aspects of these themes.[307] They could occasionally go beyond this, especially with regard to the feature of love, but for the rest remained restricted to the course of the narratives they vernacularised. The medieval versions therefore illustrate what must be termed at the most incipient or episodic fictionality. Two works show no signs of this at all,[308] but even the others suffer marked restrictions. Benoît may convey meaning by linking one episode with another far removed, but his technique, however ambitious, is still based on isolated episodes. The French and German romances of Aeneas go well beyond Virgil in developing the figure of Lavinia and the love-theme connected with her, but still conform to Virgil's plot in its essentials. Fictional features in the Alexander theme concern separate episodes or individual wonders, however fabulous. By contrast, the *matière de Bretagne* provided opportunities for creative innovations on a far greater scale.

MATIÈRE DE BRETAGNE

As with the *matière de Rome*, our task in this section will be to see how fiction, more far-reaching in this case, arose from contact with history (or what was held to be history). A modern scholar has cautiously concluded that there 'may have been a supreme British commander of genius in the late fifth century who bore the Roman-derived name of Arthur', and although no historian would accept the truth of medieval sources about him, they throw light on the interests of their authors, if not on the period on which they write.[309] They are therefore 'historical' at one remove.

Although Gildas mentions the battle of Mount Badon, later traditionally connected with Arthur, he does not refer to him by name as the leader of the Britons against the Saxons, and the same is true of Bede's history in the following century.[310] Only in the ninth century does the *Historia Brittonum* associate this battle, together with many others precisely localised so as to heighten the impression of historical accuracy, with a *dux bellorum* (war-leader) with the name of Arthur.[311] This named historical figure (now elevated to the rank of king) also recurs in the *Annales Cambriae*, again in association with the same battle, dated 516, but also with another (537) against Medraut, later known in Arthurian literature as Mordred.[312] This historiographical tradition, according to which Arthur was a successful warrior leader of the Britons, reaches the twelfth century with the eminent historian William of Malmesbury. He knows also of Arthur's nephew Gawain (Walwen) and is acquainted with fabulous tales circulating about Arthur amongst the Celts which he rejects in favour of the *veraces historiae* (true histories) which this historical figure rightly merits.[313] Another tradition, just as historical in medieval eyes, is represented by Celtic saints' *vitae* in which Arthur plays a minor part (*Vita Cadoci, Vita Iltuti* and *Vita Gildae*).[314] The occurrence of king Arthur in these legends imbues him with the credibility attaching to legends in the Middle Ages.[315] If the saints were held to be historical figures and their *vitae* to conform to events that had actually taken place, then the same aura of historicity attaches to Arthur, too.

It is on to this historiographical tradition that Geoffrey of Monmouth latches in his *Historia regum Britanniae*, even though what he has to say inflates Arthur to world-historical importance (in the extent of his European conquests, even taking up arms against Rome). True to the tradition to which, despite all his unheard-of novelties, he purports to conform, Geoffrey is at pains to present his work as a piece of historical writing. He seeks (like William of Malmesbury and Ordericus Vitalis) to join the Anglo-Saxon historical tradition; he shows parallels with the traditional learning of Wales; and, as befits one writing for an Anglo-Norman audience, he appears to have been stimulated by Norman historiography (Dudo of Saint-Quentin).[316] By his choice of title he ranks himself with the *Gesta regum Anglorum* of William of Malmesbury and the *Historia Anglorum* of Henry of Huntingdon, to both of whose works he claims to add something new, a history of the kings of the Britons.[317] This history he presents reign by reign, covering just short of a hundred kings of Britain from Brutus to Cadwallader, with Arthur as the focal point, continuously and in the correct chronological sequence (*ordo naturalis*).[318] As a historical writer Geoffrey also synchronises details in his British history with events in world history (antiquity, Old Testament, Christian period).[319]

The high-ranking members of Anglo-Norman society to whom Geoffrey dedicated his work and whose patronage he was possibly seeking[320] are also likely to have regarded his work as historically of interest. By the twelfth century the Normans had become aware of their imperfect knowledge of their new country's past.[321] Where others presented a link between present and Anglo-Saxon past, Geoffrey went much further, into the British past, but with the same historiographical aim of legitimising the Anglo-Norman present, not merely in regard to the Normans' position in Britain, but also as an act of image-boosting vis-à-vis the French royal house.[322] In serving the political interests of a ruling élite in need of historical legitimation Geoffrey may well have felt that a pseudo-history was called for. It may therefore be a fabrication or deception, but there is no sign that he intended his work to be seen through or that he invited its recipients to be complicit with him in any kind of fictional contract.[323] To be effective, propaganda has to be believed as true; no propagandist can afford the counter-productive luxury of winking openly at those whose interests he serves, implying that they know as well as he that he does not present the factual truth. In view of this we may take Geoffrey's work, as most of his contemporaries did,[324] as (fabricated or imperfect) history, but not, as is occasionally the case in scholarship, as fiction in the technical sense with which we are concerned.[325]

So novel a depiction of insular history as Geoffrey's, providing pre-Roman material hitherto unheard of and difficult to reconcile with what was attested of Anglo-Saxon history, invited both enthusiastic and sceptical responses.[326] His critics, however, were fewer than those who accepted his account as historically credible. In either case, Geoffrey was judged in the twelfth century by historiographical criteria: accepted as reliable despite doubts over details or found wanting by historical standards. The initial response was an effort to incorporate his *Historia* into comprehensive surveys, then from the middle of the twelfth century to reconcile it with prior authorities. From 1200 his work provided the standard framework for early British history.[327] In what follows I differentiate the reception of the *Historia* into various reactions to the truth of his claims.

Already before the appearance of Geoffrey's work William of
Malmesbury had expressed doubts about the historicity not of Arthur
himself, but of what was reported of him.[328] He distinguishes a historical nucleus (the figure of Arthur and the battles in which he was
victorious, worthy of *veraces historiae*) from untrustworthy accretions
(*fallaces fabulae*, deceiving fables) that have attached themselves to him
in Celtic tradition (*Britonum nugae*, the trifles of the Britons).[329] This
remark establishes that popular lore had seized upon Arthurian material
before Geoffrey's *Historia*, but it clearly cannot be used as evidence that
his account was also regarded as untrustworthy.

Nor is this the case with a wide range of twelfth-century authors,
mostly historians themselves, who for various reasons accept the historicity of Geoffrey's work, at least in its main outlines.[330] Henry of
Huntingdon, far from rejecting Geoffrey's *Historia* out of hand as worth-
less, appends his *Epistola* to Warinus Brito (on his discovery of the
Historia at Bec and with excerpts from it) to his own *Historia* and finds
it worthwhile to correct details in Geoffrey's work in the light of his own
work and other historical sources.[331] Robert of Torigni, another early witness to the reception of Geoffrey, says in his continuation of Sigebert of
Gembloux's chronicle that the *Historia* is one of the three histories he
will use to supplement Sigebert's account.[332] Ordericus Vitalis quotes
from the prophecies of Merlin in his own *Historia Ecclesiastica* because
'they can be seen to coincide with events of our own times'.[333] Similarly,
Giraldus Cambrensis places Geoffrey's Merlin in the company of the
biblical prophets and makes much use of the *Historia* in his own work.[334]
For the first part of his *Gesta regum*, with its sketch of the British past
from Brutus onwards, Gervase of Canterbury relies on Geoffrey, to
whom he betrays what has even been termed a reverential attitude.[335]
Gervase shows no awareness of any conflict between what Geoffrey reports on the Britons and what he (Gervase) learns from other sources
about the Anglo-Saxons: both Geoffrey and William of Malmesbury
are for him reliable authorities for two aspects of insular history. In the
historical writings of Ralph of Diceto there is no trace of any mistrust of
Geoffrey's factual reliability: recent events in his *Ymagines historiarum*
are seen as the fulfilment of Merlin's prophecies, and Ralph makes an
abstract of Geoffrey's *Historia*, very much as had Henry of Huntingdon
in his *Epistola*.[336] Roger of Wendover takes the step of integrating

Geoffrey's conception of history into universal history, correlating the *Historia* with other sources on other strands of history.[337] In doing this he paves the way for Matthew Paris, who in his *Flores historiarum* inserts a narrative, dependent on Geoffrey, on British history from the fall of Troy to the wanderings of Brutus and his building of Troja Nova, the capital of Britain, into what is otherwise biblical history, alternating between Jewish and British history.[338] An authority is thereby conferred on Geoffrey's *Historia* which parallels that of the bible.

The conclusion from this compressed survey of the twelfth-century reception of Geoffrey's work by Latin, largely historiographical scholarship should be clear. However inventive, even fraudulent, modern scholarship may know the *Historia* to be, for his contemporaries in Anglo-Norman society as well as in Latinate historical scholarship his version of the Britons' past was regarded as credible, providing a framework within which the present could be understood.[339] It was so successful in meeting this need for historical orientation that it soon came to lie at the heart of vernacular and even Latin textual culture in England.[340] As a result, the figure of Arthur, as presented by Geoffrey, was held to be historically real and, despite the occasional combat with giants, no figment of the imagination.[341] So undoubted was his reality in the past that henceforth English rulers could legitimise their status and political actions by appealing to him as a precedent, above all in the Plantagenets' claims to rule over Wales and Scotland.[342]

Even one exception to the readiness to accept Arthur's historicity is more apparent than real. This concerns the frequently expressed doubts about the fable of Arthur's presumed death, his disappearance and possible return as a future liberator of his people. Although, before Geoffrey, William of Malmesbury's criticism of the fables (*fallaces fabulae*) surrounding the historical Arthur is couched in general terms, he must also have had this particular belief of the Britons in mind, for he later refers in similar terms to the belief in Arthur's return.[343] Later allusions are more specific, however. Hermann of Tournai reports from the continent that Frenchmen and Bretons quarrel over this particular point,[344] whilst Joseph of Exeter is more scathing in his rejection of such folly ('Sic Britonum ridenda fides et credulus error', this is the laughable belief and credulous error of the Britons),[345] as is Giraldus Cambrensis in his dismissal of these *fabulae* ('maiori etiam fatuitate et infelicitate decepti', deceived by folly and ill fortune).[346] References to the primitive superstition of the Britons on this score are also to be found in Gervase of Tilbury and especially in William of Newburgh.[347] They also find their way into vernacular literature, first in Wace, but then in Chrétien's *Yvain* and Hartmann's *Iwein* (even though these latter rationalise the earlier superstition into a belief that it is Arthur's renown that is immortal).[348] Common to all these doubts about this particular Arthurian detail is the fact that the criticism is directed at the Britons or Bretons (they are explicitly mentioned in every case), not at Geoffrey's *Historia*, since he had not committed himself on this point, implying rather that Arthur had in fact died.[349] This range of sceptical evidence therefore throws no adverse light on Geoffrey's historical reliability in the eyes of his contemporaries.

Elsewhere doubts about the truth of what is reported on Arthur are voiced, but with no mention of Geoffrey. Aelred of Rievaulx refers to made-up fables circulating about Arthur ('in fabulis, quae vulgo de nescio quo finguntur Arcturo', fables that are everywhere made up about a certain Arthur), but his addition of *vulgo* suggests popular tales (similar to the Britons' tradition of Arthur's return), not learned Latin historiography.[350] The same is true of Peter of Blois when he alludes reproachfully to the fictive stories (*fabulosa quaedam*) recited (*recitantur*) by minstrels (*histriones*) about Arthur, Gawein and Tristan.[351] Not merely the mention of Tristan, but the background of what is presumably vernacular recital at court[352] takes us beyond the context of Geoffrey's *Historia*.

In other cases authors may express doubts about certain aspects of the *Historia*, whilst still making use elsewhere of the work as a whole, so that we approach the position exemplified by William of Malmesbury before Geoffrey: rejection of isolated points need not impair the historicity of Geoffrey's wider concept. Robert of Torigni admittedly goes much further in hesitating to intercalate the chronological framework of the *Historia* into his own work, but nonetheless his wish to reconcile Geoffrey with traditional chronology implies that he regarded the *Historia* as historical writing (which is why he included Henry of Huntingdon's epistolary summary without demur).[353] Although Giraldus Cambrensis, as we have seen, made full use of Geoffrey's work as a serious source, this did not stop him from criticising it, in terms that undo the traditional rhetorical categorisation, as a 'fabulous history' ('sicut fabulosa Galfridi Arthuri mentitur historia').[354] This barb (perhaps aimed by one court cleric at another) comes, however, after a lengthy passage in which Giraldus relied closely on Geoffrey, even copying him literally, with no hint of criticism.[355] Another remark by Giraldus ('Et Arturi nostri famosi, ne dicam fabulosi', our famous Arthur, or should I say fabulous) need not amount to questioning whether the figure of Arthur was historically true, since *fabulosus* meant not only 'unreal, therefore unhistorical', but also 'known to us in fables'.[356] In this sense Giraldus could have maintained, like William of Malmesbury, that Arthur was renowned as a historical figure, but also celebrated in story. The untruth of the latter need not affect the truth of the former.

In one case only in the twelfth century are the doubts directed specifically and without reserve at Geoffrey's *Historia*. William of Newburgh criticised not merely the superstition of the Britons about Arthur's return (on which Geoffrey could not be faulted), but also Geoffrey's work at large in no uncertain terms as *fabula* and *figmenta*, and the author as a *fabulator*.[357] This does not mean, however, that William as a historian is accusing Geoffrey of writing fiction (in the technical sense of the word), since he is judging him by the yardstick of historiography. Seen in this light, Geoffrey is faulted for including events that are nowhere attested in historical sources, for his offences against established chronology, for dishonouring the name of history by presenting British fables in the Latin tongue.[358] In summing up his criticism (Geoffrey 'contra fidem historicae veritatis deliravit', drivelled against the trustworthiness of historical truth) William as a lone voice in his day is a witness against his will to the success of Geoffrey's (pseudo-) historical presentation of Arthur.[359]

This leaves the gap between the *Historia* and the fictional Arthurian romances that arose in its train still wide open. We shall see that the adventures of the Round Table were later found a home in a period of twelve years' peace in Arthur's campaigns, but this interval was not filled by Geoffrey himself with a depiction of these adventures.[360] He therefore provided, even if unintentionally, the opportunity for later fiction, but not the fictional exploits themselves. Geoffrey, it is true, fabricates a source (the 'Britannici sermonis librum uetustissimum', most ancient book in the British tongue) to account for his inventions, but that was common practice in the Middle Ages, including historiography.[361]

Such fabrications, amounting to factual untruth, can as little be equated with fiction as can lying with irony. Both fiction and irony have to be intentionally made recognisable as such to their recipients, they need to be equipped with signals to this effect.[362] At the conclusion of his *Historia* Geoffrey aligns himself with other historians, even in a spirit of competition.[363] It is on this ground that he sought to be received (and believed), even if it was on this ground that William of Newburgh attacked and rejected him. Others did not.

This is true also of the two authors who transpose Geoffrey's work into the vernacular, for both Gaimar and Wace regard their own work as historical writing. We know of two histories by Gaimar: the *Estoire des Engleis*, based largely on the *Anglo-Saxon Chronicle*, and the *Estoire des Bretuns*.[364] Although the latter has not survived (it was possibly eclipsed by Wace's version), Gaimar refers to it in an epilogue to the former in terms that agree so closely with Geoffrey of Monmouth that his *Historia* is almost certainly the work translated by Gaimar.[365] With these works he presents the earliest examples of historiography in French, tuned to the needs of second-generation Normans with historical awareness and a wish to integrate themselves historically into their new territory.[366] The features of Gaimar's historical writing that are true of his extant work are likely to apply also to his rendering of Geoffrey's *Historia*. He refers to his writing with the historiographical terms *estoire* and *geste*; he gives the dates at which many of the events took place; and, true to an innovation in twelfth-century historical writing, he is at pains to comment on the sources (in different languages and even in variant versions) he has studied and to invest his work with the authority of verifiable *auctores*.[367] He presents himself as a scholar and his vernacular history as a work of learning, not merely meant for entertainment. With such credentials he can claim at the end of his extant work what must also apply to his rendering of Geoffrey, namely that his work presents historical truth (Appendix, v. 15, p. 207: 'Ne vilainie ne mençonge;/N'est pas cest livre ne fable ne sunge,/Ainz est de veire estoire estrait', this book is neither villainy nor lie, neither a fable nor a dream, but is drawn from true history). He thereby forestalls the kind of objection raised by William of Malmesbury, but if he claims a place for himself amongst professional historians[368] he also criticises another colleague, David, for omitting the courtly aspects (love, hunting, ceremony) of Henry I's life from his account.[369] Such features are important for Gaimar's historical writing: he regards them as facts to be recorded, not just as 'fanciful romance elements, unbefitting a work of history'.[370]

For Wace's *Roman de Brut*, too, the principal source was Geoffrey's *Historia*.[371] It is presented as a translation of what was considered a historical text, which justifies Wace in claiming the truth of his version (7: 'Maistre Wace l'ad translaté / Ki en conte la verité', Master Wace has translated it, who recounts the truth about it). True to his source and to historiographical practice, Wace proposes a chronological sequence of historical events (5: *en ordre*), recounting successive rulers of England in the *ordo naturalis* (1 ff.), but also, like Geoffrey again, correlating the events in his narrative with historical ones in biblical and classical history.[372] In another work of his (the *Roman de Rou*, a history of the Normans) Wace distances himself from the accounts of *ioculatores* (1355: 'Jeo ni di mie fable ne ieo ne voil fabler', what I say is no fable and I have no wish to tell a fable) in claiming the truth for himself (1371–2). He is anxious to maintain the same for his *Roman de Brut* by sometimes voicing criticism of his sources over details, particularly over Arthur's final disappearance and the tales that cluster around him,[373] so that, like William of Malmesbury, he distinguishes between the historical figure and the *fabulae* attaching to him.[374] It was presumably as a historian that Wace was commissioned to write both his works by Henry II, in such a way that past glory, especially in the figure of Arthur, was seen to be reflected in the Anglo-Norman present.[375] This is particularly relevant to the description of courtly splendour in which Wace largely goes beyond what is found in Geoffrey's text.[376] In locating these descriptions mainly in the twelve-year period of Arthurian peace Wace demonstrates their topicality, for the cultural hegemony of Henry II's court (in literature as well as historiography) was largely made possible, as for Arthur, by a period of peace at the beginning of the king's reign when Wace was writing.[377] As with Gaimar (but more pronouncedly), Wace's courtly embellishments are no mere fanciful elements simply added to history, they serve as historical links between past and present. This amounts to an unmistakable change of emphasis by comparison with Geoffrey but, as with the *matière de Rome*, still within the unchanged framework of historical events.[378] These details concern descriptions, they do not constitute a fictional re-fashioning of the course of the narrative.

Covering French narrative literature of the twelfth century in a broad sweep, Wolfzettel argues that these narratives arose under the auspices of history.[379] He talks of the transition from the chronicle to the utopian romance, of the emancipation of the romance from history.[380] This emergence of fictional possibilities from history, restricted in scope in the case of classical themes fixed in their outlines since antiquity, is more marked in the *matière de Bretagne*, characterised by a process of dehistoricisation in its presentation of a folktale world, divorced from real time and space and removed from history.[381] This process we must now illustrate from a few early examples.

To start with Wace again is not so anomalous as it might seem in the light of what has just been said about him. As a historian, Wace does not indulge in fiction himself, but is aware of it in connection with Arthur, both in theoretical terms (as in our definition of fictionality)[382] and in his placing of its genesis within his historical narrative. He locates the stories about Arthur, dismissed by him as fables, neither true nor untrue, in the twelve-year period of peace in the midst of campaigning that he found in Geoffrey's *Historia*, unexploited because an eventless period was of no historiographical interest.[383] This is re-emphasised by Wace who, by having Gauvain speak up against Cador in favour of the delights of peace, confers a positive role on this interval.[384] For Gauvain it is a period in which love encourages knights to undertake individual adventures on behalf of their ladies[385] (as distinct from the massed campaigns in Arthur's wars of conquest) and in which Arthur's court is the focus of court entertainments (10749: 'A gas, a deduit e a fables, / E a altres geus deportables', joking, entertainment, fables and other amusing pastimes).[386] Both these adventures and the tales told about them are regarded as non-historical by Wace, who therefore does not include them in his own account, but makes it clear that he is alluding to other works with which he can assume his audience to be acquainted.[387] Wace therefore locates what he regards as Arthurian fiction in this pause in Geoffrey's *Historia*; he recognises the existence of fiction without practising it himself, but instead provides a historiographical seedbed from which Arthurian fiction sprang. This is the achievement of Chrétien, who follows Wace in placing the action of his first romance chronologically in the historiographically empty period of Arthurian peace.[388]

However much Wace may be judged as the intermediary between Geoffrey's history and Arthurian fiction, the decisive step was taken only by Chrétien. Negatively, in the sense that the 'historical' conquests of Arthur throughout Europe, vastly more important than any interval of peace in Geoffrey's and Wace's accounts, fade into the background in Chrétien's romances in favour of a fictionalised depiction focused on the years of peace that had earlier been an interlude to be passed over.[389] Positively, however, in that the *conteürs* (storytellers) rejected by Wace (9795 ff.) may also be criticised by Chrétien (*Erec* 20ff.), who however makes ready use of their narrative material. Although not for reasons of historiographical completeness, Chrétien thus fills the gap left by Wace.[390] He sees in it an opportunity to create a fictional realm where, 'freed from the constraints of history, he could address the concerns that occupied him and his audience'.[391] He realizes this opportunity by ignoring the historical framework of Wace's account and by filling a gap in it with the material of *fabula* rejected by the historian.

Chrétien points to the fictionality of his narratives in different ways.[392] In his *Erec*, in a manner befitting the first Arthurian romance of all, he makes no secret of the tale's divorce from history and thereby from historical truth. From the beginning of Chrétien's authorship of romances the Arthurian world is cut off from the historical context in which Geoffrey and Wace had placed it, even from any sense of past time. Erec may be the son of Lac (just as later Yvain is the son of Urien), but we learn nothing of his past, he lives for us in the eternal present of the Round Table.[393] The Arthurian narrative therefore opens not in chronological, but in cyclical, liturgical time (27: 'Un jor de Pasque, au tans novel, / A Caradigan, son chastel, / Ot li rois Artus cort tenue' One Easter day, in springtime, king Arthur held court at his castle of Cardigan), far from the sphere of Arthur's campaigning and therefore presumably in an interval of peace of no historiographical interest for Geoffrey.[394] Chrétien is fully aware, even proudly so, that he is emancipating his story from history. He concludes his prologue by claiming that the story (*estoire*) he is about to begin will be preserved in memory (*memoire*) as long as Christianity lasts (23 ff.). With this boast the author inverts the function of two established historiographical concepts, relegating the truth of the past to a secondary status.[395] Instead of the standard claim to preserve the memory of the past Chrétien maintains that the future will preserve the memory of his work, the product of his own artistry and deriving no authority from past history or written transmission.[396] This abandonment of history in favour of fictional creation is also brought out semantically in the prologue, for Chrétien uses *estoire* not to mean 'history' or the source that transmits historical truth, but to refer to his own 'story'.[397]

In *Cligés* Chrétien changes tack. Instead of an indeterminate Arthurian geography with often fantastic places he locates his action within an authentic topography, with English place-names like Southampton and Windsor reminiscent of the Angevin lands ruled over by Henry II, but also extending to Constantinople and Saxony.[398] Similarly, as opposed to the cyclical sense in *Erec*, time is reckoned in *Cligés* by months, weeks and days.[399] Chrétien seems to fall back further from the innovative position of his first romance by now adducing a written source as unimpeachable chronicle-like authority for the truth of his account (18 ff.) whereas in the prologue to *Erec* he had dispensed with any reliance on a written source or claim for factual veracity.[400] However, what undermines the appearance of geographical and historical reality in *Cligés* is the sovereign way in which antiquity, the Arthurian world, and the topical present are freely jumbled together by an artist ringing the changes on various subject matters.[401] Moreover, the plot at vital turning-points hinges on obviously fabulous motivation such as the *morte vivante*, the use of magical potions and the improbable, but convenient death of an unwanted husband.[402] In suggesting that he was dependent on a written model Chrétien appears to be abandoning authorial control over his plot, but this historical ploy is rather to be seen as a smokescreen. The actual model used in the construction of the plot is the story of Tristan, not followed slavishly, but re-cast for the individual purpose of parody.[403] Chrétien's intertextual references to Tristan, like Wolfram's to Hartmann, are fiction building on fiction, so that behind a supposedly historical model there lies a fictional one, treated with the freedom which an author of fiction can claim for himself.[404]

In *Yvain* Chrétien makes use of parody for a different purpose: not to criticise another literary theme behind a smokescreen of historical veracity, but more challengingly to polemicise, on behalf of fictional writing, against the traditional view that the historian's truth-claim rested on his status as an eyewitness.[405] Once more he achieves his goal by intertextual means, this time with reference to the *Roman de Rou* of Wace, the vernacular historian from whom an author developing Arthurian fiction would most obviously have to distance himself. Wace had reported on the fables told by Bretons about a magic spring in the forest of Broceliande and had gone there to check on their veracity in person, as an eyewitness.[406] In criticising himself for foolishly believing that the fables might be true he in reality establishes his claim as a reliable historian, no mere dupe of fables.[407] This is taken up by Chrétien in *Yvain* when Calogrenant reports on his visit to a magic well in Broceliande, which he has seen for himself, as well as the marvels that this time did occur (disastrously for him), so that his account, however fabulous, should be accepted as (historical) truth.[408] The terms in which Calogrenant maintains his eyewitness veracity:

> Car ne vuel pas parler de songe,
> Ne de fable ne de mançonge,
> Don maint autre vos ont servi,
> Ainz vos dirai ce, que je vi
> (171 ff.)
>
> (for I shall not speak of a dream, a fable or a lie, which many others have offered you, but instead I shall speak of what I saw)

are terms with which historians conventionally established their reliability.[409] Behind him, of course, stands Chrétien, whose purpose (as a writer of fiction, not history) it is to question the eyewitness truth-claims of historiography. By having Calogrenant (in a work of fiction) contradict Wace's account of the non-marvellous nature of Broceliande Chrétien is doing nothing less than appropriating the truth-claims made of history for his own fable. In playing havoc in this episode with the conventional distinction between *historia* and *fabula* he is making polemical use of intertextuality to demonstrate what he had condensed into one word in the prologue to *Erec* by employing *estoire* of his own fiction.[410]

For a last French example I turn to one of the Breton *lais* of Marie de France, to *Lanval*, of particular interest because the action is placed in an Arthurian setting.[411] In this tale Marie agrees with Wace in presenting Arthur and his Round Table as historical entities, but also with Chrétien's *Cligés* in plotting a narrative transition from *historia* to *fabula*. The action of *Lanval* begins not with the indefiniteness of a folktale ('Once upon a time'), but carefully synchronised with the beginning of Arthur's reign, who is at Kardoel (Carlisle) because the Scots and Picts are ravaging the land of Logres (5 ff.). This chronological placing in the first year of Arthur's kingship agrees with the historical account of his wars, as given by Geoffrey and Wace.[412] The precise dating of the opening of the narrative, as part of Arthur's campaigns and not within any interval of peace, means that Arthur's sojourn at Kardoel (5–6), even if it falls conventionally at Whitsun (11–12), cannot be compared with the typical Arthurian opening in cyclical time at Easter (as in Chrétien's *Erec*).[413] Instead, the plausibility of Arthur's presence at Kardoel in order to deal with the threat from the North confers even more historical probability on the Arthurian setting.

It is from this setting, real in time and in place, that Lanval sets out on an adventure that takes him into a manifestly fictitious Other World. Like the other adventures in Marie's *lais* it is of Breton origin (as she repeatedly makes clear) and therefore as fabulous as those rejected time and again by twelfth-century historians. The folktale elements in Lanval's adventure are unmistakable: a fairy mistress who characteristically remains anonymous throughout (whilst figures in the Arthurian world are given names); an adventure that begins with typical temporal imprecision (41: 'Un jur', one day) and involves crossing a mysterious border into a different realm (45–6: the knight comes to a stream, his horse trembles violently).[414] Other fabulous motifs are the miraculous boon bestowed on him by the fairy mistress (135 ff.: an unending supply of gold and silver); her ability to appear before him without being seen or heard by others (169–70); and the unexplained condition she attaches to their love (143 ff.). The ending of the *lai* completes for good this transition to an unreal world: Lanval accompanies his mistress to her realm, never to return (641 ff.), but in terming it 'Avalon, as the Bretons tell us', Marie underlines finally its fabulous nature. In finishing mysteriously in this realm *Lanval* differs from the return to topical history which is found in Chrétien's *Erec* and *Cligés*. The transition from *historia* to *fabula* is irreversible.

Two examples, Hartmann's *Iwein* and Gottfried's *Tristan*, must suffice to illustrate a similar state of affairs in the German romance.[415] Hartmann was debarred from directly imitating the intertextual play with the *Roman de Rou* that Chrétien could afford in his Calogrenant

episode,[416] but nonetheless, independently of Chrétien, he makes clear
the distance separating his fiction from history in the following episode,
in Iwein's repeat performance of Kalogreant's adventure at the spring.
Hartmann's episode may be a different one, but he makes the same point
as Chrétien by setting his fiction pointedly against the truth-claim of
the historian *qua* eyewitness.[417] When Iwein meets Ascalon in combat
at the spring the narrator claims inability to describe the encounter in
any detail on the grounds that Iwein, the solitary survivor, was too well-
bred to have boasted of his victory (1039ff.), but also because no one
else had been present as a possible eyewitness informant (1032: 'sî wàren
dâ beide, / unde ouch nieman bî in mê / der mir der rede gestê', these two
were there, but no one else besides who could stand in for the account;
1035: 'sît ez nieman sach', since no one saw it; 1068: 'sô er mit niemen
enmöhte / erziugen dise geschiht / (wan dône was der liute niht)', he
could produce no one as witness for his story, since there were no people
there). Hartmann may well have had other reasons for not expatiating
on this encounter,[418] but by driving home so emphatically the point that
no eyewitness was present on whose evidence his account could be said
to be based he indicates his deliberate distance from Isidore of Seville's
definition of the historian ('Apud veteres nemo conscribebat historiam,
nisi is qui interfuisset, et ea quae conscribenda essent vidisset', Among
the ancients no one wrote history who had not been present and
witnessed what was to be written).[419] By turning his back on any possible
claim for historical veracity in this episode (could the doubt, thus raised,
not apply to other episodes as well?) Hartmann brings home to his
audience the fictional nature of his work.[420]

The force of Hartmann's technique is thus to play down any historical dimension and to make it subservient to his fiction,[421] but against
this Kellermann has argued unconvincingly for the historicity of the
Iwein narrative.[422] Her argument rests on two points: first, that the
narrative is provided with a historical foundation by the programmatic
distinction in the prologue between the world of king Arthur, set firmly
in the past, and the present;[423] secondly, that this foundation is soon
afterwards strengthened by the way in which Kalogreant describes his
adventure as having taken place ten years ago, ten years before Iwein's
repeat performance.[424] Doubts are permissible as to how far this difference between past and present represents historicity. On the first point,

we must make the distinction proposed already in the twelfth century by William of Malmesbury between recognition of the historical figure of Arthur and the stories and beliefs associated with him, not merely by the Britons, but also by the story-tellers with whom Wace would have no truck.[425] William of Malmesbury is rightly followed on this point by Haug when he points out in general terms that, although Arthur may count as a historical figure, what the historians report about him is absent from Arthurian romances around 1200, which instead are concerned with the adventures of his knights, not treated by the historians.[426] On the second point, it is doubtful how far the historicity of Arthur can be extended to Iwein, too (through the mediation of Kalogreant's story). Some of the Arthurian figures in Hartmann's romance may already occur in Geoffrey's *Historia* (e.g. Gawein, Ginover, Keie), but can we attribute the same degree of historicity to those who may be mentioned by Geoffrey only marginally (such as Iwein himself)[427] or not at all (Kalogreant)? Kellermann's argument at this stage is based on Kalogreant's claim to be recounting the historical truth of what befell him as an eyewitness (258: 'ichn wil iu keine lüge sagen./Ez geschach mir, dâ von ist ez wâr', I do not intend to tell you any lie. It happened to me and therefore it is true).[428] It is doubtful, however, whether we can take this historicising *attestatio rei visae* at face value (Kellermann elsewhere concedes that Hartmann may not have intended to be taken seriously).[429] First, because both Chrétien and Hartmann, as we have seen, parody the eyewitness basis of historical truth-claims in this work (Chrétien with regard to Calogrenant, Hartmann in the case of Iwein). Secondly, because although a work can be authenticated as *historia* by an author using external referentiality (as when Wace goes to the magic spring in Broceliande), the same is by no means true when a similar claims is made self-referentially by a (fictitious) character within that work (as with Kalogreant). The presence of fictionality in *Iwein*, admitted by Kellermann in principle,[430] goes further in undermining its apparent historicity than she is prepared to concede.[431]

With regard to our second German example it was claimed long ago that Gottfried in his *Tristan* wished to be regarded as a *historiographus*, not as a *poeta*, and this view has found widespread assent.[432] In accordance with this the German author, basing himself on the version of Thomas as the only reliable one, describes his predecessor in terms of historical source-scholarship (152: 'und an britûnschen buochen las/aller der lanthêrren leben', and read in British books the lives of all the princes). In this wording Gottfried probably depends directly on Thomas, applying to him the same historical reliability that Thomas had attributed to Breri (Douce 849: 'Ky solt les gestes e les cuntes/De tuz les reis, de tuz les cuntes' , who knew the deeds and the accounts of all the kings and counts).[433] In arguing for the historical authenticity of Thomas, whose version he follows rather than any other (146ff.), Gottfried is claiming a similar virtue for his own story. By implying historical sources for the Tristan story Gottfried suggests that its figures existed in historical reality and that the story was 'founded on, but not reducible, to history'.[434] In opening his prologue with the need for re-membrance (1 ff.) Gottfried also employs a *topos* of historical writing (cf. the argument for remembering and against forgetting advanced by Benoît de Sainte-Maure, *Roman de Troie* 1 ff.), and suggests thereby a historical dimension for his work.[435] This dimension can also be insinu-ated by verbal details that must have struck a German audience with all the more force for being new coinages by Gottfried. He is the first to use the key term *istôrje* (story, history) in German, four times with reference to his source (if not to his own work, as Chrétien had done in *Erec*).[436] Of these four examples three concern events that are presented as be-longing to the historical background of the Tristan story, as conceived by Gottfried, and two of these in turn are connected with the figure of Gurmun whom we have already considered as a 'historical' character.[437] In addition, Gottfried is the first to use the word *geste* in German (only once), likewise a term with historical implications.[438] The force of these historical terms, used in isolation, scattered throughout the work and referring only to the background of the main story, is to suggest that this story, dealing with the two lovers, is embedded in history.[439] Gottfried can even adopt the role of the historian concerned with factual truth and scornful of *fabulae* (to which he refers by another technical loanword, *fabelen*) when he refuses to narrate anything of Tristan's knightly deeds in banishment (18459ff.).[440] If such *fabulae*, according to the stereotyped definition, were neither true nor probable, the same objection would have to be made against cases of strikingly implausible motivation in the traditional story for Tristan's journey to Ireland (the swallow with the golden hair and the journey by miraculous chance to Ireland).[441]

Gottfried accordingly re-motivates, but not without a historical-critical attack on the fabulous nature of these other versions, represented by Eilhart von Oberge, even if he is not named (8605 ff.).

To regard Gottfried as a *historiographus*, however, is only part of the picture, for we have to ask what function he hoped this role would play. Bertau has been followed by others when he talks of Gottfried's 'imaginary historicity', of an appearance of being historical-critical which is in fact a rhetorical move to suggest that *res fictae* are in fact *res gestae*.[442] We may ask of Gottfried's romance what, following William of Malmesbury, we have already asked of the Arthurian romance: whether the insertion of figures regarded as historical in a work means that the narrative of that work is also historical.[443] The mention of 'historical' figures like Gurmun and Corineus at isolated points may suggest that the whole narrative is likewise historical, but certainly cannot establish it. Similarly, the implication that Tristan and Isold existed in historical reality (222: 'al eine und sîn si lange tôt', even if they have long been dead) does not mean of itself that the story told about them is based on historical fact,[444] as little as when William of Malmesbury drew a line between the historicity of Arthur and the fabulous tales connected with him. Another question concerns Gottfried's relationship with his source, for if the historicity of the German version derived from the historical authenticity of Thomas then any deviation by Gottfried must raise insistent doubts. This is indeed what we find with the German author's radical changes not merely to the traditional story, but even to Thomas's version.[445] It is telling that some of Gottfried's historical source-references may well be meant ironically. Is the use of *geste* (8945: 'dâ was des trachen heimwist, / alsô man an der geste list', the dragon's lair was there, as one reads in the history) really meant to provide historical authentication for a dragon's lair, and therefore for the existence of a fabulous beast?[446] The same is true when 'diu wâre istôrje' (the true story) testifies not simply to Tristan's courage, but also to the presence of an equally fabulous giant (1519ff.), a reference that has been described as ironically authenticating what cannot be authenticated.[447] Gottfried's role as a critical historian rejecting implausible motivation can be seen for the pose that it is when we place it alongside other cases in his work of fabulous, improbable narration. If classical authors, already in antiquity, could be accused of composing *ficta* or *fabulosa* in introducing the gods into their accounts of human affairs,[448] the same must be said of Gottfried's employment of a mythological apparatus, including figures from antiquity such as 'diu gotinne Minne', the goddess of Love (4807), Apollo (4869) and Vulcan (4930), but also such others as fairies (4698), at home in the Avalon (15812) that was the object of scepticism already in the twelfth century, and the goddess who gave the magic dog Petitcreiu to Gilan (15810ff.).[449] By introducing what in his day could be recognised as fabulous features Gottfried reveals that his historical stance is not an end in itself, that he uses history without historiographic intentions.[450] For him the past is a point of departure for the narration of a love-story, not for the reconstruction of history.[451]

When dealing with Chrétien and Hartmann we saw that they shared a method for differentiating their fictional writing from historiography by referring expressly to the eyewitness truth-claim of the latter, only to undermine it in their own case. The same is true of Gottfried at one point where, at the close of his description of the love-grotto, he affirms the truth of what he has just said (17104: 'Diz weiz ich wol, wan ich was dâ', I know this indeed, for I was there),[452] a formulation with the same force of eyewitness testimony as Kalogreant's in *Iwein* (259: 'Ez geschach mir, dâ von ist ez wâr', it happened to me and therefore it is true). The passage in *Tristan* which this line opens has therefore been interpreted as an *attestatio rei visae*, conforming to Isidore's definition of the basis of historical writing.[453] That this is not the case, however, is brought out by the narrator's final comment that he has known the love-grotto since his eleventh year, even though he has never been to Cornwall (17140ff.). With that his truth-affirmation is transposed from the sphere of historical, factual eyewitness testimony to that of the personal experience of love,[454] meant figuratively and therefore divorced from time (history) and space (Cornwall). If that were not enough to call into question the historical function of the narrator's apparent eyewitness stance, we could apply here, too, what was true of Hartmann's Kalogreant. If in a written work of literature the narrator is a fictional entity, then Gottfried's *ich* (17104) is as fictional as Kalogreant. But only the witness standing outside a narrative can give historical testimony to its truth – its conformity to external reality – whilst this is impossible for anyone, be he Gottfried's narrator or Hartmann's Kalogreant, who is part of the fiction himself. With Gottfried, as with

Chrétien and Hartmann,[455] the historiographer's eyewitness gives way to a fictional figure.

GENESIS OF MEDIEVAL FICTIONALITY

With the rise of fiction in Greek literature the focus of discussion was its relationship to disciplines such as history and philosophy.[456] When Aristotle compares the universalising nature of fiction to the particularisations of history he grants higher value to the former on the grounds that it is more philosophical.[457] His position on this score has been summed up: 'Fiction mediates between history, whose concern is with the particular, and philosophy, which deals in disembodied universals.'[458] In the Middle Ages the situation was simpler in that, as this chapter has tried to show, fiction set itself apart from historical writing alone, without the kind of philosophical dimension opened up by Aristotle's disagreement with Plato. We may conclude this chapter by correlating history with fiction in yet another way, asking what factors may have accounted for the emergence of vernacular fictionality around 1200. Of the wide range of contributory factors I choose but two for discussion in what makes no claim to be a complete and systematic survey. The first is more formal in nature (what opportunities presented themselves for this innovation in the twelfth century?), and the second is historical (what conditions made this possible?).

With the formal question we shall be concerned with windows of opportunity, with gaps or 'Freiräume' in previous narratives that later provided scope for free invention. These are of three kinds: non-fiction (invention which is a fabrication, not meant to be seen through or called into question and therefore not fiction in the technical sense); incipient or episodic fiction (such as we saw with the *matière de Rome*); and fiction fully fledged (as with the *matière de Bretagne*, where the fiction was more far-reaching and was meant to be recognisable).

Lacunae that provide opportunities for non-fictional invention can occur in religious as well as non-religious tradition. An important religious example is apocryphal literature, if we regard this as a meeting-point for the needs of popular piety on the one hand, crying out for more information than is otherwise provided on the life of Christ, and the New Testament on the other hand, with gaps likewise crying out to be filled. This need accounts for the mass of apocryphal literature added to the bible in the form of gospels, epistles and autobiographies attributed to the apostles, to Joseph or to Mary.[459] A clear example of a time-gap waiting to be filled is illustrated by the Gospel of Nicodemus, reporting on Christ's descent into Hell and thus filling in the period between the crucifixion and the resurrection, or the Acts of Peter, details of which are carefully chosen to harmonise with biblical accounts so as to produce the appearance of unquestioned historicity[460] (in a manner reminiscent of Wolfram's intertextual harmonisation with Hartmann). Doubts could certainly arise about the truth of such accounts (for they are, after all, *apocryphal* accounts, not accepted as canonical).[461] Nonetheless, the undecided statement in the prologue to the Gospel of Pseudo-Matthew ('The truth of this statement I leave to the author of the preface and the faith of the writer; for myself, while pronouncing it doubtful, I do not affirm that it is clearly false'), however similar to the more throw-away remarks by romance authors, cannot be regarded as a defence of fiction, since 'it concerns not avowed fiction but a historical narrative', uncertain but possibly true.[462]

Similar inventiveness, coupled with doubts about what it produced, can be observed with medieval legends. Again the starting-point is the need to fill a gap with detailed information, as with the development of the Simon Magus legend from the fact that, although the Acts of the Apostles may mention him (8.9ff.), they are silent about his subsequent history, the course of which can then be supplied by apocryphal tradition.[463] How freely such tradition could dispose of historical facts is evident in the way in which miracles performed by one saint can be attributed to another, filling in gaps in his *Vita*, on the grounds that the saints, joined to one another 'per mysterium unius corporis' (by the mystery of one body), share all things in common.[464] If this practice attracted occasional criticism in the Middle Ages, it was directed not at any employment of fiction, but at faulty historiography. Benedict of Chiusi, for example, criticises the inventive attempt of Adémar of Chabanne to promote St Martial, the first bishop of Limoges, to apostolic rank by supplementing the account of the gospels to the effect that Martial is presented as one of Christ's circle of disciples. For Benedict such inventiveness was not to be classified as fiction, since it was meant to be accepted as factually true (so much so that in 1029 St Martial was even granted the title of apostle).[465] Instead, Benedict sees this filling-in of the biblical account as a fabrication (brought into circulation like a *falsa moneta*), to be rejected in the name of what he regarded as historically true.[466]

For a secular example of an inventive, but non-fictional closing of a *lacuna* we come back again to Geoffrey of Monmouth. The reason advanced by Henry of Huntingdon for beginning his *Historia Anglorum* with Julius Caesar's conquest, omitting all before because he lacked any oral or written evidence, is taken up by Geoffrey in the prologue to his *Historia*: 'nichil de regibus qui ante incarnationem Christi inhabitauerant, nichil etiam de Arturo ceterisque compluribus qui post incarnationem successerunt repperissem' (I could not find anything about the kings who lived here before the incarnation of Christ, or indeed about Arthur and all those who followed after the incarnation).[467] Both historians are of course correct, for up to then Anglo-Saxon history existed in a vacuum because of the lack of information about the Britons,[468] but Geoffrey found it extraordinary that no history of their kings before and after the Roman occupation had ever been written. Inventively he filled out these vast *lacunae* in British history,[469] going far beyond what his predecessors (Gildas, Bede, the *Historia Brittonum*) had said about Brutus, the Roman period and the Anglo-Saxon invasion, but with nothing in between. Despite the criticism of William of Newburgh,[470] it can be said that he successfully incorporated his new material into these gaps in British history, harmonising it with existing accounts wherever necessary.[471] As with religious apocryphal literature, however, none of this inventiveness means that Geoffrey's *Historia* was written as fiction.[472] Just as Benedict of Chiusi criticised Adémar on historical grounds, so did William of Newburgh apply the historian's criteria to Geoffrey's work and found it wanting. Adémar's apocryphal work is as much a fabrication, and as little a fiction, as Geoffrey's pseudo-history, but both authors inventively supplement earlier material, filling in gaps to suit their own purpose.

We pass now to the windows of opportunity for developing episodic fiction presented by medieval adaptations of subjects from classical antiquity,[473] with the first two of which the innovation is closely connected with the growing importance of the literary theme of love in the twelfth century. In the *Roman de Troie* Benoît makes use of small-scale fictionality in developing the love-affairs of, above all, Medea and Jason on the one hand and Briseida and Troilus on the other. In his source, Dares, the journey of Jason to Colchis is narrated briefly without even a mention of Medea, but the French author, interested in the theme of love,[474] saw an opportunity for improving on this reticence, above all by incorporating what was treated as a love-encounter by Ovid in the *Heroides* and *Metamorphoses*.[475] By grafting on to his source something absent from Dares, but taken from another (professedly fictional) author, Benoît repeats what Virgil had done in his *Aeneid*, supplementing historical facts about Aeneas and Dido by re-fashioning them in the light of what Apollonius had written, a treatment recognised as fictional already by Macrobius.[476] Nor does Benoît's treatment of Briseida and Troilus have any precedent in the 'history' of Dares; instead, he again derives material from various sources, adapting it to his own needs.[477] Not only that: in this case Benoît fashions his composition with long-term effects in mind, linking this affair chiastically with the affair of Paris and Helen.[478] (The Greek Helen leaves her homeland, betraying her husband for a Trojan lover, whilst contrastingly the Trojan Briseida leaves Troy, betraying her lover for a Greek one, Diomedes, who turns out to be the husband of another woman.) In freely composing this episode as a parallel and a contrast to the earlier one Benoît utilises the advantage of fiction to convey meaning, even though his re-shaping is confined to no more than two episodes, however widely separated. But to realise this advantage he had to recognise a possible *lacuna* in his source that could be filled in this way.

The author of the *Roman d'Enéas* proceeds in a similar manner. Although his source did contain a fully worked-out love-affair, its disadvantage for a twelfth-century author preoccupied with the double theme of *amor* (love) and *militia* (knighthood) was that Virgil had 'misplaced' it, treating the affair between Aeneas and Dido at a point which brought the former no knightly renown, whilst his winning of Lavinia, although by deeds of arms, lacked the element of love.[479] If Virgil could not serve the French author as a model in this respect, he at least lent himself to expansion and provided an opportunity, again to be filled by meeting this deficiency from Ovid.[480] Where Virgil's Lavinia was a mere shadow, the French Lavine has been termed the first real Ovidian heroine in romance, conversing and soliloquising on the subject of love and her emotions, but above all one whose love must be earned by chivalric deeds.[481] What from the point of view of the twelfth century was a deficiency in Virgil's motivation is, however, only one of the gaps that could be filled with new, fictionally contrived material, for the French author also seizes upon other intervals in the narrative action. These intervals may be relatively short, but they lend themselves to adaptation to the theme of love, and the way in which this is done is tellingly reminiscent of Wace in the *Roman de Brut*. The structure of the second part of the French work articulates the long series of battles on Italian soil by dividing it into three parts, separated by truces in which the focus switches to more individual scenes devoted to Ovidian eroticism.[482] Within the overall framework of *militia* gaps are therefore carved out in which *amor* may come into its own. Thus, Lavine's long interior monologue on her growing affection for Eneas is placed within a truce of eight days, just as their desire for one another comes more to the fore in the period of truce between Camille's burial and the duel between Eneas and Turnus.[483] By creating these gaps in the fighting the author has hollowed out narrative space in which to deal with his new theme. In doing this he reminds us of how Wace (by contrast with Geoffrey of Monmouth) described a similar, but longer period of peace in Arthur's campaigning by having Gauvain advocate the pleasures of peace, including love and knightly adventures undertaken in its name (*Roman de Brut* 10771–2).[484] For both authors a gap provided by a period of peace is the place not merely for inserting the theme of love, but also for locating the fictional elaboration of love and knighthood, rejected as unhistorical by Wace but utilised in the *Enéas*.

Of the Alexander romance no more need be said in the present connection than that, dealing with the wonders of the East and of India in particular in a series of discrete episodes, it places these wonders, as was common practice in antiquity, on the horizon of the known world.[485] Since our knowledge of the world is inevitably incomplete and patchy, the gaps in it are filled with the unknown in the shape of these wonders. To the extent that Alexander's exploits could be said to incorporate episodic fiction,[486] this is made possible not so much by *lacunae* in any pre-existing narrative as by gaps in twelfth-century knowledge of the furthest reaches of the inhabited world.

The most important window of opportunity open to the authors of fully fictional works such as the Arthurian romances was provided by two gaps in the historical narrative of Geoffrey and Wace. Two periods of peace in Arthur's campaigning, one of twelve years and the other of nine, are mentioned briefly by Geoffrey,[487] but seen by Wace as the focus for the courtesy which underlies the king's renown, for the Round Table and, in Gauvain's praise of peace in contradiction to Cador, for love and knightly adventure.[488] In distancing himself in this way from Geoffrey's account, but also by refraining from narrating these adventures because of their transparently fabulous nature, Wace provided, however inadvertently, an opening in which romance fiction could establish itself.[489] What with Geoffrey and still with Wace was a gap in historical time was free to be appropriated for imaginative time by Chrétien and others when they situated their romance fictions in periods left vacant by historiography.[490] Freed from any obligation towards historical veracity, they could develop the themes of love and knighthood that concerned their audience, but had been shunned by Wace.[491]

Considering Geoffrey, Wace and Chrétien in this light reveals a progressive move away from *historia* and towards *fabula*. With Geoffrey we have a period of peace in the middle of a series of historical campaigns, but this period is not treated in any detail (apart from the occasional mention of Arthur's court). With the likewise historical work of Wace this period of peace is also an interval within Arthur's wars of conquest, but with significantly more detail (the Round Table, court life in fuller treatment, the conjunction of love and chivalry, the fables that deal with this period, even if they are rejected as untruthful). Finally, with Chrétien we find ourselves exclusively within the period of peace, with no treatment of the framing campaigns and no picture of Arthur as a *dux bellorum*. What is left in Chrétien's romances corresponds to the gap in Geoffrey's account, but now filled with the adventures that Geoffrey had not mentioned and Wace had omitted to recount. With Chrétien we have moved from the realm of history to that of fictional adventures.

Chrétien was not the only one to seize this opportunity of developing fiction from a space left empty by a predecessor. Thomas also exploited a gap in Geoffrey's *Historia*, such as he found in Wace's version, as a means of finding a place in time for his *Tristran*, more specifically for the reign of king Marc.[492] The wish to elevate Marc to a rank comparable to that of Arthur raised the problem of dating, which Thomas solved by placing Marc in what Wace had depicted as a time of troubles between the reigns of Arthur and Chadwalein, during which the Saxons called to their aid the Gormond of Ireland of whom Thomas also made use as a 'historical' figure.[493] To the extent that Thomas's romance, like Gottfried's, may be regarded as a fiction pretending to be history[494] this means that his fiction, like Chrétien's, emerges from a *lacuna* in history which gave him a suitable opportunity.

Just as Chrétien made creative use of a narrative vacancy in Wace, so could other romance authors in their turn profit inventively from gaps which they found, or imagined, in Chrétien's Arthurian world, so that their fictions now proceed not from what was regarded as history but from other fictions. One beneficiary of this spinning-out of what was latent, but not realised in Chrétien's works is the figure of Gauvain, for a number of French authors after Chrétien make it clear that they regard it as their task (or opportunity) to make good his deficiency in not having dedicated a full romance to this figure.[495] In the thirteenth century this narrative gap is closed more than once, just as other characters, mentioned only in passing by Chrétien, can receive fuller treatment.[496] German literature shares in this fictional closing of gaps in earlier fiction, as when Heinrich von dem Türlin proposes to tell what has not been told before, namely the youth of king Arthur (*Diu Crône* 141 ff.).[497] At times, as we saw with Wolfram's intertextual references to Hartmann, the deficiency which has to be made good is not simply a gap in the narrative action (even though this may have been created by Wolfram's imagination), but also a shortcoming in this predecessor's view of contemporary knighthood at large.[498]

In his discussion of *dilatatio materiae* (expansion of material) Worstbrock interprets two passages in Hartmann's *Erec* as the conscious use of fiction to provide freedom of scope for an author, otherwise tied to the narrative of a given text, to develop his own narrative meaning.[499] For Worstbrock this technique is the expansion of a scene, episode or description already present in the source, whilst the windows of opportunity we have been considering amount to an expansion of the narrative action (by adding a scene or by elaborating the implications of a given scene) or even to the creation of a whole new work (especially in the post-classical romances of the thirteenth century). Within the restricted timespan with which we are concerned, however, both Worstbrock's *dilatatio* and our windows of opportunity are at home in a conception of literature that lays less emphasis on the invention of new material[500] than on changing details while retaining the whole, or on new formal structuring of given material.[501] Even Chrétien, the creator of the new genre, took his material from elsewhere, combining different sources, and saw his task as one of structure (*conjointure*), reflecting the meaning he extracted from this material.[502]

Our second approach to the question of the emergence of vernacular fiction in the twelfth century is a historical (or literary-historical) one: what varying conditions encouraged this development? Before about 1150 German written literature had been exclusively concerned with religious and historical themes,[503] both of which had been regarded as true and hence giving no scope for fiction. From about this date, however, there are signs of attempts by laymen to break away from the hitherto dominant cultural tutelage of the clergy.[504] In literature this takes various forms: works begin to be commissioned more and more by laymen and to be written, if still largely by clerics, then by clerics active at rulers' courts, while their products are addressed to a recognisably courtly audience.[505] Laymen are assisted in this by a number of factors, amongst which must be included the first signs of lay literacy and of a written literature meant specifically for them (access to knowledge, previously a clerical monopoly, by means of lay literacy or quasi-literacy and control over it by lay patronage of court clerics).[506] This literature could be based on written or oral tradition, where the former (mainly of religious content) required a truthful adherence to source,[507] whilst the latter gave greater scope for structural innovations. Works addressed to laymen discuss above all their secular concerns, primarily the themes of knighthood and love. Whereas the military aspect of the former theme is nothing new (it was predominant in orally transmitted heroic literature), the latter is a decisive innovation of twelfth-century vernacular literature, already in the romances dealing with antique themes. Here the influence of Ovid comes into play: he was of interest not merely to school commentators on him, but also to these romance authors for reasons that are 'political, social and moral, but . . . not typically religious'.[508] For similar reasons the French antique romances, encouraged by the patronage of Henry II's court, were meant to establish this ruler's place in a far-reaching secular (not religious), classically based history.[509]

Underlying these various developments was a process of lay emancipation, most clearly visible in the growth (however gradual) of lay literacy as an attempt to escape from the inferior cultural status to which illiteracy had confined laymen.[510] Other cultural fields witness similar stirrings of independence at this time. Page has argued for the emancipation of music (or at least of musicians), and Mehtonen suggests that poetry became distinct from other branches of knowledge and thereby established its independence as a discipline.[511] Something similar can be said of the rise of fictional writing that we have been tracing in these pages. The Arthurian romance in particular (the same cannot be said of the antique romance) has been seen as the liberation of the author from being tied to history[512] (whether native, as in the heroic epic, or the Christian history of salvation), as a release from 'official historiography'.[513] In a more profound sense this cutting loose from history[514] amounts to an abandonment of the truth-telling requirements of historiography or of any strict subservience to source.[515] Not merely in the case of the antique romances, but also with regard to rhetoric and poetics, it was above all classical literature that 'liberated medieval authors to try their own hands at serious fiction'.[516] This liberation took place, however, in the face of serious clerical opposition, preaching a rejection of worldly independence or stressing the unrealistic nature of the laymen's wishful thinking and derogatorily dismissing the Arthurian romance in particular as the main proponent of fictional writing.[517] How seriously the Church took the need to deal with this threat may be seen in the prose *Lancelot*, interpreted as a clerical appropriation of a romance theme for religious purposes in an attempt to gain control of the genre inaugurated by Chrétien.[518]

These tendencies were already at work in Germany around 1150 and are reflected in German written literature, but as regards fictionality the decisive impulse came from the antique and Arthurian romances. What preceded them (and still persisted), in Jean Bodel's terminology the *matière de France*, was regarded as historically true. Bodel therefore characterises this literature as true (*voir*) and corresponding works of written history in German likewise establish their claim to veracity.[519] Their contribution to the rise of fictionality is accordingly negligible, so that we may now confine our attention to what the two romance forms had to offer.

We start by asking what advantages for fictional writing were offered by the *matière de Rome*. The transition from native epic themes in France and Germany to works dealing with classical antiquity amounted to an immense widening of literary horizons (in time and space as well as cultural presuppositions) and provided new models against which the medieval present could be interpreted.[520] Moreover, it contributed to the liberation of laymen from dependence on the monopoly of ecclesiastical teaching, providing them with a model of secular culture and a prestigious means of tracing the origins of chivalry back to the distant past.[521] The authors of these earliest romances were engaged in a task of twofold *translatio*: vernacularising their Latin sources, but also transmitting classical learning to laymen deprived of it by illiteracy.[522] Classical themes provided greater narrative freedom than native epic material by virtue of their greater remoteness in time and space. Because a lay audience would have been less versed in the details of classical themes than of native ones, authors were not bound by conventional expectations and were thus free to invent.[523] (Long ago Herodotus had argued similarly that distant space – and, we might add, time – could be a cover for fictional narrative because it did not admit refutation.)[524] Because of the freedom that his choice of a classical theme gave him it has been said that Benoît (and the same could be claimed of the author of the *Roman d'Enéas*) differed from the *chanson de geste* and also from Wace's historical writing in being in a position to dispose consciously and even intricately of his source-material as a way of conveying meaning.[525] To compare him in this respect with Chrétien, however, is only to some extent valid, since there are limits set to the freedom of structural reorganisation open to authors dealing with the *matière de Rome*.[526]

Further advantages enjoyed by this *matière* are of even wider scope for authors seeking to find voice for the concerns of the lay nobility. By depicting antiquity anachronistically in medieval terms these authors located chivalry in a pre-Christian age of undeniable cultural standing, thereby heightening the self-esteem of a secular class whose illiterate culture had for long been seen as inferior to that of the clergy and offering an alternative model to the Christian, clerical one.[527] This alternative enjoyed the prestige of antiquity and a sense of historical continuity, ranging in the vernacular works encouraged at the court of Henry II from Troy to contemporary Britain.[528] In content this new vernacular model turned to antiquity and its values, presented and discussed as a break with the traditional feudal values of the *chanson de geste* and the ethical ones of Christian historiography.[529] By depicting a world with no knowledge of Christianity these authors were able to discuss secular problems in neutral terms, illustrating the contemporary concerns of the lay nobility in a specifically secular manner, without benefit of clergy. If it was the Virgilian concept of history (with its starting-point in Troy and its *translatio imperii* to Rome) that provided the Middle Ages with the possibility of a secular view of history,[530] then these antique romances, indebted to him as well as to other classical sources, mark the emergence of a secular literature devoted primarily to laymen's interests.[531] In form as well as in content these antique romances mark the potential emancipation of vernacular literature from religious presuppositions.[532] To achieve this the patrons of this literature may still have been dependent on clerics (for only they were equipped to carry out a twofold *translatio*), but they were court clerics, employed by the court to serve its interests.[533]

For all the gains that this classical *matière* brought with it, there were definite limits set to the extent to which it could encourage the growth of fictional writing. However much authors might elaborate individual episodes in the light of contemporary interests and freely undertake structural patterning by linking one episode meaningfully to another, they were still tied to a traditional fixed narrative plot from which they could not deviate and, unlike Chrétien, they were translators or adapters of an already given story.[534] The details of this story may not have been known to all laymen in their audience, but their outlines were certainly known traditionally in Europe and, what is more, were regarded as historical and binding.[535] What these themes allowed was therefore not an overall fictionality pervading the whole work, but at the most an episodic fictionality,[536] even if this could occasionally achieve impressive long-term effects. The conviction that these classical themes dealt with events that had taken place in history, together with the Christian reinterpretation of them (especially Virgil's *Aeneid*), may well have helped to safeguard them from clerical criticism,[537] but at the same time this imposed limits on their overall adaptability to expressing the concerns of laymen in the twelfth century.[538] (The converse was true of the *matière de Bretagne*: its flexible adaptability was bought at the price of exposure to the criticism of being untrue.)

These limitations may well account for the way in which the *matière de Rome* was so soon surpassed by the *matière de Bretagne* in the process of fictionalisation. In the prologue to *Cligés* (39 ff.) Chrétien states that nobody now talks of the Greeks and Romans and that the glowing embers of such talk are extinguished. If that is meant to suggest that Chrétien intends to breathe new life into these embers, then it invites a sceptical response, for he writes only shortly after the flourishing of French antique romances, and the romance which he is about to begin is not an adaptation of a classical text, but a creatively original work.[539] We do better to regard the image of extinguished embers as a critical suggestion that the day of the *matière de Rome* is now past and that it has given way to Chrétien's own innovation, the Arthurian romance.[540] Read in this way, Chrétien's remark agrees with the complaint made by Marie de France, another author engaged in Celtic *fabulae*, that she had considered making a story by translating from Latin into French, but had decided against it, seeing no benefit in doing what so many had done already.[541] Reversing Chrétien's argument, but to the same critical effect, Walter Map complains that the dead (e.g. Aeneas) live in literary form, that the Carolingian heroes of the *chanson de geste* are celebrated by minstrels in the vernacular, but that topical heroes are neglected in song.[542] He does not mention Arthur who, whatever his historical date, was certainly topical at the Angevin court of the time. In any case, Walter's impatience with the preference given to classical heroes at the cost of later ones is of a piece with Chrétien and Marie in explaining how the antique romance could not long continue to satisfy contemporary needs.

But how were these needs, including the freedom given by fictionality, better met by the *matière de Bretagne*? However imperfectly the details of classical stories may have been known to laymen, they were initially acquainted even less with the novel themes of the *matière de Bretagne*, so that authors in this field were less tied to previous expectations and therefore enjoyed far greater freedom of scope for fictional invention. Moreover, likewise at the beginning of the new romance genre, there existed no traditional written sources in the vernacular in question

(Wace provided only the general Arthurian background, but no source for the stories that Chrétien drew out of the gap left by him). As a result romance authors were less restricted by an obligatory dependence on a source and by possible exposure to criticism for deviating from it. Also to be turned to positive fictional account was the distinction, made for example by William of Malmesbury and Wace, between the historicity of the figure of Arthur and the tales of adventure attaching to him and his knights.[543] The *fabulae* rejected as untrue by these predecessors of Chrétien were for him the material out of which he could develop his fiction. Much more important than these considerations, however, is the fact that the non-historical basis of Arthurian romances (as distinct from what was held to be their historical framework, which was in any case not presented in them) meant that authors were released from being tied to known historical material and enjoyed a far greater measure of invention than was available to those working in the *matière de Rome*. In this connection what Spiegel has said of vernacular prose chroniclers in thirteenth-century France dealing with the history of antiquity can be applied to their versifying predecessors in the *matière de Rome* of the twelfth century.[544] She questions whether they could remain faithful to the sources they were translating and still depict the chivalric code of their day. They were tied to plot outlines not of their own making whose implications were less easily adaptable to other ends than were those of 'forthrightly imaginative literature'.[545] The tension this produced meant that any chivalric model was imposed on, rather than produced by, these stories from classical antiquity and that Celtic themes, more malleable and less constrained by precedent, were more welcome as narrative vessels for fictional experimentation.[546]

The difference between these two types of romance is clear: the antique model finds room at the most for what I have termed episodic fiction within a given overall plot that cannot be changed in its outlines, whilst the Arthurian model is bound to no traditional plot and therefore disposes freely of its material.[547] This difference has given rise to divergent views as to what works (especially in French literature where the distinction was first established) may properly be called romances – as to what in fact constitutes a romance. On the one hand, there are those who, like Marichal, proceed from the etymological sense of French *roman* (a work in a vernacular translated from a Latin text), so that the adaptations of antique sources would count as the first romances,[548] soon to be followed by Arthurian works, since *roman* also came to denote any work of narrative literature written in a Romance vernacular.[549] On the other hand, there are those who, like Gallais, maintain that the romance is characterised by fictionality, so that works with antique themes, received by their audiences as historically true, cannot be called romances, a genre instituted only by Chrétien.[550] Central to this divergence of views is the feature of fictionality, and they can best be reconciled if we take into account the sliding scale between episodic or incipient fictionality (*matière de Rome*) and fully developed, thoroughgoing fictionality (*matière de Bretagne*). Even Marichal, who lumps both *matières* together as romances, concedes this kind of distinction when he sums up the antique romances as 'l'enfance du genre', whilst the works of Chrétien represent 'l'âge adulte'.[551] Ruh similarly differentiates between antique adaptations that 'auf halbem Wege stecken' and Arthurian works whose material is 'freier', 'gefügiger' and 'unbelastet'.[552] Seen in this light, both *matières* agree in being romances (as they have been termed in this book), but differ in the extent to which they realise the potentialities of fiction. The antique romance remains externally referential (its events were regarded as historically true), whilst the narrative plot of the Arthurian romance is self-referential. The antique romance was regarded as history, but with fictional insertions, whilst the Arthurian romance is fiction with the possible addition of historical details.[553]

The relatively short period in which fictional romances flourished creatively in German literature has been seen as a fictional interlude, coming between the dominance of historical themes in the twelfth century (before the rise of the romance) and their prominence in the thirteenth.[554] The idea of an interlude, however, can create a false impression, since historical works of the twelfth century, together with new biblical or legendary works (likewise *historia*) produced around 1200, continue to be transmitted in manuscripts through this 'fictional interlude'.[555] In that fictional writing in the form of the romance shared the field of literary interest with the continuing attractiveness of historical themes, fiction did not simply take over from history for a time.[556] Instead, history remained a continuous feature of literary interest through the twelfth and thirteenth centuries, giving rise, as we have seen, to fiction, but not vanishing before it in the timespan during which literary fiction flourished creatively in romance form. Fictional writing in this period cannot be regarded by itself alone, since it arose from an interplay with history. It lived side by side with historical writing, defining itself not by negating it or by leaving it behind, but by differentiating itself from it.

Notes

I. DEFINING TWELFTH-CENTURY FICTIONALITY

1 Gregory, 'Inheritance', pp. 54ff.; Jacquart, 'Thought', pp. 407ff.; Maccagnolo, 'Aristotelianism', pp. 429ff.

2 See below, n. 14.

3 On Plato's story of the cave see Havelock, *Preface*, p. 25; Murdoch, *Fire*, p. 5.

4 U. Müller, 'Dichter', p. 35, who draws attention to St Paul's criticism of pagan (and Hebrew) *fabulae*. Cf. Knapp, *Historie*, p. 161.

5 Murdoch, *Fire*, pp. 65–6; Vickers, *Defence*, pp. 133–4.

6 Havelock, *Preface*, *passim*; Murdoch, *Fire*, pp. 21ff., 30–1, 87. Cf. Trimpi, *Traditio* 30 (1974), 29.

7 Rösler, *Poetica* 12 (1980), 283ff.; 'Schriftkultur', pp. 109ff.

8 Green, *Listening*, pp. 237ff.

9 Feeney, 'Epilogue', p. 232. Potts goes so far as to give his translation of the *Poetics* the title *Aristotle on the art of fiction*, while Trimpi, *Traditio* 27 (1971), 1ff., repeatedly equates *poesis* with fiction. That this equation was known to the Middle Ages is clear from a twelfth-century commentary on Horace: 'Nam poio pois est fingo fingis. Inde poesis uel poetria, id est fictio uel figmentum, et poeta id est fictor' (hence poems or poetry, that is fiction or figment, and poet, that is fiction-maker) (Friis-Jensen, *CIMAGL* 60 [1990], 338). Cf. also Mehtonen, *Concepts*, pp. 50–1.

10 Potts, *Aristotle*, p. 72; Müller, 'Dichter', p. 36; Knapp, *Historie*, pp. 101ff. (with a qualification by von Moos).

11 Gill, 'Plato', pp. 74f.; Knapp, *Historie*, p. 103. Cf. Trimpi, *Traditio* 30 (1974), 43.

12 Suggested, with qualifications, by Gill, 'Plato', p. 75. Cf. Rösler, *Poetica* 12 (1980), 310.

13 Trimpi, *Traditio* 27 (1971), 14ff., 56ff.; Gill, 'Plato', pp. 77–8.

14 Minnis and Scott, *Theory*, pp. 277ff.; Knapp, *Historie*, pp. 80–1, 104, 113ff., 153ff.

15 Here I follow Müller, 'Dichter', pp. 34ff.

16 The Roman historian Velleius Paterculus therefore complains of love-poets that they declaim nothing in their own person ('nihil ex persona poetae disserunt'). Cf. Bond, *Subject*, pp. 7 and 209, n. 16.

17 See pp. 11–12.

18 Another example is Horace's *Ars Poetica*. On its influence in the Middle Ages see pp. 28–31.

19 That even such an isolated case as this could nonetheless be influential in the Middle Ages is clear from the example of Baudri de Bourgueil. See p. 21.

20 Boehm, 'Ort', p. 678; Seifert, *AfB* 21 (1977), 229; Grünkorn, *Fiktionalität*, p. 42; Knapp, *Historie*, pp. 104–5; Mehtonen, *Concepts*.
21 Grünkorn, *Fiktionalität*, p. 48.
22 Mehtonen, *Concepts*.
23 Ibid., pp. 114ff. (Bernard of Utrecht's commentary on the *Ecloga Theodoli*).
24 See below, pp. 179–80.
25 Mehtonen, *Concepts*, pp. 42–3.
26 See pp. 28–9.
27 Cf. Lamarque and Olsen, *Truth*, p. 15, but also Kermode, *Sense*, pp. 40–1.
28 Searle, *Expression*, pp. 58ff.; Rorty, 'Problem', pp. 67ff.; Newsom, *Story*; Currie, *Nature*; Walton, *Mimesis*, Lamarque and Olsen, *Truth*.
29 Gombrich, *Art*; Walton, *Mimesis*.
30 Currie, *Nature*, pp. 48, 49.
31 Searle, *Expression*, p. 72; Walton, *Mimesis*, p. 79; Lamarque and Olsen, *Truth*, p. 284. For a medieval theoretical parallel cf. Alanus ab Insulis, *De planctu* 8, 137: 'Poete tamen aliquando hystoriales eventus ioculationibus fabulosis quadam eleganti sutura confederant, ut ex diuersorum competenti iunctura ipsius narrationis elegantior pictura resultet' (However, poets sometimes elegantly sew together historical events and fabulous inventions, so that a more elegant word-picture of the narrative may result from the fitting conjunction of different things.). On the possible relevance of *iunctura* to Chrétien's *conjointure* see Kelly, *Art*, pp. 21ff.
32 *Truth*, p. 80. Cf. also Bruck, *ZGL* 6 (1978), 294.
33 On the transition from the real geographical world to a fabulous one (and therefore on their conjunction within the same work) see Green, 'Alexanderlied', pp. 246ff., and *Viator* 8 (1977), 145ff. Schilling, 'Minnesang', pp. 109–10, points out that even those who stress the fictional status of Ulrich von Liechtenstein's *Frauendienst* concede that it contains references to historically attested events and persons as well as a real geographical setting and chronology. Without using the term *argumentum* Schilling sums up the position accordingly: 'Ulrich beschreibt zwar nicht, was tatsächlich war, wohl aber, was hätte sein können.'
34 See below, pp. 146 (Prester John) and 153 (Dares and Dictys).
35 Martin, *Philosophy* 57 (1982), 229, quoted by Lamarque and Olsen, *Truth*, p. 292.
36 *Poetics* 9 (cf. Rösler, *Poetica* 12 [1980], 317, fn. 98).
37 See pp. 153–4 and also Minnis and Scott, *Theory*, p. 114.
38 Rösler, *Poetica* 12 (1980), 319; Knapp, *Historie*, p. 25.
39 See pp. 14–15.
40 Baswell, *Virgil*, pp. 64, 312. The wording makes it clear that many, but not all, historical facts were suppressed.
41 Cf. Walton, *JAAC* 37 (1978), 12. Stierle, *Poetica* 7 (1975), 345ff., terms this approach a quasi-pragmatic reception of fiction.
42 Cf. J.-D. Müller, 'Ritual', pp. 50–1, with the interesting reference to a 'Märe' by Der Stricker, *Die Minnesänger*, whose point rests on the fictive convention of the love-poet's stance being taken as true.
43 Even though more sophisticated clerical criticisms of poetry attack it for being untrue, it is still by the irrelevant criterion of truth or untruth that they judge it.
44 See p. 136, but also Morgan, 'Make-believe', p. 189.
45 *Etymologiae* I 44, 5.
46 Cf. Moser, 'Problem', p. 21, and 'Mythos', p. 32, who suggests the possibility of scepticism as well as credulity. Knapp, 'Überlegungen', p. 124, also points to the possibility of

two different attitudes to such motifs, but stresses, p. 125, that this uncertainty excludes them as a possible criterion. Cf. also Rider, 'Worlds', p. 121: 'The "marvels" that one finds in the fictive worlds of the romances . . . are indeed "marvelous" to the fictive characters who inhabit those worlds, just as they would be to the audiences of the romances if they encountered them in their everyday world, but they are not truly marvelous to the members of these audiences – whether medieval or modern – because they know that these fictive marvels are "caused" by the author of the romances.'

47 My earlier suggestion of a multiple, not merely twofold audience (*'Rîtr'*, pp. 8ff.) was based on the feature of literacy, but can be reinforced by that of fictionality, without the grouping necessarily being identical.

48 Kugler, 'Geographie', p. 133, but cf.also his comment on Wittkower, 'Marvels', on p. 112, fn. 14.

49 Knapp, *Tierepos*, pp. 30 (quoting Brinkmann), 39.

50 Quintilian, *Institutio* v 11, 19; Isidore, *Etymologiae* I 40, 1.

51 Haug and Vollmann, *Literatur*, pp. 1250, 1257, 1259ff.

52 v. 34ff.

53 Isidore, *Etymologiae* I 41, 1; Konrad von Hirsau, *Dialogus* 135. Cf. Green, *Listening*, pp. 226, 238; Haug and Vollmann, *Literatur*, pp. 1267–8.

54 Haug and Vollmann, *Literatur*, p. 1268 (against Trillitzsch, *Ecbasis*, p. 47).

55 v. 1229. Cf. Trillitzsch, *Ecbasis*, p. 156.

56 See pp. 26–7.

57 Bernard, *Commentum*, p. 63; Konrad, *Dialogus* 171. On the Horatian recommendation of plausibility in fiction (*Ars poetica* 119: 'aut famam sequere aut sibi convenientia finge', either follow tradition or make up consistently; 338: 'proxima veris', close to the truth) and its medieval survival cf. Mehtonen, *Concepts*, pp. 97ff., 130ff. ('mentiri debemus probabiliter', we must lie plausibly). On the plausibility of *argumentum* cf. Quintilian, *Institutio* II 4, 2: 'argumentum, quod falsum sed vero simile' (false, but like the truth). For Isidore the difference between fiction and untruth rests on this, cf. *Differentiae* I 221: 'Falsum est ergo quod verum non est; fictum quod verisimile est' (False is what is not true; fictional is what is like the truth).

58 Chinca, *History*, pp. 100–1. On the middling position of *argumentum* cf. also Mehtonen, *Concepts*, p. 92.

59 Chinca, *History*, pp. 104ff.

60 v. 4545ff. On this episode cf. Christ, *Rhetorik*, pp. 305ff.

61 v. 4589ff., 4595, 4610, 4824ff., 4851ff.

62 Green, *Listening*, p. 260.

63 v. 7493. Cf. Green, *Listening*, p. 257.

64 *Biographia Literaria* II 6. Rösler, *Poetica* 12 (1980), 311, fn. 80, reminds us that Goethe used the phrase 'selbstbewußte Illusion'. Cf. also Burrichter, *Wahrheit*, p. 12.

65 E.g., Huber, *AfdA* 99 (1988), 64; Feeney, *Gods*, p. 230; Latré, 'Yelping', p. 188.

66 Walton, *Mimesis*, p. 240; Searle, *Expression*, pp. 60–1.

67 Latré, 'Yelping', pp. 187–8, argues that the medieval listener and the modern reader are expected to suspend their disbelief here, but the romance's reference to trust or belief (v. 94) on which he relies is internal to the fiction (Arthur is to believe it); it does not apply to the audience of the romance. They retain their disbelief.

68 Currie, *Nature*, p. 30 (cf. also p. 196).

69 Newsom, *Story*, p. 134.

70 Morgan, 'Make-believe', pp. 194, 195.

71 For this reason I have reservations about Haug's description of heroic legend as a 'form of fictionalised reality' ('Mündlichkeit', p. 382). If the fictional contract means that both parties consciously adopt a fictive stance, can the term fiction be applied to heroic tradition which, as Haug admits, was unaware of its fictional status and was presented as historical truth?

72 E.g. Morgan, 'Make-believe', p. 180 ('tacit agreement'); Lamarque and Olsen, *Truth*, pp. 37, 43 ('collaboration', 'convention'); Iser, 'Akte', p. 135 ('Kontrakt'); Warning, 'Diskurs', p. 194 ('Kontrakt'). On 'connivance' see pp. 14–15.

73 *Truth*, pp. 43, 55, 77 and *passim*. Cf. Otter, *Inventiones*, p. 7: 'for fiction to be recognized as such, there must be a "contract" that suspends or "brackets" truth claims and therefore protects the speaker from the charge of lying, although in a strictly referential reading his or her assertions may not correspond with reality'. Otter's use of the term 'referential' is important for the distinction between factual or historical writing on the one hand and fiction on the other. Whereas the former has a referent – refers to something outside itself held to be true – the latter has no such external referent: its only presumed witness is the fictional work itself. But such fiction does not merely depend on the absence of other evidence, it also presupposes a contract with the audience according to which referential reading is suspended. The mutual convention to dispense with a referential response constitutes fiction, as has been argued already for the Greek romance by Konstan, 'Invention', pp. 3 ff.

74 Green, 'Erkennen', pp. 35 ff.

75 Currie, *Nature*, p. 73. Cf. Grünkorn, *Fiktionalität*, p. 19 (point 2).

76 Sidney, *Apology*, p. 31. For a medieval parallel (Arnulf of Orléans) cf. Zeeman, 'Schools', p. 171 Mehtonen, *Concepts*, p. 55, fn. 42; and for a modern statement to the same effect cf. Grünkorn, 'Verständnis', p. 30. Mehtonen, *Concepts*, p. 40, also draws attention to a commentator's distinction beween orators, who seek to persuade, and poets, whose aim is not to convince their audience of the truth of their fables: 'ut velint fabulis suis credi sed ad delectationem' (so that they might wish their stories to be believed, but rather for delight). Similarly, with reference to Augustine's view that it is the intention to deceive, not just the absence of objective referents, that makes the liar, she says (p. 128) that the defenders of *poesis* constantly emphasise the non-affirmative nature of poetic statements. 'The aim of the poet is not to lead readers astray, and the reader should not conceive of the narrated events as being true'. Zeeman, 'Schools', pp. 155 ff., also draws a contrast between the affirmative discourse of a discipline such as history and the non-affirmative stance of poetry. Cf. Ronen, *Worlds*, p. 36: 'When truth is regarded as a relation between an extralinguistic state of affairs and a linguistic expression, it cannot be applied to fiction since fiction does not commit itself to extralinguistic states.'

77 Morgan, 'Make-believe', p. 179.

78 Chinca, *History*, p. 103. One of our difficulties in understanding medieval authors using Latin is to tell whether, as rigorists, they use terms like *fictio*, *figmentum* and *fabula* to mean 'lies, untruth' and therefore equivalent to *mendacium* or whether, as with humanists of the twelfth century, they use them to mean 'fiction' and therefore not to be seen in terms of the dichotomy truth: untruth.

79 Loomis, 'Diffusion', p. 59; Duggan, 'Epic', p. 305; Opitz, *Geschichte*, pp. 86–7.

80 See pp. 26–7.

81 Burrichter, *Wahrheit*, p. 129.

82 Fichte, 'Fakt', pp. 45, 56, 61.

83 Ibid., pp. 58, 61. Talking of two modern examples, Bruck, *ZGL* 6 (1978), 296, makes a comparable distinction between a fictional and a pseudo-scholarly text, saying of the

latter: 'Der Text ist also keine literarische Fiktion, sondern eine Fiktion im allgemeinen, gebrauchssprachlichen Sinne.'

84 Johanek, *FMS* 21 (1987), 346ff. For a recent summary of Geoffrey's position within Norman historiography and affiliations in Anglo-Norman England cf. Ingledew, *Speculum* 69 (1994), 681ff., 691–2.

85 In what follows I am dependent on Feeney, *Gods*, pp. 229ff.

86 *Saturnalia* v 17, 4.

87 See pp. 158–9.

88 Feeney, *Gods*, p. 187.

89 *Policraticus* VIII 14, 768d.

90 Von Moos, 'Fictio', p. 761.

91 Ibid.: 'sich . . . kooperativ zu verhalten' and 'gebildeter Komplize'.

92 Chinca, *History*, pp. 92–3; Keck, *Liebeskonzeption*, pp. 139–40.

93 In classical antiquity it was the grammarians who interpreted literary texts in the light of their desire to be certain either of the truth or of the falsehood of their statements (Trimpi, *Traditio* 20 [1974], 47). On the relationship between fictionality and lies in medieval theory cf. Mehtonen, *Concepts*, pp. 123ff.

94 Oral history: Green, *Listening*, pp. 242ff.; Geoffrey of Monmouth: see p. 170.

95 Knapp, *GRM* 48 (1998), 243, refers to 'einer wahrheitsindifferenten poetischen Fiktion'. Cf. Otter, *Inventiones*, p. 16: 'The development of . . . a third category beside "truth" and "falsehood" is the specific contribution of vernacular narrative in the twelfth century.'

96 Wood, 'Prologue', p. xvi; Bowie, 'Lies', p. 3. Cf. Gill, 'Plato', p. 39: 'Fictional discourse is different in kind from factual: its statements (and other forms of expression) do not constitute truth-telling or lying, and in this sense fiction has no truth-status', and also Reardon, *Form*, p. 57: 'Fiction lies somewhere between the ideas of true and false, between fact and non-fact.'

97 Chinca, *History*, pp. 103–4; Mehtonen, *Concepts*, p. 92.

98 *Roman de Brut* 1247ff. (discussed by Burrichter, *Wahrheit*, pp. 125ff.).

99 See p. 171.

100 Haug, *Literaturtheorie*, pp. 100ff. Rather than diverge from my argument at this point I must anticipate later stages in suggesting what I mean by narrative or fictional truth. As opposed to the fortuitous shapelessness of history from which the historian may strive to extract a pattern, the author of fictional narrative shapes his material in order to convey a meaning. Whereas historical writing must be internally consistent, but also depends for its truth-status on external referentiality, the narrative logic of fictional writing can be based on self-referentiality or internal consistency alone. Fictional truth builds on this internal consistency, on the plausible organisation of structure to suggest verisimilitude. Fiction as a factually untrue narrative conveys a truth on a different plane, frequently of an ethical or exemplary nature (despite his reservations Thomasin says of the court romance, *Welscher Gast* 1124: 'wan si bezeichenunge hât/der zuht unde der wârheit', because it signifies correct behaviour and the truth).

My description of fictional truth around 1200 proceeds negatively by differentiating it from what it is not, from *historia*. This reflects the fact that at this time vernacular fiction, struggling for recognition, had to set itself apart form this alternative form of narrative. Cf. Fromm, 'Verräter', pp. 160–1, on the new valuation of Virgil in the twelfth century, whose *veritas* is seen not as the facticity of *res gestae*, but as the meaning that the *poeta-philosophus* conveys, teaching us to understand human behaviour and the truths about life.

101 See p. 171.

102 Burrichter, *Wahrheit*, p. 129. In a much wider context Adrian Stevens is preparing a book in which he argues that the romance is to be regarded as a *genus mixtum*, combining history and fable, truth and fiction.

103 How close this agreement can be, even in formulation, is shown by Bruck, *ZGL* 6 (1978), 286. Since the truth-status of a statement depends on its referentiality, its agreement with the empirical world, statements with no referentiality (to which poetry belongs) have no such truth status: 'Sie sind nicht entweder wahr oder falsch, sondern "weder wahr noch falsch".'

104 Walton, *Journal of Philosophy* 75 (1978), 7.

105 Morgan, 'Make-believe', p. 225.

2. VERNACULAR FICTION IN THE TWELFTH CENTURY

1 Cf. Lamarque and Olsen, *Truth*, p. 38.

2 Ridder, 'Inszenierung', p. 240, fn. 7; *Wolfram-Studien* 15 (1998), 193, fn. 83.

3 Rösler, *Poetica* 12 (1980), 283ff.; 'Schriftkultur', pp. 109ff.

4 Havelock, *Revolution*, *Preface*.

5 Gill, 'Plato', pp. 79, 80–1 and fn. 113.

6 Contrast Haug, 'Wandlungen', p. 255 ('Im 12. Jahrhundert entsteht in Frankreich eine neue, genuin – d.h. nicht-allegorische – fiktionale Literatur') or 'Entdeckung', p. 239 ('Entdeckung der Fiktionalität') with *Literaturtheorie*, p. 91 ('den ersten vulgärsprachlichen Roman des Mittelalters, den man als fiktiv bezeichnen darf') and 'Literatur', p. 34 (*Ruodlieb* as against Chrétien's *Erec*).

Bäuml, *Speculum* 55 (1980), 262–3, concedes in general terms that Latin writing could practise fiction, but stresses that the use of Latin raised other expectations than in vernacular fictional narratives. A more radical position is taken up implicitly by Haidu, *MLN* 92 (1977), 882, 885, for whom fiction is the voice of vernacular emancipation from Latin, the language of the literature of the Church. Cf. also Bezzola, *Origines*, II 242–3.

7 On Chrétien cf. Haug, 'Literatur', p. 32; on the experimental nature of *Ruodlieb*: Dronke, *Individuality*, pp. 34, 35.

8 Vollmann, *Ruodlieb*, pp. 62–3; Haug, 'Ruodlieb', pp. 218, 219ff. On the fictional nature of this folktale type see also later, pp. 122–3.

9 Vollmann, *Ruodlieb*, pp. 44, 74. *Fabliau*: Dronke, *Individuality*, pp. 48–9; Vollmann, *Ruodlieb*, p. 71. Romances of antiquity: Knapp, *Ruodlieb*, p. 241.

10 Dronke, *Individuality*, p. 42; Haug, 'Ruodlieb', pp. 207, 208. On the fictive nature of this device, see also pp. 96–8.

11 Vollmann, *Ruodlieb*, p. 65.

12 Ibid., pp. 63, 70.

13 Ibid., p. 69.

14 Heroic tradition: Knapp, *Ruodlieb*, p. 240; knowledge of the past: Green, *Listening*, pp. 239ff.

15 Knapp, *Ruodlieb*, p. 250; Vollmann, *Ruodlieb*, p. 44 ('Reich der Phantasie').

16 Ruh, *Epik* I 29–30.

17 Haug, 'Ruodlieb', p. 223; Haug and Vollmann, *Literatur*, pp. 1310–11.

18 Haug, 'Weisheit', p. 18 ('frei erfunden').

19 Haug, 'Ruodlieb', pp. 201, 225; Haug and Vollmann, *Literatur*, p. 1306.

20 Bowie, 'Lies', p. 3.

21 Minnis and Scott, *Theory*, p. 47.
22 Isidore: *Etymologiae* I 40, 2; Konrad von Hirsau: Minnis and Scott, *Theory*, pp. 47ff.; Engelbert von Admont: Knapp, *Historie*, pp. 87–8.
23 Haug, 'Entdeckung', p. 239.
24 Baudri de Bourgueil, *Carmina* 85, 35ff. Cf. Bond, *Subject*, pp. 8–9.
25 *Carmina* 7–8, 97–8. Cf. Bond, *Subject*, pp. 61–2.
26 See above, p. 3.
27 *Carmina* 99, 185–95. Cf. Jaeger, *Love*, pp. 99–100, 158.
28 Offermanns, *Wirkung*, p. 18 and fn. 1 (last sentence); Bond, *Subject*, p. 9. On the middle ground see above, p. 16.
29 Otter, *Inventiones*.
30 Ibid., pp. 93–4, 109, 128, 129.
31 Ibid., pp. 6 ('tentative'), 12 ('temporarily', 'partially', 'for a short time', 'possibility'), 94 ('episodes'), 110. When Otter stresses that her authors display sophistication (p. 2) and literary self-awareness (pp. 41, 93), it must be added that these qualities may be a necessary, but are not a sufficient, condition for fictionality. On my reason for doubting whether Geoffrey of Monmouth was engaged in fiction at all see later, p. 170.
32 Ibid., pp. 1, 17.
33 Von Moos, 'Antwort', pp. 431ff.
34 Grünkorn, *Fiktionalität*, pp. 49ff.
35 Burrichter, *Wahrheit*, pp. 11 and 18 (against Jauss, 'Genese', p. 423).
36 See above, pp. 3–4. Cf. also, however briefly, von Moos, *Geschichte*, p. 276.
37 Zeeman, 'Schools', pp. 151ff., especially p. 174.
38 See below, p. 168.
39 Haug, 'Mündlichkeit', p. 379.
40 Knapp, *Ruodlieb*, pp. 238–9; Vollmann, *Ruodlieb*, pp. 42–3, 64; Haug and Vollmann, *Literatur*, pp. 1311, 1312.
41 Vollmann-Profe, *Wiederbeginn*, p. 171.
42 On the fictive tradition of journeys to the East see also pp. 164–5.
43 Haug, *Literaturtheorie*, pp. 102–3.
44 See p. 171.
45 Bromwich, 'Transmission', pp. 284, 285.
46 Cf. n. 2, above.
47 Vitz, *Orality*, *passim*.
48 Haug, 'Wandlungen', p. 256.
49 Meyer, *Verfügbarkeit*, pp. 10, fn. 38, and 271, has criticised Haug for making an absolute of Chrétien's double cycle. By establishing this as a norm which other authors of the thirteenth century failed to recognise or achieve Haug remains a prisoner of the former view that these later authors were epigones. On other forms of fictional structure see pp. 93ff.
50 C. Huber, *AfdA* 99 (1988), 64–5 ('das Spiel zwischen Autor und Publikum'). On the fictional contract, see above, pp. 11–12.
51 Haug, *Literaturtheorie*, pp. 24, 126. Such independence has also been questioned, from a slightly different point of view, by Mehtonen, *Concepts*, p. 20. Cf. also Patey, *Probability*, p. 142 (only in the eighteenth century did the shift from external to internal criteria of probability lead to the view that a work of literature was autonomous).
52 Haug, 'Wandlungen', p. 257 ('Eine gewisse Autonomie'); *Literaturtheorie* (second edition), p. 126, fn. 9.
53 Schmolke-Hasselmann, *Versroman*, pp. 190ff.; Heinzle, *PBB* 112 (1990), 62–3. On Geoffrey see later, p. 170.

54 C. Huber, *ZfdA* 115 (1986), 82–3, 87ff.; *AfdA* 99 (1988), 65. Cf. also Warning, 'Diskurs', p. 197.

55 Haug, *Literaturtheorie* (second edition), p. 126, fn. 9.

56 See pp. 153 ff.

57 Riley, *Theory*.

58 Greek romance: Gill, 'Plato', pp. 41, 79; Morgan, 'Make-believe', p. 176; Feeney, 'Epilogue', p. 232, fn. 6. Medieval romance: Knapp, *Historie*, pp. 79, 101, 175.

59 Antiquity: Trimpi, *Traditio* 30 (1974), 1 ('borrowed vocabulary'); Kuch, 'Herausbildung', pp. 13–14; Morse, *Truth*, p. 258, n. 77; Feeney, 'Epilogue', p. 231. Middle Ages: Haug, *Literaturtheorie*, pp. 104–5, 125; Knapp, *GRM* 48 (1998), 243.

60 Morgan, 'Make-believe', p. 176.

61 Voelker, *ZfrPh* 10 (1886), 485 ff.; *FEW* 10 ii, 452ff. The spread of different genres covered by the term *romanz* includes religious works (Proverbs, Song of Songs, a saint's *vita*), history (Livy, Dares, Wace's *Roman de Rou*), a bestiary, ethics (*Disticha Catonis*), philosophy (Boethius), *chansons de geste*, and the Arthurian romance. Conversely, other non-specific terms such as *conte, estoire, oevre, livre* could be used of the romance (Payen and Diekstra, *Roman*, p. 21).

62 The material was first collected by Schwietering, 'Singen', pp. 43 ff., but then brought up to date and corrected by Düwel, *Werkbezeichnungen*. The range of genres covered by the term *âventiure*, in addition to what we should call a romance, includes the heroic epic (or parts of an epic), the saint's legend, and (later) the chronicle.

63 Grubmüller, *FMS* 12 (1978), 160. On the border between history and fiction see pp. 142ff.

64 Grubmüller, *FMS* 12 (1978), 163. On truth and hagiography see Schreiner, *AfK* 48 (1966), 1 ff.; *Saeculum* 17 (1966), 131 ff., and also later, p. 137.

65 Concerning hagiography: Schreiner, *AfK* 48 (1966), 4 (Petrus Damiani); *Saeculum* 17 (1966), 156, 161.

66 Thomasin, *Welscher Gast* 1121 ff. (Grubmüller, *FMS* 12 [1978], 168; Huber, *ZfdA* 115 [1986], 83, 84–5; Schirmer, 'Wahrheitsauffassung', pp. 64f.); Johann von Würzburg, *Wilhelm von Österreich* 19506ff. (Grubmüller, *FMS* 12 [1978], 168; von Ertzdorff, *ZfdPh* 86 [1967], 388–9).

67 Burrow, *Writers*, p. 18.

68 *Ars poetica* 333 ff.

69 In his commentary Brink expressly equates what Horace says about poetry with fiction: *Ars poetica*, pp. 354, 504.

70 On the verisimilar cf. v. 338: 'ficta voluptatis causa sint proxima veris' (for the sake of pleasure let your fiction be close to the truth).

71 A range of representative examples would include the following: Priscian, *Praeexercitamina*, pp. 551–2 (Manning, *JEGPh* 59 [1960], 407); Isidore of Seville, *Etymologiae* I 40 (Olson, *Literature*, p. 27); *Scholia Vindobonensia*, p. 41, 27ff. (Knapp, *Historie*, p. 38, fn. 121); Konrad von Hirsau, *Dialogus*, p. 24 (Manning, *JEGPh* 59 [1960], p. 407); Marbod of Rennes, *Liber decem capitulorum*, col. 1693, vv. 38–9 (Suchomski, *Delectatio*, p. 70); Bernardus (Silvestris?), *Commentum*, p. 2 (Olson, *Literature*, p. 36; see also Knapp, *Historie*, p. 66); Walter Map, *De nugis*, p. 37 (Olson, *Literature*, p. 114); Dominicus Gundissalinus, *De divisione*, pp. 54, 56 (Olson, *Literature*, p. 28); John of Capua, *Directorium*, p. 80 (Manning, *JEGPh* 59 [1960], p. 410).

72 On Old French examples see Hunt, *NM* 80 (1979), 17ff. (and Manning, *JEGPh* 59 (1960), 414); on Chaucer see Manning *JEGPh* 59 [1960], 403 ff. (and Olson, *Literature*, pp. 145–6, 157).

73 This is not to say that the prescription to please and instruct was the only Horatian contribution to medieval fictionality. Mehtonen, *Concepts*, has shown that this prescription was in harmony with the three rhetorical types of narrative (p. 34), as is also made clear by Dominicus Gundissalinus (see above, p. 4). She also stresses the importance for the concept of fictionality of Horace's maxim 'aut famam sequere aut sibi conuenientia finge', either follow tradition or make up consistently (pp. 96, 102) and of his doctrine of verisimilitude (p. 102). For Friis-Jensen, *CIMAGL* 60 (1990), 319ff., a twelfth-century commentary on Horace's *Ars poetica* is a bridge between the classical poetics and the new arts of poetry in the twelfth century.

74 Suchomski, *Delectatio*, pp. 72, 73.

75 v. 333–4.

76 Augustine, *De civitate Dei* II 8 (Manning, *JEGPh* 59 [1960], 407).

77 Olson, *Literature*, pp. 39ff., 90ff., 128ff.

78 Ibid., p. 89.

79 Ibid., pp. 64ff. (here, p. 75).

80 *De reductione*, pp. 38ff. (Olson, *Literature*, pp. 70–1). I have not been able to consult the edition referred to by Olson.

81 *Summa confessorum*, p. 292 (Faral, *Jongleurs*, pp. 67ff.; Suchomski, *Delectatio*, pp. 71–2; Olson, *Literature*, pp. 73–4; Page, *Owl*, pp. 23–4, 28).

82 Olson, *Literature*, pp. 94, 102.

83 *De nugis*, p. 210 (Olson, *Literature*, pp. 114–15).

84 *Summa de sacramentis*, pp. 176–7 (Page, *Owl*, pp. 22–3, 28).

85 *Soliloquia*, MPL 32, 894 (Olson, *Literature*, p. 25).

86 *Commentarii*, p. 5 (Manning, *JEGP* 59 [1960], 406).

87 *Etymologiae* I 40 (Olson, *Literature*, p. 27).

88 *Scholia Vindobonensia*, p. 40 (Manning, *JEGPh* 59 [1960], 411–12); Dominicus Gundissalinus, *De divisione*, pp. 54ff. (Olson, *Literature*, p. 28); *accessus* to Ovid's *Amores*, cf. Ghisalberti, *JWCI* 9 [1946], 46 (Olson, *Literature*, p. 30).

89 Olson, *Literature*, gives a range of examples of authors who are uneasy with and even disapproving of literature that claims no other function than to provide entertainment (cf. p. 155). See also Hunt, *NM* 80 (1979), 20.

90 Suchomski, *Delectatio*, p. 67 (necessary relaxation), 276, n. 207 (bait for moral instruction), 67 (diversion from higher things).

91 v. 1ff. (Olson, *Literature*, pp. 149f.). Knapp, *GRM* 48 (1998), 241, makes it clear that Denis, in rejecting *Partonopeus de Blois* as a 'matire de fable e de menceonge', fabulous and lying subject-matter (= 'materia fabulae et mendacii') and as a dream that could never take place (31: 'Kar iceo ne put unkes estre'), is making use of the established definition of *fabula* ('quae nec facta est nec fieri potest', which has not happened and cannot happen).

92 *Miracles* III 267 (Hunt, *NM* 80 [1979], 23).

93 Jaeger, *Origins*, Echard, *Narrative*.

94 Echard, *Narrative*, pp. 14–15.

95 Jaeger, *Origins*, pp. 162ff.; Echard, *Narrative*, pp. 17–19, 23.

96 Jaeger, *Origins*, pp. 168ff.; Echard, *Narrative*, p. 15.

97 Green, *Irony*, pp. 359ff., 365ff. Jaeger, *Origins*, p. 165, qualifies my view of the clerical poet's status at court by saying that irony and wit were the rule at court, not the response of an outsider. I expressly admit this aspect of the language of courtesy (pp. 365ff.), but see no necessary conflict between that and the poet's status.

98 Cf. von Moos, *Fictio*, p. 751, fn. 31. On Augustine's definition of *mendacium* and the narrow, but still possible licence it granted to meaningful, but fictional narrative cf. Mehtonem, *Concepts*, p. 124.
99 Vincent-Cassy: 'Recherches', pp. 172–3.
100 Augustine, *Soliloquia*, MPL 32, 892 (Olson, *Literature*, p. 25).
101 Lucian, *True History*, preface 1.2 (Romm, *Edges*, p. 212). Cf. also Wiseman, 'Historians', pp. 131–2.
102 Wagenvoort, *Studies*, pp. 30ff.
103 *Dedicatio* 7: 'Et, cum sis certe vario lassata labore, / Ludens dignare hos modulos legere', and, when worn out by various labour, deign to read these verses for entertainment.
104 Haug and Vollmann, *Literatur*, pp. 1188–9.
105 *Ecbasis*, v. 1226: 'Nimirum sapere est abiectis utile nugis / Et tempestivum psalmis concedere ludum' (Indeed, it is useful to lay aside these trifles and be intelligent, and it is time to let entertainment give way to psalm-singing.). Cf. also Knapp, *Tierepos*, pp. 34, 35.
106 Vollmann, *Ruodlieb*, pp. 73, 74.
107 *Policraticus* VIII 12, col. 768 (Echard, *Narrative*, pp. 15, 237. Cf. also Suchomski, *Delectatio*, p. 51).
108 *Gesta* I 16 (Echard, *Narrative*, p. 95). Cf. Knapp, *Historie*, pp. 82–3 (Thomas Aquinas) and 89–90 (Engelbert von Admont).
109 *Vita Merlini* 1: 'Fatidici vatis rabiem musamque jocosam / Merlini cantare paro', I make ready to sing the playful Muse, the ravings of the prophet Merlin (Echard, *Narrative*, pp. 217–18). An anonymous Latin poem (Dronke, *Love-lyric*, pp. 450ff.) likewise invokes the Ovidian *Musa iocosa*, significantly in conjunction with 'carmina … fingere', to compose fictive poems (1–2). Baudri de Bourgueil also uses this phrase in a context (*Carmina* 193, 97–107) that makes it clear that the words of his love-poems are not to be taken as face-value. Jaeger, *Love*, p. 119, translates the phrase as 'ironic muse', but it could equally be seen as 'fictive muse'.
110 *Policraticus* 1, prologue, col. 387: 'qui non omnia, quae hic scribuntur, vera esse promitto; sed sive vera, seu falsa sunt, legentium usibus inservire' (I do not promise that all that is written here is true, but that, whether true or false, it serves the interests of readers); VII, prologue, col. 657: 'Sic enim nugis seria immiscentur, et falsa veris, ut ad summae veritatis cultum, omnia ex proposito referantur', for the frivolous is mixed with the serious, so that all can be turned to the cultivation of truth (Echard, *Narrative*, pp. 15–16, 24). Cf. also von Moos, 'Fictio', pp. 752, 754, 760.
111 *Vie de saint Edmund* 38, 43ff. (Burrichter, *Wahrheit*, pp. 17–18). Bertau, *Literatur*, p. 524, suggests that the *lais* of Marie de France could be regarded as a declaration of independence by literary fiction.

3. FICTIVE ORALITY

1 Green, *Listening*.
2 See above, pp. 8–10.
3 Green, *Listening*, pp. 169ff., 203ff.
4 Ibid., pp. 27–8, 29, 93–4, 141–2, 225ff.
5 Ibid., pp. 146–7, 173, 174.
6 Ibid., pp. 84ff. on *lesen* used in this sense.
7 Kartschoke, *IASL* 8 (1983), 253ff.

8 Kartschoke, *Arbitrium* 1997, p. 161.
9 *IASL* 8 (1983), 258. Cf. Green, *Listening*, p. 142.
10 Ibid., pp. 142ff.
11 If a German nobleman recited at court himself it was in the aristocratic genre of the love-lyric. Cf. Mertens, 'Kaiser', pp. 455ff., and Kasten, *Frauendienst*, pp. 234ff.
12 Green, *Listening*, p. 144.
13 Ibid., p. 138.
14 Coleman, *Reading*.
15 This situation Coleman designates as 'aurality', which she defines (ibid., p. 228) as applied 'to the reading aloud of a written text to one or a group of listeners'.
16 Ibid., p. 28 and *passim*.
17 Ibid., pp. 16–17, 56.
18 Ibid., pp. xiii, 55, 109–10.
19 Ibid., pp. 1, 20, 27–8.
20 Ibid., pp. 28–9, 31, 80, 89, 123, 221.
21 Green, *Listening*, pp. 63ff.
22 Coleman, *Reading*, pp. 22, 37, 81–2, 96, 102, 117, 145, 214, 215, 220.
23 Ibid., pp. 87, 198–9.
24 Ibid., p. 152.
25 Green, *Listening*, pp. 27–8, 29, 93.
26 Ibid., p. 225.
27 Ibid., p. 230.
28 Coleman, *Reading*, p. 61 ('Chaucer invites his audience . . . to *hear* what he has written' – Coleman's italics).
29 Scholz, *Hören*, pp. 70ff. (*Mariengrüße*: p. 73).
30 Coleman, *Reading*, pp. 149ff.
31 Ibid., pp. 61, 100, 102, 103, 152–3, 177.
32 Green, *Listening*, pp. 152ff.
33 Ibid., pp. 123f., 131ff., 142ff., 296–7.
34 Coleman, *Reading*, pp. 145f., 196–7.
35 Green, *Listening*, pp. 150ff., 179ff., 299ff.
36 Scholz, 'Hörerfiktion', pp. 135ff.
37 Ibid., pp. 141, 142.
38 Ibid., p. 146 ('bisweilen', 'gelegentlich').
39 Ibid., pp. 142, 143.
40 Ibid., pp. 142, 143, 146.
41 Ibid., p. 143 ('fern von jeder Realität').
42 Ibid., pp. 143–4.
43 Ibid., p. 144 (stanza 1627).
44 Green, *Listening*, pp. 14 (together with p. 330, n. 142), 389, n. 242.
45 Scholz, *Hören*, pp. 107–8.
46 Ibid., p. 92. Cf. Green, *Listening*, p. 174.
47 In a much wider context cf. Goetsch, *Poetica* 17 (1983), 202: 'Mündlichkeit in geschriebenen Texten ist nie mehr sie selbst, sondern stets fingiert und damit eine Komponente des Schreibstils und oft auch der bewußten Schreibstrategie des jeweiligen Autors.'
48 Grünkorn, *Fiktionalität*, p. 31. On Hartmann's *Iwein* see Dittmann, 'Begriff', pp. 150ff., and on Wolfram Nellmann, *Erzähltechnik*, p. 28.
49 Nellmann, *Erzähltechnik*, pp. 1–2.

50 Ibid., pp. 1, 26.
51 On this aspect of Wolfram's *Parzival* cf. ibid., pp. 8, 31, 42, 68, but also Grünkorn, *Fiktionalität*, p. 33.
52 Green, *Listening*, p. 263. See also later, pp. 76ff.
53 Green, *MLR* 81 (1986), 357ff., and *Listening*, pp. 186ff.
54 Drube, *Hartmann*, p. 61, fn. 1; Scholz, *Hören*, p. 94; Green, *Listening*, p. 73.
55 Scholz, *Hören*, pp. 96–7. On the twofold reception of Rudolf's works see Green, *ZfdA* 115 (1986), 151 ff.
56 E.g. Peter of Blois, *De confessione, MPL* 207, 1088. On this cf. Green, *Listening*, p. 108.
57 Coleman, *Reading*, pp. xii, 59.
58 Coleman, ibid., p. 71, rightly says of the logic of this argument that it is of the 'heads I win, tails you lose' variety.
59 Ibid., pp. 56–7.
60 Scholz, 'Hörerfiktion', p. 145.
61 In Coleman's drastic words, *Reading*, p. 60: 'the idea of fictive orality collapses under the weight of aural reality'.
62 Ibid., pp. 57–8, with reference to Burrow, *Poetry*, p. 36. Burrow argues similarly in *Writers*, pp. 54–5.
63 Cf. the criticism made by Finnegan, *Poetry*, p. 18, of the view that composition-in-performance (or recital from memory) is the only kind of performance.
64 Coleman, *Reading*, pp. 58–9, refers to similar views expressed by D. Pearsall and D. Mehl on English literature in the Middle Ages.
65 Scholz, 'Hörerfiktion', pp. 142, 146.
66 Green, *Listening*, p. 269.
67 Vitz, *Orality*.
68 Ibid., pp. 26–7.
69 Ibid., pp. 54ff.
70 Ibid., pp. 165 ff., 180ff.
71 The word 'exclusively' is italicised by Vitz herself (ibid., p. 164), but she contradicts this later when discussing some cases of reading aloud in festive settings (pp. 173 ff.).
72 After discussing these few cases of reading aloud Vitz claims (ibid., p. 214) that they represent virtually the only ones. We remain uninformed what precisely she means by 'virtually'.
73 Vitz suggests (ibid., p. 200) that Chrétien may have composed his works for performance at such festive occasions as court weddings. Thus, his *Erec*, whose hero and heroine have to balance the demands of marriage with social obligations, lent itself well to a marriage-feast, she argues, but equally, since the couple are crowned at the end, to a coronation. But there are limits to the possibility of invoking the context of a wedding, as Vitz recognises in the case of the adulterous theme of *Lancelot*, but not in the equally tricky case of *Cligés*. As regards the composition of *Erec* for a festive occasion Vitz seems to be unacquainted with the suggestion of Schmolke-Hasselmann, *Versroman*, pp. 190ff., that it may have been intended to celebrate the engagement of the son of Henry II of England. On a further difficulty for Vitz's view of Chrétien which this interpretation presents see below, n. 119.
74 Scholz, *Hören*, pp. 57ff., 70ff. See also Green, *Listening*, pp. 79ff., 82ff.
75 Vitz, *Orality*, p. 61 (*Roman de Thèbes* 8796).
76 Ibid., p. 67 (*Roman de Thèbes* 7823).
77 Ibid., p. 32 (*Tristan* 1790). On the association of verbs of seeing with reading see Scholz, *Hören*, pp. 116ff. and Green, *Listening*, pp. 139ff.

78 Green, *Listening*, pp. 316ff.
79 Vitz, *Orality*, pp. 113–14 (*Yvain* 1414).
80 Green, *Listening*, p. 319.
81 Grundmann, *AfK* 40 (1958), 1 ff.
82 Vitz, *Orality*, p. 49 (cf. also pp. 89, 113).
83 Ibid., pp. 124–5. (*Perceval* 49).
84 Green, *Listening*, pp. 8ff.
85 Vitz, *Orality*, pp. 32–3 (*Tristan* 1268).
86 Isidore, *Etymologiae* 1 3 ('Vsus litterarum repertus propter memoriam rerum', writing was invented to remember things); Einhard, *Vita* 29, pp. 33–4 ('scripsit memoriaeque mandavit', he wrote and entrusted to historical memory); Wace, *Roman de Rou* 1 ff.; *Lai de l'aubépine* 1 ff. (these last two passages are even quoted by Vitz, *Orality*, pp. 107, 173).
87 Ibid., pp. 228ff.
88 Ibid., p. 229 and fn. 3.
89 Ibid., pp. 234, 236.
90 As Vitz once recognises in passing (p. 241), without drawing any conclusion from it.
91 Ibid., pp. 244ff.
92 Ibid., p. 228.
93 Ibid., p. 250; Lord, *Singer*, pp. 99ff.
94 Vitz, *Orality*, p. 243.
95 Green, 'Aspects'.
96 Vitz, *Orality*, p. 87.
97 Faral, *Jongleurs*, pp. 199, 218ff.
98 Bumke, *Mäzene*, pp. 71–2 (the earliest authors of German romances were clerics at least in the sense of having had a training in literacy).
99 Cf. Karnein, 'Renaissance', p. 124, and Kasten, *Frauendienst*, p. 167, for French literature and Peters, 'Hofkleriker', pp. 31 ff., for German.
100 Vitz, *Orality*, p. 107.
101 Ibid., p. 108.
102 Ibid., pp. 95 and fn. 18 (referring to Green, *Listening*, pp. 115–16), 108–9.
103 Ibid., pp. 111–12.
104 Ibid., pp. 75–6.
105 Ibid., pp. 89–90, 93.
106 Ibid., p. 180.
107 Ibid., p. 91.
108 Cf. Green, *Listening*, pp. 242ff., 244ff., 310ff.
109 Vitz, *Orality*, pp. 117–18.
110 Ibid., pp. 173–4.
111 Ibid., p. 179.
112 See later, pp. 93ff.
113 Vitz, *Orality*, p. 47, fn. 1.
114 See pp. 169, 171.
115 Green, *Listening*, pp. 79ff., 115 ff., 130ff., 135 ff.
116 Vitz, *Orality*, p. 208; Green, *Listening*, p. 86.
117 Vitz, *Orality*, p. 213; Green, *Listening*, pp. 85–6.
118 Vitz, *Orality*, p. 213–14; Green, *Listening*, pp. 88–9.
119 Vitz, *Orality*, pp. 120ff. She also mentions in this connection that Chrétien was neither an Anglo-Norman nor worked in the Anglo-Norman realm, but was from France, and sees in this confirmation of his 'retarded' literacy. However, this takes no account of

Schmolke-Hasselmann's argument, *Versroman*, pp. 184ff., that Chrétien's *Erec* (and *Cligés*?), together with many other romances in French, Arthurian or not, were composed for Anglo-Norman patrons. Vitz's reluctance to engage critically with different views is also apparent elsewhere. She nowhere discusses Krueger, *Readers*, for whom women were not simply a noticeable part of the audience for romances, but were also active as readers. At the least Krueger's opening general chapter and that devoted to Chrétien's *Yvain* and *Lancelot* should have been taken into account. Although Vitz makes many references to Coleman's book she nowhere takes issue with the fact that Coleman's argument (with whatever restrictions) rests on reading a written text in two different ways (aloud to others or to oneself). Coleman also rightly maintains, p. 81, that what she has established for the late Middle Ages can also be found much earlier in Latin and Anglo-Norman. Nor does Vitz, finally, face up to the challenge of Hindman, *Parchment*, for whom the illuminated manuscripts of Chrétien's work, standing between an oral and a literate culture, represent a 'crisis in reading' as society passed from a period of public performance to one of private reading.

120 Vitz, *Orality*, pp. 165, fn. 2; 205, fn. 60; 217, fn. 78.
121 Ibid., p. 165, fn. 2.

4. FICTION AND WOLFRAM'S *PARZIVAL*

1 Kern, *Artusromane*, pp. 92ff.; Currie, *Nature*, pp. 86, 171.
2 Currie, *Nature*, pp. 176–7.
3 Kern, *Artusromane*, p. 92. Maddox, *Romances*, pp. 119ff., goes further in seeing Chrétien's romances as together constituting a 'multitextual totality' (p. 119), a design 'that conveys meaning through the comprehensive dimension created by all five fictions' (p. 122).
4 Cormeau, *Kapitel*, p. 202; Schmolke-Hasselmann, *Versroman*, pp. 174–5.
5 Cormeau, *Kapitel*, p. 184.
6 Ibid., p. 202.
7 Green, 'Namedropping', pp. 104f., 115–16; Kern, *Artusromane*, p. 95; Wand, *Wolfram*, p. 56.
8 Kern, *Artusromane*, p. 95.
9 Schmid, *Familiengeschichten*, pp. 35ff., 171ff.
10 Kern, *Artusromane*, pp. 95–6.
11 Kern, *Artusromane*, on Der Pleier and Cormeau, *Kapitel*, on Heinrich von dem Türlin.
12 Green, 'Namedropping', pp. 91–2, 112–13; Schmolke-Hasselmann, *GRM* 31 (1981), 1ff.; Schirok, *LiLi* 18 (1988), Heft 69, p. 14.
13 *Parzival* 125, 11; *Iwein* 5680. Cf. Wand, *Wolfram*, p. 124.
14 *Iwein* 263, 925. Cf. Wand, *Wolfram*, pp. 124 and 237, n. 324.
15 Wand, *Wolfram*, p. 125.
16 Kern, *Artusromane*, p. 102.
17 See pp. 63–4 and also Schirok, *LiLi* 18 (1988), Heft 69, 12.
18 Kern, *Artusromane*, pp. 117ff.
19 Ibid., pp. 102 ('als fülle er lediglich weiße Flecken auf einer im übrigen vorgezeichneten Landkarte aus'), 121 ('Lücken in der vorgegebenen Erzählwelt ausfindig zu machen und sie ... auszufüllen'), but also p. 98 (under point 6).
20 v. 164ff. (cf. Schirok, *LiLi* 18 [1988], Heft 69, 14, 16). On this background to French romances devoted to Gauvain see Schmolke-Hasselmann, *Versroman*, pp. 86ff. Outside

the romance genre, in her discussion of the 'traitor translator', Morse, *Truth*, p. 209, points to a similar tendency: 'In addition, amplifications include the introduction of new characters and incidents . . . new adventures for known characters are always fitted into chronological periods for which nothing is recorded, like the Harrowing of Hell or the Apocryphal gospels which invent the childhood of Christ.'

21 Kern, *Artusromane*, p. 98 (point 7).

22 Morse, *Truth*, p. 238.

23 To complete the second quotation from Kern given above in n. 19: 'sie so auszufüllen, daß seiner Erfindung noch der Anschein verbürgter Wahrheit zukommt'.

24 Draesner, *Wege*, pp. 217, 433; Kern, 'Leugnen', p. 21. Cf. also Kern, *Artusromane*, p. 97.

25 Wand, *Wolfram*, pp. 125, 130.

26 Draesner, *Wege*, p. 434; Ridder, *Aventiureromane*, p. 30, and *Wolfram-Studien* 15 (1998), 175. Cf. also Cormeau, *Kapitel*, p. 244 ('Die literarische Gattung bezieht sich auf sich selbst zurück') and Meyer, *Verfügbarkeit*, p. 290, for whom 'Selbstbezüglichkeit' is a pointer to the elaboration of a fictional realm. On the similar position with the Hellenistic romance cf. Morgan, 'Make-believe', pp. 215, 222, 223, 224.

27 Cf. Wand, *Wolfram*, p. 130 (and also implicitly Draesner, *Wege*, p. 434: 'von Teilen eines zeitgenössischen Publikums durchschaut'), but also Kern, 'Leugnen', pp. 11 ff.

28 Green, *'Rîtr'*, pp. 7ff. Knapp, 'Subjektivität', argues against a categorial distinction between educated and illiterate recipients, but elsewhere ('Überlegungen', pp. 123–4), he concedes that the romances of Chrétien and Hartmann were recognised as fictional by at least part of their audience (but not by all of it?).

29 Cf. Irvine, *Making*, p. 243, on the position with Virgil: 'the intelligibility and ultimate meaning of Vergil's works depends upon a reader's intertextual competence'. Cf. also, with specific reference to *Reinfried von Braunschweig* but also more generally applicable, Ridder, 'Erzählstruktur', pp. 343–4.

30 Kelly, *Art*, pp. 48.

31 Cormeau, *Kapitel*, p. 176 (cf. also Kern, 'Leugnen', pp. 24–5).

32 Kern, *Artusromane*, p. 96; Nellmann, *Poetica* 28 (1996), 333 ff.

33 Wand, *Wolfram*, p. 15.

34 Ibid., pp. 15–16; Draesner, *Wege*, pp. 203–4.

35 Wand, *Wolfram*, pp. 17, 237, n. 337; Draesner, *Wege*, p. 204.

36 Wand, *Wolfram*, pp. 17ff.; Draesner, *Wege*, pp. 204ff.

37 Wand, *Wolfram*, p. 17; Draesner, *Wege*, pp. 204–5.

38 Green, *Irony*, p. 63, n. 3.

39 Wand, *Wolfram*, pp. 17–18; Draesner, *Wege*, pp. 206–9.

40 Nellmann, *Poetica* 28 (1996), 336–7, has shown similarly how, basing himself on knowledge of Chrétien's *Cligés*, Wolfram has imaginatively developed the figure of Clîas (334, 11), fitting him into the details of his own work, as part of his own invention. The patterning that this reveals agrees with what Morgan has shown in the case of the Greek romances and of which he has said that such 'self-conscious manipulation of plot exposes . . . the controlling mind behind the fiction, and hence its fictionality' ('Make-believe', p. 228).

41 *Parzival* 178, 11 ff.

42 *Erec* 951 ff. (defeat of Iders), 9315 ff. (defeat of Mabonagrin).

43 Green, 'Homicide', pp. 11 ff. (especially pp. 52–3); Rosskopf, *Traum*, pp. 186–7; Brackert, 'Parzival', pp. 143 ff.

44 *Erec* 204ff.

45 Green, *Irony*, pp. 64–5; Draesner, *Wege*, pp. 238–9, 240.

46 Wand, *Wolfram*, p. 31.
47 Draesner, *Wege*, pp. 235 ff.
48 Draesner, ibid., p. 241, calls into question Wand's view (*Wolfram*, p. 218, n. 82) that it is impossible to locate the killing of Lascoyt chronologically.
49 Wand, *Wolfram*, p. 32.
50 Chrétien, *Erec* 590ff.; Hartmann, *Erec* 214ff.
51 Draesner, *Wege*, pp. 242, 244, n. 106.
52 Green, 'Homicide', pp. 52f.; *Irony*, pp. 63 ff.; Wand, *Wolfram*, pp. 30ff.; Draesner, *Wege*, pp. 235 ff.
53 Green, 'Homicide', pp. 52–3; *Irony*, pp. 63–4; Draesner, *Wege*, p. 246 and n. 110.
54 *Erec* 9645; *Parzival* 210, 5.
55 Green, 'Homicide', p. 53.
56 Draesner, *Wege*, p. 243; Brunner, 'Artus', p. 70.
57 See pp. 65–7 on Wolfram's address to Hartmann (143, 21 ff.). On the fictional status of Hartmann's romances see Green, *Listening*, pp. 256–7.
58 Nellmann, *Poetica* 28 (1996), 333 ff.
59 Draesner, *Wege*, p. 240.
60 As is suggested by Nellmann, *Poetica* 28 (1996), 333 ('historisches Relief'), 335. See also my doubts on such a 'historical' dimension, pp. 84ff.
61 Wand, *Wolfram*, pp. 23 ff.; Draesner, *Wege*, pp. 217ff.
62 Wand, *Wolfram*, p. 28; Draesner, *Wege*, p. 218.
63 See p. 83.
64 Wand, *Wolfram*, pp. 28–9; Draesner, *Wege*, p. 219.
65 Draesner, *Wege*, p. 219. What Cormeau, *Kapitel*, p. 196, says of Heinrich von dem Türlin in the passage referred to (n. 63) can also be applied to Hartmann and Wolfram in the present context: 'Die Figuren sind Geschöpfe des Autors, der Autor is verantwortlich für ihr Schicksal.'
66 Cf. Ridder, *Wolfram-Studien* 15 (1998), 176: 'Der Parzival-Erzähler und Hartmann werden hier als Autoren inszeniert, die in eigener Verantwortung Figuren entwerfen und agieren lassen. Die Bindung an eine Quellenvorlage spielt in dieser Reflexion keine Rolle.'
67 Nellmann, *Erzähltechnik*, p. 54. Cf. Draesner, *Wege*, p. 403.
68 Ernst, 'Formen', p. 185.
69 Besch, *PBB* 94 (1972), Sonderheft, p. 755.
70 Butzer, *Euphorion* 89 (1995), 182.
71 Nellmann, *Erzähltechnik*, p. 52 arrives at a total of 78, but Lofmark, *MLR* 67 (1972), 824, using different criteria, suggests the higher figure.
72 Nellmann, *Erzähltechnik*, p. 50, although his reference to medieval Latin practice needs to be qualified in the light of Gompf, 'Figmenta', p. 53.
73 Nellmann, *Erzähltechnik*, p. 51. On re-drawing the boundary: Green, *Listening*, pp. 312–13.
74 Nellmann, *Erzähltechnik*, pp. 51–2.
75 See p. 80 and Draesner, *Wege*, p. 387.
76 Wand, *Wolfram*, p. 62.
77 Cf. Cormeau, *Kapitel*, p. 119, on Wirnt von Gravenberc in *Wigalois,* and p. 207, on the brevity of intertextual references in *Diu Crône* of Heinrich von dem Türlin.
78 Draesner, *Wege*, p. 220, n. 62.
79 Curschmann, *PBB* 106 (1984), 233, makes the important point that Wolfram, in drawing his audience into the process of narration (on this see later, pp. 76–8, 81–2) as part of his

fiction, does this to a certain extent with their understanding and agreement ('gewissermaßen im Einvernehmen mit ihm').

80 Wand, *Wolfram*, p. 132.
81 Draesner, *Wege*, p. 387, n. 23. Cf. also Lofmark, *Wolfram-Studien* 4 (1977), 60.
82 Green, '*Rîtr*', pp. 7ff.; *Listening*, pp. 293ff.
83 What Hagenlocher, *NdJb* 102 (1979), 27ff., has said about source-references in vernacular chronicles is largely applicable to vernacular literature at large.
84 Ibid., p. 29.
85 Ibid., p. 30. Cf. Gottfried (with reference to Ovid as a source, Ganz ed. II 330), *Tristan* 17900: 'deist wâr, wan daz hân ich gelesen' (that is true, because I have read it).
86 Hagenlocher, *NdJb* 102 (1979), 28, 64, n. 125.
87 Green, *Listening*, pp. 243–4.
88 Ibid., p. 162.
89 Ibid., p. 163.
90 Ibid., p. 108. (On Chrétien cf. Kelly, *Art*, pp. 80–1.).
91 E.g. 14249: 'wan alse ich'z von dem buoche nim' (except for what I take from the book); 244: 'als ich ez las' (as I read); 6881: 'als uns diu wârheit/ie hât gesaget und hiute seit' (as the true source always and still maintains).
92 Chrétien concludes his *Yvain* (6814ff.) by claiming that to give anything more than what he has heard about this story would mean adding a lie.
93 8946: 'alsô man an der geste list' (as one reads in the history); 5884: 'als ich an der istôrje las,/und als daz rehte maere seit' (as I read in the history and as the true account says). On the use to which Gottfried puts such historical terminology see later, pp. 183–7.
94 In autobiographical terms (was Wolfram himself illiterate or not?), with regard to the wider cultural world, lay or clerical, to which he belonged, and as regards the literate status of his audience and hence the nature of their reception of his work. Cf. Green, *Listening*, p. 190.
95 Nellmann, *Erzähltechnik*, pp. 26f., 53; Green, 'Oral', pp. 232–3.
96 Wand, *Wolfram*, pp. 202ff.
97 Green, *Listening*, p. 164.
98 9019, 9723: 'als ich ez las' (as I read).
99 Nellmann, ed. II 517 (note on 115, 28–30).
100 Green, 'Rezeption', pp. 271ff.
101 Wand, *Wolfram*, pp. 204, 205–6. Cf. Haug, *Literaturtheorie*, p. 185.
102 Schausten, *Erzählwelten*, pp. 287–8, sums up her survey of four variant German *Tristan* romances (Eilhart, Gottfried, Ulrich von Türheim, Heinrich von Freiberg) by saying that they depart from a common authoritative tradition in favour of developing their own distinctive readings. She describes this situation, using the title of Meyer's book, as the 'Verfügbarkeit der Fiktion'.
103 How far the doubt thus expressed was seized upon as a means of playing with source-references (or even fabricating a fictive source) can be seen in Der Stricker's *Daniel* 7ff., where not merely are the words of the *Alexanderlied* quoted, but the source of this earlier work is even preposterously claimed as the source for *Daniel*. See Kern, *ZfdPh* 93 (1974), Sonderheft, pp. 26f.; Haug, *Literaturtheorie*, p. 276; Mertens, 'Verhältnis', pp. 93f.; Meyer, *Verfügbarkeit*, p. 22; Butzer, *Euphorion* 89 (1995), 181–2. On other cases in German literature see Mackert, *Alexandergeschichte*, p. 90, fn. 75, whose interpretation of the two lines from the *Alexanderlied*, however, differs from mine.

104 See later, pp. 164–5. Even in antiquity not everything that was reported of Alexander could be accepted at face value. Cf. the quotation from the preface of Arrian's *Anabasis*, given by Wiseman, 'Historians', pp. 135–6.

105 Cf. also *König Rother* 16: 'iz ne haben die bŏche gelogen' (unless the books have lied). To establish one's veracity by appealing to a book-source that could conceivably have lied is not exactly straightforward.

106 See later, pp. 177 ff.

107 Cf. Otter, *Inventiones*, p. 16 ('vernacular narrative emancipates itself – not immediately, but gradually over the course of the twelfth century – from the truth-telling requirements that bind Latin writing; it frees itself from truth claims that rest on prior texts or in theologically revealed truth that is accessible through allegory'). However, what we have seen of fictional writing in Latin from the eleventh century (pp. 7–8, 19–20) should make us dubious about the simple equation of Latin writing with truth-telling requirements.

108 Lofmark, *MLR* 67 (1972), 820–1. The requirement not to add to or omit from the source derives its authority from Revelation 22, 18–19. (and still informs the *Rolands-lied*, 9084–5). Wolfram leaves his attitude in doubt by concluding *Parzival* with a similar claim (827, 12: 'niht mêr dâ von nu sprechen wil/ich Wolfram von Eschenbach,/wan als dort der meister sprach', I, Wolfram von Eschenbach, will tell no more of this now than the master told). The only *meister* recently mentioned is Chrétien (827, 1), who did not complete his *Perceval* and to whose fragment Wolfram made considerable additions. By contrast, the Kyot who, according to Wolfram, did complete the work (827, 5: 'endehaft' (to the end); 827, 11: 'dirre âventiure endes zil', the final conclusion of this story) is not termed a *meister* and is presented elsewhere in the work as very much a fictive source. See pp. 78 ff.

109 Lofmark, *Wolfram-Studien* 4 (1977), 33 ff.

110 *Parzival*: Lofmark, *MLR* 67 (1972), 825. *Erec*: Pörksen, *Erzähler*, p. 62, n. 14; Arndt, *Erzähler*, p. 46.

111 Lofmark, *MLR* 67 (1972), 825, 831. Falk, *LwJb* 9 (1968), 13 and 15, betrays a similar confusion of thought when, arguing against those who regard Kyot as a fictive invention, he claims that, whether this may have been meant ironically or as a fiction, Wolfram would not have gone against the truth in deceiving his audience. Neither irony nor fictionality involves deception. On irony cf. Weinrich, *Linguistik*, pp. 59 ff.; Green, *Irony*, pp. 7 ff. On fictionality see p. 12. Cf. also Green, 'Erkennen', pp. 38 ff.

112 *Wolfram-Studien* 4 (1977), 60, where Lofmark refers to Wolfram's knowing audience as 'Mitschuldige(n)', 'mitwissend' and 'mitlachend', all as part of what I understand as the fictional contract.

113 *Der welsche Gast* 1118 ff. Chronicles: Hagenlocher, *NdJb* 102 (1979), 65.

114 Green, 'Âventiure', pp. 110 ff., especially 119. It is not by chance that the occasion (*Erec* 9209–10) when Hartmann is equivocal about the truth he supposedly derives from his source Chrétien refers to a hyperbolic description.

115 Green, 'Âventiure', pp. 114–15.

116 Nellmann, *Erzähltechnik*, p. 54.

117 Pörksen, *Erzähler*, p. 62; Panzer, *Zitieren*.

118 Kern, 'Leugnen', p. 20.

119 Lofmark, *MLR* 67 (1972), 826–7; Green, 'Âventiure', p. 117. On the further implications of this see pp. 86–7.

120 Lofmark, *MLR* 67 (1972), 828–9. In n. 2 Lofmark makes the important point that dependence on a source for the hyperbolic use of light-imagery in 638, 15 ff. is hardly

called for when this stylistic mannerism is so typical of Wolfram himself (cf. Huber, *Licht*, pp. 48 ff.). Cf. also Lofmark, *Wolfram-Studien* 4 (1977), 67.

121 Düwel, *Werkbezeichnungen*, p. 103.

122 Lofmark, *MLR* 67 (1972), 826.

123 Ridder, *Wolfram-Studien* 15 (1998), 171, 181.

124 Stevens, 'Fiction', p. 108. Cf. also, in more general terms, Haug, 'Ästhetik', p. 211: 'Entdeckung der Fiktionalität bedeutet, daß man nicht mehr vorgegebenen Stoffen verpflichtet war, sondern sich das Recht nahm, frei über die literarishcen Materilien, wo immer sie herkommen mochten, zu verfügen.'

125 Stevens, 'Fiction', pp. 106, 113.

126 See pp. 9–10.

127 Knapp, 'Subjektivität', suggests that passages where Wolfram involves his audience in telling his story are meant ironically, so that they are not really invited into collusion with him. If signals are called for in the case of fictionality, they are also requisite for irony. Knapp does not establish any, but instead contents himself with rhetorical questions and hypotheses. What he says elsewhere in arguing against *Parzival* as fiction 'Überlegungen', p. 119 – this 'müßte man für das Mittelalter erst nachweisen' – applies equally in this case.

128 Nellmann, *Erzähltechnik*, p. 40.

129 Ibid.

130 Ibid., p. 41.

131 Hartmann: *Erec* 6902 ('waz welt ir daz der künec tuo?', what would you like the king to do?), 9263; *Iwein* 3309. *Le Bel inconnu*: Bauschke, 'Auflösung', pp. 108, 111.

132 On this concept see Ridder, *Aventiureromane*, pp. 89 f., 279–80, 285 ff. and Dietl, 'Fiktionalität', p. 181.

133 The fictional collusion summed up in this passage has been emphasised more than once: Nellmann, *Erzähltechnik*, p. 68 ('gemeinsam'); Lofmark, *Wolfram-Studien* 4 (1977), 60 ('mitwissend und mitlachend', 'mitschuldig'); Haug, *Literaturtheorie*, p. 166 ('Komplizen').

134 Wilhelm, *PBB* 33 (1908), 286 ff., discussed critically by Kolb, *Munsalvaesche*, pp. 188 ff. Speyer, *Fälschungen*, pp. 69 ff., also discusses source-fabrications (letters from heaven and books mysteriously found in graves or archives) in classical and early Christian antiquity. On fabricated source-references see also Wild, 'Manuscripts', pp. 203 ff. Lofmark, *Wolfram-Studien* 4 (1977), 58, has also pointed out that Chrétien's successors in France make frequent use of fabricated source-references.

135 Although Wilhelm uses 'fiction' of Wolfram's work (ibid., pp. 288, 289), he also unjustifiably talks of his 'absicht sie [seine Leser] zu täuschen' (p. 288).

136 Ibid., pp. 289, 339.

137 Ibid., pp. 330 ff. On fabricated written sources claimed for heroic epics or *Spielmannsepen* based on oral transmission cf. Green, *Listening*, pp. 161 ff. To imply the literate status of the source served as a guarantee of truth when oral tradition was under clerical attack for its unreliability. This is not so irrelevant to the romance as Kolb, *Munsalvaesche*, p. 189, suggests, for this genre also had to deal with criticism because of its fictionality.

138 Cf. Draesner, *Wege*, pp. 393, 394–5.

139 On this division in scholarship between 'Kyotisten' and 'Fiktionisten' (sometimes amplified by a third group taking into account other sources of *Parzival*) see Grünkorn, *Fiktionalität*, p. 100; Draesner, *Wege*, p. 382; Butzer, *Euphorion* 89 (1995), 179.

140 Lofmark, *Wolfram-Studien* 4 (1977), 34.

141 Schirok, 'Passagen', p. 141.
142 Nellmann, *Erzähltechnik*, p. 55. Cf. Draesner, *Wege*, p. 383.
143 Lofmark, *Wolfram-Studien* 4 (1977), 35–6.
144 Ibid., pp. 41, 47. On Anglo-Norman historiography see Leckie, *Passage*; Ingledew, *Speculum* 69 (1994), 665 ff.; Otter, *Inventiones*, Damian-Grint, *Historians*.
145 Nellmann, *Erzähltechnik*, pp. 55, 57.
146 *Wolfram-Studien* 4 (1977), 36ff. On other reasons for doubting the literal truth of what Wolfram claims about his source cf. Ernst, *WW* 35 (1985), 177ff.. The force of Ernst's points is quite independent of the specific proposal he goes on to make.
147 Chenu, *Théologie*, p. 387, quotes Adelard to this effect. Chenu describes this as 'camoufler sous des autorités pseudonymes ou sous le patronage des Arabes l'énoncé de ses recherches'. I owe this reference to Schreiner, *Saeculum* 17 (1966), 157–8.
148 Lofmark, *Wolfram-Studien* 4 (1977), 47, 58.
149 Nellmann, *Erzähltechnik*, pp. 58f.; Schirok, 'Passagen', p. 141.
150 *Erzähltechnik*, p. 57, and also the note on 453, 5–455, 22 in his edition (II 664). Cf. also Draesner, *Wege*, p. 389.
151 Lofmark, *Wolfram-Studien* 4 (1977), 62–3.
152 Lofmark, *MLR* 67 (1972), 843, n. 1, points out that Wolfram's dislike of painted ladies is characteristic of him and was well known to his audience, thus needing no support from a source.
153 Attention has been drawn to this suspicious triviality of what is authenticated by Ridder, *Wolfram-Studien* 15 (1998), 181, n. 44.
154 Lofmark, *Wolfram-Studien* 4 (1977), 67.
155 Green, *Art, passim*.
156 Lofmark, *Wolfram-Studien* 4 (1977), 69. Wyss, 'Erzählstrukturen', p. 267, regards the fabulous source Kyot as Wolfram's declaration of independence as an author of romance fiction.
157 Schirok, 'Passagen', p. 142.
158 Feeney, *Gods*, p. 186.
159 On this see above all Cormeau, *Kapitel*, pp. 189ff., and Kern, *Artusromane*, pp. 117ff.
160 Cormeau, *Kapitel*, pp. 195–6, 214.
161 On an intertextual reference to *Parzival* in *Seifried Helbling* see p. 88.
162 Like Nellmann, *ZfdA* 117 (1988), 44, I still take this whole passage to belong to Gottfried's polemics against Wolfram.
163 Ibid., pp. 46ff., summed up on p. 49.
164 Although Krohn, 'Finden', pp. 43ff., rightly emphasises the conventional and practical restrictions on the medieval poet's creative inventiveness, he nonetheless adduces a number of examples where *vunt* or *vinden* implies an original invention rather than finding something already present in a source. These include Der Marner on Reinmar von Zweter (p. 51), and other examples concerning Der Marner himself, Berthold von Regensburg, and Gottfried, *Tristan* 19204–5 (p. 52). Cf. also Meyer, *Verfügbarkeit*, pp. 71–2.
165 Schröder, *ZfdA* 104 (1976), 320, 332, 336.
166 As in the case of Veldeke's 'meisterlîchen fünde', masterly inventions (4741).
167 Chinca, *History*, p. 114, suggests that *vinden* here recalls 'the rhetorical *inventio*, defined by the *Rhetorica ad Herennium* (1.2.3) as 'excogitatio rerum verarum aut veri similium, quae causam probabilem reddunt' (devising true or verisimilar details that render a case probable).

168 4663 ff.
169 Green, *Listening*, pp. 237–8.
170 *Etymologiae* I 41.
171 *Dialogus*, p. 17.
172 Strasser, 'Fiktion', p. 69. That history could be subverted in this way in antiquity is suggested by Wiseman, 'Historians', p. 123. He quotes Seneca's impersonation of the irresponsible historian, claiming to record, of all things, what was transacted in heaven, laughing at the idea of a historian producing sworn referees and recommending the inquirer to 'ask the man who saw Drusilla on her way to heaven'. Eyewitness authentication is rendered here as impossible, and therefore irrelevant, as in Hartmann's case.
173 Green, *Listening*, p. 256.
174 Ibid.
175 Knape, *Historie*, pp. 168 ff.
176 Green, *Listening*, pp. 258–9.
177 Christ, *Rhetorik*, pp. 313–14.
178 Green, *Listening*, p. 258.
179 Cf. Nellmann, *Erzähltechnik*, p. 68. When Lofmark, *MLR* 67 (1972), 832, refers to what he regards as the angry, impatient tone of this passage he introduces a surmise too biographical to be convincing.
180 Green, *Listening*, pp. 247, 261–2.
181 Ruh, *Epik* II 122, 133 f.; Ernst, 'Formen', p. 183. See also later, pp. 144–6.
182 Nellmann, *Poetica* 28 (1996), 327 ff., especially 344: 'Parzival war für Wolfram, so glaube ich, eine historische Figur.'
183 Cf. Stevens, 'Fiction', p. 116: '*Parzival*, for all that it may at times look like history, advertises itself repeatedly as a fictional construct.'
184 Ibid., p. 335.
185 Ibid., pp. 333 ff.
186 See above, pp. 57–8.
187 *Poetica* 28 (1996), 338 ff.
188 See p. 250, n. 385.
189 *Poetica* 28 (1996), 340.
190 See pp. 5–6.
191 See later, p. 176. Keck, *Liebeskonzeption*, pp. 140–1, 141–2, suggests that Thomas put forward his *Tristan* version as historical, basing herself on Breri, who like Wace was seen as a historian of the rulers of Britain (Douce 848 ff.) and into whose historical framework Thomas' characters are inserted. This may place the *Tristan* story in a historical context, but it does not make the action of the story itself historical. We need to follow William of Malmesbury in distinguishing between a general context, which may be *historia*, and particular events narrated, which are *fabulae*. The same kind of distinction was made by Bernardus 'Silvestris' between the historical nucleus of the Trojan War and the fabulous accretions concerning Aeneas (see below, p. 241, n. 224). It is also made by Jacob van Maerlant in his *Spiegel historiael*, where he argues that despite the minstrels' invention of fabricated stories about Arthur the truth about the king should not be disdained. He will therefore not write about such non-historical characters as Lancelot, Perceval and Agravain, but distinguishes them from figures like Walewein, Mordred and Keye, about whom he has reliable information in Latin sources (by which he most probably meant Geoffrey of Monmouth, whose *Historia* was known to him and who includes the latter group of names, but not the former).

Cf. Besamusca, 'Material', p. 189, but also Gerritsen, 'Jacob', pp. 368ff. Jürgen Wolf, in a book he is preparing on vernacular book-culture, argues that Wolfram 'historicises' *Parzival*, but adds: 'Allerdings betrifft dies primär wohl nur den unmittelbaren Horizont des Werks selbst und nicht dessen historische Akzeptanz außerhalb eines engen literaturhistorischen Diskurses.' I thank Wolf for allowing me to see an early draft of his work.

192 We are on even less contested ground when William of Malmesbury, *Gesta* III 287 (p. 342), attests the historicity of Gawein. Cf. Burrichter, *Wahrheit*, pp. 34–5.

193 Knapp, *Historie*, pp. 150–1.

194 See later, pp. 113ff.

195 *Historie*, p. 151, n. 44.

196 Heinzle, *Wandlungen*, pp. 105–6; Green, *Listening*, pp. 265ff. See also p. 200.

197 Nor does Knapp, for he refers to them as purely fictional (p. 150).

198 Knapp, *DVjs* 70 (1996), 363ff.; Brunner, *Wolfram*, pp. 94ff.

199 Knapp, *DVjs* 70 (1996), 366–7 and n. 48. Wyss, 'Erzählstrukturen', p. 271, also disagrees with Knapp's view that we are in fact dealing with *historia* and says instead: 'Der Roman tut so, als wäre er Geschichtsschreibung.' For Wyss the rounded structure of the romance stamps it as fiction, rather than history. On the way in which *Parzival* concludes, however, by opening out onto the stories of Prester John and Loherangrin Wyss says (p. 272): 'Als Roman vermag er auch politische Reminiszenzen wie die Stammsage der Brabanter Herzöge oder den fiktiven Presbyterbrief zu verarbeiten, ohne daß er damit Geschichte erzählen muß.'

Elsewhere Knapp (*Subjektivität*) argues that the historical echoes at the beginning and close of *Parzival* are not merely a historical framework, but make of the whole work a *historia*. Wolfram then filled this out with freely invented details, as was allowed to the medieval historian (cf. pp. 146ff.). By contrast, Nellmann, *Poetica* 28 (1996), 343, sees these details as an opening and closing historical anchorage for what is consciously fictional writing. Although he recognises the fundamental difference between 'functional' and 'pure' fiction (cf. pp. 151–2), Knapp associates *Parzival* with the former, whereas I classify it with the latter.

200 See later, pp. 142ff.

201 Haug, *Literaturtheorie*, pp. 174ff.

202 Knapp, *DVjs* 70 (1996), 365.

5. FICTION AND STRUCTURE

1 On the criticism of rhyme for its lack of conformity to the truth see Haug, *Literaturtheorie*, pp. 236f., 243ff.; Spiegel, *Romancing*, pp. 55ff., 340, n. 34; Burrichter, *Wahrheit*, p. 163; Damian-Grint, *Historians*, pp. 172ff.

2 Von Moos, *PBB(T)* 98 (1976), 117; Mehtonen, *Concepts*, p. 19.

3 Von Moos, *PBB(T)* 98 (1976), 93ff. (here, p. 117).

4 Lactantius, *Opera* 1.11.23–4 (cf. Trimpi, *Traditio* 30 (1974), 73–4). See also Zeeman, 'Schools', pp. 155–6.

5 Grünkorn, *Fiktionalität*, pp. 56ff.

6 In his *Poetics*, Chapter 7, Aristotle argues that an art-form (he is talking of tragedy, but also of fables at large) must constitute a whole, with a beginning, a middle, and an end, by contrast with history (Chapter 23), whose writers present not a single action, but a single period in which there is a purely accidental relationship of one event to

others. Cf. also Fichte, 'Fakt', p. 46, on the *Poetics*, Chapter 9. The twentieth-century scholar is Daiches, *Study*, p. 55 (quoted by Lacy, *Craft*, p. 113).

7 Morgan, 'Make-believe', pp. 220, 221. The indication that a plot has been consciously planned constitutes a signal to the audience that they are dealing with fiction, and also an invitation to them to adopt a fictive stance.

8 Busby, *Chrétien*, p. 87.

9 Haug, 'Epos', pp. 84ff.

10 Green, *Listening*. On complex structures and fictionality cf. Haug, 'Epos', p. 86: 'Die Realisierung derart komplexer Strukturen ist selbstverständlich nur mehr im Raum freier Fiktionalität möglich.'

11 Lamarque and Olsen, *Truth*, p. 448.

12 Morgan, 'Make-believe', pp. 224, 228.

13 Gallais, *CCM* 14 (1971), 70–1.

14 Dietl, 'Fiktionalität', p. 182.

15 Ibid.

16 Schmolke-Hasselmann, *Versroman*.

17 Köhler, *Ideal*, pp. 236ff; Emmel, *Formprobleme*, pp. 11 ff., 41 ff.

18 Baehr, *Sprachkunst* 2 (1971), 43 ff.

19 Hartmann's *Erec*: Green, *Irony*, pp. 317–18; Wolfram's *Parzival*: Schneider, *Parzival-Studien*.

20 Kelly, *Viator* 1 (1970), 196; *Art*, p. 17.

21 Kelly, *MPh* 67 (1970), 9ff. (here, p. 9).

22 Cf. the *Rolandslied* (9084–5) for a clerical example of this attitude.

23 Kelly, *MPh* 67 (1970), 17.

24 Faral, *Arts*, pp. 55 ff.

25 Lucan and Statius: von Moos, *PBB(T)* 98 (1976), 95. Engelbert, *Speculum virtutis* x 17 (p. 343), quoted by Knapp, *Historie*, p. 85.

26 *Dialogi* ii 35 (p. 130). Cf. Wolpers, *Heiligenlegende*, p. 63.

27 Knape, *Historie*, pp. 168 ff.

28 *Vita s. Guthlaci*, p. 64.

29 *Vita s. Wulfstani*, p. 2. Strunk, *Kunst*, p. 155, quotes a comparable example from the *Vitae abbatum Acaunensium*, especially interesting because it opposes the *ordo naturalis* to the *artificialis*, at home in *confusis fabulis*.

30 *Gesta* ii 518.

31 *Historia* [2] p. 1.

32 *Commentum* ii 97 (quoted by Groos, *MLN* 87 [1972], 393).

33 *Commentarii* i 4f. Cf. Singerman, *Clouds*, p. 2.

34 *Ars poetica* 148–9. Cf. Singerman, *Clouds*, pp. 2–3.

35 *Scholia Vindobonensia*, p. 5. Cf. Singerman, *Clouds*, pp. 3–4.

36 Fromm, 'Eneasromane', pp. 31 f. In other words, what is dislocated from its actual point in time by the *ordo artificialis* need not be an actual account of events, it can also be details necessary for their full understanding. (On the relevance of this to Wolfram's technique of delaying the release of information in *Parzival* see p. 102.) Furthermore, the account of events out of their natural time-sequence need not always be given by the narrator, for sometimes a character in the story can stand in for him. This is already the case in the *Aeneid*, where Aeneas recounts the past to Dido in Books ii and iii, and Anchises the future to Aeneas in Book vi.

37 Konrad von Hirsau, *Dialogus*, pp. 18, 194–8 (cf. Fromm, 'Eneasromane', p. 30); Geoffrey of Vinsauf, *Poetria nova* 101 ff. (cf. also Groos, *MLN* 87 [1972], 394).

38 See later, pp. 160, 162. Lacy, 'Typology', pp. 36–7, also points out that authors of shorter texts, freed from the constraints of simultaneous narratives, can adopt the *ordo naturalis*, presenting events in linear progression.

39 *Accessus*, ed. Huygens, p. 148 (cf. von Moos, *PBB(T)* 98 [1976], 95).

40 This term is used by Bernard of Utrecht, *Commentum in Theodolum*, quoted by Faral, *Arts*, p. 57.

41 Singerman, *Clouds*, pp. 26ff. (quotation p. 28).

42 Green, *Irony*, p. 133.

43 Steinhoff, *Darstellung*.

44 Green, *Irony*, p. 133. Kellermann, *Aufbaustil*, p. 43, fn. 1, asks whether Chrétien was dependent on Virgil for this, but he could equally well depend on the handbooks and commentaries that so often quote Virgil's example.

45 Green, *Art*, p. 15, fn. 57, and in more detail *Wolfram-Studien* 6 (1980), 92ff.

46 Examples also occur already in *Erec*. For example, when after recounting the defeated Yder's despatch to Arthur's court the narrator reverts to Erec his use of *ancor* makes it clear that we are being taken back to pick up the narrative thread where we left him (1244–5: 'Or redevons d'Erec parler,/Qui ancor an la place estoit,/Ou la bataille feite avoit', now we must speak of Erec again who was still at the place where he had done combat).

47 *Yvain* 175 ff., where the opening line stresses that with this account we are moving back seven years to a point even before Chrétien's story began. Cf. Kelly, *Art*, p. 269. On other aspects of *Yvain* see Kullmann, 'Formen', pp. 31 ff.

48 *Yvain* 3601 ff.

49 Ibid., 4821 ff.

50 The switch to the Harpin strand is governed by a review of past events by the lord of the castle (3851 ff.) and that to the *Pesme Aventure* by a similar account (5256ff.) which opens with an explicit flashback ('il avint mout grant pieç'a', it happened a long time ago).

51 Ruh, 'Interpretation', pp. 44ff.; Cormeau, *Wolfram-Studien* 5 (1979), 67. Lacy, 'Typology', p. 43, points to a similar feature in Chrétien's *Lancelot*: 'Lancelot, having offended the Queen by delaying (however slightly) his entry into the cart, repeatedly encounters adventures that threaten to delay or divert him once again.'

52 Ryding, *Structures*, pp. 140–1. On shorter parallel narratives in *Perceval* see also Kullmann, 'Formen', pp. 24ff.

53 Weigand, *Parzival*, pp. 35–6; Busby, *Chrétien*, p. 69.

54 Another example is 6514ff. (a switch from Perceval to Gauvain).

55 Baumgartner, 'Vers', p. 7. (Cf. also Kullmann, 'Formen', pp. 44f.) The term 'gliding transitions' (or *iuncturae subtiles*) comes from Kelly, *Viator* 1 (1970), 198.

56 Gruenter, 'Bauformen', pp. 40ff.; Rathofer, *ZfdA* 95 (1966), 27ff.; Green, *Irony*, pp. 137ff.

57 Although Gottfried's words (17351: 'Des selben morgens') may count as one of Kelly's gliding transitions, for they apply to both strands of the narrative, Gottfried also makes use of an explicit switch similar to those in Chrétien's *Perceval*. Cf. *Tristan* 3748ff. as a switch from Tristan back to Rual, where *zehant*, straightaway (3756) at the start of the new strand makes it clear that we have gone back in time to the point immediately after Tristan's kidnapping.

58 *Perceval* 412ff.

59 See the notes on the opening of this Book in the editions of Bartsch and Marti (i 311) and of Nellmann (ii 603).

60 Green, *Art*, pp. 176ff.
61 Worked out in greater detail by Sauer, *Parzival.*
62 Fromm, 'Eneasromane', p. 33.
63 It is conceivable that Hartmann was alerted to the possibilities of such a feature by an example in Chrétien's *Yvain* (3782: 'Assez an savroiz la reison/Une autre foiz, quant leus sera', you will hear enough about this matter another time, when the occasion arises), especially if Hartmann, when composing his *Erec*, was also acquainted with *Yvain* (cf. Piquet, *Etude*, pp. 231 f.).
64 Green, *Art*, pp. 28ff.
65 *Ars poetica* 42ff. Cf. Singerman, *Clouds*, p. 3.
66 Groos, *MLN* 87 (1972), 393; Simon, *Einführung*, p. 211. Although she does not refer to the *ordo narrationis* the same point is made by Hirschberg, *Untersuchungen*, p. 317. By contrast, Spitz, 'Bogengleichnis', pp. 271 ff., interprets this passage in terms of typology; for my grounds for disagreeing with him on this see Green, *Art*, p. 35, fn. 138.
67 Green, *Art*, p. 33 ff.
68 Ibid., pp. 35–6.
69 With regard to 805, 14f. Groos, *MLN* 87 (1972), 392, talks of the 'veracity of his [Wolfram's] assertion', but the presence of the word *maere* (tale) suggests instead the truth of his narrative.
70 Otter, *Inventiones*, pp. 139–40 (cf. also p. 131).
71 Ohly, *Bedeutungsforschung*, pp. 315–16, 363–4.
72 A passage from the *Vita s. Abbonis*, quoted by Strunk, *Kunst*, p. 131, illustrates this conjunction in the words 'idem quidem studium, sed dissimili intentione' (the same application, but with a different aim).
73 *Verus*: Kolb, *DVjs* 41 (1967), 10ff.; Wolf, *ABÄG* 6 (1974), 98; Ohly, 'Figuren', p. 133. *Novus*: Wolf, *ABÄG* 6 (1974), 100. *Noster*: Ohly, 'Figuren', p. 133.
74 Kolb, *DVjs* 41 (1967), 17–18. The fact that *supremus* can be omitted in favour of *Iupiter* alone illustrates that a signal is not always indispensable with typology.
75 See above all three essays in his *Bedeutungsforschung*: 'Synagoge und Ecclesia. Typologisches in mittelalterlicher Dichtung' (pp. 312ff.), 'Außerbiblisch Typologisches zwischen Cicero, Ambrosius und Aelred von Rievaulx' (pp. 338ff.) and 'Halbbiblische und außerbiblische Typologie' (pp. 361 ff.). For Ohly's (brief) answer to Schröder's criticism of his views see Ohly, 'Figuren', p. 144, n. 1. He is supported in this by Michel, 'Übergangsformen', pp. 43 ff., and Wandhoff, *Blick*, p. 278, fn. 93.
76 Ohly, *Bedeutungsforschung*, p. 322 ('Eva causa mortis, Maria causa salutis', Eve the cause of death, Mary the cause of salvation).
77 Pinder, *Kunst*, Abb. 370, 373; Ohly, *Bedeutungsforschung*, p. 312.
78 Solomon and Constantine: Ohly, *Bedeutungsforschung*, pp. 366, 374f., 376. Ezechias and Theodosius: ibid., p. 375, fn. 33. Exodus and crusading present: Green, *Exodus*, pp. 252, 255, 257.
79 Ohly, 'Figuren', p. 132.
80 Ulysses and Hercules: Ohly, *Bedeutungsforschung*, p. 327. Socrates: ibid., p. 366. Orpheus: Ohly, 'Figuren', pp. 133 ff.
81 Eleusis and Cithaeron: Ohly, *Bedeutungsforschung*, p. 396; Roman triumphs: ibid., p. 370.
82 Romulus and Remus, Peter and Paul: ibid., p. 316. Virgil and Juvencus: ibid., pp. 366, 379 (with the quotation from Juvencus).
83 Ohly, 'Figuren', pp. 127–8, together with p. 145, n. 10 and n. 11.
84 Ibid., p. 140; Haug, *Literaturtheorie*, p. 220.

85 That the possibility of mixing truth with falsehood is a feature of fictionality we have seen in our definition (cf. pp. 16–17); it was well known both to Horace and to Macrobius (cf. p. 204, n. 57, and pp. 14–15).

86 Ohly, *Bedeutungsforschung*, pp. 329–30 and fn. 21 (where the text is given).

87 Ibid., p. 343.

88 Ibid., p. 379. Other examples come from Sedulius (cf. Strunk, *Kunst*, p. 134) and Aelred of Rievaulx (cf. Ohly, *Bedeutungsforschung*, p. 350).

89 Fontaine, *Sulpice* 132; Ohly, *Bedeutungsforschung*, p. 394.

90 Fontaine, *Sulpice* 123 ff.; Ohly, *Bedeutungsforschung*, p. 393–4.

91 *Vita s. Martini*, c. 4 (p. 260).

92 Fontaine, *Sulpice* 126, 132, refers to 'stylisation typologique' and to 'artifices littéraires'.

93 Green, *FMS* 14 (1980), 408.

94 Heinzle, 'Stellung', p. 106, has also interpreted the relationship between Lancelot and Galaad in the prose *Lancelot* in typological terms. This work may claim historical truth for itself (cf. Heinzle, ibid., pp. 104 ff.; Green, *Listening*, p. 267), but its characters and their relations with one another come from the fictional realm of the Arthurian romance and it also shows literary artifice, as in the *Vita s. Martini* (on the dimension of time, crucial for typology, see Ruberg, *Raum*, pp. 105 ff.). To that (limited) extent this typology operates within a fictional work, as with *Parzival*.

95 Cf. Ohly, *Bedeutungsforschung*, pp. 317, 332; Wolf, *Gottfried*, pp. 111 ff.; Wandhoff, *Blick*, p. 281. Schausten, *Erzählwelten*, pp. 145 ff., discusses the prefiguration of Tristan and Isold by Riwalin and Blanscheflur, expressly distancing herself from biblical typology. (Does she mean by this that *Tristan* is for her an example of secular typology?) Significantly, she regards the prehistory not as a mere prelude or anticipation of the main story, but rather as being surpassed by it (pp. 155, 159, 162, 166, 168).

96 Speckenbach, *Studien*, p. 66; Schindele, *Tristan*, p. 49; Keuchen, *Strukturen*, pp. 76–7; Wessel, *Probleme*, p. 356.

97 Keuchen, *Strukturen*, p. 77.

98 Wolf, *Gottfried*, p. 122.

99 Marke's spring festival, at which Riwalin plays a dominant part, has been related typologically to the eternal springtime of the *locus amoenus* landscape of the love-grotto. Cf. Krohn, *Gottfried* 161; Wessel, *Probleme*, p. 385, fn. 1146.

100 Speckenbach, *Studien*, p. 66, fn. 54; Wessel, *Probleme*, p. 329; Wolf, *Gottfried*, p. 121.

101 Ibid., p. 118.

102 Nauen, *Bedeutung*, pp. 57 f.; Keuchen, *Strukturen*, pp. 169–70; Wessel, *Probleme*, pp. 328–9; Tomasek, *Utopie*, p. 183.

103 *Morgenrôt*: 7296, 8285, 9462, 10890, 10894, 11026, 11512. *Sunne*: 8284, 9460, 10165, 10891, 11010, 11026, 11512, 12570, 17587.

104 Cf. Keuchen, *Strukturen*, p. 152.

105 Ibid., pp. 167 ff.; Ohly, 'Figuren', p. 128; Wessel, *Probleme*, pp. 333 ff.; Tomasek, *Utopie*, p. 184.

106 Schwietering, *Dichtung*, p. 192.

107 Wolf, *ABÄG* 6 (1974), 99, 103.

108 The passage from Notker Balbulus is quoted by Ohly, 'Figuren', p. 128.

109 Hahn, *Raum*, pp. 131–2; Rathofer, *ZfdA* 95 (1966), 29 ff.; Wolf, *ABÄG* 6 (1974), 101–2, 109; Keuchen, *Strukturen*, pp. 179 ff.; Wessel, *Probleme*, pp. 461–2; Tomasek, *Utopie*, pp. 184–5.

110 Virgil, *Aeneid* IX 571; XII 208; Geoffrey of Monmouth, *Historia* [17] p. 10, and elsewhere.

111 *Hol*: 16688, 16693, 16705, 16765. *Klûse*: 16810, 17083, 17206, 17227. Within the love-grotto episode Tristan and Isold are also presented as typologically surpassing the lovers of classical antiquity whom they commemorate there (Keuchen, *Strukturen*, pp. 185 ff.; Wessel, *Probleme*, pp. 373, 465).

112 Hahn, *AfdA* 75 (1964), 172; Keuchen, *Strukturen*, p. 245; Tomasek, *Utopie*, p. 186.

113 Hahn, *AfdA* 75 (1964), 173. The 'edeliu herzen' (noble hearts) take the lesson of the ful-filment represented by Tristan and Isold to heart by imitating their example (Rathofer, 'Hirsch', p. 374 and fn. 15; Keuchen, *Strukturen*, pp. 164 f.; Tomasek, *Utopie*, p. 186). In the same way biblical typology acknowledges no possibility of surpassing Christ's transcendence of earlier types, but only the individual believer's *imitatio Christi*.

114 Tomasek, *Utopie*, p. 186.

115 Gottfried asserts the truth of his narrative by typological signals such as 'der wâre Êlikôn', the true Helicon (4895) and *bewaeret*, shown to be true (17232).

116 See later, pp. 123 ff.

117 Warning, 'Formen', pp. 36–7, 38, fn. 16, 39. Cf. also Michel, 'Übergangsformen', pp. 66–7; Wandhoff, *Blick*, pp. 276 ff.

118 E.g. Wolf, *ABÄG* 6 (1974), 93 ('figurales Denken'), 94 ('typologisches Denken', 'Denkform'), 99 ('typologische Denkweise'), 120 ('typologisches Denkschema'); Wolf, *Gottfried*, p. 122 ('Analogien zu typologischen Relationen'); Haug, *Literaturtheorie*, p. 217 ('Denkmuster . . . der Typologie verpflichtet'); Ohly, *Bedeutungsforschung*, p. 363 ('typologische Denkart').

119 E.g. Wolf, *ABÄG* 6 (1974), 112 ('eine Art säkularisierter Typologie', cf. p. 129). Ohly talks of 'säkularisierte Denkformen' in his contribution to the discussion of Michel, 'Übergangsformen', p. 72.

120 Wessel, *Probleme*, p. 410.

121 Wandhoff, *Blick*, pp. 290–1, basing himself on Warning, 'Formen', p. 39.

122 Morse, *Truth*, pp. 27–8.

123 Ruh, *Epik* I 132 (criticising P. W. Tax), 135 (disagreeing with B. Willson).

124 Chydenius, *Problem*, pp. 41 ff.

125 Notker Balbulus echoes this in describing God, arranging for Bede to appear as a *novus sol*, as 'naturarum dispositor Deus' (Ohly, 'Figuren', p. 128).

126 Ohly, *Bedeutungsforschung*, p. 365.

127 Tigerstedt, *CLS* 5 (1968), 468.

128 Cramer, *Daphnis* 15 (1986), 263.

129 Ibid., pp. 264–5. Tomasek, *Utopie*, sees utopianism as central to Gottfried's *Tristan* romance, but also touches briefly on Hartmann and Wolfram (pp. 35 ff.).

130 Quoted by Lüthi, *Volksmärchen*, p. 5.

131 Jauss, 'Genese', p. 428, who talks revealingly here of a 'gewußte Fiktion'. Cf. also Damian-Grint, *Historians*, p. 86, on the different functions of wonders in historical and fictional writing.

132 Propp, *Morphologie*, p. 9.

133 Lüthi, *Volksmärchen*, pp. 25, 78–9.

134 Ibid., pp. 20, 21. The same is true of the Arthurian romance whose conventional setting is an equally unspecified springtime.

135 Green, *Wolfram-Studien* 6 (1980), 89–90.

136 Lüthi, *Volksmärchen*, pp. 31, 50, 51.

137 Ibid., p. 33; Lüthi, *Märchen*, p. 24.

138 Propp, *Morphologie*, p. 74.

139 Nolting-Hauff, *Poetica* 6 (1974), 144.

140 See later, pp. 115–17.

141 Simon, *Einführung*, pp. 35 ff.

142 Lüthi, *Märchen*, p. 38.

143 On Wace as a historian see later, p. 176. On the connection between Wace and Chrétien see Wolf, '*Fol*', pp. 205 ff.

144 Ruh, *Epik* I 117.

145 Baehr, *Sprachkunst* 2 (1971), 55; Green, *Irony*, p. 114.

146 To make a happy ending possible Fénice's husband dies conveniently, but hardly persuasively.

147 Haidu, *Distance*, pp. 100ff.; Putter, *Gawain*, pp. 144ff. In his *Tristan* Gottfried made use of folktale elements, but also criticised some of them.

148 Jackson, 'Observations', p. 79; Green, *Irony*, p. 234. This concluding passage echoes an earlier one on the occasion of the wedding of Iwein and Laudine (2426ff.), with a similar string of conditions and use of *waenlich*. If the earlier wish did not stand up to the realities of their married life we are led to wonder whether the concluding wish will turn out any differently.

149 See above, pp. 62–5.

150 Bumke, *DVjs* 65 (1991), 236ff.

151 Killy, *Kitsch*, p. 31.

152 Alanus ab Insulis, *De planctu* 2, 845, 17ff. (quoted and discussed by Huber, *Aufnahme*, p. 101); Thomasin von Zerclaere, *Der welsche Gast* 1023ff., 1079ff. (cf. also Düwel, *Fabula* 32 [1991], 67ff.; Green, *Listening*, p. 143).

153 Mertens, 'Verhältnis', p. 103, n. 4.

154 Nolting-Hauff, *Poetica* 6 (1974), 129ff.

155 Meyer, *Die Verfügbarkeit der Fiktion*.

156 *Poetica* 6 (1974), 151 ff.

157 Ibid., pp. 161 ff.

158 Ibid., pp. 164ff.

159 Cormeau, *Wolfram-Studien* 5 (1979), 63 ff.

160 Ibid., pp. 66, 71.

161 Simon, *Einführung*, (He has been criticised by Wild, *Erzählen*, p. 44, for drastically reducing the number of functions in Propp's folktale scheme in order to accommodate his theory with the double cycle structure. On reservations about the double cycle see later, pp. 123 ff.).

162 Simon, *Einführung*, pp. 47ff.

163 Ibid., pp. 18ff., 121, 167.

164 Ibid., pp. 65 ff.

165 Ehrismann, *PBB* 30 (1905), 45 ff.

166 Simon, *Einführung*, pp. 65 f.

167 Ehrismann, *PBB* 30 (1905), 18; Green, *FMS* 14 (1980), 360ff.

168 *Perceval* 455 ff.

169 Green, *FMS* 14 (1980), 361.

170 Ibid., p. 364.

171 Ibid. and fn. 75.

172 Propp, *Morphologie*, p. 91.

173 Mohr, *Fabula* 1 (1958), 201 ff.

174 Propp, *Morphologie*, p. 92.

175 On folktale elements in Gawan's adventures (from Book x) see Neugart, *Wolfram*.

176 Green, *FMS* 14 (1980), 365.

177 Green, 'Advice', pp. 64ff.
178 Seiler, *Ruodlieb*, p. 47; Morse, *Truth*, p. 143.
179 Green, *FMS* 14 (1980), 374.
180 Ibid., p. 375.
181 Ibid., pp. 376–7.
182 Lüthi, *Volksmärchen*, pp. 36, 95.
183 Green, *FMS* 14 (1980), 397–8.
184 Ibid., p. 398, with a reference to Green, *Weg*, p. 13: 'die glückliche Fügung, die dem Märchenhelden günstig gesinnt ist'.
185 Green, *FMS* 14 (1980), 398–9.
186 Ibid., p. 399, fn. 212.
187 Ibid., p. 400. In agreement with this, references to Parzival as the son of Gahmuret, which occur throughout the whole work, are not used haphazardly in Books III and IV. They are all applied to him in a clearly knightly context and at turning-points in his path to chivalry. In attaining this status the son follows the father. Cf. Green, 'Namedropping', pp. 34–5; *FMS* 14 (1980), 402–3.
188 Green, *FMS* 14 (1980), 405, fn. 235.
189 Ibid., pp. 405 ff. Because Herzeloyde belongs to the Grail dynasty Parzival can meaningfully be referred to as her son in the context of the Grail, but such references are withheld while he is depicted as entering upon his father's inheritance. Cf. Green, 'Namedropping', pp. 135 ff.; *FMS* 14 (1980), 407–8.
190 *Märchen von den guten Ratschlägen*: Seiler, *Ruodlieb*, pp. 48ff.; Le Rider, *Chevalier*, pp. 44ff.; *Parzival*: Green, 'Advice', pp. 33–4.
191 Ibid., pp. 39ff., 54ff.
192 The evidence for this I have assembled ibid., pp. 64–5.
193 Ibid., pp. 67ff.
194 Nolan, *Chaucer*, p. 45, quoting a commentary of Servius on Virgil's first Eclogue, says of it: 'Here according to Servius, the author presents himself through his characters, not to reveal his personality, but to serve his argument.'
195 Wehrli, *Formen*, p. 167.
196 Kuhn, '*Erec*,' pp. 133 ff. The importance of the distribution of Arthurian scenes was earlier stressed by Kellermann, *Aufbaustil*, pp. 11 ff.
197 Hirschberg, *Untersuchungen*, p. 245.
198 Schmid, 'Doppelweg', p. 77 (the title of the essay is 'Weg mit dem Doppelweg'!); Wyss, 'Erzählstrukturen', p. 262.
199 Schmolke-Hasselmann, *Versroman*, p. 47 ('Das Prinzip der strengen Artusszenen-Struktur gilt schon bei Chrestien nicht für alle Romane. Der erste Artusdichter bietet verschiedene strukturelle Prototypen'); Lacy, *Craft*, pp. 88, 105 (on *Lancelot* and *Perceval*); Wolfzettel, 'Doppelweg', p. 141.
200 Adams, 'Shape', pp. 141, 143, stresses that the double cycle was not sacrosanct even in France after Chrétien.
201 Ibid., pp. 144–5; Wild, *Erzählen*, p. 82, and 'Symbolstruktur', p. 296; Wolfzettel, 'Doppelweg', p. 126; Wyss, 'Erzählstrukturen', p. 271.
202 Unzeitig-Herzog, *Überlegungen*, pp. 233 ff. Schmolke-Hasselmann, *Versroman*, pp. 42, 45–6, also points out that the turning-point in a bipartite romance need not always coincide with an Arthurian scene.
203 Lacy, *Typology*, p. 41; Guerin, *Fall*, pp. 87ff., 140ff.; Wolfzettel, 'Doppelweg', pp. 127ff.; Unzeitig-Herzog, 'Überlegungen', p. 243. Cf. also Schmolke-Hasselmann, *Versroman*,

pp. 48 ff. On this feature of Chrétien's works at large see also Maddox, *Romances*, pp. 120 ff.

204 Most clearly presented by Ruh, *Epik* I 126, with modifications of Kuhn, 'Erec', p. 142.

205 Erec does not seek out the three adventures in the second sub-cycle, in the same sequence as those in the first, as a conscious intention to repeat the test. Rather is he led to these encounters by *âventiure* (3111–12), standing here for the controlling hand of the author. The duplication of the first triad of adventures in the second in itself points to a deliberately artificial pattern.

206 Kuhn, 'Erec', p. 139; Ruh, *Epik* I 127; Haug, *Literaturtheorie*, p. 95.

207 This pattern is reminiscent of the folktale, combining a tripartite structure with a climactic conclusion. See above, p. 114.

208 Ruh, *Epik* I 128–9. Cf. also Ohly, *Struktur*, pp. 72–3.

209 Ruh, *Epik* I 130, 131, but also Ohly, *Struktur*, pp. 75, 80, 81.

210 Kuhn, 'Erec', p. 145; Ruh, *Epik* I 127.

211 Ibid., 134; Cormeau, 'Bedeutungssetzung', pp. 194 ff.

212 Kuhn, 'Erec', pp. 135 f.; Ruh, *Epik* I 113.

213 Discussed by Hanning, *Individual*, pp. 54 f., as the 'chivalry topos'.

214 Ruh, *Epik* I 122–3; Simon, *Einführung*, p. 14.

215 Kuhn, 'Erec', p. 147; Ohly, *Struktur*, p. 90; Haug, *Literaturtheorie*, pp. 95–6 (with reference to Chrétien).

216 Ruh, *Epik* I 142; Cormeau and Störmer, *Hartmann*, pp. 217–18.

217 Hirschberg, *Untersuchungen*, pp. 289–90.

218 Ruh, *Epik* I 148–9, 153, 156; Hirschberg, *Untersuchungen*, pp. 285–6; Simon, *Einführung*, pp. 47, 57 ff. A first step in this direction had already been taken in the conclusion of Hartmann's *Erec*, based on what the German poet already knew of the conclusion of Chrétien's *Yvain*. Cf. Green, *Irony*, p. 316 and Simon, *Einführung*, p. 55 (although whether this conclusion away from Arthur's court can be regarded as belonging to the structure of the genre, as Simon claims, is another matter).

219 See above, pp. 99–100.

220 Ruh, *Epik* I 152–3, 155. Cf. also Ohly, *Struktur*, pp. 115–16, 130–1.

221 Lacy, *Craft*, p. 12; Wolfzettel, 'Doppelweg', pp. 124–5.

222 Fourrier, *Courant*, pp. 124 ff.; Baehr, *Sprachkunst* 2 (1971), 43 ff.; Zaddy, *Chrétien*, pp. 175 f.

223 Wolfzettel, 'Doppelweg', p. 124.

224 Baehr, *Sprachkunst* 2 (1971), 55.

225 Ibid., p. 54.

226 Fourrier, *Courant*, pp. 144; Baehr, *Sprachkunst* 2 (1971), 55; Green, *Irony*, p. 113; Zaddy, *Chrétien*, pp. 174 ff.

227 See below, p. 179.

228 Wolfzettel, 'Doppelweg', pp. 127–8.

229 Kelly, *Sens*, pp. 169–70, commenting critically on Kellermann, *Aufbaustil*, pp. 11 ff.

230 Kelly, *Sens*, pp. 170, 171.

231 Ibid., pp. 166 ff., especially pp. 178–9, 184.

232 Wolfzettel, 'Doppelweg', p. 128–9.

233 Emmel, *Formprobleme*, p. 49; Burrichter, 'Zweiteilung', p. 96.

234 Ibid., p. 96.

235 Emmel, *Formprobleme*, pp. 58, 62.

236 Ibid., pp. 60, 61.

237 In this I differ from Hirschberg, *Untersuchungen*, pp. 239ff., who proceeds from the view that the double cycle structure, modified though it may be, still informs *Parzival*, and agree more with Haug who, even though he views Chrétien's *Perceval* as a development of the double cycle in *Erec* and *Yvain*, interprets Wolfram's work as a dissolution of this pattern, breaking decisively with it. Cf. Haug, 'Symbolstruktur', pp. 483ff., and '*Parzival*', pp. 133ff. (specifically against the equation of the Trevrizent episode in Book IX with the interim stay at Arthur's court, as in the second part of *Erec*).

238 Emmel, *Formprobleme*, pp. 73, 76, 78; Green, *Irony*, p. 320.

239 Emmel, *Formprobleme*, pp. 85, 86; Green, *Irony*, p. 321.

240 Emmel, *Formprobleme*, pp. 114–15.

241 Ibid., pp. 131–2, 135, 137.

242 Schneider, *Parzival-Studien*, pp. 32ff.

243 One specific example of Wolfram's inventiveness in constructing his own fiction concerns the figure of Sigune, for he goes much further than Chrétien by expanding her role in one episode in the French work to four in the German (Ruh, *Epik* II 76, 90–1). Wolfram's first Sigune episode is structurally counterpoised to his first Jeschute scene (cf. Emmel, *Formprobleme*, pp. 76–7). This episode has therefore been carefully worked out and initiates the expansion of the Sigune story within *Parzival* and ultimately in *Titurel*. This narrative invention on the basis of one scene with Chrétien is a further example of fiction arising out of fiction.

244 *Craft*, pp. 74–5.

245 Schmolke-Hasselmann, *DVjs* 57 (1983), 421.

246 Interlace: Lacy, *Craft*, pp. 67f., 94f., 105 (cf. Ryding, *Structures*, p. 139); analogy: Lacy, pp. 68ff., 78f., 106ff.; parallelism: Lacy, pp. 82–3 (cf. Haidu, *Distance*, pp. 63ff.; Brand, *Chrétien*, pp. 34ff.); symmetry: Lacy, p. 73 (cf. Kelly, *Sens*, pp. 166ff.); progression: Lacy, pp. 75, 94, 97; binary division: Lacy, p. 84 (cf. Burrichter, 'Zweiteilung', pp. 87ff.).

247 Lacy, *Craft*, pp. 67, 88, 105.

248 Haug, '*Tristan*', pp. 57–8. On the additive, episodic nature of *Tristan* cf. Fuchs, *Tristanroman*, pp. 33, 73; Stein, *DVjs* 51 (1977), 344; Wolf, *Gottfried*, pp. 19ff.; Wandhoff, *Blick*, p. 271; Keck, *Liebeskonzeption*, p. 36; Schausten, *Erzählwelten*, p. 112.

249 Mertens, 'Verhältnis', pp. 85ff.

250 See above, pp. 112–13.

251 Chrétien's *Yvain*, for example, makes combined use of the *ordo artificialis*, a sequence of folktales, and an (adapted) double cycle structure. Gottfried's *Tristan* follows for part of the narrative an additive composition, but also employs typology and incorporates what Simon has termed a *Feenmärchen*; Simon has also discussed other constituent structures in this work (*ZfdPh* 109 [1990], 354ff.). In Wolfram's *Parzival* only fragmentary remnants of the double cycle pattern are detectable, but alongside these a folktale structure, typology and the *ordo artificialis* are employed. This takes no account of other structural patterns that it was not possible to discuss in this chapter.

6. FICTION AND HISTORY

1 Knapp, *Historie*.

2 In a more specific context Lutz, 'Herrscherapotheosen', p. 100, fn. 50, speaks of the 'Vermittlung zwischen Historiographie und Roman'.

3 See above, pp. 3–4.

4 See above, p. 4.

5 Mehtonen, *Concepts*.

6 *Rhetorica ad Herennium* I 8, 13; Cicero, *De inventione* I 19, 27; Quintilian, *Institutio* II 4, 2.

7 Isidore, *Etymologiae* I 44, 5; *Scholia Terentiana* 167, 30ff.; Bernard of Utrecht, *Commentum*, p. 63, 127ff.; John of Garland, *Poetria*, 100, 317ff.

8 Heitmann, '*Verhältnis*', p. 221. Cf. also Mehtonen, *Concepts*, p. 49, on an anonymous commentary on the *Rhetorica ad Herennium*.

9 Mehtonen, *Concepts*, pp. 63ff.

10 Hence the phrasing in our definition of twelfth-century fictionality: 'events that were held to have actually taken place' (see above, p. 4). Cf. Charles-Edwards, 'Arthur', p. 18, on Dumville's distinction between a modern historian and the mentalities and political and other interests of medieval historical writers.

11 Spiegel, *Romancing* p. 341, n. 40, rightly qualifies the manner in which Goody regards the homeostatic view of history, the collapsing of past with present, as specifically characteristic of oral cultures alone.

12 For example, the historical events surrounding the death of Roland in the eighth century were later made to serve very different ends, including the interests of religious houses on the pilgrim route to Santiago de Compostela, the military campaigns in Spain encouraged by Cluny, the feudal ties between ruler and princes and, in the case of the *Rolandslied*, the rivalry between Henry the Lion and the Hohenstaufen. On a comparable adaptation of the Guillaume theme to the interests of the monastic foundation of Gellone (Saint-Guilhem-le-Désert) see Remensnyder, *Remembering*, pp. 188ff.

13 Knapp, *Historie*, pp. 22f., and Grünkorn, *Fiktionalität*, p. 44, on the divine sanction granted to the authority of *historia*. Cf. also Boehm, 'Ort', pp. 666, 686. On the bible as *historia* cf. Seifert, *AfB* 21 (1977), 243ff. and Knape, *Historie*, pp. 134–5. On the truth of religious writing see Mackert, *Alexandergeschichte*, p. 88, fn. 65.

14 Cicero, *De oratore*, p. 224, refers to *historia* as 'testis temporum, lux veritatis' (the witness of time, the light of truth). Lucan is praised in the high Middle Ages for his 'veritas historiae absque fictione', truth of history without fiction (von Moos, *PBB(T)* 98 [1976], 106). Servius, discussing the relationship between historical truth and invention in Virgil's *Aeneid*, revealingly varies between 'a veritate discedere' (deviate from truth) and 'ab historia discedere', deviate from history (Zeeman, 'Schools', pp. 166–7).

15 *Etymologiae* I 44, 5.

16 Lacroix, *L'historien*, p. 133.

17 Damian-Grint, *ANS* 18 (1995), 63ff.; *MÆ* 66 (1997), 189ff. (especially p. 198); *Historians*, pp. 211ff.

18 Chinca, *History*, pp. 64, 66.

19 On *argumentum* see Mehtonen, *Concepts*, pp. 91ff.

20 *Rhetorica ad Herennium* I 8, 13; Bernard of Utrecht, *Commentum*, pp. 63, 139; John of Garland, *Poetria*, 100, 327–8.

21 Verisimilitude: Chinca, *History*, pp. 86ff.; consistent plausibility: Mehtonen, *Concepts*, p. 100, with reference to Horace, *Ars poetica* 119: 'sibi convenientia finge' (make up consistently). See also above, pp. 8–10.

22 Mehtonen, *Concepts*, pp. 119ff.

23 Macrobius, *Commentarii* I 2, 7; Isidore, *Etymologiae* I 40.

24 Suchomski, *Delectatio*, p. 282, n. 266.

25 Konrad von Hirsau, *Dialogus* 386 (cf. Mehtonen, *Concepts*, p. 125). Engelhert von Admont: Knapp, *Historie*, p. 87. Cf. also the juxtaposition 'fabulis et mendaciis' (fables and lies) in Aelred of Rievaulx, *De speculo caritatis*, II 51.
26 Jordan Fantosme, *Chronicle* 115–16. Cf. Damian-Grint, *Historians*, p. 224.
27 Fragments of truth: Morse, *Truth*, p. 60 (cf. Horace, *Ars poetica* 151: 'atque ita mentitur, sic veris falsa remiscet', lies in such a way that the false is mixed with the true). Feelings rather than facts: Morse, p. 62. Suppression of facts: Morse, *Truth*, p. 96. On aspects of rhetoric held to be of dubious value see later, pp. 148–9.
28 Gompf, 'Figmenta', p. 53; Manning, *JEGPh* 59 (1960), 406 (cf. also p. 407).
29 Sedulius: Gompf, 'Figmenta', p. 54; Arator: Klopsch, *Einführung*, p. 12; Notker Balbulus: Gompf, 'Figmenta', p. 55.
30 Bernard of Clairvaux: Köhler, 'Selbstauffassung', p. 13; Herrad von Landsberg: ibid.; Greiner, *Poetica* 24 (1992), 300. For this illustration from the *Hortus deliciarum* see the frontispiece.
31 Schirmer, 'Wahrheitsauffassung', pp. 52ff.
32 Ibid., pp. 54ff. Cf. Hauck, 'Heldendichtung', pp. 118ff.; Green, *Listening*, pp. 239–40.
33 Schirmer, 'Wahrheitsauffassung', pp. 54–5; Green, *Listening*, pp. 241ff.
34 Knape, *Historie*, pp. 163ff.
35 Schirmer, 'Wahrheitsauffassung', pp. 56ff.
36 These sceptical reactions are discussed by Schreiner, 'Discrimen', pp. 10ff., under the significant heading 'sporadische Zweifel'.
37 *Kaiserchronik* 27ff. Cf. Ohly, *Sage*, pp. 31–2.
38 Schirmer, 'Wahrheitsauffassung', pp. 59ff.
39 Ibid., pp. 63ff.
40 *Aiol* 1 ff. Cf. Mölk, *Literarästhetik*, p. 4.
41 *L'Histoire ancienne* 251 ff. (no modern edition, but cf. Singerman, *Clouds*, p. 154).
42 *Fable* and *verité* (or *voir*): *Ami et Amile* 5–6 (cf. Mölk, *Literarästhetik*, p. 9); Graindor de Douai, *Antioche* 58–9 (Mölk, p. 19); Jean Renart, *L'Escoufle* 14–15 (Mölk, p. 53). *Fable* and *mençonge*: Gautier de Douai, *Louis le roi: Destruction de Rome* 4 (Mölk, p. 4); *Roman des Sept Sages* 4 (Mölk, p. 45); Gervaise, *Bestiaire* 19ff. (Mölk, p. 79); Denis Piramus, *Vie de saint Edmund* 29 (Mölk, p. 93).
43 Jean Bodel, *Chanson des Saisnes* 6ff. Cf. Mölk, *Literarästhetik*, pp. 6–7.
44 Duggan, 'Epic', p. 311; Green, *Listening*, pp. 239–40.
45 Duggan, 'Epic', p. 304; Green, *Listening*, p. 162.
46 Schmolke-Hasselmann, *Versroman*, pp. 246–7; *GRM* 32 (1982), 388; Morris, 'Arthur', pp. 118–19.
47 Knapp, *Historie*, pp. 13–14.
48 Köhler, 'Selbstauffassung', p. 10.
49 Cf. Guiette, *Romania* 88 (1967), 1ff.
50 Ibid., pp. 1, 10.
51 On Augustine see above, p. 29, and on Denis Piramus p. 31.
52 Guiette, *Romania* 88 (1967), 2, 10.
53 *OLD*, p. 2010, under 2 and 3. Guiette, *Romania* 88 (1967), 2, himself lists Latin *vanum*, used substantivally, as meaning 'mensonge'.
54 *Aeneid* 6.283–4, 896. *Roman d'Enéas* 2416 (cf. Fromm, 'Unterwelt', p. 109). Isidore, *Etymologiae* VIII 11, 29. For a medieval Latin example cf. Aelred of Rievaulx, *De speculo caritatis* II 50, who talks of 'uana carmina' (vain songs) that are composed fictively (*fingitur*) and deal with an imaginary person (*fabulosus*), but contrasts them with

what truly (*uere*) happens before one's own eyes. See also Sims-Williams, *Romania* 116 (1998), 88.
55 *FEW* 14, 164.
56 *Vies des Pères* 29ff. (cf. Mölk, *Literarästhetik*, p. 95); *Bestiaire* 15ff. (Mölk, p. 79).
57 On Bodel's attitude to the *matière de Bretagne* cf. Uitti, *RPh* 22 (1969), 477 ('as less "true" and, on balance, as more "fictional"') and Knapp, *Historie*, p. 59 ('das Lügenhafte und bloß Unterhaltende').

The political implications of Bodel's claim for the truth of the *chanson de geste* in support of the French royal house have been taken further by Thomas, *ZfdPh* 108 (1989), 66–7. He correlates all three literary genres with three contemporary areas of political sovereignty: not merely the *matière de France* with the French dynasty and the *matière de Bretagne* with the Anglo-Normans, but also the *matière de Rome* with the German Empire in continuation of the Roman. Seen in this wider context, Bodel's argument for the truth of 'his' genre and the untruth of the Arthurian romance acquires even more force.

Wolfzettel, 'Probleme', pp. 343–4, has also drawn attention to the passage in *Ille et Galeron* 931 ff., whose author Gautier d'Arras, a rival of Chrétien, proclaims the truth of his own work by denying that it contains anything fantastic (*fantome*) or untrue (*mençonge*), by contrast with *lais* (which he compares with dreams). By this explicit mention of a genre belonging to the *matière de Bretagne* Gautier could be distinguishing his own work, hagiographical and historical, from the *merveilleux* of Chrétien's Arthurian romances. The untruth of Chrétien's romances can also be read out of what Jürgen Wolf (in a book not yet published) has called 'das Ende der Chrétienschen Erfolgsstory', the rapid break in the manuscript tradition of his works after the thirteenth century and their inability to hold their own against the truth-claims of the prose romance.
58 Also from Dutch literature, as when Jacob van Maerlant in his *Spiegel historiael* rejects 'the nonsense of the Grail, the lies about Perceval, the trifles of Lanval, and many other false stories' (Besamusca, 'Material', p. 189).
59 *Welscher Gast* 1026ff. See also Knapp, *Historie*, pp. 43, 58.
60 That others, too, could see the classical theme of Alexander as fictional (at least in part) has been suggested in the case of Rudolf von Ems by Hagenlocher, *NdJb* 102 (1979), 65, on the basis of this poet's use of *âventiure* in connection with his *Alexander* in contrast with his avoidance of this term for his *Weltchronik*.
61 Okken, *Kommentar* II 651.
62 Christ, *Rhetorik*, p. 299.
63 Chinca, *History*, pp. 49ff.
64 See later, pp. 183 ff.
65 Cf. Schreiner, *Saeculum* 17 (1966), 131 ff. The examples discussed there make it clear that the authors concerned were well aware that they were deviating from the historical facts known to them: they transpose the argument from the historical to the metahistorical plane, they feel it necessary to defend their procedure, and, as the quotation from Augustine makes clear, they realise that factual truth is not on their side. In other words, these conscious deviations from history are not to be equated with what medieval authors, as distinct from modern historians, took to be historical facts (see above, p. 135).
66 Ibid., p. 139.
67 Ibid., p. 145.

68 Ibid., p. 162.
69 Aesop: Minnis and Scott, *Theory*, p. 119. *Ecbasis captivi*: see above, p. 8.
70 Ridder, *Aventiureromane*, p. 10, dealing with a group of later romances, talks of a 'Historisierung der Fiktion' and a 'Fiktionalisierung der Geschichte', but comments, p. 235, that these tendencies had set in earlier.
71 In talking of the fictionality of historiography I am not advocating for medieval historical writing anything at all similar to the postmodernism of Hayden White and others (cf. Lamarque and Olsen, *Truth*, pp. 301 ff.), for whom historical facts become constructed artefacts, so that fact and fiction are indistinguishable and the historian becomes an author like any fabulist. For a polemical discussion of such views see Evans, *Defence*.
72 *Ars poetica* 119.
73 See above, pp. 55 ff., especially p. 59 on the fictional nature of this world.
74 On this conclusion of *Erec* see Schmolke-Hasselmann, *Versroman*, pp. 190ff.; *CCM* 24 (1981), 241 ff.; Morris, *FSt* 42 (1988), 267; Huber, 'Herrscherlob', pp. 470f.; Mertens, *Artusroman*, pp. 42 f.
75 Schmolke-Hasselmann, *Versroman*, p. 192.
76 On Henry II's intellectual interests see Schirmer and Broich, *Studien*, pp. 17ff., 28ff.
77 Knapp, *Historie*, p. 122.
78 Gottfried explicitly refers to his source at this point (5884–5), and the agreement between Gottfried's version and the *Tristrams saga* (Bédier, *Tristan* I 71, fn. 1) suggests that both followed Thomas here. On Gottfried's inventive elaboration see Stevens, 'Giants', pp. 423 ff.
79 Metzner, *PBB(T)* 95 (1973), 219ff.
80 Geoffrey, *Historia* [184], pp. 133–4. The mention of Isembardus and the Franks connects Thomas' Gurmun with the *chanson de geste Gormond et Isembard*, itself based on a conflation of historical events that include the battle of Saucourt from which the Old High German *Ludwigslied* is derived. (Metzner has shown that the *Gormond et Isembard* tradition goes back to two historical events, around 500 and 891 respectively, conflated because they share a number of comparable features.)
81 Wace, *Roman de Brut* 13379ff. Cf. also Stevens, 'Giants', pp. 417ff.
82 See later, p. 176.
83 Stevens, 'Giants', p. 409.
84 *Tristrant* 5129ff.
85 Fourrier, *Courant*, pp. 43–4, 97, 124. Cf. also Bédier, *Tristan* I 307–8.
86 Ibid., pp. 81–2, 84.
87 Stevens, 'Giants', p. 415–16.
88 Cf. Kugler, 'Geographie', pp. 116ff., who starts by saying that Wolfram incorporated his Arthurian world into the real world of his present. I place the emphasis conversely: both Chrétien in *Erec* and Wolfram in *Parzival* incorporate details from their present into their fictional constructs.
89 Ibid., pp. 116–17.
90 Kugler, ibid., p. 120, therefore talks of the 'universalhistorischen und universalräumlichen Dimensionen der Wolframschen Romanwelt'.
91 Brunner uses the term 'immanente Historizität' in the subtitle to his article ('Artus', pp. 61 ff.) and talks of a 'romanimmanente Historizität' on p. 62. Even when historically referential allusions to events of Wolfram's own day are given (cf. the commentary on 21, 21 in Nellmann's edition) they concern only details, not the longer course of narrative action which remains chronologically floating.

92 *Parzival* 65, 25 ff.
93 Of the knights mentioned by Wolfram in the context of Kanvoleis only some are known from Geoffrey's *Historia*: Utherpendragon, Arturus, Loth, Gualguanus. For the majority, however, no claim for historicity can be made by an appeal to Geoffrey's authority.
94 See later, pp. 171, 172, 176, 177.
95 Brunner, *GRM* 72 (1991), 375.
96 Bumke, *DVjs* 65 (1991), 236f., 256. In other words, Wolfram raises the same kind of critical questions about the conclusion of his own romance as those he had prompted by intertextual means in the case of Hartmann (see above, p. 61).
97 Ibid., p. 262.
98 Kolb, *Munsalvaesche*, pp. 74ff.; Schmid, 'Priester', pp. 75ff.; Kugler, 'Geographie', pp. 131ff.; Bumke, *DVjs* 65 (1991), 244ff.
99 Kolb, *Munsalvaesche*, pp. 53ff.; 'Schwanrittersage', pp. 23ff.; Brunner, *GRM* 72 (1991), 369ff.; Bumke, *DVjs* 65 (1991), 255ff.
100 Bumke, *DVjs* 65 (1991), 261.
101 Ibid., pp. 250ff.
102 Ibid., p. 255.
103 Ibid., pp. 240, fn. 6, 263, 264.
104 Morgan, 'Make-believe', p. 200. In my assessment of the relationship between *historia* and fiction in *Parzival* I differ from Knapp, who inclines more towards the former (see above, pp. 90–91). Even he, however, with explicit reference to Prester John and Loherangrin, hesitates to align *Parzival* so clearly with *Willehalm* in this respect. See Knapp, *DVjs* 70 (1991), pp. 366f. and fn. 48.
105 *Rhetorica ad Herennium* I 8, 13; Isidore of Seville, *Etymologiae* I 41. On history as a linguistic construct, a text, cf. Otter, *Inventiones*, pp. 10–11; Opitz, *Geschichte*, pp. 189, 190–1.
106 Morse, *Truth*, pp. 98, 258, n. 1. Cf. also Knapp, 'Überlegungen', p. 118.
107 Morse, *Truth*, p. 9.
108 See above, pp. 8–10.
109 On the truth-status of apocryphal writings see later, pp. 187–8.
110 Morse, *Truth*, p. 148. Aubin, 'Reversing', pp. 257ff., argues that the apocryphal *Acts* transform features of the romance so as to subvert its guiding ideology.
111 Morse, *Truth*, pp. 209, 283, n. 38.
112 The following is largely based on Moles, 'Truth', pp. 88ff.
113 See above, p. 2, and also Fleischman, *History and Theory* 22 (1983), 292f.
114 Moles, 'Truth', p. 105.
115 Wiseman, 'Historians', pp. 122ff. (with reference to Seneca on p. 122).
116 Moles, *Truth*, p. 115.
117 Livy, *Ab urbe condita*, *Praefatio* 6. Cf. Morse, *Truth*, pp. 93–4.
118 Seneca, *Apocolocyntosis* I 1–2. Cf. Wiseman, 'Historians', p. 123.
119 *Erec* 8946ff. See also above, p. 85.
120 Morse, *Truth*, pp. 152, 186; Wiseman, *Cosmetics*, pp. 34–5.
121 Morse, *Truth*, p. 83.
122 *De oratore* II 35. Cf. Wiseman, *Cosmetics*, p. 34.
123 See above, p. 59, and Green, 'Erkennen', pp. 35ff.
124 *De inventione* I 46. Cf. Morgan, 'Make-believe', pp. 187–8.
125 See above, p. 4.

126 The standard argument for the latter policy was put forward by Augustine in *De doctrina christiana*. On this see Morse, *Truth*, pp. 27, 252, n. 21 ('Christian writers are to be trained in classical rhetoric . . . in order to transmute this "Egyptian gold" into a more holy word').

127 Morse, *Truth*, pp. 8, 196.

128 Ibid., pp. 129, 130; Feeney, *Gods*, p. 13. Chinca, *History*, p. 87, quotes Quintilian's approval of Cicero's oratory on the grounds that he 'iudicem fefellerit' (deceived the judge).

129 *Vita s. Wulfstani* I 16. Cf. Morse, *Truth*, p. 156.

130 Chinca, *History*, p. 2. Morse, *Truth*, p. 135, refers to Sulpicius Severus' use of Sallust and Jerome's of Suetonius and says that the 'prestige of these two early Christian writers established the legitimacy of classical rhetorical models'.

131 Cicero: Morse, *Truth*, p. 97. Philippe de Commynes: ibid., p. 106, and *MLR* 80 (1985), 264–5.

132 Schreiner, *Saeculum* 17 (1966), 161.

133 Cf. von Ertzdorff, *ZfdPh* 86 (1967), 383. Other examples, Latin and vernacular, are quoted by Raynaud de Lage, *MA* 63 (1957), 279 (*L'histoire ancienne jusqu'à César*) and Kellermann, *GRM* 73 (1992), 12 (*Historia troiana*, Lupus of Ferrières, and *Historia peregrinorum*).

134 Morse, *Truth*, pp. 86–7, 108, 177.

135 Nelson, *Fact*, p. 27.

136 Worstbrock, *FMS* 19 (1985), 3; Partner, 'Cornificius', pp. 11 f.; Morse, *Truth*, p. 8.

137 Ibid., p. 6 ('it could have happened like this').

138 Ibid., p. 64; Fichte, 'Fakt', p. 50. A criticism of this rhetorical practice by Hugo of St Victor is quoted by von Moos, *PBB(T)* 98 (1976), 122, fn. 60.

139 Cicero, *De inventione* I 9. Cf. Wiseman, 'Historians', p. 142, and on rhetorical invention at large Morse, *Truth*, p. 96.

140 Brooke, *Renaissance*, p. 174.

141 The difference between historiography and fiction in this respect lies of course in the material to be structurally organised, because only the historian could justifiably claim to be dealing with actual facts as opposed to inventions.

142 Morse, *Truth*, p. 87: 'Admixtures of invention, elaboration, and embellishment were a method of stylization *in order to* make the past comprehensible.'

143 Partner, 'Cornificius', p. 16.

144 Southern, *TRHS* 20 (1970), 188. Cf. also von Moos, *PBB(T)* 98 (1976), 96. As a modern historian, Evans, *Defence*, pp. 25, 80, has stressed the 'interconnectedness' of events and the 'larger patterns' that the historiographer, as distinct from the chronicler, seeks to establish.

145 Burrichter, *Wahrheit*, pp. 13, 15 ff., 19 ff.

146 Cf. Knapp, *GRM* 48 (1998), 241–2.

147 In this connection von Ertzdorff, *ZfdPh* 86 (1967), 386, fn. 33, quotes Quintilian, *Institutio* X 1, 31: 'ideoque et verbis remotioribus et liberioribus figuris narrandi taedium evitat' (. . . avoids tedium in the narrative by more unusual diction and freer figures of speech).

148 Burrichter, *Wahrheit*, pp. 19–20. On Lucan's *Pharsalia* see von Moos, *PBB(T)* 98 (1976), 93 ff.

149 Ibid., 117–18.

150 Burrichter, *Wahrheit*, p. 26.

151 Ibid., p. 62. See also later, p. 174.

152 Morgan, 'Make-believe', pp. 186–7. Morgan then adds an important qualification ('We are still a long way from a novel, because the vital ingredient of plot is missing') that is also applicable in the Middle Ages to the different fictional status of the *roman antique* and the Arthurian romance. See later, p. 199.

153 Ibid., p. 197.

154 Ibid., p. 199.

155 On this phenomenon see above, pp. 61 ff. (Wolfram's intertextual references to Hartmann), and also later, pp. 187ff.

156 Morgan, 'Make-believe', p. 178.

157 Green, *Listening*, pp. 242ff.

158 Because he mainly confines his attention to express authorial statements Haug has omitted the first two themes from his survey and given only cursory treatment to the *Alexanderlied* (*Literaturtheorie*, pp. 85ff.).

159 For this reason I omit the *Roman de Thèbes*.

160 Lengenfelder, *Liet*, p. 99, n. 10; Feeney, *Gods*, pp. 44f.; Lienert, *Geschichte*, p. 13.

161 From antiquity these historians include, for example, Eusebius, Augustine and Orosius and from the Middle Ages Isidore, Bede, Frutolf von Michelsberg and Otto von Freising.

162 Worstbrock, *ZfdA* 92 (1963), 251–2; Singerman, *Clouds*, pp. 147–8.

163 Wolff, *GRM* 20 (1932), 60.

164 Isidore of Seville, *Etymologiae* I 42. Cf. Lienert, *Geschichte*, pp. 13f.

165 Time-references: Eley, 'Aspects', pp. 140–1. *Ordo naturalis* : Singerman, *Clouds*, p. 175.

166 *Commentum, Praefatio*, p. 1. Cf. von Ertzdorff, *ZfdPh* 86 (1967), 383, and Knape, *Historie*, p. 81. Raynaud de Lage, *MA* 63 (1957), 279, illustrates a similar mistrust of the effects of poetry on historical veracity from *L'histoire ancienne jusqu'à César* : 'Por beau parler est mainte choze contee e dite que n'est mie voire en tote traitie d'estoire' (For the sake of beautiful diction many things are recounted and said in works of history that are not true).

167 Pastré, *BDBA* 10 (1992), 119–20.

168 Ibid., pp. 120ff.; Ingledew, *Speculum* 69 (1994), 677.

169 On these early misgivings see Wolff, *GRM* 20 (1932), 53 ff. Cf also Fromm, 'Verräter', p. 143.

170 Wolff, *GRM* 20 (1932), 54; Wittkower, *JWCI* 5 (1942), 160, fn. 2; Romm, *Edges*, p. 96; Worstbrock, *ZfdA* 92 (1963), 252; Opitz, *Geschichte*, p. 22.

171 As was recognised by Benoît de Sainte-Maure in his *Roman de Troie*, for whom Homer 'fu clers merveillos', was a wonderful clerk (45), but his book did not always speak the truth (51: 'Mais ne dist pas sis livres veir').

172 *Confessiones* I 14, 23 and I 13, 22. Cf. von Ertzdorff, *ZfdPh* 86 (1967), 384.

173 Ermenrich von Ellwangen, *Vita b. Soli*, p. 157. Cf. Wolff, *GRM* 20 (1932) 62–3; Worstbrock, *ZfdA* 92 (1963), 250.

174 Feeney, *Gods*, pp. 13, 40–1.

175 Bowie, 'Lies', pp. 9, 17. With reference to the tales told by Odysseus (known by the audience to be untrue) cf. Bowie, p. 37 (the 'poet too is aware that stories can be created, or creatively adapted, and that his own role is not wholly different from that of his fictionalizing Odysseus') and Gill, 'Plato', p. 70 ('The fact that Homer's poem contains a figure of this type has implications for the status of Homer's poem: if Odysseus can create "fictions", so, by implication, can Homer').

176 Bowie, 'Lies', p. 10.

177 Rösler, *Poetica* 12 (1980), 307; Feeney, *Gods*, p. 14, and 'Epilogue', p. 233.

178 Dares, *Historia*, prologue, p. 1; Benoît, *Roman de Troie* 60ff. On the *Aeneid* cf. the *accessus* attributed to Anselm of Laon (Baswell, *Virgil*, p. 313).

179 Romm, *Edges*, p. 172. Romm seems to me to be overscrupulous in qualifying his statement with the word 'loosely', for his subsequent argument strengthens his case notably. On p. 173 he refers to the storyteller's prerogative of 'saying what is said' without necessarily affirming (what Aristotle had recommended to writers of fiction). Cf. also pp. 187 ('the voyage of Odysseus had been removed into the fabulous realm of Ocean for purely aesthetic purposes') and 188 ('the *Odyssey* in the outermost zone of a concentric scheme of narrative fictions, a zone here specifically identified with Ocean and therefore with absolute poetic license').

180 *Accessus ad auctores*, p. 20. Cf. Lengenfelder, *Liet*, p. 104, n. 47.

181 Eley, *MÆ* 68 (1999), 81; she also argues that Benoît's *Chronique* contains a number of romance elements (regarded as fictional), although fewer than in the *Roman de Troie*.

182 *Roman de Troie* 87ff.

183 Ibid., 104ff. Cf. also Nolan, *Chaucer*, p. 30. The medieval definition of the historian comes from Konrad von Hirsau, *Dialogus* 138. On this view of history see Green, *Listening*, pp. 237ff.

184 *Roman de Troie* 139ff., 2076ff.

185 Raynaud de Lage, 'Romans', p. 178.

186 Marichal, 'Naissance', p. 464.

187 Franks: Tatlock, *History*, pp. 427–8; Ebenbauer, 'Historiographie', pp. 77, 82, 87. Britons: ibid., p. 83. Normans: Southern, *TRHS* 20 (1970), 192; Burrichter, *Wahrheit*, pp. 22–3.

188 Bezzola, *Origines* III 1, 182–3, 193, 288ff.

189 Cf. Singerman, *Clouds*, p. 322, n. 78.

190 Baumgartner, 'Vers', p. 2. Zink, *Invention*, pp. 26–7, interprets this passage as opening the door to personal creation while still benefiting from the authority of the source; as displacing this authority, which shifts from the source to the romance, just as the subject's originality shifts to that of Benoît's own work.

191 Nolan, *Chaucer*, p. 24.

192 Ibid., pp. 24, 26. Zink, *Invention*, p. 27, says of Benoît's artistry: 'In this way he imposed his presence and lent to his function as translator an authority that would not be his if, as he pretended to assert, only the story's truthfulness mattered.'

193 See above, p. 28.

194 Nolan, *Chaucer*, p. 27, who goes on to say that Benoît's theory of poetic composition anticipates Chrétien's elaboration of a theory of *matiere*, *sen* and *conjointure*.

195 Adler, *RF* 72 (1960), 14ff. This theme (termed the 'chivalry topos') has been treated by Hanning, *Individual*, pp. 54ff. for the twelfth-century romance in France.

196 Mertens, 'Liet', pp. 156, 158–9.

197 Nolan, *Chaucer*, p. 96, but also p. 99 ('dynamic interplay between a carefully developed poetics of private Ovidian love and the larger epico-historical narrative').

198 Ibid., p. 77.

199 Nolan, ibid., p. 310, n. 57, stresses that most *accessus* to the *Heroides* emphasise the fictive character of Ovid's epistles. This was also well known to Baudri de Bourgueil (see above, p. 21).

200 See above pp. 14–15.

201 Nolan, *Chaucer*, p. 117.

202 Nolan, ibid., pp. 104ff., has worked out in detail, for example, how Benoît sets the beginning of the affair between Paris and Helen significantly in a temple of Venus on

the island of Cythera, but also, nearly 20,000 verses later at the time of Paris's death, brings two other temples, of Juno and Minerva, into play. From Venus' temple at the beginning we therefore move to the temples of the goddesses long ago spurned in Paris' judgment, as proof of the tragic outcome of his choice. Benoît relates these three settings symbolically to one another and impresses on his audience's attentiveness the consequences of Paris' action, but also the need for them to be alert to such tacit allusions, operative over a wide span of his narrative.

For a likewise carefully orchestrated chiastic relationship between Briseida's betrayal and the affair of Paris and Helen see also Nolan, ibid., p. 110, and above, pp. 189–90.

203 Cf. Raynaud de Lage, 'Romans', p. 178 ('Benoît amplifie sans innover, ou s'il innove, c'est à l'intérieur d'un cadre reçu') and Baumgartner, 'Vers', p. 2 ('les auteurs des romans antiques ne semblent pas être allés jusqu'au bout de l'aventure de la fiction').
204 Southern, *TRHS* 20 (1970), 189–90; *Annolied* 6, 1; 22, 1 ff.; 23, 19ff.
205 Wehrli, *Geschichte*, p. 250.
206 Huschenbett, 'Literaturtradition', p. 304; Mertens, *'Liet'*, pp. 152–3; Fromm, *PBB* 115 (1993), 245.
207 *Ordo naturalis*: Lengenfelder, *Liet*, p. 21. Time-pattern: ibid., pp. 17ff., especially pp. 20–1. Benoît: Eley, 'Aspects', pp. 144, 145.
208 Henkel, 'Kurzfassungen', p. 42; Lengenfelder, *Liet*, p. 23. On the presence of wonders in Benoît's version cf. Kelly, *Art*, p. 130.
209 Mertens, *'Liet'*, pp. 160, 162, 165; Kistler, *Veldeke*, p. 200.
210 Strohschneider, *ZfdA* 120 (1991), 436–7.
211 Wolf, *Kultur*, pp. 259ff.; Vollmann-Profe, *Wiederbeginn*, pp. 59ff., 153ff.; Heinzle, *Wandlungen*, pp. 105f.
212 Eberhard, *Laborintus*, p. 359 (cf. Knape, *Historie*, p. 80); Konrad von Hirsau, *Dialogus* 1561ff. (cf. Knapp, *Historie*, p. 24); 'Anselm of Laon': Baswell, *Virgil*, p. 66.
213 Singerman, *Clouds*, p. 99.
214 Kistler, *Veldeke*, p. 196. Cf. also Patterson, *Negotiating*, p. 159.
215 *Annolied* 22, 1ff. and 23, 1ff. (cf. Nellmann's edition pp. 95–6); *Kaiserchronik* 343ff.
216 *Aeneid* 4. 621ff. Cf. Singerman, *Clouds*, p. 113; Patterson, *Negotiating*, p. 181 (saying that the avenger to come would have been identified by any Roman as Hannibal).
217 On Macrobius' reading of Virgil see above, pp. 14–15.
218 *Aeneid* 6. 756ff. Cf. Kistler, *Veldeke*, pp. 38f.; Ingledew, *Speculum* 69 (1994), 670–1.
219 Feeney, *Gods*, p. 162; Singerman, *Clouds*, p. 111; Patterson, *Negotiating*, p. 161.
220 Patterson, *Negotiating*, p. 169.
221 Servius, *Commentarii* 1 382 (cf. Irvine, *Making*, p. 240); Otto von Freising, *Gesta*, p. 12 (cf. Chinca, *History*, p. 61). On Bernardus 'Silvestris' see also Knapp, *Historie*, p. 55.
222 Fromm, 'Verräter', pp. 139ff.
223 Bernardus 'Silvestris', *Commentum*, p. 1: 'non usque secundum historie veritatem, quod Frigius describit', not always, as with Dares, in accord with the truth of history (cf. Knape, *Historie*, p. 81; Baswell, *Virgil*, p. 19).
224 Bernardus 'Silvestris', *Commentum*, p. 15: 'Est enim historia quod Greci Troiam devicerunt, quod vero Enee probitas enarratur fabula est', it is historical that the Greeks conquered Troy, but fabulous what is recounted of the honesty of Aeneas. (cf. Singerman, *Clouds*, pp. 148–9). This distinction parallels what William of Malmesbury says of the *matière de Bretagne*: he accepts the historicity of Arthur, but not of the tales about him. See later, p. 171.
225 Cf. the *accessus* quoted by Lengenfelder, *Liet*, p. 104, n. 47, where Virgil in the second part of his epic is said to have imitated the *Iliad*, itself described as a *fabula*. On

criticism of Homer see above, p. 154. By rewriting Homer's two epics Virgil also appropriates Greek legend and makes it part of Rome's legendary history.

226 In the *accessus* attributed to Anselm of Laon (Baswell, *Virgil*, p. 313) the conjunction of divine and human figures in the *Aeneid* is described as 'uera cum fictis' (true mixed with fictitious), while the role played by Venus and Mercury is 'compositum et ficticium' (invented and fictitious). On criticism on this score see also Servius, *Commentarii* I 4, in the same terms as the Anselm *accessus* (cf. Feeney, *Gods*, pp. 35–6), but also, when Virgil's Venus talks to herself, I 86: 'hoc fictum est ... unde sciret poeta?', this is fictitious. How should the poet know? (cf. Zeeman, 'Schools', p. 167). With regard to the *Histoire ancienne* cf. Singerman, *Clouds*, pp. 176, 178.

227 Medieval commentators: e.g. Bernardus 'Silvestris', *Commentum*, p. 1: 'ut Augusti Cesaris gratiam lucraretur' (to win the favour of Augustus); Dares preferred: see above, n. 223; Anselm *accessus*: 'ad laudem scripsit augusti cesaris' (wrote to flatter Augustus) and 'Verum quia ad laudem augusti scripsit, idcirco de ueritate historie multa reticendo poetice quedam figmenta satis competenter apponit', since he wrote in praise of Augustus, hence suppressed much of the truth, he quite fittingly added a number of poetic fictions (Baswell, *Virgil*, p. 313).

228 Macrobius: see above, pp. 14–15; Medea and Dido: ibid. and Patterson, *Negotiating*, pp. 166–7; 'contemporaries': Courcelle, *Lecteurs* I 376 and n. 714 (with references to Servius, *Commentarii* IV 459, and John of Salisbury, *Policraticus* VIII 14); Dido's chastity: Courcelle, *Lecteurs* I 376 (John of Salisbury: 'pudicissima', most chaste); Baswell, *Virgil*, pp. 20f.; Carthage: Servius, *Commentarii* I 159: 'fictus secundum poeticam licentiam', invented in accord with poetic licence (cf. Chinca, *History*, pp. 71–2; Zeeman, 'Schools', pp. 166f.).

229 West, 'Bough', pp. 224ff., argues that Servius' explanation (Virgil indicates by this detail that what he said is false) is not acceptable, since the prophecies given to Aeneas had already been fulfilled before Virgil wrote. Instead, VI 893ff. is one of Virgil's many disclaimers, a way of distancing himself from assertions he wishes to make, but not to be taken as believing.

230 Servius, *Commentarii* I, pp. 4–5 (cf. Singerman, *Clouds*, pp. 2–3). Cf. also Singerman, p. 7, on Konrad von Hirsau, but also von Moos, *PBB(T)* 98 (1976), 95; Knape, *Historie*, p. 81; Fromm, 'Eneasromane', pp. 27ff.; Opitz, *Geschichte*, p. 95.

231 E.g. Hrabanus Maurus (cf. von Moos, *PBB(T)* 98 [1976], 105, n. 22). When Konrad von Hirsau, *Dialogus* 1562ff., accuses Virgil of lying he adds that no one did it in a more polished way (cf. Mehtonen, *Concepts*, pp. 137–8).

232 John of Salisbury, *Policraticus* II 415, refers to Virgil's art of presentation 'under the cloak of fictional invention' ('sub involucro fictitii commenti'). Cf. Singerman, *Clouds*, p. 22, and Knapp, *Historie*, p. 47.

233 Bernardus, *Commentum*, p. 1 (cf. Huber, *ZfdA* 115 (1986), 89); Anselm, cf. n. 227, second quotation.

234 Baswell, *Virgil*, p. 74.

235 *Enéas* 2950ff. (cf. Singerman, *Clouds*, pp. 100–1).

236 *Enéas* 93ff., 10131ff. (cf. Baswell, *Virgil*, p. 201).

237 Singerman, *Clouds*, pp. 119ff.; Baswell, *Virgil*, pp. 11, 20. In three manuscripts *Enéas* is copied with *Brut* (Singerman, *Clouds*, pp. 124–5), so that with this historical link the *matière de Rome* touches the *matière de Bretagne*.

238 Patterson, *Negotiating*, pp. 179–80; Baswell, *History*, p. 168.

239 Bezzola, *Origines* III, part 1, pp. 280ff.

240 Singerman, *Clouds*, pp. 100, 114–15.

241 Fromm, 'Eneasromane', pp. 33 f. On historiography and eyewitnesses see Green, *Listening*, pp. 237–8.

242 Raynaud de Lage, 'Roman', p. 175; Blask, *Geschehen*.

243 Poirion, *CCM* 19 (1976), 213 ff.; Singerman, *Clouds*, p. 53.

244 Singerman, *Clouds*, pp. 105, 110ff.

245 Ibid., pp. 101–2. Cf. also Marichal, 'Naissance', pp. 471–2.

246 Singerman, *Clouds*, pp. 48, 113 f.; Patterson, *Negotiating*, p. 182.

247 Singerman, *Clouds*, p. 38. Cf. also Wittig, *CL* 22 (1970), 242.

248 Virgil's Lavinia: Singerman, *Clouds*, pp. 51–2. On the theme of love Opitz, *Geschichte*, has too little to say, but cf. pp. 40, 46, 52. On *amor et militia* cf. Kistler, *Veldeke*, pp. 183–4, and in more general literary-historical terms Hanning, *Individual*, pp. 54ff. (under what he terms the 'chivalry topos').

249 Singerman, *Clouds*, p. 94; Kasten, *DVjs* 62 (1988), 243; Baswell, *Virgil*, p. 186 ('an *altera Dido*').

250 See above, pp. 14–15. Whereas Virgil's fictional Dido could be made to serve a historical purpose, the reverse is almost the case in the French work, where the historical extension of the narrative backwards to include the judgment of Paris is harnessed to the theme of love in giving the first illustration of the power of Venus in a work in which love plays so important a role. Cf. Kistler, *Veldeke*, pp. 34–5.

251 Jones, *Theme*, p. 36 ('The situation in Virgil lent itself to adaptation and expansion'); Raynaud de Lage, 'Roman', p. 176; Kistler, *Veldeke*, p. 122 ('... die Leere füllen, die Vergils bloße Andeutung der Situation hinterließ').

252 Singerman, *Clouds*, pp. 50–1. Likewise, another interlude of peace, whose wider importance we consider later, is seen by Gauvain in Wace's *Roman de Brut* 10765 ff. as the occasion for love and the chivalric deeds that it inspires. The new theme of love, like the fictionality that makes use of it, seeks out such niches for expression.

253 Singerman, *Clouds*, pp. 51–2; Nolan, *Chaucer*, pp. 80, 85, 89, 90, 96.
    Nolan, *Chaucer*, pp. 81 ff., has also shown how light is thrown on Dido in the *Roman d'Enéas* by structural re-disposition of material. The French author differs from Virgil at the beginning of his work by interrupting Eneas' departure from Troy with an interpolated account of the judgment of Paris, not merely as an explanation of the Trojan War, but also to allow us to assess actions and motives elsewhere in the work. The French author reads Virgil in the light of Ovid's *Heroides* in having Paris, choosing between various bribes, opt for love (Helen) instead of *pris de chevalerie* (*hardement, proëce*) or *richece*, bravery, prowess, riches (137ff.), the prerequisites for effective rulership. The author's own judgment on Paris (neglecting other values for the sake of love) informs his discussion of the two love-affairs (Dido, Lavine) of the work. This opening passage prepares us for the assessment of the nature of Dido's love nearly 2000 lines later, much as, in the opening scene in Chrétien's *Erec*, Erec's choice to remain with the queen instead of displaying valour with other knights on the hunt implicitly foreshadows his *recréantise* with Enide (cf. Lacy, *Craft*, pp. 70, 74). The relevance of Paris' choice to the events at Carthage is suggested when Dido's successful reign there is seen in terms of her *richece* and *proëce* (403–4), implying the equilibrium of qualities called for in rulership. Suddenly this balance is upset by the queen's obsessive love for Eneas, a choice as foolish and disastrous in the author's eyes as that made by Paris. Inviting us tacitly to consider whether Dido's choice echoes Paris', he uses verbal echoes when describing Dido's subjects lamenting the loss of her *richece* and *proëce* (2125 ff.). The consequences of love which in the case of Dido Ovid had described as *stultus*, foolish (*Heroides* 7, 28) and the French poet as *fol*, foolish

(2143) are then examined again, this time positively, in the case of Eneas and Lavine, harmonising the demands of *proëce* and *richece* with *amor*, as Paris and Dido had not been able to. In this long-range structural technique, making use of verbal echoes, the author of the *Enéas* foreshadows what Chrétien accomplished on a much more complex level, but operating with greater freedom, as early as his *Erec*.

254 Nolan, *Chaucer*, p. 310, n. 57, quotes a twelfth-century glossator to the effect that Ovid wrote the letters 'sub personis illarum grecarum nobilium mulierum' (in the roles of those noble Greek women), and Baudri de Bourgueil already understood him in that light (see above, p. 21). This building of fiction on a predecessor's fiction can be compared with Wolfram's intertextual references to Hartmann (see above, p. 59).

255 Fromm, 'Eneasroman', p. 90.

256 Wolf, *Kultur*, p. 321. Cf. also Wenzelburger, *Motivation*, pp. 270f.; Fromm, 'Unterwelt', p. 321; Kistler, *Veldeke*, pp. 39, 196; Kartschoke, ed. p. 874.

257 Gottfried von Viterbo, *Speculum*, pp. 21 and 92 (cf. Thomas, *ZfdPh* 108 [1989], 78ff.); Pastré, *BDBA* 10 (1992), 127; *Carmen de gestis*, pp. 67ff. (cf. Willaert, 'Luisterlied', pp. 184f.).

258 On the first *Stauferpartie* see Heinrich von Veldelce, *Eneasroman*, ed. Kartschoke, pp. 800–1; ed. Fromm, pp. 857f.; Pastré, *Auffindung*, pp. 107ff. On the second *Stauferpartie* cf. *Eneasroman*, ed. Kartschoke, pp. 822–3; ed. Fromm, pp. 899–900.

259 Opitz, *Geschichte*, p. 68. On Veldeke's associations with the Hohenstaufen in his lyrics see Willaert, 'Luisterlied', pp. 65ff.; 'Veldeke', pp. 33ff.; 'Thesen', p. 309ff. In his *Servatius*: Koldeweij, *Servas*, pp. 28f.; Leusden, *NT* 79 (1986), 134ff.; Willaert, 'Luisterlied', pp. 87 and 184, n. 9; 'Veldeke', pp. 41ff. In the *Eneasroman*: Willaert, 'Luisterlied', p. 67.

260 Willaert, 'Veldeke', p. 48; Thomas, *ZfdPh* 108 (1989), 73ff.

261 *Ordo naturalis*: Fromm, 'Eneasromane', p. 29; Opitz, *Geschichte*, pp. 107–8. Eyewitness account: Fromm, 'Eneasromane', pp. 33f. Pagan gods: Kartschoke, ed., p. 876; Fromm, 'Eneasroman', pp. 90–1; Opitz, *Geschichte*, pp. 149–50, 169 (with a reference to Veldeke's concern for historical credibility).

262 Henkel, 'Kurzfassungen', p. 57; Opitz, *Geschichte*, p. 108, fn. 244.

263 Bastert, *ZfdA* 128 (1999), 364. In my review of Opitz in *MLR* 95 (2000), 459ff., I likewise criticise her historical interpretation for allowing the fictional dimension to go by default.

264 Bastert, *ZfdA* 128 (1999), 364f. Veldeke's phrasing about Virgil (354, 25: 'ne louch her niht, sô is ez wâr', if he did not lie, then it is true), like that of other authors in his time, could even imply a doubt about the historical reliability of his material. See above, p. 72, and Schirmer, 'Wahrheitsauffassung', pp. 61f.

265 Bastert, *ZfdA* 128 (1999), 366.

266 Syndikus, *PBB* 114 (1992), 57ff., argues that Veldeke's changes of emphasis are far-reaching enough to establish his independence of Virgil and the French *Enéas*. Even though he may play off Ovid against one or both of these, Ovid is a means of reinterpreting his material. He may not invent himself, but goes a new way by selection from and compilation of different sources.

267 Kistler, *Veldeke*, has shown that the German author often differs from Virgil and the French version, but agrees with Ovid, whom he has most probably adapted to his own needs.

268 Bastert, *ZfdA* 128 (1999), 365. Only towards the end of her book does Opitz, *Geschichte*, p. 225, acknowledge this, but without drawing any conclusion from it. By contrast, Kistler, *Veldeke*, shows herself throughout to be aware of the two dimensions in

Veldeke's work. Cf. p. 238: 'Der Aeneasstoff ist für Veldeke nicht bloß *fabula*, nicht allein Abenteuer- und Liebesroman, sondern darüber hinaus ist er wie die "Aeneis" eingebunden in eine historisch-politische Dimension.'

269 Alexander, born in 356 BC and died in 323, invaded India in 326.

270 Wittkower, *JWCI* 5 (1942), 161;Green, *GLL* 28 (1975), 246. Cf. Wiseman, 'Historians', p. 131.

271 Cary, *Alexander*, pp. 14–15; Romm, *Edges*, pp. 110ff.

272 Quintus Curtius: Ehlert, *Alexanderdichtung*, pp. 13–14; Justinus and Orosius: ibid., p. 14. Cf. also Fischer, *Alexanderliedkonzeption*, p. 13. Honorius Augustodunensis: Wittkower, *JWCI* 5 (1942), 169, 170, fn. 6 (with reference to the *Weltchronik* of Rudolf von Ems); Vincent of Beauvais: ibid., p. 170, fn. 3; Roger Bacon: ibid., p. 171, fn. 2. Cf. also Wittkower, p. 180, and Schnell, 'Alexander', pp. 51, 52. Knape, *Historie*, pp. 119, 170, points out that texts in the Alexander tradition can be termed *historia* and regarded as belonging to historiography.

273 Fischer, *Alexanderliedkonzeption*, pp. 53 f.; Shaw, *Epos*, p. 280.

274 Green, *GLL* 28 (1975), 247. Schnell, 'Alexander', pp. 58, 59, points to the codicological evidence for several Alexander texts being transmitted in manuscripts containing mainly historical works.

275 Kugler, 'Geographie', p. 110. Natural history: Wittkower, *JWCI* 5 (1942), 159; Cary, *Alexander*, pp. 335–6; geography (Ebstorf and Hereford *mappae mundi*): Wittkower, *JWCI* 5 (1942), 174–5; Kugler, 'Geographie', p. 109. For the same 'factual' reason they also find a place in so many medieval encyclopaedias (Wittkower, *JWCI* 5 [1942], 169–70).

276 Romm, *Edges*, pp. 85 ff., who also makes the point, pp. 93–4, that this expectation would have been shared by Alexander on his march into the East.

277 Ibid., pp. 173, 174.

278 Ruh, *Epik* I 34; Perry, *Romances*, pp. 381–2; Stoneman, *Alexander*, pp. 1 ff.

279 Strabo: Wittkower, *JWCI* 5 (1942), 165; Aulus Gellius: ibid., pp. 165–70. Similar criticism could be voiced in the Middle Ages. For James of Vitry cf. Henkel, *Studien*, p. 145 (but see also Grubmüller, *FMS* 12 [1978], 174) and for Albertus Magnus see Wittkower, *JWCI* 5 (1942), 171, fn. 1.

280 Romm, *Edges*, p. 202.

281 Photius: ibid., pp. 209–10. (Romm also stresses, p. 214, how easily truth and fiction could change places with each other and that only in a fluid medium like this could a safe haven be found for imaginative fiction.) Later Alexander romances: Green, *GLL* 28 (1975), 256–7 (on the Strassburg version of the *Alexanderlied*).

282 Romm, *Edges*, p. 95, interprets Strabo on 'the writers on India' as meaning not that they were truly ignorant, but 'fictionalizers, who use ignorance as a ploy in order to achieve a literary effect'.

283 Fictional contract: Romm, *Edges*, pp. 197 ('the mendacity . . . was obvious to all'), 200 ('all are aware of their intent to deceive'), 203 ('the right to invent *thaumata* candidly'). Blurring the boundary: pp. 204('deliberately fuses the language of poetry and science, emphasizing perhaps the permeability of the boundary between the two'), 205 ('as a way of mediating between the poles of geography and fiction, or perhaps as a way of questioning whether any real distinction could be drawn between the two categories'). Romm gives this whole chapter the title 'Geography and Fiction' (p. 172).

284 Ehlert, *Alexanderdichtung*, pp. 13–14, 19.

285 Roncaglia, 'L'Alexandre', p. 42. Cf. Frappier, 'Roman', pp. 153–4; Mackert, *Alexandergeschichte*, p. 111.

286 Roncaglia, 'L'Alexandre', pp. 37ff.

287 Szklenar, *Studien*, p. 28; Kelly, *Art*, pp. 251–2; Mackert, *Alexandergeschichte*, pp. 76ff.

288 Cary, *Alexander*, pp. 219–20; Jones, *Theme*, p. 63; Frappier, 'Roman', p. 165.

289 Kelly, *Art*, p. 127.

290 Szklenar, *Studien*, pp. 87–8; Frappier, 'Roman', p. 159. *Contra naturam*: Isidore, *Etymologiae* I 44.

291 Frappier, 'Roman', pp. 158, 163.

292 Green, *GLL* 28 (1975), 248.

293 This Frankish tradition goes back to Fredegar (cf. Southern, *TRHS* 20 [1970], 189f.) and is attested in German in Otfrid, *Evangelienbuch* I 1, 88 (cf. Vollmann-Profe, *Kommentar*, pp. 144–5; *Otfrid*, pp. 225–6), but also in the *Annolied* 22,1 ff. and 23, 1 ff. and the *Kaiserchronik* 325 ff. (where kinship with Alexander is attributed to the Saxons instead), 343 ff.

294 Ehlert, *Alexanderdichtung*, pp. 29, 30, 35, 36–7, 38ff. Whatever may be the reason for Albéric's rejection of the rival view that Nectanebus, rather than Philip of Macedon, was the father of Alexander, we may be sure that in Lamprecht's case it was because this fable conflicted with the bible (Macc. 1.1).

295 Fischer, *Alexanderliedkonzeption*, p. 61; Green, *GLL* 28 (1975), 248.

296 Szklenar, *Studien*, pp. 32ff.; Green, *GLL* 28 (1975), 252; Ehlert, *Alexanderdichtung*, pp. 40–1.

297 View of world-history: Fischer, *Alexanderliedkonzeption*, p. 62; Szklenar, *Studien*, pp. 29, 51, 58. Vorau manuscript: Fischer, *Alexanderliedkonzeption*, p. 59; Shaw, 'Epos', pp. 280–1; Ehlert, *Alexanderdichtung*, pp. 41–2; Mackert, *Alexandergeschichte*, pp. 32, 229–30 (whose view is, however, quite different).

298 See above, p. 72.

299 Ehlert, *Alexanderdichtung*, pp. 28ff.; Schirmer, 'Wahrheitsauffassung', p. 61.

300 See later, p. 171, for the similar differentiation with Arthur, whose historical status could be accepted alongside scepticism about the tales that attached themselves to him.

301 Szklenar, *Studien*, pp. 51 ff.

302 Vollmann-Profe, *Wiederbeginn*, p. 165; Ehlert, *Alexanderdichtung*, pp. 78–9.

303 Szklenar, *Studien*, p. 62.

304 On *wunder* in the Strassburg text: Green, *GLL* 28 (1975), 257–8; on their literary function: Szklenar, *Studien*, pp. 110ff.

305 Ibid., pp. 85ff., 105–6; Ehlert, *Alexander*, pp. 81 ff.

306 Green, *GLL* 28 (1975), 250ff.

307 Cf. Nykrog, 'Rise', p. 594: 'it was the scholarly writer who groped his way toward fiction, not the oral storyteller who simply resorted to writing'.

308 Those by Herbort von Fritzlar and Lamprecht (Vorau text).

309 Jackson, 'Arthur', pp. 10–11; Charles-Edwards, 'Arthur', p. 18. Both these authors deal with the Arthur of history.

310 Gildas: Bezzola, *Origines* II 529; Jackson, 'Arthur', pp. 2–3; Leckie, *Passage*, pp. 11–12; Burrichter, *Wahrheit*, p. 32. Bede: Bezzola, *Origines*, II 529; Leckie, *Passage*, pp. 13 ff., 52; Burrichter, *Wahrheit*, p. 32.

311 Bezzola, *Origines* II 529ff.; Jackson, 'Arthur', pp. 4ff.; Leckie, *Passage*, pp. 16–17, 61–2; Burrichter, *Wahrheit*, pp. 32f.

312 Jackson, 'Arthur', pp. 4–5; Burrichter, *Wahrheit*, pp. 33–4.

313 Burrichter, *Wahrheit*, pp. 34–5. On *veraces historiae* and fabulous tales see later, p. 171.

314 *Vita Cadoci*: Johanek, *FMS* 21 (1987), 369ff.; Echard, *Narrative*, pp. 198ff.; Roberts, 'Triads', pp. 83–4. *Vita Iltuti*: Johanek, *FMS* 21 (1987) 371–2. Echard, p. 198;

Roberts, 'Triads', pp. 82 ff. (Roberts points out that the saint is presented as a cousin of Arthur, whose court is of magnificent splendour). *Vita Gildae*: Burrichter, *Wahrheit*, p. 35.

315 Whilst it is true that criticisms of some saints' lives and doubts about the historical veracity of their miracles could be expressed in the Middle Ages (cf. Schreiner, *AfK* 48 [1966], 10 ff.), we should not generalise this. References to doubters who are put in their place enhance credibility, and the criticisms voiced are sporadic. The case of Robert of Auxerre is informative (ibid., pp. 17–18), for what he calls into doubt as unhistorical is not the legend of the finding of the Cross as such, but rather one legend that attributed it to Cyriacus instead of Helena. Such a criticism is not general, but specific; it is not sceptical on principle, but takes the historicity of the legend seriously.

316 Anglo-Saxon historical tradition: Burrichter, *Wahrheit*, p. 29 (Geoffrey refers to Gildas and Bede in his prologue, [1] p. 1). Traditional learning of Wales: Roberts, 'Geoffrey', pp. 101, 113. Norman historiography: Ingledew, *Speculum* 69 (1994), 681 ff. (cf. also the way in which Geoffrey supplements William of Malmesbury and Henry of Huntingdon by his explicit mention of them at the close of his work, [208] p. 147). See also Flint, *Speculum* 54 (1979), 455, and Otter, *Inventiones*, p. 79.

317 Burrichter, *Wahrheit*, pp. 29–30. On historical models that Geoffrey follows see Barron, Le Saux and Johnson, 'Chronicles', pp. 15–16.

318 Geoffrey, *Historia* [1] p. 1 ('librum uetustissimum qui a Bruto primo rege Britonum usque ad Cadualadrum filium Caduallonis actus omnium continue et ex ordine perpulcris orationibus proponebat', a very ancient book that set out the deeds of all the rulers, from Brutus, the first king of the Britons, to Cadwallader, the son of Cadwallo, in unintempted sequence and in an attractive style). What Geoffrey says here of his purported source applies to his own work, too. Cf. Burrichter, *Wahrheit*, pp. 41, 42, 46.

319 Flint, *Speculum* 54 (1979), 456–7; Shichtman and Finke, *AL* 12 (1993), 12; Chinca, *History*, p. 30; Barron, Le Saux and Johnson, 'Chronicles', p. 15.

320 Ingledew, *Speculum* 69 (1994), 691–2; Burrichter, *Wahrheit*, p. 44. Burrichter, ibid., p. 64, fn. 5, and Roberts, 'Geoffrey', p. 99, also stress that these men were politically powerful, but also proven patrons of historical writing.

321 Roberts, 'Geoffrey', p. 100; Damian-Grint, *Historians*, pp. 43 ff.

322 Legitimising the present: Shichtman and Finke, *AL* 12 (1993), 15; Ingledew, *Speculum* 69 (1994), 686; Burrichter, *Wahrheit*, pp. 50, 53 ff. Image-boosting vis-à-vis the French royal house: Gerould, *Speculum* 2 (1927), 33 ff.; Tatlock, *History*, pp. 426 ff.; Knight, *Literature*, pp. 44–5; Brooke, 'Geoffrey', pp. 103–4.

323 Even if Geoffrey may have expected that some contemporaries, such as Henry of Huntingdon, might see through his fabrication, can he be said to have given them signals that he was indulging in fiction? A lie or forgery that is seen through by its potential victim as mendacious is not converted into fiction by that fact alone.

324 Johanek, *FMS* 21 (1987), 353: 'An der Authenzität dieses Arthurbildes hat das Mittelalter, trotz gelegentlicher Kritik an Einzelelementen, grundsätzlich nicht mehr gezweifelt.'

325 Burrichter, *Wahrheit*, p. 46 ('Diese Intention legt es nahe, daß Geoffrey die *Historia Regum Britanniae* wirklich als Geschichtswerk verstanden wissen wollte und nicht die Absicht hatte, ein fiktionales Werk zu schreiben'); Knapp, *GRM* 48 (1998), 242 ('Nichts im Text weist darauf hin, daß Geoffrey seinem Publikum damit einen Hinweis auf die Fiktionalität des Erzählten liefern wollte. Er hat ganz eindeutig eine Geschichtsfälschung in großem Stil zu politischen Zwecken inszeniert und damit auch

Erfolg gehabt'). When others talk of Geoffrey's 'fiction' this is acceptable only in the general, non-technical sense of the word (see above, p. 13). Cf. Clanchy, *Memory*, p. 256 ('fictions or half-truths'); Flint, *Speculum* 54 (1979), 457 ('fictional passage'); Leckie, *Passage*, p. 59 ('the success of this fiction'); Brooke, 'Geoffrey', p. 100 ('to hide a fiction'); Jackson, *Chivalry*, p. 3 ('shot through with fiction'). We need to make a clear distinction between the everyday and specialist usages of the word 'fiction'.

326 Leckie, *Passage*, pp. 21, 43.
327 Ibid., pp. 21–2, 27.
328 William of Malmesbury, *Gesta regum Anglorum* I § 8 (I 11). Cf. Johanek, *FMS* 21 (1987), 376; Leckie, *Passage*, p. 62; Echard, *Narrative*, p. 69.
329 Johanek refers to such accretions as 'Einzelelemente' or 'erzählerisches Beiwerk' (*FMS* 21 [1987], pp. 353, 378). A similar distinction was made between the historical figure of Alexander and the *fabulae* attaching to him. See above, pp. 167–8. The same is true of Aeneas (see above, p. 159).
330 Morse, *Truth*, p. 89; Shichtman and Finke, *AL* 12 (1993), 7; Burrichter, *Wahrheit*, p. 61.
331 Johanek, *FMS* 21 (1987), 352 and fn. 31; Wright, 'Place', pp. 71 ff.; Burrichter, *Wahrheit*, p. 61; Echard, *Narrative*, pp. 75–6. Where Wright, 'Place', p. 91, sees in the *Epistola* 'a first, faint adumbration of the misgivings', Leckie, *Passage*, p. 78, says: 'If Henry harboured doubts as to Geoffrey's veracity, no trace of such misgivings has survived.'
332 Otter, *Inventiones*, p. 77.
333 Howlett, *Arthuriana* 5 (1995), 53; Burrichter, *Wahrheit*, p. 61; Echard, *Narrative*, p. 78.
334 Ingledew, *Speculum* 69 (1994), 679; Burrichter, *Wahrheit*, p. 61; Echard, *Narrative*, p. 74; Otter, *Inventiones*, p. 152 (at n. 78).
335 Leckie, *Passage*, pp. 93 ff.
336 Ibid., pp. 97–8; Burrichter, *Wahrheit*, p. 61, n. 2 and 5.
337 Leckie, *Passage*, p. 98.
338 Ingledew, *Speculum* 69 (1994), 696 ff.; Burrichter, *Wahrheit*, p. 61.
339 Short, *Speculum* 69 (1994), 341.
340 Ingledew, *Speculum* 69 (1994), 701–2.
341 Johanek, *FMS* 21 (1987), 356.
342 Ibid., pp. 360 ff.
343 *Gesta regum Anglorum* III § 287 (II 342): 'unde antiquitas naeniarum adhuc eum venturum fabulatur' (the antiquity of these fables still puts about the tale that he will return). Cf. Howlett, *Arthuriana* 5 (1995), 42. To *nugae* and *fabulae* in an earlier passage (I 11–12) there correspond *naeniarum* and *fabulatur* in the later.
344 Johanek, *FMS* 21 (1987), 373. From the fact that Frenchmen and Bretons quarrel about whether Arthur is still alive we may assume that for the former this was unacceptable. On Hermann and Arthur see also Bezzola, *Origines* II 535–6.
345 Johanek, *FMS* 21 (1987), 374, fn.141.
346 Ibid., p. 376, fn. 154.
347 Gervase of Tilbury: Chambers, *Arthur*, p. 276. William of Newburgh: Echard, *Narrative*, p. 77.
348 Wace, *Roman de Brut* 13275 ff., imputes the belief in Arthur's survival and eventual return to the Britons, which is not exactly historically reliable in view of his earlier remark about Arthur (9752): 'Dont Bretun dient mainte fable' (about whom the Britons tell many fables). Cf. Burrichter, *Wahrheit*, pp. 123–4. Chrétien, *Yvain* 37–8. Hartmann, *Iwein* 8 ff. (cf. Kern, *WW* 23 [1973], 249; 'Leugnen', p. 17).
349 Although Geoffrey says that Arthur was carried off to Avalon 'ad sananda uulnera', for the healing of his wounds [178] p. 132, he says in the same breath that he was

mortally wounded ('letaliter uulneratus') and confirms this by the addition: 'Anima eius in pace quiescat' (May his soul rest in peace). Cf. Burrichter, *Wahrheit*, p. 124, fn. 2. In his edition, p. lix, Wright points out that this addition occurs only in the Bern manuscript, whose scribe presumably had no time for the Breton hope that Arthur might return.

350 Johanek, *FMS* 21 (1987), 378, fn. 166. Cf. Fichte, 'Fakt', p. 45, fn. 1.

351 Johanek, *FMS* 21 (1987), 378, fn. 167.

352 Green, *Listening*, p. 108.

353 Leckie, *Passage*, pp. 47ff.

354 *Descriptio* VI 179. Cf. Otter, *Inventiones*, p. 152.

355 Echard, *Narrative*, p. 73.

356 *Descriptio* VI 208. I now question my earlier view, *Listening*, p. 251, that this implies a doubt about Arthur's historicity. On the range of meaning of *fabulosus* see *OLD*, p. 665.

357 *Historia rerum Anglicarum*, pp. 11, 12–13, 16, 18. Cf. Leckie, *Passage*, p. 25.

358 Morse, *LSE* 13 (1982), 96; Johanek, *FMS* 21 (1987), 377; Burrichter, *Wahrheit*, p. 62; Echard, *Narrative*, pp. 75ff.

359 *Historia rerum Anglicarum*, p. 13. Leckie, *Passage*, p. 95, concludes that William's attack on Geoffrey was occasioned by the readiness with which his view of British history was being accepted, while Wolfzettel, *ZfrPh* 100 (1984), 444, argues that the failure of William's criticisms to register is itself a witness to Geoffrey's success.

360 See later, p. 192. With Geoffrey this interval of peace, [153] p. 107, is filled with a description of the renown and splendour of Arthur's court, [154] p. 107, not of any adventures. Cf. Burrichter, *Wahrheit*, p. 54.

361 Geoffrey, *Historia* [1] p. 1. Historiography: see above, p. 153, on Dares and Dictys, and Spiegel, *Romancing*, pp. 69, 76, on the *Pseudo-Turpin Chronicle*.

362 Green, 'Erkennen', pp. 35ff. If we assessed Wolfram's fabrication of a source for *Parzival* in the form of Kyot (see above, pp. 78–82) as part of his fictional strategy, this was because of other signals to fiction inviting the audience's knowing collusion.

363 *Historia* [207] p. 147. Howlett, *Arthuriana* 5 (1995), 43, refers to 'literary oneupmanship'.

364 Short, 'Gaimar', pp. 155ff.; *Speculum* 69 (1994), 323ff.; Howlett, *Arthuriana* 5 (1995), 47ff.

365 Short, *Speculum* 69 (1994), 327, 338; Damian-Grint, *Historians*, pp. 50–1.

366 Short, *Speculum* 69 (1994), 323–4.

367 *Estoire, geste*: Damian-Grint, *Historians*, pp. 255–6, 258. Dating of events: Burrichter, *Wahrheit*, p. 72. Comments on sources: Short, 'Gaimar', pp. 158–9; *Speculum* 69 (1994), 323; Burrichter, p. 73; Damian-Grint, *MÆ* 66 (1997), 191. The historian Gaimar's recourse to sources in various languages (6435ff.) is reminiscent of the historiographical front put up by Gottfried, *Tristan* 155ff. (cf. Chinca, *History*, pp. 49ff.).

368 Howlett, *Arthuriana* 5 (1995), 54.

369 Short, *Speculum* 69 (1994), 326; Burrichter, *Wahrheit*, p. 71. On this formulation by Gaimar cf. Press, 'Courtesy', pp. 267ff., for whom it amounts to a new historiographical concept.

370 Blacker, *Faces*, pp. 29–30. Cf. also Meneghetti, *MR* 2 (1975), 232ff. and Damian-Grint, *Historians*, p. 101.

371 Leckie, *Passage*, p. 116; Sturm-Maddox, *Studies in Philology* 81 (1984), 28–9; Howlett, *Arthuriana* 5 (1995), 55.

372 *Ordo naturalis*: Burrichter, *Wahrheit*, pp. 119–20. Chronological correlations: Eley, 'Aspects', pp. 144–5; Burrichter, pp. 120–1.

373 Criticism of details: Lofmark, 'Credulity', p. 6; Burrichter, *Wahrheit*, pp. 121–2; Damian-Grint, *Historians*, pp. 54, 55, fn. 74. Arthur's disappearance: see above, n. 348. Tales about Arthur: Burrichter, *Wahrheit*, pp. 125–6.

374 Wace's canny scepticism also underlies his checking on Celtic fables in going to the 'magic' well in the forest of Broceliande (*Roman de Rou* 6415 ff.).

375 Burrichter, *Wahrheit*, pp. 130–1, but also 91–2; Barron, Le Saux and Johnson, 'Chronicles', p. 18.

376 These have been discussed in detail by Bezzola, *Origines* III 1, particularly concerning Arthur himself (pp. 154–5), Guinevere (pp. 156–7), Arthur's court (pp. 160–1), Martia (p. 170), and the theme of love (pp. 171–2). Cf. also Marichal, 'Naissance', p. 472, and Meneghetti, *SLF* 3 (1974), 26ff. Burrichter, *Wahrheit*, has shown that whereas Geoffrey refers to the *facetia* of the court, Wace sees it repeatedly in terms of *corteisie* (pp. 104ff.). Nykrog, 'Rise', p. 598, pertinently says of such details that for all the narrative imagination displayed 'this is not fiction but translation (adaptation) in the formal framework of history or chronicle'.

377 Burrichter, *Wahrheit*, pp. 90, 95–6.

378 Ibid., pp. 96, 114.

379 Wolfzettel, 'Probleme', p. 341: 'Die Entstehung einer volkssprachlichen erzählenden Literatur in Frankreich im 12. Jahrhundert vollzieht sich im Zeichen der Geschichte.'

380 Ibid., p. 345.

381 Chinca, *History*, p. 29.

382 See above, pp. 16–17.

383 *Roman de Brut* 9787ff. ('En cele grant pais . . .', in that great peace). Geoffrey knows of two such periods of peace, one lasting twelve years and the other nine: *Historia* [153] p. 107, [155] p. 109. Cf. Putter, *MÆ* 63 (1994), 1 ff.; Burrichter, *Wahrheit*, pp. 96ff.

384 Cador: 10737ff.; Gauvain: 10765 ff. By contrast, Geoffrey has only Cador's words critical of the effects of too long a period of peace:[158] p. 113.

385 10771: 'Pur amistié e pur amies / Funt chevaliers chevaleries' (For love and their ladies knights perform deeds of chivalry). Cf. Burrichter, *Wahrheit*, p. 97. That these adventures, as later recounted in Chrétien's romances, belong to this period was recognised by the scribe of a thirteenth-century manuscript (Bibl. nat. fr. 1450). Cf. Walters, *Romania* 106 (1985), 303ff.; Huot, *Song*, pp. 27ff.; Morris, *FSt* 42 (1988), 257ff.; Putter, *MÆ* 63 (1994), 5 ff. In thus 'historicising' Chrétien (inserting his romances in a collective manuscript that runs chronologically from the *Roman de Troie* and the *Roman d'Enéas* to Wace's *Roman de Brut*, placing them precisely in the period of Arthurian peace) the scribe goes against both Wace's view that such adventures are fables and against Chrétien's conception of non-historical literary fiction. At least he confirms that it was at this point in Arthur's historical career, as recounted by Wace, that Chrétien's fiction originated.

386 In opting for *fables* rather than *tables* (dicing) I follow the reading of Arnold and Pelan, instead of Weiss, even though the latter's decision in favour of *tables* is closer to Geoffrey's *alee*, *Historia* [158] p. 113. Wace shows enough independence at this point (introducing Gauvain's praise of peace) to make this change credible. Cf. Burrichter, *Wahrheit*, pp. 96f., 127–8, who makes the point that *fables* as literary entertainment at court provides a further link between Arthur and Henry II.

387 Burrichter, *Wahrheit*, p. 127 and n. 2 (against Zink, *CCM* 24 [1981], 19). Cf. *Roman de Brut* 9788 ('Ne sai si vus l'avez oï', I do not know if you have heard it), 9791 (the use of *tant* goes well beyond Wace's text), 9795 (*tant* again, and *li conteür*).

388 See later, pp. 191–2.

389 Jauss, *Alterität*, p. 322 ('Fiktionalisierung').
390 Morris, *FSt* 42 (1988), 257ff., but see Putter, *MÆ* 63 (1994), 4–5, on her suggestion that Chrétien may have done this to make his fictions more credible.
391 Putter, *MÆ* 63 (1994), 5, who also suggests that this amounts to a liberation of narrative from the linear dimensions of the chronicle (p. 4) and that authors of romances thereby cleared or appropriated imaginative space in the chronicle for their own inventions (p. 13).
392 One suggestion of fictionality need not be expressly pointed out by Chrétien. If, as Jürgen Wolf argues in a forthcoming book, his audience knew of a 'real' Arthurian history from which Chrétien's accounts deviate they would be in a position similar to that described by Macrobius for Virgil's audience (see above, pp. 14–15), accepting as part of a fictional contract what does not conform to their historical knowledge.
393 Baumgartner, 'Vers', pp. 3–4. Neither in Geoffrey nor in Wace is there any mention of Erec or his father Lac, attesting them 'historically'. Yvain and Urien are mentioned, but the former very much in passing.
394 Burrichter, *Wahrheit*, pp. 133–4. For the medieval historian time stands still in such a period of peace, there are no *gesta* to be recounted. If Chrétien's *Erec* returns to topical history in the concluding allusions to Nantes (see pp. 142–3), this is as if to underline that what preceded it had been outside history.
395 Spiegel, *Romancing*, p. 63. On *historia* and *memoria* cf. Isidore of Seville, *Etymologiae* I 41: 'Historiae autem ideo monumenta dicuntur, eo quod memoriam tribuant rerum gestarum' (Histories are called memorials because they hand down the memory of what happened).
396 Spiegel, *Romancing*, p. 63; Zink, *Invention*, p. 29. Cf. also Wolfzettel, 'Probleme', p. 345. Warning, 'Diskurs', p. 194, makes the further point that in this prologue there speaks the cleric's pride in his literacy, but also the author's discovery of himself and his role. He adds: 'Der höfische Roman hat nicht etwa den Erzähler entdeckt. Den Erzähler gab es auch in der "oral tradition". Entdeckt hat er die fiktive Erzählerrolle, und zwar über den schreibenden Autor als Subjekt dieses Rollenspiels.'
397 Köhler, 'Selbstauffassung', pp. 13–14; Knapp, *Historie*, p. 61. Damian-Grint, *MÆ* 66 (1997), 195, argues that the use of *estoire* in the twelfth century to refer to an author's own text seems to be confined to historical works. Of the use of *estoire* by Béroul and Thomas he says that it means their source, but he misses the case of Chrétien's *Erec* and its importance for that author's distance from historical writing.
398 Frappier, *Chrétien*, p. 107; Maddox, 'Discourse', pp. 11, 15; Morris, *FSt* 42 (1988), 264.
399 Maddox, 'Discourse', pp. 16, 23 (n. 36).
400 Ibid., pp. 13–14. Cf. also Zink, *CCM* 24 (1981), 19–20.
401 Bertau, *Literatur*, p. 498.
402 Maddox, *Discourse*, pp. 11, 12.
403 Fourrier, *Courant*, pp. 124ff.; Baehr, *Sprachkunst* 2 (1971), 43ff.
404 Maddox, *Discourse*, p. 12, points out that 'reminiscences of historical events and descriptive realism pervasive early in *Cligés* eventually thin out and give way to *évasion*'. If, like *Erec*, *Cligés* concludes by reverting to present-day history (6645ff.: because of Fénice's deception of her husband Byzantine emperors keep their wives guarded by eunuchs), this pseudo-history is not meant to be taken seriously. Cf. Maddox, p. 18.
405 On the historian's status as an eyewitness see above, p. 153 (on the standing of Dares as a historiographer of the Trojan War) and also Green, *Listening*, pp. 237–8.
406 *Roman de Rou* 6395ff. Wace expressly refers to the fables of the Bretons (6374: 'Donc Breton vont sovent fablant', about whom the Bretons often tell fables) and to the

magical quality of the spring (6387: *fees*, fairies; 6389: 'E altres merveilles plusors', and several other marvels). He goes to see this for himself (6393: 'La alai jo merveilles querre, / Vi la forest e vi la terre', I went there seeking marvels, I saw the forest and saw the land).

407 On the historian as an eyewitness in twelfth-century historical writing, Latin as well as vernacular, see Damian-Grint, *Historians*, pp. 68 ff.

408 On the intertextual connections between the passages in *Yvain* and in the *Roman de Rou* see Wolf, 'Löwenritter', pp. 205 ff.; Green, *Listening*, pp. 254–5. Like Wace in search of marvels, Calogrenant goes in search of *avantures* (176 f.), closely related to *merveilles* (362 ff., 432), but which he, unlike Wace, actually beheld (174: 'ce, que je vi', which I saw). Albeit for different reasons, both Wace and Calogrenant accuse themselves of folly in going to the spring (6396 ff.; 577 f.).

409 On historians' truth-claims based on the denigration of others for their untruth (*songe, fable, mançonge*) cf. Damian-Grint, *Historians*, pp. 114 ff., and, specifically with regard to Arthurian material, Green, *Listening*, p. 251: William of Malmesbury (*somniarent, fabulae*), William of Newburgh (*fabula*), Giraldus Cambrensis (*fabulosa, mentitur*), Aelred of Rievaulx (*fabulae mendaciae*), Peter of Blois (*fabula*).

410 In quite a different way, as Stevens, 'Giants', p. 412 (cf. also p. 415), has shown, Thomas makes intertextual use of a giant-killing episode in Wace's historical account for his own fictional purpose. The freely inventive way in which he proceeds is shown by the detailed chiastic and highly artificial structure Thomas creates in setting off Arthur, Tristran and Marc against one another.

411 Here I largely follow Burrichter, *Wahrheit*, pp. 147 ff.

412 Geoffrey, *Historia* [143] p. 101; Wace, *Roman de Brut* 9033 ff.

413 See above, p. 178.

414 Burrichter, *Wahrheit*, p. 150.

415 For Germany the transition of Arthurian material from history to fiction was assisted by the fact that, whereas the historicity of the theme was bolstered by its dynastic, political role in the Anglo-Norman realm and to a lesser extent in France (or in parts of France), such factors did not come into play in Germany. This weakening of historical connections opened the door to the possibility of a more fictional treatment.

416 Two faint traces remain (258: 'ichn wil iu keine lüge sagen. / Ez geschach mir, dâ von ist ez wâr', I do not intend to tell you any lie. It happened to me and therefore it is true; 795: 'Ich hân einem tôren glîch getân', I acted like a fool), but without any adaptation of the *Roman de Rou* in Germany they have lost the intertextual function they had with Chrétien.

417 Green, *Listening*, p. 256.

418 To avoid a prolonged description, to put forward Iwein in flattering terms, to pretend his own trustworthiness as an author. Cf. Christ, *Rhetorik*, p. 317.

419 *Etymologiae* I 41.

420 Hartmann also parodies eyewitness truth-claims for his own fictional purposes in *Erec* 8946 ff. (Green, *Listening*, p. 256).

421 A similar observation has been made of Chrétien's *Yvain* by Uitti, *RPh* 22 (1969), 480, 481.

422 Kellermann, *GRM* 42 (1992), 1 ff.

423 Ibid., p. 8, although the author concedes, p. 23, n. 72, that for Dittmann, 'Begriff', p. 160, the prologue nowhere touches upon the question of historical reality.

424 Kellermann, *GRM* 42 (1992), 16.

425 See above, p. 171.

426 Haug, 'Ästhetik des Widerspruchs', p. 212. Cf. Nykrog, 'Rise', p. 603.
427 Geoffrey, *Historia* [177] p. 130 ('Hiwenus, filius Uriani'). Cf. Gaimar, *Estoire des Engleis* 1 ff., Wace, *Roman de Brut* 13189, but also Sims-Williams, *Romania* 116 (1998), 94–5.
428 *GRM* 42 (1992), 9–10.
429 Ibid., p. 16.
430 Ibid., p. 17.
431 Nor is Kellermann's argument made more convincing when she suggests that Hartmann legitimised his work not merely by *historia*, but also by providing an *exemplum* (ibid., p. 16). She rightly refers to the function of *exempla* in the historiography of antiquity (p. 6: Sallust, Livy) and points out that they were also central to historical and religious writing in the Middle Ages (p. 7). That does not mean, however, that they are a feature of history alone, as some of her references make clear. Aristotle recognised two types, dealing with actual events or fictitious ones (p. 20, n. 39), Quintilian makes a similar distinction (p. 6: 'res gesta aut ut gesta', deeds that were performed or could have been), whilst the *bilde* (examples) recommended to young men and women by Thomasin (*Der Welsche Gast* 1029 ff.) likewise include both historical and fictitious characters. The exemplary function of a work of literature can therefore place it either with history or with fiction. It does not suffice to settle the issue by itself.
432 Sawicki, *Gottfried*, p. 158. Cf. also Huber, *Gottfried* (1986), p. 36; Knapp, *Historie*, pp. 31–2.
433 Chinca, *History*, p. 92.
434 Ibid., p. 53. On the historical existence of Gottfried's figures cf. also p. 46, as well as Huber, *Gottfried* (1986), p. 36. Two figures, albeit marginal ones, whose 'historicity' was well established by their occurrence in Geoffrey's *Historia* and Wace's *Roman de Brut* are Gurmun (see above, pp. 143–4) and Corineus (cf. Chinca, *History*, p. 48, and Stevens, *Giants*, pp. 417 ff.).
435 On the theme of *memoria* in Gottfried's work cf. Chinca, *History*, pp. 53 ff.
436 448, 5884, 15919, 18696. On these usages cf. Knape, *Historie*, pp. 112 ff., and on the first example see Stevens, 'Giants', pp. 420–21.
437 Historical background: 448, 5884, 18696. Gurmun: 448, 5884. See also above, pp. 143–4.
438 8946. On the historical implications of this word cf. *Rhetorica ad Herennium* I 8, 3: 'Historia est gesta res' (History is what happened), but also Damian-Grint, *Historians*, pp. 221 ff., on its use in Anglo-Norman historiography.
439 Chinca, *History*, p. 49.
440 Christ, *Rhetorik*, p. 299.
441 Ibid., pp. 296 ff.; Chinca, *History*, pp. 95–6.
442 Bertau, *Literatur*, pp. 920–21. Knapp, *Historie*, p. 32, whilst agreeing with Sawicki's view of Gottfried as a *historiographus*, expresses doubts whether this is the whole story. Whereas Huber, *Gottfried* (1986), p. 36, says pointblank that Gottfried and Thomas were historians, in *Gottfried* (2000), p. 43, this is qualified by 'gewissermaßen'. Cf. also Jaffe, *Gottfried*, p. 302 ('historicizing posture'); Christ, *Rhetorik*, p. 297 ('nur als Haltung'); Chinca, *History*, p. 89 ('allegedly historical').
443 See above, p. 171.
444 Chinca, *History*, pp. 46–7.
445 Krohn, 'Finden', p. 56.
446 Düwel, *Werkbezeichnungen*, p. 125.
447 Ibid., pp. 126–7.

448 See above, pp. 154 (Homer), 159 (Virgil).

449 Chinca, *History*, pp. 68–9.

450 Ibid., p. 58.

451 Ibid., p. 57. By demonstratively varying his narrative between *historia* and *fabula*, but also by constructing it in accordance with *argumentum* (see above, pp. 8–10), Gottfried reveals his acquaintance with the three *genera narrationis* and their importance for his fictional writing.

452 Christ, *Rhetorik*, pp. 312 ff.; Green, *Listening*, pp. 258–9.

453 See the note to v. 17142 in Ganz's edition of *Tristan*, II 330.

454 Christ, *Rhetorik*, p. 314, sees Gottfried's line 17140 ('ich hân die fossiure erkant', I have known the grotto) as meaning 'Ich kenne mich in der Liebe aus'.

455 To these could of course be added Wolfram. See above, pp. 86–7.

456 Without specifying, Haug, *Literaturtheorie*, p. 105, says that Greek fiction arose from the 'Auseinandersetzung zwischen Wissenchaft und Dichtung'.

457 See above, p. 2.

458 Morgan, 'Make-believe', p. 182.

459 Nelson, *Fact*, p. 17.

460 On this harmonisation cf. Fuhrmann, 'Wunder', pp. 219–20.

461 Cf. Schreiner, *AfK* 48 (1966), 17 (with reference to 'apocrifas . . . scripturas' and 'ineptas superfluitates' apocryphal writings, useless superfluities) and *Saeculum* 17 (1966), 147 (with the telling contrast between *vera* and *apocrifa*).

462 Nelson, *Fact*, p. 21. Cf. also p. 22: 'The apocryphal tales created a substantial precedent for a kind of imaginative literature which was presented not as fiction but as documented history'. On the throw-away remarks of romance authors see above, pp. 72–3.

463 Dorn, *Heilige*, pp. 138–9.

464 Schreiner, *Saeculum* 17 (1966), 138.

465 Schreiner, *AfK* 48 (1966), 29 ff.

466 Ibid., pp. 30, 31.

467 Henry of Huntingdon, *Epistola ad Warinum*, p. 65 ('Respondeo igitur tibi quod nec voce nec scripto horum temporum saepissime notitiam quaerens invenire potui', My reply to you is that, however much I sought, I could find no report, by word of mouth or in writing, on that period); Geoffrey, *Historia* [1] p. 1.

468 Leckie, *Passage*, pp. 11–12, 15, 29–30.

469 Hanning, *Vision*, p. 124; Wiseman, *Cosmetics*, p. 21.

470 See above, p. 174.

471 Leckie, *Passage*, p. 20; Echard, *Narrative*, pp. 34–5.

472 See above, pp. 174–5.

473 Cf. Baswell, 'Marvels', p. 33; 'They thereby generate a comparatively safe imaginative space within ancient story to register aspects of their own time.'

474 Benoît creates an opportunity for treating four love-affairs in all (see above, p. 156). These have been discussed at length by Nolan, *Chaucer*, p. 96 ff.

475 Ibid., p. 99.

476 See above, pp. 14–15.

477 Nolan, *Chaucer*, pp. 109 ff.

478 Ibid., p. 110.

479 Kistler, *Veldeke*, p. 110.

480 Ibid. Kistler argues, p. 122, that the French poet (and Veldeke, too) made use of the figure of Scylla in Ovid's *Metamorphoses* to flesh out his depiction of Lavine. Of this

procedure she says: 'Ovids Scylla . . . konnte genau die Leere füllen, die Vergils bloße Andeutung der Situation hinterließ.'

481 Singerman, *Clouds*, p. 52.

482 Ibid., pp. 50–1.

483 Baswell, *Virgil*, pp. 170–1, 211.

484 See above, p. 177. Cf. also Wolf, *Kultur*, p. 317.

485 Stierle, 'Fiktion', p. 177; Romm, *Edges*, pp. 82ff.

486 See above, pp. 164, 167–8.

487 Geoffrey, *Historia* [153] p. 107 and [155] p. 109.

488 Wace, *Roman de Brut* 9729ff., 10133ff. Cf. Bezzola, *Origines* III 1, 161–2; Meneghetti, *SLF* 3 (1974), 40f.; Burrichter, *Wahrheit*, pp. 96–7.

489 Ibid., p. 140.

490 Putter, *MÆ* 63 (1994), 1ff.

491 Ibid., p. 5. That the adventures recounted in Chrétien's romances belong in this period of peace was recognised by a thirteenth-century scribe. See above, n. 385.

492 Fourrier, *Courant*, pp. 43–4; Keck, *Liebeskonzeption*, pp. 141–2; Stevens, 'Giants', pp. 409ff.

493 Fourrier, *Courant*, p. 44. See also above, pp. 143–4.

494 Keck, *Liebeskonzeption*, p. 142, suggests that Thomas, like Gottfried, intended his work to be regarded as historical rather than fictional. I should rather see them both as using historical information, but without historiographical intention (cf. Chinca, *History*, p. 49 and also p. 89: 'allegedly historical').

495 Schmolke-Hasselmann, *Versroman*, pp. 86ff.; *DVjs* 57 (1983), 424.

496 Frank, 'Varianten', p. 124, quotes for example the *Bliocadran* prologue in which the story of Perceval's parents and brothers, only hinted at by Chrétien, is elaborated.

497 Schirok, *LiLi* 18 (1988), Heft 69, 14.

498 See above, pp. 61–5.

499 Worstbrock, *FMS* 19 (1985), 1ff.

500 On Wolfram, *Parzival* 4, 9 ('maere . . . niuwen', tell a story again) see Nellmann's edn, II 52, but also Wolf, *Kultur*, pp. 20, 21.

501 Zeeman, 'Schools', p. 162, on Servius ('frequenter . . . variant fabulas poetae', poets frequently vary fables) and p. 164 on the same commentator's use of *tangere* to indicate the poet's 'power to choose from these various materials or discourses without any obligation to employ them as they are customarily used in their original contexts'.

502 Ibid., p. 151: 'Romance composition is a creative reworking of other materials'. On the general implications of this see Worstbrock, 'Wiedererzählen', pp. 128ff.

503 These two themes are of course closely interconnected: the bible (and religious literature based on it) was regarded as *historia*, while historiography was concerned with *historia salutis* (history of salvation).

504 Vollmann-Profe, *Wiederbeginn*, pp. 88ff. Cf. Meyer, *Verfügbarkeit*, pp. 6 ('der Weg aus der Vorherrschaft der klerikal beherrschten Literatur heraus', with reference to Kuhn and Haug) and 10 ('Versuch der Emanzipation aus klerikalen Denkmustern').

505 Vollmann-Profe, *Wiederbeginn*, pp. 89ff.

506 Green, *Listening*, pp. 270ff.; Bumke, *Mäzene*, pp. 70ff.; Fleckenstein, 'Miles', pp. 302ff.

507 Vollmann-Profe, *Wiederbeginn*, p. 155, who points out the difference when the written source was in another vernacular (French): since it lacked the clerically based authority and truth-status of Latin such a source was more open to creative adaptation.

508 Nolan, *Chaucer*, p. 76.

509 Ibid., p. 8.

510 Green, *Listening*, pp. 313–14.

511 Page, *Owl*, pp. 19ff., 29ff.; Mehtonen, *Concepts*, pp. 27ff.

512 Wehrli, *Geschichte*, p. 273 ('... bedeutet der Artusroman die Befreiung der Erzähler von aller geschichtlichen Bindung').

513 Wandhoff, *Blick*, p. 288.

514 Wehrli, *Geschichte*, p. 273, calls this a 'Vorgang der Enthistorisierung'.

515 Otter, *Inventiones*, p. 16, speaks instead more globally of the 'truth-telling requirements that bind Latin writing', but this goes too far if we take account of early attempts at fictional writing in Latin (see above, pp. 7–8, 19–20). Otter herself comes to acknowledge this later (p. 95) when voicing disagreement with Haidu.

516 Morse, *Truth*, p. 242. She makes this point with regard to Henryson, but it is of more general import.

517 Green, *Listening*, pp. 310ff.; Wandhoff, *Blick*, p. 288. Cf. also Vollmann-Profe, *Wiederbeginn*, pp. 91–2, 158; Kartschoke, *Geschichte*, p. 387; Bumke, *Geschichte*, pp. 89–90; Gaunt, 'Romance', p. 55 (on the *Queste del Saint Graal*).

518 Knapp, *Ritterideal*, pp. 22ff. (also in abbreviated form in *CCM* 32 [1989], 263ff.); Heinzle, 'Stellung', pp. 104ff.

519 Green, *Listening*, pp. 244ff.

520 Spiegel, *Romancing*, p. 101; Wandhoff, *Blick*, pp. 110, 114.

521 Spiegel, *Romancing*, p. 109 (what she says here of thirteenth-century vernacular histories of antiquity is also applicable to the antique romances of the preceding century).

522 Ibid., pp. 61–2.

523 Nolan, *Chaucer*, p. 64. Cf. also Spiegel, *Romancing*, p. 62, who, commenting that emphasis on the art of translation displaced the authority of the Latin source to the romance and made way for the author's personal creativity, adds: 'By drawing attention to the centrality of literary expression, the romance author / translator liberated himself and his text from dependence on classical models ... and created a distance between source and translation in which the creative imagination of the writer found legitimate room for play'.

524 Romm, *Edges*, p. 172.

525 Nolan, *Chaucer*, p. 127. On Benoît's meaningful disposition of his material see above, n. 202, and on the same in the *Roman d'Enéas* see n. 253.

526 See later, pp. 197–8.

527 Spiegel, *Romancing*, pp. 115, 152–3; Brownlee, 'Romance', p. 254 (on Spanish antique romances).

528 Nolan, *Chaucer*, p. 8.

529 Ibid., p. 9.

530 Patterson, *Negotiating*, p. 160.

531 Raynaud de Lage, *MA* 67 (1961), 250–1 (cf. also Patterson, *Negotiating*, p. 158). It is significant that Albéric's *Roman d'Alexandre* should be the first work in French literature whose subject-matter is not religious, and that, for all his qualms, the same should be the case with Lamprecht's *Alexanderlied* in Germany (cf. Kugler, 'Geographie', p. 114, fn. 22).

532 Opitz, *Geschichte*, pp. 53–4.

533 Fleckenstein, 'Miles', pp. 302ff.

534 Nykrog, 'Rise', p. 597 (with regard to the *Roman de Thèbes*).

535 Opitz, *Geschichte*, p. 8. Clerically trained authors would have presumably known of traditional doubts about the historicity of classical themes, but how far can we assume

such knowledge in their audience? If they did not possess it, there can have been no fictional contract for them. Bertau, *Literatur*, p. 429, also remarks that the Anglo-Norman antique romances must be seen in conjunction with the vernacular chronicles (*Brut, Rou*). All serve a historiographical purpose.

536 The episodic nature of such fictionality could be seen on the same plane as the fictional interludes in twelfth-century historical writing in England discussed by Otter, *Inventiones*, who significantly talks of flirting with fictionality, tentatively, temporarily or partially (pp. 6, 9, 12). Such reservations could also be applied to the antique romances.

537 Greiner, *Poetica* 24 (1992), 301.

538 Ruh, *Epik* i 100–1.

539 Spiegel, *Romancing*, pp. 100–1.

540 Bertau, *Literatur*, pp. 498–9, 550, 553. Arthur and his court may play a restricted role in *Cligés*, but classical antiquity plays none at all.

541 Lais, *Prologue* 28ff.

542 *De nugis*, p. 404.

543 A similar distinction between the historicity of a figure and what was dubiously reported of him could also be made occasionally in the case of Aeneas and Alexander (cf. pp. 159 and 167).

544 Spiegel, *Romancing*, p. 158.

545 See above, n. 203. Cf. also Jackson, 'Material', p. 280: 'the very lack of historiographical encumbrance helped Arthurian literature to express imaginatively the contemporary concerns of authors, patrons and public'.

546 Haug, 'Spiel', p. 104.

547 Knapp, 'Überlegungen', p. 119, for all his doubts about fictional writing in the Middle Ages, acknowledges it in the case of Chrétien's romances and distinguishes them from the *historia* of the antique romances.

548 Marichal, 'Naissance', p. 452 (true to his etymological understanding of *roman* he includes Wace's *Brut*, as a translation of Geoffrey's Latin *Historia*). See also Damian-Grint, *Historians*, p. 229, who sees the primary meaning of the word as linguistic (vernacular as opposed to Latin), not literary.

549 On this widening of the term see Voelker, *ZfrPh* 10 (1887), 485ff., especially pp. 497–8; Payen and Diekstra, *Roman*, p. 21 (and fn. 4 on Chrétien's usage). For this reason the statement by Damian-Grint, *Historians*, p. 231 ('the term *romanz* is linguistic in the twelfth century') is much too restrictive.

550 Gallais, *CCM* 14 (1971), 70 ('Qui dit roman dit fiction, création de l'imagination, et qui dit création dit possibilité de créer, liberté de créer; absence de modèle précis qu'on se bornerait à imiter'). This leads Gallais to deny the term to Wace's *Brut* and to the antique romances (p. 71). Cf. also Zink, *CCM* 24 (1981), 19 ('Mais il faut encore, bien sûr, que l'Histoire considérée comme avérée soit remplacée par une histoire reconnue comme douteuse. Cette histoire douteuse, c'est la matière arthurienne, opposée à la matière antique') and 21 ('pour que le roman pût imposer seul sa propre vérité, il fallait renoncer à la vérité antique et lui préférer la fable bretonne, comme Chrétien l'a fait systématiquement') and Gerritsen, 'Avond', pp. 164–5.

551 Marichal, 'Naissance', p. 452.

552 Ruh, *Epik*, i 101.

553 With specific regard to Wolfram's *Parzival* Ernst, 'Formen', p. 183, says: 'Wenngleich z.B. in der Vorgeschichte nach Art der Chanson de geste an Historisches angeknüpft

wird, so ändert das, funktions- und gattungsgeschichtlich betrachtet, am Status der Fiktionalität ebensowenig wie das Vorkommen fiktionaler Reden in historischen Werken der Antike am Status der Historiographie.'

554 Heinzle, *Wandlungen*, pp. 105–6; Green *Listening*, pp. 265–6.
555 Strohschneider, *ZfdA* 120 (1991), 433 ff.; Henkel, 'Kurzfassungen', p. 58, and 'Erzählen', pp. 2, 3, 20–1; Haustein, *ZfdPh* (Sonderheft) 116 (1997), 118–19, 127, 129.
556 As suggested by von Ertzdorff, *ZfdPh* 86 (1967), 388.

Bibliography

PRIMARY SOURCES

Works are listed here under the name of the author, where this is known, or under the name of the work itself. Occasionally, where they are referred to in the course of the argument, more than one edition is cited.

Greek and Latin sources

Accessus ad auctores, ed. R. B. C. Huygens, Brussels 1954

Accessus to Lucan, ed. R. B. C. Huygens, *Accessus ad auctores. Bernard d'Utrecht; Conrad d'Hirsau, Dialogus super auctores*, Leiden 1970, pp. 39ff.

Accessus to Ovid's Amores, ed. F. Ghisalberti, 'Mediaeval biographies of Ovid', *JWCI* 9 (1946), 10ff. (here pp. 45ff., Appendix E)

Aelred of Rievaulx, *De speculo caritatis, MPL* 195, 505ff.

Alanus ab Insulis, *De planctu Naturae*, ed. N. M. Häring, in: *Studi Medievali* ser. III 19 (1978), 2, 797ff.

Aristotle, *Poetics*, ed. S. Halliwell, Cambridge, Mass. 1995

Augustine, *De civitate Dei, MPL* 41, 13ff.

  Confessiones, ed. M. Skutella, Stuttgart 1969

  Soliloquia, MPL 32, 869ff.

Baudri de Bourgueil, *Carmina*, ed. K. Hilbert, Heidelberg 1979

Bernard of Utrecht, *Commentum in Theodolum*, ed. R. B. C. Huygens, *Accessus ad auctores. Bernard d'Utrecht; Conrad d'Hirsau, Dialogus super auctores*, Leiden 1970, pp. 55ff.

Bernardus (Silvestris?), *Commentum super sex libros Eneidos Virgilii*, ed. J. W. and E. F. Jones, Lincoln, Nebraska 1977

Bonaventure, *De reductione artium ad theologiam*, ed. E. T. Healy, St Bonaventure, New York 1940

Carmen de gestis Frederici I. imperatoris in Lombardia, ed. I. Schmale-Ott, Hanover 1965

Cicero, *De inventione*, ed. H. M. Hubbell, London 1949

  De oratore, ed. E. W. Sutton and H. Rackham, London 1942

Dares Phrygius, *De excidio Troiae historia*, ed. F. Meister, Leipzig 1873

Dominicus Gundissalinus, *De divisione philosophiae*, ed. L. Baur, Münster 1903

Bibliography

Eberhard the German, *Laborintus*, ed. E. Faral, *Les arts poétiques du XIIe et du XIIIe siècle*, Paris 1924, pp. 386ff.

Ecbasis cuiusdam captivi per tropologiam, ed. W. Trillitzsch, Leipzig 1964. Also by B. K. Vollmann, in: W. Haug and B. K. Vollmann, *Frühe deutsche Literatur und lateinische Literatur in Deutschland 800–1150*, Frankfurt 1991, pp. 300ff.

Einhard, *Vita Karoli*, ed. O. Holder-Egger, MGH SS rerum Germanicarum in usum scholarum, Hanover 1922

Engelbert von Admont, *Speculum virtutum moralium*, ed. B. Pez, *Bibliotheca ascetica* III, Regensburg 1724, pp. 1ff.

Ermenrich von Ellwangen, *Vita b. Soli*, MGH SS 15, 156ff.

Felix of Crowland, *Vita s. Guthlaci*, ed. B. Colgrave, Cambridge 1956

Geoffrey of Monmouth, *Historia regum Britannie*, (Bern, Burgerbibliothek, MS 568), ed. N. Wright, Cambridge 1984

Geoffrey of Vinsauf, *Poetria nova*, ed. E. Faral, *Les arts poétiques*, Paris 1924, pp. 197ff.

Giraldus Cambrensis, *Descriptio Kambriae*, ed. J. E. Dimock, *Giraldus Cambrensis, Opera*, London 1868, vol. VI

    Speculum ecclesiae, ed. J. S. Brewer, *Giraldus Cambrensis, Opera*, London 1873, vol. IV

Gottfried von Viterbo, *Speculum regum*, MGH SS 22, 21ff.

Gregory the Great, *Dialogi*, ed. U. Moricca, Rome 1924

Henry of Huntingdon, *Epistola ad Warinum*, extracts in R. Howlett, *Chronicles of the reigns of Stephen, Henry II, and Richard I*, London 1886, vol. IV, pp. 65ff.

Horace, *Ars poetica*, ed. H. R. Fairclough, Cambridge, Mass. 1966

Hrotswitha, ed. P. von Winterfeld, MGHSS Rerum Germanicarum in usum scholarum 34, Hanover 1902

Isidore of Seville, *Differentiarum sive de proprietate sermonum libri duo*, MPL 83, 9ff.

    Etymologiae, ed. W. M. Lindsay, Oxford 1910

John of Capua, *Directorium humanae vitae*, ed. L. Hervieux, *Les fabulistes latins*, Paris 1899, vol. V, pp. 79ff.

John of Garland, *Poetria*, ed. T. Lawler, New Haven 1974

John of Salisbury, *Policraticus, MPL* 199, 385ff.

Joseph of Exeter (Joseph Iscanus), ed. L. Gompf, Leiden 1970

Konrad von Hirsau, *Dialogus super auctores*, ed. R. B. C. Huygens, Berchem 1955. Cf. also Huygens, ed., *Accessus ad auctores. Bernard d'Utrecht; Conrad d'Hirsau, Dialogus super auctores*, Leiden 1970, pp. 71ff.

Lactantius, *Opera omnia*, ed. S. Brandt and G. Laubmann, Vienna 1890–7

Livy, *Ab urbe condita*, ed. R. S. Conway and C. F. Walters, Oxford 1914

Macrobius, *Commentarii in Somnium Scipionis*, ed. J. Willis, Leipzig 1970

    Saturnalia, ed. J. Willis, Leipzig 1963

Marbod of Rennes, *Liber decem capitulorum, MPL* 171, 1693ff.

Otto von Freising, *Gesta Friderici I. imperatoris*, ed. G. Waitz, MGH SS rerum Germanicarum in usum scholarum, Hanover 1912

Ovid, *Amores*, ed. G. Showerman, Cambridge, Mass. 1986

    Heroides, ed. H. P. Dörrie, Berlin 1971

    Metamorphoses, ed. F. J. Miller, Cambridge, Mass. 1984

    Tristia, ed. G. P. Goold, Cambridge, Mass. 1988

Bibliography

Peter of Blois, *De confessione*, MPL 207, 1078ff.

Petrus Cantor, *Summa de sacramentis et animae consiliis*, ed. J.-A. Dugauquier, vol. III 2a (*Liber casuum conscientiae*), Louvain 1963

Priscian, *Praeexercitamina*, ed. C. Halm, Leipzig 1863

Quintilian, *Institutio oratoria*, ed. H. E. Butler, London 1966ff.

Remigius of Auxerre, *Commentum in Martianum Capellam*, ed. C. E. Lutz, Leiden 1965

Rhetorica ad Herennium, ed. H. Caplan, London 1954

Ruodlieb, ed. F. P. Knapp, Stuttgart 1977

Scholia Terentiana, ed. F. Schlee, Leipzig 1893

Scholia Vindobonensia ad Horatii Artem poeticam, ed. J. Zechmeister, Vienna 1877

Seneca, *Apocolocyntosis*, ed. P. T. Eden, Cambridge 1984

Servius Grammaticus, *Aeneidos Commentarii*, ed. G. Thilo and H. Hagen, Leipzig 1878–84

Thomas of Chobham, *Summa confessorum*, ed. F. Broomfield, Louvain 1968

Virgil, *Aeneid*, ed. R. A. B. Mynors, Oxford 1969

Vita s. Martini, ed. J. Fontaine, Paris 1967

Vita Merlini, ed. B. Clarke, Cardiff 1973

Vitae abbatum Acaunensium, MGH SS rerum Merovingicarum 3, 322ff.

Walter Map, *De nugis curialium*, ed. M. R. James, rev. C. N. L. Brooke and R. A. B. Mynors, Oxford 1983

Waltharius, ed. K. Strecker, Berlin 1947

William of Malmesbury, *Gesta regum Anglorum*, ed. W. Stubbs, London 1887ff.

    Vita s. Wulfstani, ed. R. R. Darlington, London 1928

William of Newburgh, *Historia rerum Anglicarum*, ed. R. Howlett, London 1884

William of Rennes, *Gesta regum Britannie*, ed. N. Wright, *The Historia regum Britannie of Geoffrey of Monmouth*, vol. v, Cambridge 1991

Vernacular sources

Aiol, ed. W. Foerster, Heilbronn 1876

Albéric de Pisançon, *Alexandre*, ed. A. Foulet, in: *The medieval French Roman d'Alexandre* (Elliott Monographs, 38), vol. III, pp. 37ff., Princeton 1949

Annolied, ed. E. Nellmann, Stuttgart 1986

Benoît de Sainte-Maure, *Roman de Troie*, ed. L. Constans, Paris 1904ff.

Béroul, *Tristan*, ed. A. Ewert, Oxford 1967, 1970

Li Chevalier as deus espees, ed. W. Foerster, Halle 1877

Le Chevalier à l'épée, ed. R. C. Johnson and D. D. R. Owen, *Two Old French Gauvain romances*, Edinburgh 1972, pp. 30ff.

Chrétien de Troyes, *Cligés*, ed. A. Micha, Paris 1957

    Erec, ed. W. Foerster, Halle 1934

    Perceval, ed. K. Busby, Tübingen 1993

    Yvain, ed. W. Foerster, Halle 1926

Denis Piramus, *La vie saint Edmund*, ed. H. Kjellman, repr. Geneva 1974

Eilhart von Oberge, *Tristrant*, ed. F. Lichtenstein, Strassburg 1887

Bibliography

Gaimar, *L'Estoire des Engleis*, ed. A. Bell, Oxford 1960

Gautier d'Arras, *Ille et Galeron*, ed. Y. Lefèvre, Paris 1988

Gautier de Coinci, *Miracles de Nostre Dame*, ed. V. F. Koenig, Geneva 1966

Gawain and the Green Knight, ed. J. R. R. Tolkien and E. V. Gordon (second edition by N. Davis), Oxford 1968

Gottfried von Strassburg, *Tristan*, ed. P. Ganz, Wiesbaden 1978

Hartmann von Aue, *Erec*, ed. A. Leitzmann, Tübingen 1963

    Iwein, ed. G. F. Benecke, K. Lachmann and L. Wolff, Berlin 1968

Heinrich von dem Türlin, *Diu Crône*, ed. G. H. F. Scholl, Amsterdam 1966

Heinrich von Veldeke, *Eneasroman*, ed. D. Kartschoke, Stuttgart 1986. Also ed. K. Fromm, Frankfurt 1992

Herzog Ernst, ed. K. Bartsch, Vienna 1869

Hunbaut, ed. M. Winters, Leiden 1984

Jean Bodel, *Chanson des Saisnes*, ed. F. Menzel and E. Stengel, Marburg 1906

Johann von Würzburg, *Wilhelm von Österreich*, ed. E. Regel, Berlin 1906

Jordan Fantosme, *Chronicle*, ed. R. C. Johnston, Oxford 1981

Kaiserchronik, ed. E. Schröder, MGH Deutsche Chroniken I, part I, Berlin 1964

König Rother, ed. J. de Vries, Heidelberg 1922

Konrad von Fussesbrunnen, *Kindheit Jesu*, ed. H. Fromm and K. Grubmüller, Berlin 1973

Lai de l'aubépine, ed. A. Micha, *Lais féeriques des XIIe et XIIIe siècles*, Paris 1992, pp. 226ff.

Lamprecht, Pfaffe, *Alexanderlied*, ed. K. Kinzel, Halle 1884

Marie de France, *Lais*, ed. J. Rychner, Paris 1966 (*Lanval*: pp. 72ff.)

Otfrid von Weissenburg, *Evangelienbuch*, ed. O. Erdmann, Halle 1882

Reinbot von Durne, *Der heilige Georg*, ed. C. von Kraus, Heidelberg 1907

Rolandslied, ed. D. Kartschoke, Stuttgart 1993

Roman d'Enéas, ed. J.-J. Salverda de Grave, Paris 1964

Roman de Thèbes, ed. G. Raynaud de Lage, Paris 1966, 1968

Rudolf von Ems, *Alexander*, ed. V. Junk, Leipzig 1928, 1929

Seifried Helbling, ed. J. Seemüller, Halle 1886

Der Stricker, *Daniel von dem blühenden Tal*, ed. M. Resler, Tübingen 1983

Thomas, *Tristan*, ed. B. H. Wind, Geneva 1960

Thomasin von Zerclaere, *Der welsche Gast*, ed. H. Rückert, Quedlinburg 1852. Also ed. W. von Kries, Göppingen 1984–5

Väterbuch, ed. K. Reissenberger, Berlin 1914

Veldeke, *see* Heinrich von Veldeke

Wace, *Roman de Brut*, ed. J. Weiss, Exeter 1999. Reference is also made to the (partial) edition of I . D. O. Arnold and M. M. Pelan, *La partie arthurienne du Roman de Brut*, Paris 1962

    Roman de Rou, ed. A. J. Holden, Paris 1970–3

Wolfram von Eschenbach, *Parzival*, ed. K. Lachmann, Berlin 1926. Reference is also made to the editions by K. Bartsch and M. Marti, Leipzig 1929–35, and by E. Nellmann, Frankfurt 1994

Bibliography

SECONDARY LITERATURE

Endnote references in the text of this book give a key word (normally the first noun in the title) which enables the entry in the bibliography to be recognised.

Adams, A., 'The shape of Arthurian verse romance (to 1300)', in: N. J. Lacy, D. Kelly and K. Busby (ed.), *The legacy of Chrétien de Troyes*, Amsterdam 1987, I 141ff.

Adler, A., '*Militia et amor* in the *Roman de Troie*', *RF* 72 (1960), 14ff.

Arndt, P. H., *Der Erzähler bei Hartmann von Aue. Formen und Funktionen seines Hervortretens und seine Äusserungen*, Göppingen 1980

Aubin, M., 'Reversing romance? The *Acts of Thecla* and the ancient novel', in: R. F. Hock, J. Bradley Chance and J. Perkins (ed.), *Ancient fiction and early Christian narrative*, Atlanta, Ga. 1998, pp. 257ff.

Baehr, R., 'Chrétien de Troyes und der Tristan', *Sprachkunst* 2 (1971), 43 ff.

Barron, W. R. J., Le Saux, F. and Johnson, L. 'Dynastic chronicles', in: W. R. J. Barron (ed.), *The Arthur of the English. The Arthurian legend in medieval English life and literature*, Cardiff 1999, pp. 11 ff.

Bastert, B., Review of K. Opitz, *Geschichte im höfischen Roman*, *ZfdA* 128 (1999), 361ff.

Baswell, C., *Virgil in medieval England. Figuring the Aeneid from the twelfth century to Chaucer*, Cambridge 1995

'Marvels of translation and crises of transition in the romances of Antiquity', in: R. L. Krueger (ed.), *The Cambridge companion to medieval romance*, Cambridge 2000, pp. 29ff.

Baumgartner, E., 'Vers, prose et fiction narrative (1150–1240)', in: FS for E. Kennedy, Cambridge 1994, pp. 11ff.

Bäuml, F. H., 'Varieties and consequences of medieval literacy and illiteracy', *Speculum* 55 (1980), 237ff.

Bauschke, R., 'Auflösung des Artusromans und Defiktionalisierung im "Bel Inconnu". Renauts de Beaujeu Auseinandersetzung mit Chrétien de Troyes', in: V. Mertens and F. Wolfzettel (ed.), *Fiktionalität im Artusroman*, Tübingen 1993, pp. 84ff.

Bédier, J., *Le roman de Tristan par Thomas. Poème du XIIe siécle*, Paris 1902

Bertau, K., *Deutsche Literatur im europäischen Mittelalter. Band I: 800–1197*, Munich 1972

Besamusca, B., 'The medieval Dutch Arthurian material', in: W. H. Jackson and S. A. Ranawake (ed.), *The Arthur of the Germans. The Arthurian legend in medieval German and Dutch literature*, Cardiff 2000, pp. 187ff.

Besch, W., 'Vers oder Prosa? Zur Kritik am Reimvers im Spätmittelalter', *PBB* 94 (1972), Sonderheft, pp. 745 ff.

Bezzola, R. R., *Les origines et la formation de la littérature courtoise en Occident (500–1200)*, 3 vols., Paris 1958ff.

Blacker, J., *The faces of time. Portrayal of the past in Old French and Latin historical narrative in the Anglo-Norman regnum*, Austin 1994

Blask, D. J., *Geschehen und Geschick im altfranzösischen Eneas-Roman*, Tübingen 1984

Boehm, L., 'Der wissenschaftliche Ort der historia im frühen Mittelalter', in: FS for J. Spörl, Munich 1965, pp. 663ff.

Bond, G. A., *The loving subject. Desire, eloquence, and power in Romanesque France*, Philadelphia 1995

Bowie, E. L., 'Lies, fiction and slander in early Greek poetry', in: C. Gill and T. P. Wiseman (ed.), *Lies and fiction in the ancient world*, Exeter 1993, pp. 1ff.

Brackert, H., 'der lac an riterschefte tôt. Parzival und das Leid der Frauen', in: FS for G. Schweikle, Stuttgart 1989, pp. 143ff.

Brand, W., *Chrétien de Troyes. Zur Dichtungstechnik seiner Romane*, Munich 1972

Brink, C. A., *Horace on poetry. The 'Ars poetica'*, Cambridge 1971

Bromwich, R., 'The first transmission in England and France', in: R. Bromwich, A. O. H. Jarman and B. F. Roberts (ed.), *The Arthur of the Welsh. The Arthurian legend in medieval Welsh literature*, Cardiff 1991, pp. 273ff.

Brooke, C. N. L., *The twelfth-century Renaissance*, London 1976
    'Geoffrey of Monmouth as a historian', in: *id.*, *The Church and the Welsh border in the central Middle Ages*, Woodbridge 1986, pp. 95ff.

Brownlee, M. S., 'Romance at the crossroads: medieval Spanish paradigms and Cervantine revisions', in: R. L. Krueger (ed.), *The Cambridge companion to medieval romance*, Cambridge 2000, pp. 253ff.

Bruck, J., 'Zum Begriff literarischer Fiktion', *ZGL* 6 (1978), 283ff.

Brunner, H., 'Artus der wise höfsche man. Zur immanenten Historizität der Ritterwelt im "Parzival" Wolframs von Eschenbach', in: D. Peschel (ed.), *Germanistik in Erlangen. Hundert Jahre nach der Gründung des Deutschen Seminars*, Erlangen 1983, pp. 61ff.
    'Wolfram von Eschenbach: "Parzival" – zum Verhältnis von Fiktion und außerliterarischer Realitätserfahrung', in: A. Weber (ed.), *Handbuch der Literatur in Bayern*, Regensburg 1987, pp. 89ff.
    'Von Munsalvaesche wart gesant/den der swane brahte. Überlegungen zur Gestaltung des Schlusses von Wolframs *Parzival*', *GRM* 72 (1991), 369ff.

Bumke, J., *Mäzene im Mittelalter. Die Gönner und Auftraggeber der höfischen Literatur in Deutschland 1150–1300*, Munich 1979
    Geschichte der deutschen Literatur im hohen Mittelalter, Munich 1990
    'Parzival und Feirefiz – Priester Johannes – Loherangrin. Der offene Schluß des *Parzival* von Wolfram von Eschenbach', *DVjs* 65 (1991), 236ff.

Burrichter, B., *Wahrheit und Fiktion. Der Status der Fiktionalität in der Artusliteratur des 12. Jahrhunderts*, Munich 1996
    '"Ici fenist li premier vers" (*Erec et Enide*) – noch einmal zur Zweiteilung des Chrétienschen Artusromans', in: F. Wolfzettel (ed.), *Erzählstrukturen der Artusliteratur. Forschungsgeschichte und neue Ansätze*, Tübingen 1999, pp. 87ff.

Burrow, J. A., *Ricardian poetry*, London 1971
    Medieval writers and their work. Middle English literature and its background 1100–1500, Oxford 1982

Busby, K., *Chrétien de Troyes. Perceval (Le Conte du Graal)*, London 1993

Butzer, G., 'Das Gedächtnis des epischen Textes. Mündliches und schriftliches Erzählen im höfischen Roman des Mittelalters', *Euphorion* 89 (1995), 151ff.

Cary, G., *The medieval Alexander*, Cambridge 1956

Bibliography

Chambers, E. K., *Arthur of Britain*, Cambridge 1964

Charles-Edwards, T., 'The Arthur of history', in: R. Bromwich, A. O. H. Jarman and B. F. Roberts (ed.), *The Arthur of the Welsh. The Arthurian legend in medieval Welsh literature*, Cardiff 1991, pp. 15ff.

Chenu, M.-D., *La théologie au douzième siècle*, Paris 1957

Chinca, M. G., *History, fiction, verisimilitude. Studies in the poetics of Gottfried's 'Tristan'*, London, 1993

Christ, W., *Rhetorik und Roman. Untersuchungen zu Gottfrieds von Straßburg 'Tristan und Isold'*, Meisenheim 1977

Chydenius, J., *The typological problem in Dante. A study in the history of medieval ideas*, Societas Scientiarum Fennica. Commentationes Humanarum Litterarum xxv, 1, Helsinki 1958

Clanchy, M. T., *From memory to written record. England 1066–1307*, London 1979

Coleman, J., *Public reading and the reading public in late medieval England and France*, Cambridge 1996

Coleridge, S. T., *Biographia literaria*, ed. J. Shawcross, Oxford, second edition 1979

Cormeau, C., *'Wigalois' und 'Diu Crône'. Zwei Kapitel zur Gattungsgeschichte des nachklassischen Aventiureromans*, Munich 1977

'Artusroman und Märchen. Zur Beschreibung und Genese der Struktur des höfischen Romans', *Wolfram-Studien* 5 (1979), 63ff.

'Joie de la Curt. Bedeutungssetzung und ethische Erkenntnis', in: W. Haug (ed.), *Formen und Funktionen der Allegorie*, Stuttgart 1979, pp. 194ff.

Cormeau, C. and Störmer, W., *Hartmann von Aue. Epoche – Werk – Wirkung*, Munich 1985

Courcelle, P., *Lecteurs païens et lecteurs chrétiens de l'Enéïde. I: Les témoignages littéraires*, Paris 1984

Cramer, T., *'Solus creator est Deus*. Der Autor auf dem Weg zum Schöpfertum', *Daphnis* 15 (1986), 261ff.

Currie, G., *The nature of fiction*, Cambridge 1990

Curschmann, M., 'Hören – Lesen – Sehen. Buch und Schriftlichkeit im Selbstverständnis der volkssprachlichen literarischen Kultur Deutschlands um 1200', *PBB* 106 (1984), 218ff.

Daiches, D., *A study of literature*, Ithaca 1948

Damian-Grint, P., 'Truth, trust, and evidence in the Anglo-Norman *estoire*', *ANS* 18 (1995), 63ff.

'*Estoire* as word and genre: meaning and literary usage in the twelfth century', *MÆ* 66 (1997), 189ff.

The new historians of the twelfth-century renaissance. Authorising history in the vernacular revolution, Woodbridge 1999

Dietl, C. 'Du bist der aventeûre fruht. Fiktionalität im "Wilhelm von Österreich" Johanns von Würzburg', in: V. Mertens and F. Wolfzettel (ed.), *Fiktionalität im Artusroman*, Tübingen 1993, pp. 171ff.

Dittmann, W., 'Dune hâst niht wâr, Hartman! Zum Begriff der "wârheit" in Hartmanns "Iwein"', in: FS for U. Pretzel, Berlin 1963, pp. 150ff.

Bibliography

Dorn, E., *Der sündige Heilige in der Legende des Mittelalters*, Munich 1967

Draesner, U., *Wege durch erzählte Welten. Intertextuelle Verweise als Mittel der Bedeutungskonstitution in Wolframs 'Parzival'*, Frankfurt 1993

Dronke, P., *Medieval Latin and the rise of European love-lyric*, 2 vols., Oxford 1965–6
Poetic individuality in the Middle Ages. New departures in poetry 1000–1150, Oxford 1970

Drube, H., *Hartmann und Chrétien*, Münster 1931

Duggan, J. J., 'Medieval epic as popular historiography: appropriation of historical knowledge in the vernacular epic', in: A. Biermann *et al.* (ed.), *La littérature historiographique des origines à 1500 (GRLMA* 11, 1), Heidelberg 1986, pp. 285 ff.

Düwel, K., *Werkbezeichnungen der mittelhochdeutschen Erzählliteratur (1050–1200)*, Göttingen 1983
'Lesestoff für junge Adlige. Lektüreempfehlungen in einer Tugendlehre des 13. Jahrhunderts', *Fabula* 32 (1991), 67 ff.

Ebenbauer, A., 'Historiographie zwischen der Spätantike und dem Beginn volkssprachlicher Geschichtsschreibung im Mittelalter', in: A. Biermann *et al.* (ed.), *La littérature historiographique des origines à 1500 (GRLMA* 11, 1), Heidelberg 1986, pp. 57 ff.

Echard, S., *Arthurian narrative in the Latin tradition*, Cambridge 1998

Ehlert, T., *Deutschsprachige Alexanderdichtung des Mittelalters. Zum Verhältnis von Literatur und Geschichte*, Frankfurt 1989
'Alexander und die Frauen in spätantiken und mittelalterlichen Alexander-Erzählungen', in: W. Erzgräber (ed.), *Kontinuität und Transformation der Antike im Mittelalter*, Sigmaringen 1989, pp. 81 ff.

Ehrismann, G., 'Märchen im höfischen Epos', *PBB* 30 (1905), 14 ff.

Eley, P., 'How long is a Trojan War? Aspects of time in the *Roman de Troie* and its sources', in: FS for E. Kennedy, Cambridge 1994, pp. 139 ff.
'History and romance in the *Chronique des ducs de Normandie*', *MÆ* 68 (1999), 81 ff.

Emmel, H., *Formprobleme des Artusromans und der Graldichtung. Die Bedeutung des Artuskreises für das Gefüge des Romans im 12. und 13. Jahrhundert in Frankreich, Deutschland und den Niederlanden*, Bern 1951

Ernst, U., 'Kyot und Flegetanis in Wolframs "Parzival". Fiktionaler Fundbericht und jüdisch-arabischer Kulturhintergrund', *WW* 35 (1985), 176 ff.
'Formen analytischen Erzählens im *Parzival* Wolframs von Eschenbach. Marginalien zu einem narrativen System des Hohen Mittelalters', in: F. Wolfzettel (ed.), *Erzählstrukturen der Artusliteratur. Forschungsgeschichte und neue Ansätze*, Tübingen 1999, pp. 165 ff.
'Die natürliche und die künstliche Ordnung des Erzählens. Grundzüge einer historischen Narratologie', in: FS for D. Weber, Cologne 2000, pp. 179 ff.

Ertzdorff, X. von, 'Die Wahrheit des höfischen Romans des Mittelalters', *ZfdPh* 86 (1967), 375 ff.

Evans, R. J., *In defence of history*, London 1997

Falk, W., 'Wolframs Kyot und die Bedeutung der "Quelle" im Mittelalter', *LwJb* 9 (1968), 1 ff.

Bibliography

Faral, E., *Les arts poétiques du XIIe et du XIIIe siècle*, Paris 1924

　　Les jongleurs en France au moyen âge, Paris, second edition 1971

Feeney, D. C., *The gods in epic. Poets and critics of the classical tradition*, Oxford 1991

　　'Epilogue: towards an account of the ancient world's concepts of fictive belief', in: C. Gill and T. P. Wiseman (ed.), *Lies and fiction in the ancient world*, Exeter 1993, pp. 230ff.

Fichte, J. O., '"Fakt" und Fiktion in der Artusgeschichte des 12. Jahrhunderts', in: V. Mertens and F. Wolfzettel (ed.), *Fiktionalität im Artusroman*, Tübingen 1993, pp. 45ff.

Finnegan, R., *Oral poetry. Its nature, significance and social context*, Cambridge 1977

Fischer, W., *Die Alexanderliedkonzeption des Pfaffen Lambrecht*, Munich 1964

Fleckenstein, J., 'Miles und clericus am Königs- und Fürstenhof. Bemerkungen zu den Voraussetzungen zur Entwicklung und zur Trägerschaft der höfisch-ritterlichen Kultur', in: *id.* (ed.), *Curialitas. Studien zu Grundfragen der höfisch-ritterlichen Kultur*, Göttingen 1990, pp. 302ff.

Fleischman, S., 'On the representation of history and fiction in the Middle Ages', *History and Theory* 22 (1983), 278ff.

Flint, V. I. J., 'The *Historia Regum Britanniae* of Geoffrey of Monmouth: parody and its purpose. A suggestion', *Speculum* 54 (1979), 447ff.

Fontaine, J., *Sulpice Sévère, Vie de Saint Martin, Tome I*, Paris 1967

Fourrier, A., *Le courant réaliste dans le roman courtois en France au moyen-âge. I: Les débuts (XIIe siècle)*, Paris 1960

Frank, B., 'Varianten, Fortsetzungen, Neubearbeitungen. Zur Textgeschichte des *Conte del Graal* von Chrétien de Troyes', in: H. L. C. Tristram (ed.), *Text und Zeittiefe*, Tübingen 1993, pp. 117ff.

Frappier, J., *Chrétien de Troyes*, Paris 1957

　　'Le *Roman d'Alexandre* et ses diverses versions au XIIe siècle', in: J. Frappier and R. R. Grimm (ed.), *Le roman jusqu'à la fin du XIIIe siècle* (*GRLMA* 4), Heidelberg 1978, pp. 149ff.

Friis-Jensen, K., 'The Ars Poetica in twelfth-century France. The Horace of Matthew of Vendôme, Geoffrey of Vinsauf, and John of Garland', *CIMAGL* 60 (1990), 319ff.

Fromm, H., 'Die Unterwelt des Eneas. Topographie und Seelenvorstellung', in: *id., Arbeiten zur deutschen Literatur des Mittelalters*, Tübingen 1989, pp. 101ff.

　　'Der Eneasroman Heinrichs von Veldeke', in: *id., Arbeiten zur deutschen Literatur des Mittelalters*, Tübingen 1989, pp. 80ff.

　　'Eneas der Verräter', in: FS for W. Haug and B. Wachinger, 2 vols., Tübingen 1992, II 139ff.

　　'Herbort von Fritslar', *PBB* 115 (1993), 244ff.

　　'Die mittelalterlichen Eneasromane und die Poetik des *ordo narrandi*', in: H. Haferland and M. Mecklenburg (ed.), *Erzählungen in Erzählungen. Probleme der Narration in Mittelalter und früher Neuzeit*, Munich 1996, pp. 27ff.

Fuchs, W., *Der Tristanroman und die höfische Liebesnovelle*, diss. Zürich 1967

Bibliography

Fuhrmann, M., 'Wunder und Wirklichkeit. Zur Siebenschläferlegende und anderen Texten aus christlicher Tradition', in: D. Henrich and W. Iser (ed.), *Funktionen des Fiktiven*, Munich 1983, pp. 209ff.

Gallais, P. 'De la naissance du roman. A propos d'un article récent', *CCM* 14 (1971), 69ff.

Gaunt, S., 'Romance and other genres', in: R. L. Krueger (ed.), *The Cambridge companion to medieval romance*, Cambridge 2000, pp. 45ff.

Gerould, G. H., 'King Arthur and politics', *Speculum* 2 (1927), 33ff.

Gerritsen, W. P., 'Jacob van Maerlant and Geoffrey of Monmouth', in: K. Varty (ed.), *An Arthurian tapestry. Essays in memory of Lewis Thorpe*, Glasgow 1981, pp. 368ff.
'Een avond in Ardres. Over middeleeuwse vertaalkunst', in: F. van Oostrom *et al.* (ed.), *Grote lijnen. Syntheses over Middelnederlandse letterkunde*, Amsterdam 1995, pp. 157ff.

Ghisalberti, F., 'Mediaeval biographies of Ovid', *JWCI* 9 (1946), 45ff.

Gill, C., 'Plato on falsehood – not fiction', in: C. Gill and T. P. Wiseman (ed.), *Lies and fiction in the ancient world*, Exeter 1993, pp. 38ff.

Goetsch, P., 'Fingierte Mündlichkeit in der Erzählkunst entwickelter Schriftkulturen', *Poetica* 17 (1983), 202ff.

Gombrich, E. H., *Art and illusion. A study in the psychology of pictorial representation*, London 1962

Gompf, L., 'Figmenta poetarum', in: FS for K. Langosch, Darmstadt 1973, pp. 53ff.

Green, D. H., *The Millstätter Exodus. A crusading epic*, Cambridge 1966
Der Weg zum Abenteuer im höfischen Roman des deutschen Mittelalters, Göttingen 1974
'The *Alexanderlied* and the emergence of the romance', *GLL* 28 (1975), 246ff.
'The pathway to adventure', *Viator* 8 (1977), 145ff.
'Homicide and *Parzival*', in: D. H. Green and L. P. Johnson, *Approaches to Wolfram von Eschenbach*, Bern 1978, pp. 11ff.
'The concept *âventiure* in *Parzival*', in: D. H. Green and L. P. Johnson, *Approaches to Wolfram von Eschenbach*, Bern 1978, pp. 82ff.
'Oral poetry and written composition. (An aspect of the feud between Gottfried and Wolfram)', in: D. H. Green and L. P. Johnson, *Approaches to Wolfram von Eschenbach*, Bern 1978, pp. 163ff.
Irony in the medieval romance, Cambridge 1979
'The art of namedropping in Wolfram's "Parzival"', *Wolfram-Studien* 6 (1980), 84ff.
'Parzival's departure – folktale and romance', *FMS* 14 (1980), 352ff.
The art of recognition in Wolfram's Parzival, Cambridge 1982
'Advice and narrative action. Parzival, Herzeloyde and Gurnemanz', in: FS for L. Forster, Baden-Baden 1982, pp. 33ff.
'The reception of Hartmann's works: listening, reading or both?', *MLR* 81 (1986), 357ff.
'On the primary reception of the works of Rudolf von Ems', *ZfdA* 115 (1986), 151ff.
'Zur primären Rezeption von Wolframs "Parzival"', in: FS for W. Schröder, Tübingen 1989, pp. 271ff.

Bibliography

Medieval listening and reading. The primary reception of German literature 800–1300, Cambridge 1994

'*Vrume rîtr und guote vrouwen/und wîse phaffen*. Court literature and its audience', in: FS for R. Wisbey, Tübingen 1994, pp. 7ff.

'Zum Erkennen und Verkennen von Ironie- und Fiktionssignalen in der höfischen Literatur', in: D. Peil, M. Schilling and P. Strohschneider (ed.), *Erkennen und Erinnern in Kunst und Literatur*, Tübingen 1998, pp. 35ff.

Review of K. Opitz, *Geschichte im höfischen Roman, MLR* 95 (2000), 549ff.

'Three aspects of the Old Saxon biblical epic, the *Heliand*', to appear

Gregory, T., 'The Platonic inheritance', in: P. Dronke (ed.), *A history of twelfth-century western philosophy*, Cambridge 1988, pp. 54ff.

Greiner, T., 'Das Erzählen, das Abenteuer und "ihre sehr schöne Verbindung". Zur Begründung fiktionalen Schreibens in Chrétiens de Troyes *Erec*-Prolog', *Poetica* 24 (1992), 300ff.

Groos, A. B., 'Wolfram von Eschenbach's "bow metaphor" and the narrative technique of *Parzival*', *MLN* 87 (1972), 391ff.

Grubmüller, K., 'Überlegungen zum Wahrheitsanspruch des Physiologus im Mittelalter', *FMS* 12 (1978), 160ff.

Gruenter, R., 'Bauformen der Waldleben-Episode in Gottfrieds Tristan und Isold', in: FS for G. Müller, Bonn 1957, pp. 21ff.

Grundmann, H., 'Litteratus – illitteratus. Der Wandel einer Bildungsnorm vom Altertum zum Mittelalter', *AfK* 40 (1958), 1ff.

Grünkorn, G., 'Zum Verständnis von fiktionaler Rede im Hochmittelalter. Das Verhältnis von lateinischer Kommentartradition und höfischem Roman', in: V. Mertens and F. Wolfzettel (ed.), *Fiktionalität im Artusroman*, Tübingen 1993, pp. 29ff.

Die Fiktionalität des höfischen Romans um 1200, Berlin 1994

Guerin, M. V., *The fall of kings and princes. Structure and destruction in Arthurian tragedy*, Stanford 1995

Guiette, R., 'Li conte de Bretagne sont si vain et plaisant', *Romania* 88 (1967), 1ff.

Hagenlocher, A., 'Quellenberufungen als Mittel der Legitimation in deutschen Chroniken des 13. Jahrhunderts', *NdJb* 102 (1979), 15ff.

Hahn, I., *Raum und Landschaft in Gottfrieds Tristan. Ein Beitrag zur Werkdeutung*, Munich 1963

Review of P. W. Tax, *Wort, Sinnbild, Zahl im Tristanroman. Studien zum Denken und Werten Gottfrieds von Straßburg, AfdA* 75 (1964), 171ff.

Haidu, P., *Aesthetic distance in Chrétien de Troyes: Irony and comedy in Cligès and Perceval*, Geneva 1968

'Repetition: modern reflections on medieval aesthetics', *MLN* 92 (1977), 875ff.

Hanning, R. W., *The vision of history in early Britain from Gildas to Geoffrey of Monmouth*, New York 1966

The individual in twelfth-century romance, New Haven 1977

Hauck, K., 'Heldendichtung und Heldensage als Geschichtsbewußtsein', in: FS for O. Brunner, Göttingen 1963, pp. 118ff.

Haug, W., 'Epos (Epik, Episierung)', in: K. Ranke (ed.), *Enzyklopädie des Märchens. Handwörterbuch zur historischen und vergleichenden Erzählforschung*, vol. IV, Berlin 1982, cols. 73 ff.

Literaturtheorie im deutschen Mittelalter. Von den Anfängen bis zum Ende des 13. Jahrhunderts. Eine Einführung, Darmstadt 1985. (Second edition, Darmstadt 1992)

'Der "Ruodlieb"', in: *id., Strukturen als Schlüssel zur Welt. Kleine Schriften zur Erzählliteratur des Mittelalters*, Tübingen 1989, pp. 199 ff.

'Der *Tristan* – eine interarthurische Lektüre', in: F. Wolfzettel (ed.), *Artusroman und Intertextualität*, Giessen 1990, pp. 57 ff.

'Mündlichkeit, Schriftlichkeit und Fiktionalität', in: J. Heinzle (ed.), *Modernes Mittelalter. Neue Bilder einer populären Epoche*, Frankfurt 1994, pp. 376 ff.

'Weisheit, Reichtum und Glück. Über mittelalterliche und neuzeitliche Ästhetik', in: *id., Brechungen auf dem Weg zur Individualität. Kleine Schriften zur Literatur des Mittelalters*, Tübingen 1995, pp. 17 ff.

'Literatur und Leben im Mittelalter. Eine neue Theorie zur Entstehung und Entwicklung des höfischen Romans', in: *id., Brechungen auf dem Weg zur Individualität. Kleine Schriften zur Literatur des Mittelalters*, Tübingen 1995, pp. 31 ff.

'*Parzival* ohne Illusionen', in: *id., Brechungen auf dem Weg zur Individualität. Kleine Schriften zur Literatur des Mittelalters*, Tübingen 1995, pp. 125 ff.

'Die Entdeckung der personalen Liebe und der Beginn der fiktionalen Literatur', in: *id., Brechungen auf dem Weg zur Individualität. Kleine Schriften zur Literatur des Mittelalters*, Tübingen 1995, pp. 233 ff.

'Wandlungen des Fiktionalitätsbewußtseins vom hohen zum späten Mittelalter', in: *id., Brechungen auf dem Weg zur Individualität. Kleine Schriften zur Literatur des Mittelalters,* Tübingen 1995, pp. 251 ff.

'Für eine Ästhetik des Widerspruchs. Neue Überlegungen zur Poetologie des höfischen Romans', in: N. F. Palmer and H. -J. Schiewer (ed.), *Mittelalterliche Literatur und Kunst im Spannungsfeld von Hof und Kloster*, Tübingen 1999, pp. 211 ff.

'Das Spiel mit der arthurischen Struktur in der Komödie von *Yvain/Iwein*', in: F. Wolfzettel (ed.), *Erzählstrukturen der Artusliteratur, Forschungsgeschichte und neue Ansätze*, Tübingen 1999, pp. 99 ff.

Haug, W. and B. K. Vollmann, *Frühe deutsche Literatur und lateinische Literatur in Deutschland 800–1150*, Frankfurt 1991

Haustein, J., '"Herzog Ernst" zwischen Synchronie und Diachronie', *ZfdPh* (Sonderheft) 116 (1997), 115 ff.

Havelock, E. A., *Preface to Plato*, Cambridge, Mass., 1982.

The literate revolution in Greece and its consequences, Princeton 1982

Heinzle, J., 'Zur Stellung des Prosa-Lancelot in der deutschen Literatur des 13. Jahrhunderts', in: F. Wolfzettel (ed.), *Artusrittertum im späten Mittelalter, Ethos und Ideologie*, Giessen 1984, pp. 104 ff.

'Die Entdeckung der Fiktionalität. Zu Walter Haugs "Literaturtheorie im deutschen Mittelalter"', *PBB* 112 (1990), 55 ff.

Wandlungen und Neuansätze im 13. Jahrhundert (1220/30–1280/90), Tübingen 1994 (vol. II, part 2 of Heinzle [ed.], *Geschichte der deutschen Literatur von den Anfängen bis zum Beginn der Neuzeit*)

Bibliography

Heitmann, K., 'Das Verhältnis von Dichtung und Geschichtsschreibung in älterer Theorie', in: B. Haupt (ed.), *Zum mittelalterlichen Literaturbegriff*, Darmstadt 1985, pp. 201 ff.

Henkel, N., *Studien zum Physiologus im Mittelalter*, Tübingen 1976
'Kurzfassungen höfischer Erzähldichtung im 13./14. Jahrhundert. Überlegungen zum Verhältnis von Textgeschichte und literarischer Interessenbildung', in: J. Heinzle (ed.), *Literarische Interessenbildung im Mittelalter*, Stuttgart 1993, pp. 39 ff.
'Religiöses Erzählen um 1200 im Kontext höfischer Literatur. Priester Wernher, Konrad von Fußesbrunnen, Konrad von Heimesfurt', in: T. R. Jackson, N. F. Palmer and A. Suerbaum (ed.), *Die Vermittlung geistlicher Inhalte im deutschen Mittelalter*, Tübingen 1996, pp. 1 ff.

Hindman, S., *Sealed in parchment. Rereadings of knighthood in the illuminated manuscripts of Chrétien de Troyes*, Chicago 1994

Hirschberg, D., *Untersuchungen zur Erzählstruktur von Wolframs 'Parzival'. Die Funktion von erzählter Szene und Station für den doppelten Kursus*, Göppingen 1976

Howlett, D. R., 'The literary context of Geoffrey of Monmouth: an essay on the fabrication of sources', *Arthuriana* 5 (1995), 25 ff.

Huber, C., *Gottfried von Straßburg 'Tristan und Isolde'. Eine Einführung*, Munich 1986
'Höfischer Roman als Integumentum? Das Votum Thomasins von Zerklaere', *ZfdA* 115 (1986), 79 ff.
Review of W. Haug, *Literaturtheorie im deutschen Mittelalter*, *AfdA* 99 (1988), 60 ff.
Die Aufnahme und Verarbeitung des Alanus ab Insulis in mittelhochdeutschen Dichtungen. Untersuchungen zu Thomasin von Zerklaere, Gottfried von Straßburg, Frauenlob, Heinrich von Neustadt, Heinrich von St. Gallen, Heinrich von Mügeln und Johannes von Tepl, Munich 1988
'Herrscherlob und literarische Autoreferenz', in: J. Heinzle (ed.), *Literarische Interessenbildung im Mittelalter*, Stuttgart 1993, pp. 452 ff.
Gottfried von Straßburg: Tristan, Berlin 2000

Huber, H. M., *Licht und Schönheit in Wolframs 'Parzival'*, Zürich 1981

Hunt, T., 'Prodesse et delectare. Metaphors of pleasure and instruction in Old French', *NM* 80 (1979), 17 ff.

Huot, S., *From song to book. The poetics of writing in Old French lyric and lyrical narrative poetry*, Ithaca 1987

Huschenbett, D., 'Zur deutschen Literaturtradition in Herborts von Fritzlar "Liet von Troy"', in: H. Brunner (ed.), *Die deutsche Trojaliteratur des Mittelalters und der frühen Neuzeit*, Wiesbaden 1990, pp. 303 ff.

Ingledew, F., 'The Book of Troy and the genealogical construction of history: the case of Geoffrey of Monmouth's *Historia regum Britanniae*', *Speculum* 69 (1994), 665 ff.

Irvine, M., *The making of textual culture. 'Grammatica' and literary theory, 350–1100*, Cambridge 1994

Iser, W., 'Akte des Fingierens oder Was ist das Fiktive im fiktionalen Text?', in: D. Henrich and W. Iser (ed.), *Funktionen des Fiktiven*, Munich 1983, pp. 121 ff.

Jackson, K. H., 'The Arthur of history', in: R. S. Loomis (ed.), *Arthurian literature in the Middle Ages. A collaborative history*, Oxford 1959, pp. 1 ff.

Jackson, W. H., 'Some observations on the status of the narrator in Hartmann von Aue's *Erec* and *Iwein*', in: D. D. R. Owen (ed.), *Arthurian romance, Seven essays*, Edinburgh 1970, pp. 65 ff.

Chivalry in twelfth-century Germany. The works of Hartmann von Aue, Cambridge 1994

'The Arthurian material and German society in the Middle Ages', in: W. H. Jackson and S. Ranawake (ed.), *The Arthur of the Germans. The Arthurian legend in medieval German and Dutch literature*, Cardiff 2000, pp. 280ff.

Jacquart, D., 'Aristotelian thought in Salerno', in: P. Dronke (ed.), *A history of twelfth-century western philosophy*, Cambridge 1988, pp. 407ff.

Jaeger, C. S., *The origins of courtliness. Civilizing trends and the formation of courtly ideals 939–1210*, Philadelphia 1985

Ennobling love. In search of a lost sensibility, Philadelphia 1999

Jaffe, S., 'Gottfried von Strassburg and the rhetoric of history', in: J. J. Murphy (ed.), *Medieval eloquence. Studies in the theory and practice of medieval rhetoric*, Berkeley 1978, pp. 288ff.

Jauss, H. R., *Alterität und Modernität der mittelalterlichen Literatur. Gesammelte Aufsätze 1956–1976*, Munich 1977

'Zur historischen Genese der Scheidung von Fiktion und Realität', in: D. Henrich and W. Iser (ed.), *Funktionen des Fiktiven*, Munich 1983, pp. 423 ff.

Johanek, P., 'König Arthur und die Plantagenets. Über den Zusammenhang von Historiographie und höfischer Epik in mittelalterlicher Propaganda', *FMS* 21 (1987), 346ff.

Jones, R., *The theme of love in the romans d'antiquité*, London 1972

Karnein, A., 'Renaissance und höfische Kultur des 12. Jahrhunderts in Frankreich', in: U. Liebertz-Grün (ed.), *Aus der Mündlichkeit in die Schriftlichkeit: höfische und andere Literatur 750–1320*, Reinbek 1988, pp. 104ff.

Kartschoke, D., Review of M. G. Scholz, *Hören und Lesen, IASL* 8 (1983), 253 ff.

Geschichte der deutschen Literatur im frühen Mittelalter, Munich 1990

Review of D. H. Green, *Medieval listening and reading, Arbitrium* 1997, pp. 160ff.

Kasten, I., *Frauendienst bei Trobadors und Minnesängern im 12. Jahrhundert. Zur Entwicklung und Adaption eines literarischen Konzepts*, Heidelberg 1986

'Herrschaft und Liebe. Zur Rolle und Darstellung des 'Helden' im *Roman d'Eneas* und in Veldekes *Eneasroman*', *DVjs* 62 (1988), 227ff.

Keck, A., *Die Liebeskonzeption der mittelalterlichen Tristanromane. Zur Erzähllogik der Werke Bérouls, Eilhards, Thomas' und Gottfrieds*, Munich 1998

Kellermann, K., '"Exemplum" und "historia". Zu poetologischen Traditionen in Hartmanns "Iwein"', *GRM* 73 (1992), 1 ff.

Kellermann, W., *Aufbaustil und Weltbild Chrestiens von Troyes im Percevalroman*, Halle 1936

Kelly, F. D., *Sens and conjointure in the Chevalier de la Charrette*, The Hague 1966

'En uni dire (*Tristan* Douce 839) and the composition of Thomas's *Tristan*', *MPh* 67 (1969/70), 9ff.

'The source and meaning of *conjointure* in Chrétien's *Erec* 14', *Viator* 1 (1970), 179ff.

The art of medieval French romance, Madison 1992

Bibliography

Kermode, F., *The sense of an ending. Studies in the theory of fiction*, New York 1967

Kern, P., 'Der Roman und seine Rezeption als Gegenstand des Romans. Beobachtungen zum Eingangsteil von Hartmanns *Iwein*', *WW* 23 (1973), 246ff.

'Rezeption und Genese des Artusromans. Überlegungen zu Strickers "Daniel vom blühenden Tal"', *ZfdPh* 93 (1974), Sonderheft, pp. 18ff.

Die Artusromane des Pleier. Untersuchungen über den Zusammenhang von Dichtung und literarischer Situation, Berlin 1981

'Leugnen und Bewußtmachen der Fiktionalität im deutschen Artusroman', in: V. Mertens and F. Wolfzettel (ed.), *Fiktionalität im Artusroman*, Tübingen 1993, pp. 11ff.

Keuchen, R., *Typologische Strukturen im 'Tristan'. Ein Beitrag zur Erzähltechnik Gottfrieds von Straßburg*, diss. Cologne 1975

Killy, W., *Deutscher Kitsch. Ein Versuch mit Beispielen*, Göttingen 1961

Kistler, R., *Heinrich von Veldeke und Ovid*, Tübingen 1993

Klopsch, P., *Einführung in die Dichtungslehren des lateinischen Mittelalters*, Darmstadt 1980

Knape, J., *Historie in Mittelalter und früher Neuzeit. Begriffs- und gattungsgeschichtliche Untersuchungen im interdisziplinären Kontext*, Baden-Baden 1984

Knapp, F. P., *Ruodlieb. Mittellateinisch/Deutsch*, Stuttgart 1977

Das lateinische Tierepos, Darmstadt 1979

'*Chevalier errant' und 'fin' amor'. Das Ritterideal des 13. Jahrhunderts in Nordfrankreich und im deutschsprachigen Südosten*, Passau 1986

'De l'aventure profane à l'aventure spirituelle. Le double esprit du *Lancelot en prose*', *CCM* 32 (1989), 263ff.

'Von Gottes und der Menschen Wirklichkeit. Wolframs fromme Welterzählung *Parzival*', *DVjs* 70 (1996), 351ff.

Historie und Fiktion in der mittelalterlichen Gattungspoetik. Sieben Studien und ein Nachwort, Heidelberg 1997

Review of B. Burrichter, *Wahrheit und Fiktion*, *GRM* 48 (1998), 241ff.

'Gattungstheoretische Überlegungen zur sogenannten märchenhaften Dietrichepik', in: K. Zatloukal (ed.), *5. Pöchlarner Heldenliedgespräch. Aventiure – Märchenhafte Dietrichepik*, Vienna 2000, pp. 115ff.

'Subjektivität des Erzählers und Fiktionalität der Erzählung bei Wolfram von Eschenbach und anderen Autoren des 12. und 13. Jahrhunderts', to appear in *Wolfram-Studien* 17

Knight, S., *Arthurian literature and society*, London 1983

Köhler, E., 'Zur Selbstauffassung des höfischen Dichters', in: *id., Trobadorlyrik und höfischer Roman. Aufsätze zur französischen und provenzalischen Literatur des Mittelalters*, Berlin 1962, pp. 9ff.

Ideal und Wirklichkeit in der höfischen Epik. Studien zur Form der frühen Artus- und Graldichtung, Tübingen, second edition 1970

Kolb, H., *Munsalvaesche. Studien zum Kyotproblem*, Munich 1963

'*Der ware Elicon*. Zu Gottfrieds Tristan vv. 4862–4907', *DVjs* 41 (1967), 1ff.

'Die Schwanrittersage als Ursprungsmythos mittelalterlicher Fürstengeschlechter', in: T. Nyberg (ed.), *History and heroic tale. A symposium*, Odense 1985, pp. 23ff.

Koldeweij, A. M., *Der gude Sente Servas. De Servatiuslegende en de Servatiana: een onderzoek naar de beeldvorming rond een heilige in de middeleeuwen. De geschiedenis van de kerkschat van het Sint-Servaaskapittel te Maastricht*, Assen 1985

Konstan, D., 'The invention of fiction', in: R. F. Hock, J. Bradley Chance and J. Perkins (ed.), *Ancient fiction and early Christian narrative*, Atlanta, Ga. 1998, pp. 3 ff.

Krohn, R., *Gottfried von Straßburg, Tristan. Bd. 3: Kommentar, Nachwort und Register*, Stuttgart 1981

'Zwischen Finden und Erfinden. Mittelalterliche Autoren und ihr Stoff', in: F. P. Ingold and W. Wunderlich (ed.), *Fragen nach dem Autor. Positionen und Perspektiven*, Konstanz 1992, pp. 43 ff.

Krueger, R. L., *Women readers and the ideology of gender in Old French verse romance*, Cambridge 1993

Kuch, H., 'Die Herausbildung des antiken Romans als Literaturgattung. Theoretische Positionen, historische Voraussetzungen und literarische Prozesse', in: *id.* (ed.), *Der antike Roman. Untersuchungen zur literarischen Kommunikation und Gattungsgeschichte*, Berlin 1989, pp. 11 ff.

Kugler, H., 'Zur literarischen Geographie des fernen Ostens im "Parzival" und "Jüngeren Titurel"', in: FS for K. Stackmann, Göttingen 1990, pp. 107 ff.

Kuhn, H., '*Erec*', in: *id., Dichtung und Welt im Mittelalter*, Stuttgart 1959, pp. 133 ff.

Kullmann, D., 'Frühe Formen der Parallelhandlung in Epos und Roman. Zu den Voraussetzungen von Chrétiens *Conte du Graal*', in: F. Wolfzettel (ed.), *Erzählstrukturen der Artusliteratur. Forschungsgeschichte und neue Ansätze*, Tübingen 1999, pp. 23 ff.

Lacroix, B., *L'historien au moyen âge*, Montréal 1971

Lacy, N. J., *The craft of Chrétien de Troyes: an essay on narrative art*, Leiden 1980

'The typology of Arthurian romance', in: N. J. Lacy, D. Kelly and K. Busby (ed.), *The legacy of Chrétien de Troyes*, Amsterdam 1987, pp. 33 ff.

'The evolution and legacy of French prose romance', in: R. L. Krueger (ed.), *The Cambridge companion to medieval romance*, Cambridge 2000, pp. 167 ff.

Lamarque, P. and Olsen, S. H., *Truth, fiction, and literature. A philosophical perspective*, Oxford 1994

Latré, G., 'Yelping for Arthur: adventure and (meta)fiction in *Sir Gawain and the Green Knight*', in: W. van Hoecke, G. Tournoy and W. Verbeke (ed.), *Arturus Rex* II (Acta Conventus Lovaniensis 1987), Leuven 1991, pp. 186 ff.

Leckie, R. W., *The passage of dominion: Geoffrey of Monmouth and the periodization of insular history in the twelfth century*, Toronto 1982

Lengenfelder, H., *Das 'Liet von Troyge' Herborts von Fritzlar. Untersuchungen zur epischen Struktur und geschichts-moralischen Perspektive*, Frankfurt am Main 1975

Le Rider, P., *Le chevalier dans le Conte du Graal de Chrétien de Troyes*, Paris 1978

Leusden, A. van, 'St. Servaas, heilige tussen paus en keizer. Peilingen naar de context van Hendrik van Veldeke's *Sint Servaeslegende*', *NT* 79 (1986), 134 ff.

Lienert, E., *Geschichte und Erzählen. Studien zu Konrads von Würzburg 'Trojanerkrieg'*, Wiesbaden 1996

Lofmark, C., 'Wolfram's source references in "Parzival"', *MLR* 67 (1972), 820 ff.

Bibliography

'On medieval credulity', *Trivium Special Publications* 1, University of Wales Press 1974, pp. 5 ff.

'Zur Interpretation der Kyotstellen im "Parzival"', *Wolfram-Studien* 4 (1977), 33 ff.

Loomis, R. S., 'The oral diffusion of the Arthurian legend', in: *id.* (ed.), *Arthurian literature in the Middle Ages. A collaborative history*, Oxford 1959, pp. 52 ff.

Lord, A. B., *The singer of tales*, New York 1965

Lüthi, M., *Das europäische Volksmärchen. Form und Wesen*, Bern 1960

Märchen, Stuttgart 1962

Lutz, E. C., 'Herrscherapotheosen. Chrestiens Erec-Roman und Konrads Karl-Legende im Kontext von Herrschaftslegitimation und Heilssicherung', in: C. Huber, B. Wachinger and H.-J. Ziegeler (ed.), *Geistliches in weltlicher und Weltliches in geistlicher Literatur des Mittelalters*, Tübingen 2000, pp. 89 ff.

Maccagnolo, E., 'David of Dinant and the beginnings of Aristotelianism in Paris', in: P. Dronke (ed.), *A history of twelfth-century western philosophy*, Cambridge 1988, pp. 54 ff.

Mackert, C., *Die Alexandergeschichte in der Version des 'Pfaffen' Lambrecht. Die frühmittelhochdeutsche Bearbeitung der Alexanderdichtung des Alberich von Bisinzo und die Anfänge weltlicher Schriftepik in deutscher Sprache*, Munich 1999

Maddox, D., 'Pseudo-historical discourse in fiction: *Cligés*', in: FS for B. M. Craig, Columbia, SC 1982, pp. 9 ff.

The Arthurian romances of Chrétien de Troyes. Once and future fictions, Cambridge 1991

Manning, S., 'The Nun's Priest's morality and the medieval attitude toward fables', *JEGPh* 59 (1960), 403 ff.

Marichal, R., 'Naissance du roman', in: M. de Gandillac and E. Jeauneau (ed.), *Entretiens sur la renaissance du 12e siècle*, Paris 1968, pp. 449 ff.

Martin, G. D., 'A new look at fictional reference', *Philosophy* 57 (1982), 223 ff.

Mehtonen, P., *Old concepts and new poetics. Historia, Argumentum, and Fabula in the twelfth- and early thirteenth-century Latin poetics of fiction* (Societas Scientiarum Fennica, Commentationes Humanarum Litterarum 108), Helsinki 1996

Meneghetti, M. L., 'Ideologia cavalleresca e politica culturale nel *Roman de Brut*', SLF 3 (1974), 26 ff.

'L' "Estoire des Engleis" di Geffrei Gaimar fra cronaca genealogica e romanzo cortese', *MR* 2 (1975), 232 ff.

Mertens, V., 'Kaiser und Spielmann. Vortragsrollen in der höfischen Lyrik', in: G. Kaiser and J.-D. Müller (ed.), *Höfische Literatur, Hofgesellschaft, höfische Lebensformen um 1200*, Düsseldorf 1986, pp. 455 ff.

'"gewisse lêre": Zum Verhältnis von Fiktion und Didaxe im späten deutschen Artusroman', in: F. Wolfzettel (ed.), *Artusroman und Intertextualität*, Giessen 1990, pp. 85 ff.

'Herborts von Fritzlar *Liet von Troie* – ein Anti-Heldenlied?', in: D. Buschinger and W. Spiewok (ed.), *Heldensage – Heldenlied – Heldenepos*, Publications du Centre d'Etudes Médiévales, Université de Picardie 1992, pp. 151 ff.

Der deutsche Artusroman, Stuttgart 1998

Metzner, E. E., 'Wandalen im angelsächsischen Bereich? Gormundus rex Africanorum und die gens Hestingorum. Zur Geschichte und Geschichtlichkeit des Gormund-Isembard-Stoffes in England, Frankreich, Deutschland', *PBB(T)* 95 (1973), 219ff.

Meyer, M., *Die Verfügbarkeit der Fiktion. Interpretationen und poetologische Untersuchungen zum Artusroman und zur aventiurehaften Dietrichepik des 13. Jahrhunderts*, Heidelberg 1994

Michel, P., 'Übergangsformen zwischen Typologie und anderen Gestalten des Textbezugs', in: W. Harms and K. Speckenbach (ed.), *Bildhafte Rede in Mittelalter und früher Neuzeit. Probleme ihrer Legitimation und ihrer Funktion*, Tübingen 1992, pp. 43ff.

Minnis, A. J. and Scott, A. B., *Medieval literary theory and criticism c. 1100–1375. The commentary tradition*, Oxford 1998 (revised edition)

Mölk, U., *Französische Literarästhetik des 12. und 13. Jahrhunderts. Prologe – Exkurse – Epiloge,* Tübingen 1969

Mohr, W., 'Parzival und die Ritter. Von einfacher Form zum Ritterepos', *Fabula* 1 (1958), 201ff.

Moles, J. L., 'Truth and untruth in Herodotus and Thucydides', in: C. Gill and T. P. Wiseman (ed.), *Lies and fiction in the ancient world*, Exeter 1993, pp. 88ff.

Moos, P. von, 'Poeta und historicus im Mittelalter. Zum Mimesis-Problem am Beispiel einiger Urteile über Lucan', *PBB(T)* 98 (1976), 93ff.

'Fictio auctoris. Eine theoriegeschichtliche Miniatur am Rand der Institutio Traiani', in: *Fälschungen im Mittelalter* (Monumenta Germaniae Historica Schriften 33, 1), Hanover 1988, pp. 739ff.

Geschichte als Topik. Das rhetorische Exemplum von der Antike zur Neuzeit und die historiae in 'Policraticus' Johanns von Salisbury, Hildesheim 1988

'Was galt im Mittelalter als das Literarische an der Literatur? Eine theologisch-rhetorische Antwort des 12. Jahrhunderts', in: J. Heinzle (ed.), *Literarische Interessenbildung im Mittelalter*, Stuttgart 1993, pp. 431ff.

Morgan, J. R., 'Make-believe and make believe: the fictionality of the Greek novels', in: C. Gill and T. P. Wiseman (ed.), *Lies and fiction in the ancient world*, Exeter 1993, pp. 175ff.

Morris, R., 'Aspects of time and place in the French Arthurian verse romances', *FSt* 42 (1988), 257ff.

'King Arthur and the growth of French nationalism', in: G. Jondorf and D. N. Dumville (ed.), *France and the British Isles in the Middle Ages and Renaissance*, Woodbridge 1991, pp. 115ff.

Morse, R., '"This vague relation": historical fiction and historical veracity in the later Middle Ages', *LSE* 13 (1982), 85ff.

'Medieval biography: history as a branch of literature', *MLR* 80 (1985), 258ff.

Truth and convention in the Middle Ages. Rhetoric, representation and reality, Cambridge 1991

Moser, H., 'Zum Problem der Realität in der hochmittelalterlichen deutschen Dichtung. Dichtung und Wirklichkeit im Hochmittelalter', in: *id., Studien zur deutschen Dichtung des Mittelalters und der Romantik. Kleine Schriften II*, Berlin 1984, pp. 13ff.

Bibliography

'Mythos und Epos in der hochmittelalterlichen deutschen Dichtung', in: *id. Studien zur deutschen Dichtung des Mittelalters und der Romantik. Kleine Schriften II*, Berlin 1984, pp. 28 ff.

Müller, J.-D., 'Ritual, Sprecherfiktion und Erzählung. Literarisierungstendenzen im späteren Minnesang', in: M. Schilling and P. Strohschneider (ed.), *Wechselspiele. Kommunikationsformen und Gattungsinterferenzen mittelhochdeutscher Lyrik*, Heidelberg 1996, pp. 43 ff.

Müller, U., '"Lügende Dichter?" (Ovid, Jaufre Rudel, Oswald von Wolkenstein)', in: H. Kreuzer (ed.), *Gestaltungsgeschichte und Gesellschaftsgeschichte. Literatur-, Kunst- und musikwissenschaftliche Studien*, Stuttgart 1969, pp. 32 ff.

Murdoch, I., *The fire and the sun. Why Plato banished the artists*, Oxford 1977

Nauen, H.-G., *Die Bedeutung von Religion und Theologie im Tristan Gottfrieds von Straßburg*, diss. Marburg 1947

Nellmann, E., *Wolframs Erzähltechnik. Untersuchungen zur Funktion des Erzählers*, Wiesbaden 1975

'Wolfram und Kyot als *vindaere wilder maere*. Überlegungen zu "Tristan" 4619–88 und "Parzival" 453, 1–17', *ZfdA* 117 (1988), 31 ff.

'Zu Wolframs Bildung und zum Literaturkonzept des *Parzival*', *Poetica* 28 (1996), 327 ff.

Nelson, W., *Fact or fiction. The dilemmas of the Renaissance storyteller*, Cambridge, Mass. 1973

Neugart, I., *Wolfram, Chrétien und das Märchen. Erzählstrukturen und Erzählweisen in der Gawan-Handlung*, Frankfurt am Main 1996

Newsom, R., *A likely story. Probability and play in fiction*, New Brunswick 1988

Nolan, B., *Chaucer and the tradition of the roman antique*, Cambridge 1992

Nolting-Hauff, I., 'Märchen und Märchenroman. Zur Beziehung zwischen einfacher Form und narrativer Großform in der Literatur', *Poetica* 6 (1974), 129 ff.

Nykrog, P., 'The rise of literary fiction', in: R. L. Benson, G. Constable and C. D. Lanham (ed.), *Renaissance and renewal in the twelfth century*, Oxford 1982, pp. 593 ff.

Offermanns, W., *Die Wirkung Ovids auf die literarische Sprache der lateinischen Liebesdichtung des XI. und XII. Jahrhunderts*, Wuppertal 1970

Ohly, F., *Sage und Legende in der Kaiserchronik. Untersuchungen über Quellen und Aufbau der Dichtung*, Darmstadt 1968

Schriften zur mittelalterlichen Bedeutungsforschung, Darmstadt 1977

'Typologische Figuren aus Natur und Mythus', in: W. Haug (ed.), *Formen und Funktionen der Allegorie*, Stuttgart 1979, pp. 126 ff.

Ohly, W., *Die heilsgeschichtliche Struktur der Epen Hartmanns von Aue*, diss. Berlin FU, 1958

Okken, L., *Kommentar zum Tristan-Roman Gottfrieds von Straßburg*, Amsterdam 1984

Olson, G., *Literature as recreation in the later Middle Ages*, Ithaca 1982

Opitz, K., *Geschichte im höfischen Roman. Historiographisches Erzählen im 'Eneas' Heinrichs von Veldeke*, Heidelberg 1998

Otter, M., *Inventiones. Fiction and referentiality in twelfth-century English historical writing*, Chapel Hill 1996

Panzer, F., 'Vom mittelalterlichen Zitieren', Sitzungsberichte der Heidelberger Akademie der Wissenschaften, Phil.-hist. Klasse, 2. Abhandlung, Heidelberg 1950

Page, C., *The owl and the nightingale. Musical life and ideas in France 1100–1300*, London 1989

Partner, N. F., 'The new Cornificius: medieval history and the artifice of words', in: E. Breisach (ed.), *Classical rhetoric and medieval historiography*, Kalamazoo 1985, pp. 5 ff.

Pastré, J.-M., 'Die Auffindung des Pallas-Grabes in Veldekes *Eneide* und die *Renovatio* und *Translatio Imperii*', in: *Zum Traditionsverständnis in der mittelalterlichen Literatur. Funktion und Wertung* (*Wodan* 4, 1991), pp. 107 ff.

'L'Empire et Troie: les enjeux politiques littéraires de la *translatio regni*', *BDBA* 10 (1992), 119 ff.

Patey, D. L., *Probability and literary form. Philosophic theory and literary practice in the Augustan age*, Cambridge 1984

Patterson, L., *Negotiating the past. The historical understanding of medieval literature*, Madison 1987

Payen, J. C. and Diekstra, F. N. M., *Le roman* (Typologie des sources du moyen âge occidental, fasc. 12), Turnhout 1975

Perry, B. E., *The ancient romances. A literary-historical account of their origins*, Berkeley 1967

Peters, U., 'Hofkleriker – Stacltschreiber – Mystikerin. Zum literarhistorischen Status dreier Autorentypen', in: W. Haug and B. Wachinger (ed.), *Autorentypen*, Tübingen 1991, pp. 29 ff.

Pinder, W., *Die Kunst der deutschen Kaiserzeit bis zum Ende der staufischen Klassik. Bd. I: Bilder*, Frankfurt, second edition 1952

Piquet, F., *Etude sur Hartmann d'Aue*, Paris 1898

Poirion, D., 'De l'*Enéide* à l'*Enéas*: mythologie et moralisation', *CCM* 19 (1976), 213 ff.

Pörksen, U., *Der Erzähler im mittelhochdeutschen Epos. Formen seines Hervortretens bei Lamprecht, Konrad, Hartmann, in Wolframs Willehalm und in den "Spielmannsepen"*, Berlin 1971

Potts, L. J., *Aristotle on the art of fiction*, Cambridge 1968

Press, A. R., 'The precocious courtesy of Geoffrey Gaimar', in: G. S. Burgess (ed.), *Court and poet*, Liverpool 1981, pp. 267 ff.

Propp, W., *Morphologie des Märchens* (ed. K. Eimermacher), Munich 1972

Putter, A., 'Finding time for romance: mediaeval Arthurian literary history', *MÆ* 63 (1994), 1 ff.

Sir Gawain and the Green Knight and French Arthurian romance, Oxford 1995

Rathofer, J., 'Der "wunderbare Hirsch" der Minnegrotte', *ZfdA* 95 (1966), 27 ff.

Raynaud de Lage, G., 'Les "romans antiques" dans l'*Histoire ancienne jusqu'à César*', *MA* 63 (1957), 267 ff.

'Les romans antiques et la représentation de l'antiquité', *MA* 67 (1961), 247 ff.

(Together with J. Frappier), 'Les romans antiques', in: J. Frappier and R. R. Grimm (ed.), *Le roman jusqu'à la fin du XIIIe siècle* (*GRLMA* 4), Heidelberg 1978, pp. 145 ff.

Bibliography

Reardon, B. P., *The form of Greek romance*, Princeton 1991

Remensnyder, A. G., *Remembering kings past. Monastic foundation legends in medieval southern France*, Ithaca 1995

Ridder, K., 'Die Inszenierung des Autors im "Reinfried von Braunschweig". Intertextualität im späthöfischen Roman', in: E. Andersen, J. Haustein, A. Simon and P. Strohschneider (ed.), *Autor und Autorschaft im Mittelalter*, Tübingen 1998, pp. 239 ff.

Mittelhochdeutsche Minne- und Aventiureromane. Fiktion, Geschichte und literarische Tradition im späthöfischen Roman. 'Reinfried von Braunschweig', 'Wilhelm von Österreich', 'Friedrich von Schwaben', Berlin 1998

'Erzählstruktur und Schemazitate im *Reinfried von Braunschweig*', in: F. Wolfzettel (ed.), *Erzählstrukturen der Artusliteratur. Forschungsgeschichte und neue Ansätze*, Tübingen 1999, pp. 331 ff.

Rider, J., 'The other worlds of romance', in: R. L. Krueger (ed.), *The Cambridge Companion to medieval romance*, Cambridge 2000, pp. 115 ff.

Riley, E. C., *Cervantes's theory of the novel*, Oxford 1962

Roberts, B. F., '*Culhwch ac Olwen*, The Triads, Saints' Lives', in: R. Bromwich, A. O. H. Jarman and B. F. Roberts (ed.), *The Arthur of the Welsh. The Arthurian legend in medieval Welsh literature*, Cardiff 1991, pp. 73 ff.

'Geoffrey of Monmouth, *Historia Regum Britanniae* and *Brut y Brenhinedd*', in: R. Bromwich, A. O. H. Jarman and B. F. Roberts (ed.), *The Arthur of the Welsh. The Arthurian legend in medieval Welsh literature*, Cardiff 1991, pp. 97 ff.

Romm, J. S., *The edges of the earth in ancient thought. Geography, exploration, and fiction*, Princeton 1992

Roncaglia, A., 'L'*Alexandre* d'Albéric et la séparation entre chanson de geste et roman', in: *Chanson de Geste und höfischer Roman* (*Studia Romanica* 4), Heidelberg 1963, pp. 37 ff.

Ronen, R., *Possible worlds in literary theory*, Cambridge 1994

Rorty, R., 'Is there a problem about fictional discourse?', in: D. Henrich and W. Iser (ed.), *Funktionen des Fiktiven*, Munich 1983, pp. 67 ff.

Rösler, W., 'Die Entdeckung der Fiktionalität in der Antike', *Poetica* 12 (1980), 283 ff.

'Schriftkultur und Fiktionalität. Zum Funktionswandel der griechischen Literatur von Homer bis Aristoteles', in: A. and J. Assmann (ed.), *Schrift und Gedächtnis. Beiträge zur Archäologie der literarischen Kommunikation*, Munich 1983, pp. 109 ff.

Rosskopf, R., *Der Traum Herzeloydes und der rote Ritter. Erwägungen über die Bedeutung des staufisch-welfischen Thronstreites für Wolframs 'Parzival'*, Göppingen 1972

Ruberg, U., *Raum und Zeit im Prosa-Lancelot*, Munich 1965

Ruh, K., 'Zur Interpretation von Hartmanns *Iwein*', in: FS for W. Henzen, Bern 1965, pp. 39 ff.

Höfische Epik des deutschen Mittelalters. I: Von den Anfängen bis zu Hartmann von Aue, Berlin 1967

Höfische Epik des deutschen Mittelalters. II: 'Reinhart Fuchs', 'Lanzelet', Wolfram von Eschenbach, Gottfried von Straßburg, Berlin 1980

Ryding, W. W., *Structures in medieval narrative*, The Hague 1971

Sauer M., *Parzival auf der Suche nach der verlorenen Zeit. Ein Beitrag zur Ausbildung einer formkritischen Methode*, Göppingen 1981

Sawicki, S., *Gottfried von Straßburg und die Poetik des Mittelalters*, Berlin 1932

Schausten, M., *Erzählwelten der Tristangeschichte im hohen Mittelalter. Untersuchungen zu den deutschsprachigen Tristanfassungen des 12. und 13. Jahrhunderts*, Munich 1999

Schilling, M., 'Minnesang als Gesellschaftskunst und Privatvergnügen. Gebrauchsformen und Funktionen der Lieder im *Frauendienst* Ulrichs von Liechtenstein', in: M. Schilling and P. Strohschneider (ed.), *Wechselspiele. Kommunikationsformen und Gattungsinterferenzen mittelhochdeutscher Lyrik*, Heidelberg 1996, pp. 103 ff.

Schindele, G., *Tristan. Metamorphose und Tradition*, Stuttgart 1971

Schirmer, K.-H., 'Die Wahrheitsauffassung und ihre Wandlung in mittelalterischer deutscher Literatur', in: F. Debus and E. Dittmer (ed.), *Sandbjerg 85. Dem Andenken von Heinrich Bach gewidmet* (Kieler Beiträge zur deutschen Sprachgeschichte, 10), Neumünster 1986, pp. 51 ff.

Schirmer, W. F. and Broich, U., *Studien zum literarischen Patronat im England des 12. Jahrhunderts*, Cologne 1962

Schirok, B., 'Als dem hern Êrecke geschach. Literarische Anspielungen im klassischen und nachklassischen deutschen Artusroman', *LiLi* 18 (1988), Heft 69, 11 ff.

'Swer mit disen schanzen allen kan, an dem hât witze wol getân. Zu den poetologischen Passagen in Wolframs "Parzival"', in: FS for J. Rathofer, Cologne 1990, pp. 119 ff.

Schmid, E., 'Priester Johann oder die Aneignung des Fremden', in: D. Peschel (ed.), *Germanistik in Erlangen. Hundert Jahre nach der Gründung des Deutschen Seminars*, Erlangen 1983, pp. 75 ff.

Familiengeschichten und Heilsmythologie. Die Verwandtschaftsstrukturen in den französischen und deutschen Gralromanen des 12. und 13. Jahrhunderts, Tübingen 1986

'Weg mit dem Doppelweg. Wider eine Selbstverständlichkeit der germanistischen Artusforschung', in: F. Wolfzettel (ed.), *Erzählstrukturen der Artusliteratur. Forschungsgeschichte und neue Ansätze*, Tübingen 1999, pp. 69 ff.

Schmolke-Hasselmann, B., *Der arthurische Versroman von Chrestien bis Froissart. Zur Geschichte einer Gattung*, Tübingen 1980

'Untersuchungen zur Typik des arthurischen Romananfangs', *GRM* 31 (1981), 1 ff.

'Henri II Plantagenêt, roi d'Angleterre, et la genèse d'"Erec et Enide"', *CCM* 24 (1981), 241 ff.

'Accipiter et chirotheca. Die Artusepisode des Andreas Capellanus – eine Liebesallegorie?', *GRM* 32 (1982), 387 ff.

'Der französische Artusroman in Versen nach Chrétien de Troyes', *DVjs* 57 (1983), 415 ff.

Schneider, H., *Parzival-Studien*, Sitzungsberichte der Bayerischen Akademie der Wissenschaften, Phil.-hist. Klasse 1944/46, Heft 4, Munich 1947

Schnell, R., 'Der "Heide" Alexander im "christlichen" Mittelalter', in: W. Erzgräber (ed.), *Kontinuität und Transformation der Antike im Mittelalter*, Sigmaringen 1989, pp. 45 ff.

Bibliography

Scholz, M. G., 'Zur Hörerfiktion in der Literatur des Spätmittelalters und der frühen Neuzeit', in: G. Grimm (ed.), *Literatur und Leser. Theorien und Modelle zur Rezeption literarischer Werke*, Stuttgart 1975, pp. 135 ff.

Hören und Lesen. Studien zur primären Rezeption der Literatur im 12. und 13. Jahrhundert, Wiesbaden 1980

Schreiner, K., '"Discrimen veri ac falsi". Ansätze und Formen der Kritik in der Heiligen- und Reliquienverehrung des Mittelalters', *AfK* 48 (1966), 1 ff.

'Zum Wahrheitsverständnis im Heiligen- und Reliquienwesen des Mittelalters', *Saeculum* 17 (1966), 131 ff.

Schröder, W., *'Die von Tristande hant gelesen.* Quellenhinweise und Quellenkritik im "Tristan" Gottfrieds von Straßburg', *ZfdA* 104 (1975), 307 ff.

Schwietering, J., *Die deutsche Dichtung des Mittelalters*, Potsdam 1941

'Singen und Sagen', in: *id., Philologische Schriften* (ed. F. Ohly and M. Wehrli), Munich 1969, pp. 7 ff.

Searle, J. R., *Expression and meaning. Studies in the theory of speech acts*, Cambridge 1993

Seifert, A., 'Historia im Mittelalter', *AfB* 21 (1977), 226 ff.

Seiler, F., *Ruodlieb, der älteste Roman des Mittelalters, nebst Epigrammen*, Halle 1882

Shaw, F., 'Das historische Epos als Literaturgattung in frühmittelhochdeutscher Zeit', in: L. P. Johnson, H.-H. Steinhoff and R. A. Wisbey (ed.), *Studien zur frühmittelhochdeutschen Literatur*, Berlin 1974, pp. 275 ff.

Shichtman, M. B. and Finke, L. A., 'Profiting from the past: history as symbolic capital in the *Historia Regum Britanniae*', *AL* 12 (1993), 1 ff.

Short, I., 'Gaimar et les débuts de l'historiographie en langue française', in: D. Buschinger (ed.), *Chroniques nationales et chroniques universelles*, Göppingen 1990, pp. 155 ff.

'Gaimar's epilogue and Geoffrey of Momouth's *liber vetustissimus*', *Speculum* 69 (1994), 323 ff.

Sidney, P., *An apology for poetry*, ed. D. J. Enright, *English critical texts: sixteenth century to twentieth century*, London 1962, pp. 3 ff.

Simon, R., *Einführung in die strukturalistische Poetik des mittelalterlichen Romans. Analysen zu deutschen Romanen der matière de Bretagne*, Würzburg 1990

'Thematisches Programm und narrative Muster im Tristan Gottfrieds von Straßburg', *ZfdPh* 109 (1990), 354 ff.

Sims-Williams, P., 'Did itinerant Breton *conteurs* transmit the *matière de Bretagne?*', *Romania* 116 (1998), 72 ff.

Singerman, J. E., *Under clouds of poesy. Poetry and truth in French and English reworkings of the Aeneid, 1160–1513*, New York 1986

Southern, R. W., 'Aspects of the European tradition of historical writing. 1. The classical tradition from Einhard to Geoffrey of Monmouth', *TRHS* 20 (1970), 173 ff.

Speckenbach, K., *Studien zum Begriff 'edelez herze' im Tristan Gottfrieds von Straßburg*, Munich 1965

Speyer, W., *Die literarischen Fälschungen im heidnischen und christlichen Altertum*, Munich 1971

Spiegel, G. M., *Romancing the past. The rise of vernacular prose historiography in thirteenth-century France*, Berkeley 1993

Spitz, H.-J., 'Wolframs Bogengleichnis: ein typologisches Signal', in: FS for F. Ohly, Munich 1975, II 247ff.

Stein, P. K., 'Tristans Schwertleite. Zur Einschätzung ritterlich-höfischer Dichtung durch Gottfried von Straßburg', *DVjs* 51 (1977), 300ff.

Steinhoff, H.-H., *Die Darstellung gleichzeitiger Geschehnisse im mittelhochdeutschen Epos. Studien zur Entfaltung der poetischen Technik vom Rolandslied bis zum Willehalm*, Munich 1964

Stevens, A., 'Fiction, plot and discourse: Wolfram's *Parzival* and its narrative sources', in: W. Hasty (ed.), *A companion to Wolfram's 'Parzival'*, Columbia, SC 1999, pp. 99ff.

'Killing giants and translating empires: the history of Britain and the Tristan romances of Thomas and Gottfried', in: FS for L. P. Johnson, Tübingen 2000, pp. 409ff.

Stierle, K., 'Was heißt Rezeption bei fiktionalen Texten?', *Poetica* 7 (1975), 345 ff.

'Die Fiktion als Vorstellung, als Werk und als Schema – eine Problemskizze', in: D. Henrich and W. Iser (ed.), *Funktionen des Fiktiven*, Munich 1983, pp. 173 ff.

Stoneman, R., *The Greek Alexander romance*, Harmondsworth 1991

Strasser, I., 'Fiktion und ihre Vermittlung in Hartmanns "Erec"-Roman', in: V. Mertens and F. Wolfzettel (ed.), *Fiktionalität im Artusroman*, Tübingen 1993, pp. 63 ff.

Strohschneider, P., 'Höfische Kurzfassungen. Stichworte zu einem unbeachteten Aufgabenfeld', *ZfdA* 120 (1991), 419ff.

Strunk, G., *Kunst und Glaube in der lateinischen Heiligenlegende. Zu ihrem Selbstverständnis in den Prologen,* Munich 1970

Sturm-Maddox, S., '"Tenir sa terre en pais": social order in the *Brut* and in the *Conte del Graal* ', *Studies in Philology* 81 (1984), 28ff.

Suchomski, J., *'Delectatio' und 'Utilitas'. Ein Beitrag zum Verständnis mittelalterlicher komischer Literatur*, Bern 1975

Syndikus, A., 'Dido zwischen Herrschaft und Minne. Zur Umakzentuierung der Vorlagen bei Heinrich von Veldeke', *PBB* 114 (1992), 57ff.

Szklenar, H., *Studien zum Bild des Orients in vorhöfischen deutschen Epen*, Göttingen 1966

Tatlock, J. S. P., *The legendary history of Britain. Geoffrey of Monmouth's Historia regum Britanniae and its early vernacular versions*, Berkeley 1950

Thomas, H., 'Matière de Rome–Matière de Bretagne. Zu den politischen Implikationen von Veldekes "Eneide" und Hartmanns "Erec"', *ZfdPh* 108 (1989), Sonderheft *Literatur und Sprache im rheinisch-maasländischen Raum zwischen 1150 und 1450* (ed. H. Tervooren and H. Beckers), pp. 65 ff.

Tigerstedt, E. N., 'The poet as creator: origins of a metaphor', *CLS* 5 (1968), 455 ff.

Tomasek, T., *Die Utopie im 'Tristan' Gottfrieds von Straßburg*, Tübingen 1985

Trillitzsch, W., *Ecbasis cuiusdam captivi per tropologiam. Die Flucht eines Gefangenen (tropologisch)*, Leipzig 1964

Trimpi, W., 'The ancient hypothesis of fiction: an essay on the origins of literary theory', *Traditio* 27 (1971), 1ff.

Bibliography

'The quality of fiction: the rhetorical transmission of literary theory', *Traditio* 30 (1974), 1ff.

Uitti, K. D., 'Chrétien de Troyes' *Yvain*: fiction and sense', *RPh* 22 (1969), 471ff.

Unzeitig-Herzog, M., 'Überlegungen zum Erzählschluß im Artusroman', in: F. Wolfzettel (ed.), *Erzählstrukturen der Artusliteratur. Forschungsgeschichte und neue Ansätze*, Tübingen 1999, pp. 233ff.

Vickers, B., *In defence of rhetoric*, Oxford 1988

Vincent-Cassy, M., 'Recherches sur le mensonge au moyen âge', in: *Études sur la sensibilité. (Actes du 102e Congrès National des Sociétés Savantes*, Limoges 1977), Paris 1979, pp. 165ff.

Vitz, E. B., *Orality and performance in early French romance*, Cambridge 1999

Voelker, P., 'Die Bedeutungsentwickelung des Wortes Roman', *ZfrPh* 10 (1886), 485ff.

Vollmann, B. K., *Ruodlieb*, Darmstadt 1993

Vollmann-Profe, G., *Kommentar zu Otfrids Evangelienbuch. Teil I: Widmungen, Buch I, 1–11*, Bonn 1976

Otfrid von Weißenburg. Evangelienbuch, Stuttgart 1987

Wiederbeginn volkssprachiger Schriftlichkeit im hohen Mittelalter (1050/60–1160/70), vol. I, part 2 of J. Heinzle (ed.), *Geschichte der deutschen Literatur von den Anfängen bis zum Beginn der Neuzeit*, Tübingen 1994

Wagenvoort, H., *Studies in Roman literature, culture and religion*, Leiden 1956

Walters, L., 'Le rôle du scribe dans l'organisation des manuscrits des romans de Chrétien de Troyes', *Romania* 106 (1985), 303ff.

Walton, K., 'How remote are fictional worlds from the real world?', *JAAC* 37 (1978), 11ff.

'Fearing fiction', *Journal of Philosophy* 75 (1978), 5ff.

Mimesis as make-believe. On the foundations of the representational arts, Cambridge, Mass. 1990

Wand, C., *Wolfram von Eschenbach und Hartmann von Aue. Literarische Reaktionen auf Hartmann im Parzival*, Herne 1989

Wandhoff, H., *Der epische Blick. Eine mediengeschichtliche Studie zur höfischen Literatur*, Berlin 1996

Warning, R., 'Formen narrativer Identitätskonstitution im höfischen Roman', in: J. Frappier and R. R. Grimm (ed.), *Le roman jusqu'à la fin du XIIIe siècle* (*GRLMA* 4), Heidelberg 1978, pp. 25ff.

'Der inszenierte Diskurs. Bemerkungen zur pragmatischen Relation der Fiktion', in: D. Henrich and W. Iser (ed.), *Funktionen des Fiktiven*, Munich 1983, pp. 183ff.

Wehrli, M., *Formen mittelalterlicher Erzählung. Aufsätze*, Zürich 1969

Geschichte der deutschen Literatur vom frühen Mittelalter bis zum Ende des 16. Jahrhunderts, Stuttgart 1980

Weigand, H. J., *Wolfram's Parzival. Five essays with an introduction*, Ithaca 1969

Weinrich, H., *Linguistik der Lüge*, Heidelberg 1970

Wenzelburger, D., *Motivation und Menschenbild der Eneide Heinrichs von Veldeke als Ausdruck der geschichtlichen Kräfte seiner Zeit*, Göppingen 1974

Wessel, F., *Probleme der Metaphorik und der Minnemetaphorik in Gottfrieds von Straßburg 'Tristan und Isolde'*, Munich 1984

Bibliography

West, D. A., 'The bough and the gate', in: S. J. Harrison (ed.), *Oxford readings in Virgil's Aeneid*, Oxford 1990, pp. 224ff.

Wild, G., 'Manuscripts found in a bottle? Zum Fiktionalitätsstatus (post)arthurischer Schwellentexte', in: V. Mertens and F. Wolfzettel (ed.), *Fiktionalität im Artusroman*, Tübingen 1993, pp. 203ff.

Erzählen als Weltverneinung. Transformation von Erzählstrukturen im Ritterroman des 13. Jahrhunderts, Essen 1993

'(Pseudo-)arthurisches *recycling* oder: Wie die Symbolstruktur des Artusromans im Spätmittelalter aufgegeben ward', in: F. Wolfzettel (ed.), *Erzählstrukturen der Artusliteratur. Forschungsgeschichte und neue Ansätze*, Tübingen 1999, pp. 291ff.

Wilhelm, F., 'Antike und Mittelalter. Studien zur Literaturgeschichte. 1. Ueber fabulistische quellenangaben', *PBB* 33 (1908), 286ff.

Willaert, F., 'Van luisterlied tot danslied. De hoofse lyriek in het Middelnederlandse tot omstreeks 1300', in: F. P. van Oostrom and W. van Anrooij (ed.), *Grote lijnen. Syntheses over Middelnederlandse letterkunde*, Amsterdam 1995, pp. 65ff.

'Heinrich von Veldeke und der frühe Minnesang', in: T. Cramer and I. Kasten (ed.), *Der deutsche Minnesang. Probleme der Poetik*, Berlin 1999, pp. 33ff.

'Zwischen dem Rotten und der Souwe. Einige Thesen zur Stellung Veldekes im frühen Minnesang', in: FS for H. Beckers, Cologne 1999, pp. 309ff.

Wisbey, R., 'Living in the presence of the past: exemplary perspectives in Gottfried's *Tristan*', in: A. Stevens and R. Wisbey (ed.), *Gottfried von Strassburg and the medieval Tristan legend*, Cambridge 1990, pp. 257ff.

Wiseman, T. P., *Clio's cosmetics. Three studies in Greco-Roman literature*, Leicester 1979

'Lying historians: seven types of mendacity', in: C. Gill and T. P. Wiseman (ed.), *Lies and fiction in the ancient world*, Exeter 1993, pp. 122ff.

Wittig, J. S., 'The Aeneas–Dido allusions in Chrétien's *Erec et Enide*', *CL* 22 (1970), 237ff.

Wittkower, R., 'Marvels of the East. A study in the history of monsters', *JWCI* 5 (1942), 159ff.

Wolf, A., 'diu wâre wirtinne – der wâre Elicôn. Zur Frage des typologischen Denkens in volkssprachlicher Dichtung des Hochmittelalters', *ABÄG* 6 (1974), 93ff.

Deutsche Kultur im Hochmittelalter 1150–1250, Essen 1986

Gottfried von Straßburg und die Mythe von Tristan und Isolde, Darmstadt 1989

'Fol i allai–fol m'en revinc! Der Roman vom Löwenritter zwischen *mançonge* und *maere*', in: FS for W. Hoffmann, Göppingen 1991, pp. 205ff.

Wolff, M. J., 'Der Lügner Homer', *GRM* 20 (1932), 53ff.

Wolfzettel, F., Review of R. Morris, *The character of king Arthur*, *ZfrPh* 100 (1984), 443ff.

'Probleme der Geschichtskonstruktion im arthurischen Roman', in: H.-W. Goetz (ed.), *Hochmittelalterliches Geschichtsbewußtsein im Spiegel nichthistoriographischer Quellen*, Berlin 1998, pp. 341ff.

'Doppelweg und Biographie', in: *id.* (ed.), *Erzählstrukturen der Artusliteratur. Forschungsgeschichte und neue Ansätze*, Tübingen 1999, pp. 119ff.

Bibliography

Wolpers, T., *Die englische Heiligenlegende des Mittelalters. Eine Formgeschichte des Legendenerzählens von der spätantiken lateinischen Tradition bis zur Mitte des 16. Jahrhunderts*, Tübingen 1964

Wood, M., 'Prologue', in: C. Gill and T. P. Wiseman (ed.), *Lies and fiction in the ancient world*, Exeter 1993, pp. xiiiff.

Worstbrock, F. J., 'Zur Tradition des Troiastoffes und seiner Gestaltung bei Herbort von Fritzlar', *ZfdA* 92 (1963), 248ff.

'Dilatatio materiae. Zur Poetik des "Erec" Hartmanns von Aue', *FMS* 19 (1985), 1ff.

'Wiedererzählen und Übersetzen', in: W. Haug (ed.), *Mittelalter und frühe Neuzeit. Übergänge, Umbrüche und Neuansätze*, Tübingen 1999, pp. 128ff.

Wright, N., 'The place of Henry of Huntingdon's *Epistola ad Warinum* in the text-history of Geoffrey of Monmouth's *Historia regum Britanniae*: a preliminary investigation', in: G. Jondorf and D. N. Dumville (ed.), *France and the British Isles in the Middle Ages and Renaissance*, Woodbridge 1991, pp. 71ff.

Wyss, U. 'Erzählstrukturen im Prosaroman', in: F. Wolfzettel (ed.), *Erzählstrukturen der Artusliteratur. Forschungsgeschichte und neue Ansätze*, Tübingen 1999, 257ff.

Zaddy, Z. P., *Chrétien studies. Problems of form and meaning in Erec, Yvain, Cligés and the Charrete*, Glasgow 1973

Zeeman, N., 'The schools give a license to poets', in: R. Copeland (ed.), *Criticism and dissent in the Middle Ages*, Cambridge 1996, pp. 151ff.

Zink, M., 'Une mutation de la conscience littéraire: Le langage romanesque à travers des exemples français du xiie siècle', *CCM* 24 (1981), 1ff.

The invention of literary subjectivity, Baltimore 1985. (This volume also includes an English version of the 1981 article, not identical in all respects, so that I refer as necessary to both versions.)

Index of names

Index of names

Bernard of Utrecht, *Commentum in Theodolum*, 8, 97–8, 135, 203, 204, 225, 233

Bernardus (Silvestris), *Commentum super sex libros Eneidos Virgilii*, 153, 159, 209, 222, 239, 241, 242

Béroul, 48, 213, 214, 251

Berthold von Regensburg, 221

Blanchefleur, 100, 130

Blanscheflur, 108, 227

Bliocadran, 255

Bodel, Jean, *Chanson des Saisnes*, 138–40, 141, 152, 195, 234, 235

Boethius, 209

Boiardo, *Orlando innamorato*, 41–2

Bonaventure, St, *De reductione artium ad theologiam*, 29, 210

Brabant, 146

Brandigan, 62, 64, 116

Breri, 184, 222

Brian de Wallingford, 143

Briseida, 156, 190, 241

Britain, 169, 172, 197

Britons (Bretons), 115, 154, 155, 168, 169, 171, 172, 173, 174, 180, 181, 183, 189, 240, 248, 251

Brittany, 143

Brizljân, 57

Broceliande 180, 183

Bruianz des Illes, 143

Brutus, 169, 172, 189

Cador, 177, 192, 250

Cadwallader, 169

Caedmon, *Hymn*, 49

Callisthenes, 163–4, 165

Calogrenant, 99, 180, 181, 183, 252

Camille, 191

Candace, 165, 167

Cappadocia, 142

Carduel, 57, 181

Carmen de gestis, 162, 244

Carthage, 97, 98, 158, 159, 161, 243

Chadwalein, 193

Charles the Great, 140

Chaucer, 28, 39, 42, 46, 209, 212

Le Chevalier à l'épée, 52

Chrétien de Troyes, 17, 19, 20, 21, 24–5, 34, 47–54, 55–6, 57, 60–7, 70, 89, 91, 95, 99, 102, 111, 116, 131–2, 156, 178–80, 183, 186, 192, 193–4, 195, 196, 197, 199, 200, 203, 213, 214–15, 216, 225, 229, 235, 240, 250, 251, 255, 257

Cligés, 50, 70, 95, 99, 116, 124, 128–9, 179, 180, 181, 198, 213, 215, 216, 251, 257

Erec, 24, 25, 50–1, 60–1, 63, 72, 95, 111, 115–16, 123, 124, 127, 142–3, 145, 178, 179, 181, 184, 213, 215, 217, 225, 236, 243, 244, 251

Lancelot, 52, 56, 124, 129, 213, 215, 225, 230

Perceval, 56, 61, 73, 74, 76, 79, 90, 91, 94, 99, 100, 101, 119, 120, 124, 129–30, 214, 225, 229, 230, 232

Yvain, 4, 53, 56, 95, 99–100, 111, 115, 117–18, 124, 130, 131, 173, 179–80, 181–2, 215, 218, 225, 226, 231, 232, 248, 252

Christ, Jesus, 103, 104, 105, 108, 162, 187, 228

Cicero, 139

De inventione, 134, 149, 233, 237, 238

De oratore, 135, 148–9, 233, 237

Cithaeron, 104, 226

Clamide, 64, 65

Cligés, 128

Colchis, 190

Condwiramurs, 106, 122, 130

Constantine, 104, 226

Constantinople, 179

Corineus, 185, 253

Cornelius Nepos, 157

Cornwall, 86, 108, 143, 186

Ctesias, 164

Cundrie, 131

Cunneware, 130

Daniel, 164, 166–7

Dares Phrygius, 5, 153–7, 158, 159, 164, 190, 209, 240, 249, 251

Darius, 166–7

David, 175

Decasyllabic *Alexander*, 165

Denis Piramus, *Partonopeus de Blois*, 31

Vie de saint Edmund, 31, 34, 139, 140, 210, 211, 234

Dictys Cretensis, 5, 153, 154, 158, 164, 249

Dido, 6, 14–15, 156, 158, 159, 160, 161, 163, 190, 224, 243–4

Dietrich (von Bern), 81

Diomedes, 156, 190

Disticha Catonis, 209

Dominicus Gundissalinus, *De divisione philosophiae*, 4, 30–1, 209, 210

Drusilla, 148, 226

Dudo of Saint-Quentin, 169

Eberhard the German, *Laborintus*, 158, 241

Ecbasis captivi, 7–8, 9, 11, 20, 24, 33, 34, 142, 211, 236

Egypt, 154

Eilhart von Oberge, *Tristrant*, 71, 72, 144, 185, 218, 236

Einhard, *Vita Karoli*, 49, 214

Eleusis, 104, 226

Eneas, 160–3, 191, 243

287

Index of names

Index of names

Index of names

Index of names

CAMBRIDGE STUDIES IN MEDIEVAL LITERATURE